Lecture Notes in Artificial Int

Subseries of Lecture Notes in Computer S
Edited by J. G. Carbonell and J. Siekmann

Lecture Notes in Computer Science

Edited by G. Goos, J. Hartmanis and J. van Leeuwen

Springer

Berlin
Heidelberg
New York
Barcelona
Budapest
Hong Kong
London
Milan
Paris
Tokyo

Marco Cadoli

Tractable Reasoning
in Artificial Intelligence

Springer

Series Editors

Jaime G. Carbonell
School of Computer Science
Carnegie Mellon University
Pittsburgh, PA 15213-3891, USA

Jörg Siekmann
University of Saarland
German Research Center for Artificial Intelligence (DFKI)
Stuhlsatzenhausweg 3, D-66123 Saarbrücken, Germany

Author

Marco Cadoli
Dipartimento di Informatica e Sistemistica
Università di Roma "La Sapienza"
Via Salaria, 113, I-00198 Roma, Italy

Die Deutsche Bibliothek - CIP-Einheitsaufnahme

Cadoli, Marco:
Tractable reasoning in artificial intelligence / Marco Cadoli. -
Berlin ; Heidelberg ; New York : Springer, 1995
  (Lecture notes in computer science ; Vol. 941 : Lecture notes in
  artificial intelligence)
  ISBN 3-540-60058-2 (Berlin ...)
  ISBN 0-387-60058-2 (New York ...)
NE: GT

CR Subject Classification (1991): I.2.3-4, F.4.1, F.1.3

ISBN 3-540-60058-2 Springer-Verlag Berlin Heidelberg New York

CIP data applied for

© Springer-Verlag Berlin Heidelberg 1995
Printed in Germany

Typesetting: Camera ready by author
SPIN: 10486355   06/3142-543210 - Printed on acid-free paper

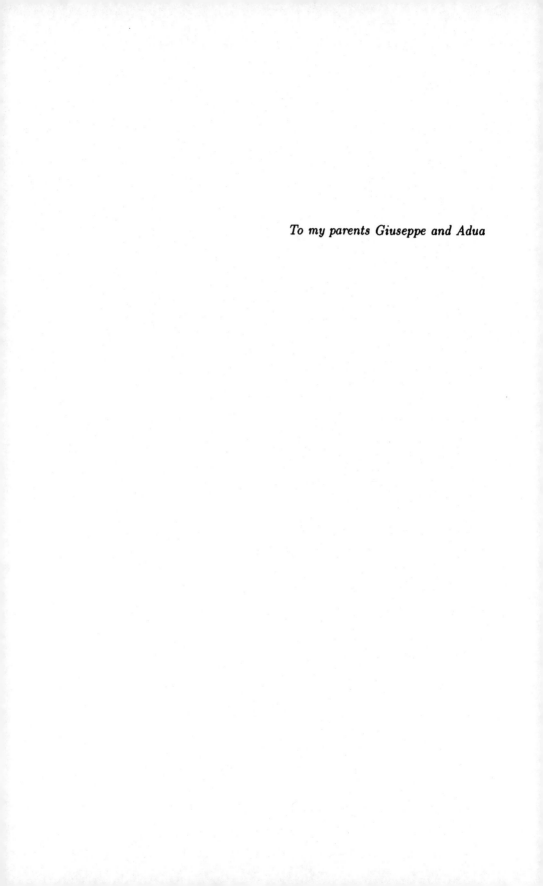

To my parents Giuseppe and Adua

Preface

Logic is one of the most popular approaches to Artificial Intelligence, as it provides a language within which it is possible to express a set of basic truths, from which other truths can be mechanically generated by applying some rules.

A potential obstacle to use of logic is its high computational complexity. Logical inference is indeed an extraordinarily powerful computational device, and problems in logic are known among computer scientists for their high computational complexity.

As efficiency of AI systems is important for their success, if we are to use logic as the major tool for AI we have to deal with its computational intractability.

This book is concerned with computational aspects of the logical approach to Artificial Intelligence. The focus is on two strategies for achieving computational tractability in Knowledge Representation and Reasoning. The first strategy is language restriction: the language used for representing knowledge is restricted so that the formalization of interesting cases is still possible, but resulting tasks are computationally feasible. The second strategy is theory approximation: we approximate a form of logic by using another one that allows weaker inferential power but is computationally feasible even with a full expressiveness in the language.

As far as the language restriction strategy is concerned, we consider a form of non-monotonic reasoning called *minimal* reasoning, which is a technique developed in the AI literature as a tool for the formalization of common-sense reasoning, now popular also in Database Theory and in Logic Programming. Closed world reasoning and circumscription are two forms of minimal reasoning addressed in our work. We analyze the tractability threshold of several problems, finding polynomially tractable cases —for which we give polynomial-time algorithms— and intractable cases. We consider propositional as well as first-order formulae, decision as well as constructive problems, modeling several reasoning patterns. Moreover we apply the complexity results to obtain efficient strategies for the solution of reasoning problems like non-monotonic inheritance and model-based diagnosis.

For what concerns theory approximation, we define a strategy for the approximation of decision reasoning problems based on multi-valued logic. The strategy is designed taking into account semantical as well as computational requirements and differs from existing ones in several aspects. The strategy is applied to a wide range of reasoning problems in propositional logic, fragments of first-order logic (concept description languages), propositional non-monotonic logics and modal logics. Moreover we provide a meta-level language for the representation of approximate knowledge owned by a non-omniscient agent.

In the last part we show some results relating the two studies. In particular we use techniques and results developed in our analysis of the tractability threshold of minimal reasoning to perform an analysis of a famous form of logic-based approximation.

As logic and computational analysis provide a ground which is common to Artificial Intelligence, Database Theory and Theoretical Computer Science, we believe that this book belongs to the intersection of the three disciplines.

The work describes research that has been carried out when the author was a doctoral student at *Università di Roma "La Sapienza"*, in the period November 1989 – February 1993.

Acknowledgments

First of all I want to thank God, who made all this possible, and wonderful.

Many colleagues deserve my deepest thanks for helping me in various ways during the preparation of this book. I am grateful to my advisor Maurizio Lenzerini, who taught me a lot, helped me very much in my research and encouraged me continuously.

Marco Schaerf was so kind to allow me to use results about the approximation techniques that we defined and studied together (now in Chapter 3 of this book.) Other friends gave me the same privilege of using portions of work done together: Thomas Eiter and Georg Gottlob (Section 2.6), Maurizio Lenzerini (Sections 2.3 and 2.7.1), Daniele Nardi and Fiora Pirri (Section 2.7.1.)

I found in *Dipartimento di Informatica e Sistemistica dell'Università "La Sapienza" di Roma* an ideal place to do my research. In particular I thank Luigia Carlucci Aiello for her continuous advice and encouragement.

Finally, many other people read this book or portions of it that have been previously published, and gave me their feedback. Some others gave me clarifications on their work. I am grateful to all of them for their useful advice. Among them, I remember of Wolfgang Bibel, Piero Bonatti, Gerd Brewka, Marta Cialdea, Pierluigi Crescenzi, Francesco Donini, Bruno Errico, Henry Kautz, Hector Levesque, Alberto Marchetti Spaccamela, Eugenio Omodeo, Riccardo Rosati, Andrea Schaerf, Torsten Schaub, Bart Selman, Carolyn Talcott.

Financial support for the preparation of the present work has been partially provided by ESPRIT Basic Research Action N.6810-COMPULOG II and *Progetto Finalizzato Sistemi Informatici e Calcolo Parallelo del Consiglio Nazionale delle Ricerche.*

Contents

List of Figures

List of Tables

List of Algorithms

Chapter 1

Introduction

The goal of this chapter is to make it clear what the premises, the scope and the results of the work are.

In particular we review the logical approach to Artificial Intelligence, recall the importance of formal computational analysis, and clarify the potential side-effects of computational intractability of logical reasoning. We give an informal definition of the two strategies for addressing intractability ("tractability via language restriction" and "tractability via theory approximation"), review the work that other researchers have done in this field, and sketch the results presented in the sequel.

1.1 What is Artificial Intelligence?

Several people attempted to define Artificial Intelligence (AI). In the first pages of three popular textbooks on AI we find possible definitions of this discipline:

- the study of how to make computers do things which, at the moment, people do better [Rich and Knight, 1991, p. X];

- the study of the computations that make it possible to perceive, reason, and act [Winston, 1992, p. 5];

- the enterprise of constructing an intelligent artifact [Ginsberg, 1993, p. 3].

Apparently different researchers have different ideas about *what* the goals of AI are. Analogously, there is obviously no consensus about *how* to achieve the goals of AI. Generally speaking, people agree that AI is both a branch of science and a branch of engineering. "As *engineering*, AI is concerned with the concepts, theory and practice of building intelligent machines [...] As *science*, AI is developing concepts and vocabulary to help us understand intelligent behavior in people and in other animals" (cf. [Genesereth and Nilsson, 1987, p. 1].)

Research in AI in the last decades lead to the proposal of a large spectrum of concepts and techniques, and the process does not seem to converge. Anyway, two ideas about how to do AI were proposed at the very beginning of the field, and still stand after many years: an intelligent system should have to do with both *knowledge representation* and *reasoning*. An informal definition of the two subjects follows [Levesque, 1986]:

Knowledge Representation deals with how to write down in some language a description that corresponds to the world;

Reasoning deals with how to use the knowledge that has been represented for obtaining reliable and useful conclusions.

The next section deals with how *logic* can be used to perform Knowledge Representation and Reasoning (KR&R).

1.2   The role of Logic in Artificial Intelligence

One of the most interesting proposals that have been made for achieving the goals of Artificial Intelligence is to use logic. As a matter of fact logic provides a language within which it is possible to express a set of basic truths, from which other truths can be mechanically generated by applying some rules (cf. Figure 1.1.) For example, mathematical logic was created as a formal system within which all mathematical propositions could be expressed and theorems could be proved. Therefore logic provides a powerful tool for performing Knowledge Representation and Reasoning.

The first researcher who proposed to use logic for the purpose of AI was probably John McCarthy. In his seminal paper [McCarthy, 1959] he showed how to use sentences of first-order predicate logic to represent everyday situations and problems, e.g., the situation in which a person is home and wants to reach the airport. He showed also how first-order deductive machinery can be used on the formal description of the situation for obtaining a plan that specifies how to achieve the solution to the problem.

First-order predicate logic is just one, and the most prominent, example of usage of logic in AI. In fact other forms of logic have been used for the purpose of KR&R. Logical languages other than first-order predicate logic are typically proposed because they can represent some aspects of the world in a more concise and/or appealing way. As an example, logics of *knowledge and belief* were designed for capturing precisely what an agent knows and/or believes, which is not necessarily what is true in the real world. Moreover what an agent knows/believes might be different from what another agent knows/believes. Such logics are also meant to represent easily *beliefs about other another agent's knowledge*, which might be different from what such an agent really knows (cf. Figure 1.2.) Nowadays several logics of knowledge and belief exist, and most of

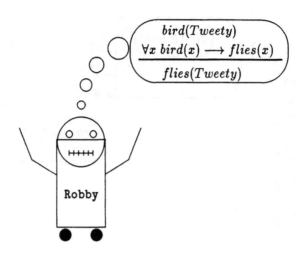

Figure 1.1: Using first-order logic for Knowledge Representation & Reasoning

them differ quite a bit from predicate logic in syntax or semantics or computational properties (or even in all of them.) The task of representing what an agent knows/believes is specially important in scenarios in which several agents are involved.

Logics of knowledge and belief have a long tradition that originated among philosophers. AI researchers have used the ideas developed in such a discipline, modifying them for the purpose of KR&R and giving also some interesting contributions. On the other hand several logical languages were born in the AI community. *Non-monotonic logics* are a noticeable example of the latter kind. The purpose of non-monotonic logics is to give a logical description of reasoning with incomplete knowledge. Since our knowledge of the world is always partial, we —and probably also the artificial agents we are going to build— are forced to take decisions on the grounds of some assumptions that we are not able to prove, but we just accept as plausible (cf. Fig 1.3.) Non-monotonic logics are meant to give a formal account of such plausible reasoning.

The field of logic for AI has become very popular and is extensively represented in AI conferences. Due to the interdisciplinary character of logic it often happens that a formal system designed for the purpose of KR&R is analyzed and used by researchers in other fields. As an example, non-monotonic logics have received much attention in disciplines such as Philosophy, Economics and Computer Science.

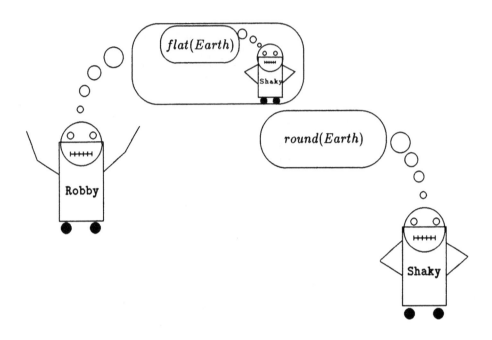

Figure 1.2: Representing somebody else's knowledge

Since the early days of AI a fascinating debate of logical vs. non-logical approach
has flourished. Some researchers in the AI community do not think formal logic
is the most adequate tool to use for achieving the goals of Artificial Intelligence.
A common objection is that the human mind probably does not work with any
form of logic. Therefore we should be inspired by real-world thinking processes
and —as opposed to use unrealistic assumptions— we should build cognitively
plausible mathematical models of such processes and design artificial agents
grounded on such models.

     Other researchers believe that very simple forms of intelligence do not need
representations of the world, and that intelligence has to be approached by
relying on interfacing to the real world through perception and action.

     None of the competing approaches has demolished the other ones, and the
debate is probably not going to stop in the near future. An interesting collection
of papers about foundations of AI appears as [Kirsh, 1991].

We now recall the benefits that are usually advocated in favor of the logical
approach [Genesereth and Nilsson, 1987, Nilsson, 1991].

Declarative character. Logical formulae represent knowledge. Logical infer-
     ence provides the mechanism for achieving conclusions. In this way *what*
     is represented is clearly distinct from *how* it is used.

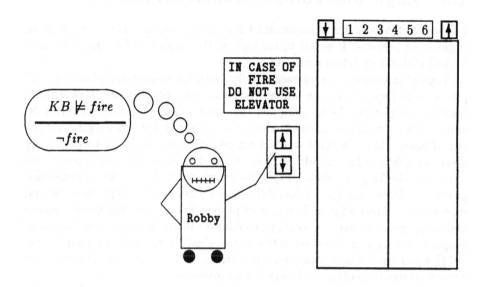

Figure 1.3: Using a plausible assumption

Building Knowledge Bases. A formula represents a piece of knowledge, which might be a specific fact or a general rule. A *Knowledge Base* (KB) can be modeled as a set of formulae. Adding knowledge to a KB or subtracting knowledge from it amounts to add or subtract formulae. This makes it possible to conceive dynamic aspects such as knowledge acquisition and revision in terms of operations on formulae.

Flexibility. Just like human knowledge is often not task-specific, a KB describing some aspects of the world can be used for several purposes. It could even be used for purposes not explicitly anticipated at the time the knowledge is assembled.

Introspectiveness. When knowledge is represented as a logical formula, a machine can answer questions about what it knows or about what it does not know.

We already mentioned some of the alleged drawbacks of the logical approach. Another one concerns the high computational complexity of logical inference, which should make it unfeasible to perform significant amounts of reasoning. We deal with such an important aspect in the following section.

1.3   Logic and computational complexity

Efficiency of AI systems is important for their success, as it is important in all
engineering projects. If we are to use logic as the major tool for KR&R we have
to deal with computational aspects.

Logical inference is an extraordinarily powerful computational device, and
problems in logic are known among computer scientists for their high computational complexity. As an example, the prototypical recursively enumerable,
non-recursive problem is to check whether a formula of first-order logic is consistent [Rogers, 1967]. In other words a reasoner that represents its knowledge by
means of a first-order formula and uses a sound and complete consistency procedure for checking the plausibility of its knowledge has as much computational
power as a Turing machine. What if the reasoner gives up full expressiveness and
represents its knowledge in formulae of propositional logic, still using a sound
and complete consistency checking procedure? To check whether a formula of
propositional logic is consistent is the prototypical NP-complete problem [Cook,
1971], which means that such a reasoner has as much computational power as a
non-deterministic, polynomial-time Turing machine.

Non-recursive problems are —from the computational point of view— definitely unfeasible, because we know that there will never be algorithms that solve
them. This means that we are not guaranteed that the above mentioned first-
order reasoner will ever be able to accomplish the task for which it has been
designed.

NP-complete problem are also commonly labeled as "intractable", or "unfeasible", although for a different reason. For understanding this we have to go
for a short digression. An idea which is commonly accepted in Computer Science is that "feasible" problems are those for which there are polynomial-time
algorithms, while everything else is an "unfeasible" problem. This assumption
is grounded on the fact that exponential functions grow faster than any polynomial. Assuming that the "feasibility world" coincides with polynomial-time
algorithms is definitely an approximation. This is because an algorithm whose
cost is exponential or super-polynomial, may be —as long as small instances are
concerned— less expensive than an algorithm whose cost is polynomial. As an
example this happens if we deal with problems of size $n < 2,000$, the exponential
[super-polynomial] cost is $O(2^{n/20})$ $[O(n^{\log n})]$ and the polynomial cost is $O(n^{10})$.
Similarly constant factors —which are disregarded in asymptotic analysis— may
have a strong impact on the efficiency of an algorithm. Anyway experience with
algorithms shows that —with few exceptions— those aspects don't undermine
the above classification of problems, because such extreme cases rarely occur (cf.
[Papadimitriou, 1994].)

Coming back to NP-complete problems, they are decidable, but currently
there are no known polynomial-time algorithms that solve them, and most researchers believe there will be none [Garey and Johnson, 1979, Johnson, 1990].
As a matter of facts, best algorithms we have for solving NP-complete problems
use exponential time in the worst case. This means that, for what concerns the
propositional reasoner we were considering previously, we are not guaranteed

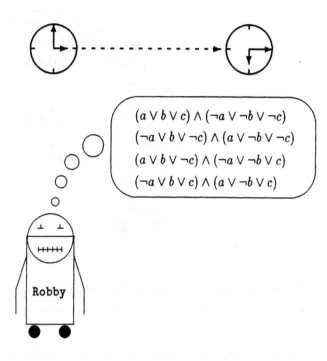

Figure 1.4: Testing if a formula of propositional logic is inconsistent is a polynomially intractable task

that it will be able to accomplish in all cases its task in time which is polynomial in the size of the Knowledge Base it deals with. Therefore, even if we know that the reasoner will finish its task sooner or later, we don't know whether this will take an amount of time that we are willing to wait for (cf. Figure 1.4.)

We mentioned consistency checking of a logical formula as a "benchmark problem" for an automated reasoner. In fact consistency checking is, for the purpose of AI, a basic task. Let's see this with an example. An autonomous robot is designed for the purpose of exploring the world and acquiring knowledge about it. The robot represents its current world of interest as a formula in logic, either propositional or first-order. A primary feature of its representational system should be to guarantee consistency of the represented formula, as it would be embarrassing to be able to prove both a fact p and its negation $\neg p$. Now imagine a highly dynamic environment, which forces the system to continuously add and/or retract pieces of knowledge to the representation. While retraction of knowledge can never cause a consistent formula to become inconsistent, addition of a new fact can (cf. Figure 1.5.)

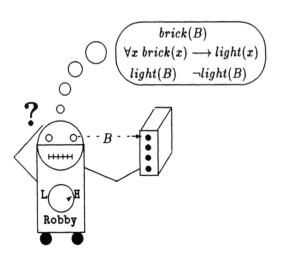

Figure 1.5: A new fact makes a Knowledge Base inconsistent

If inconsistency arises then some action has to be taken, but the very fact of detecting that there is an inconsistency is a prerequisite of any reasonable action. In this scenario the robot must solve a computationally intractable problem each time it wants to add a new piece of knowledge to its representation.

We mentioned in the previous section that sometimes "fancy" forms of logic are used as tools for Knowledge Representation. What happens to computational complexity of reasoning? Logical formalisms that are used in AI typically have higher computational complexity than classical —propositional or first-order— logic. As an example, consistency checking in propositional classical logic is NP-complete, while consistency checking in the propositional modal logic $S4$ —a logic which can be used for representing the *knowledge* modality [Hintikka, 1962]— is PSPACE-complete [Ladner, 1977].

What can we say about this aspect? High complexity of logic is not necessarily a drawback, but is rather a symptom of the exceptional power and expressiveness of such a representational formalism. By using logic, in general, we expect to spend less time in the design and development of an intelligent system, because we are able to use a highly declarative and expressive language. Using logic for the purpose of KR&R we enjoy the benefits listed in Section 1.2, but we pay a price in terms of possible loss in efficiency of the system.

Nevertheless the designer of a logic-based AI system has to give some guarantees about its performances. How to give such guarantees is the subject of this book, and it will be explained better in the next sections.

1.4 The subject of this book

This book deals with *algorithms and complexity associated with formal systems of knowledge representation and reasoning*. We commit to the logical approach to AI, and we take seriously the potential drawbacks of computational intractability.

This book is not a complete guide to computational aspects of KR&R. It is not complete in two ways: only some of the logical formalisms ever used for KR&R are considered, and only some of the possible computational problems are analyzed. Anyway we explore a large spectrum of languages, ideas and techniques, both original and defined by other authors. Our work can be seen as a collection of essays in which some important topics are addressed.

Among the KR&R formal systems we consider there are: classical logic, non-monotonic logics, modal logics, logics of knowledge and belief. Both propositional and first-order versions of such logics are analyzed. Among the computational problems we take into account there are: checking satisfiability and entailment of formulae, checking if a structure is a model of a formula, finding a model, approximating a logical formula and compiling it. We also address applications of our results to domains such as diagnosis in physical systems and inheritance of properties.

As we mentioned in the previous section, many interesting reasoning problems are computationally intractable. In Computer Science there are two techniques for handling computationally intractable classes of problems. The first is to add some constraints to the specification of the class, so that the search space has enough structure to admit fast algorithms. As an example, the problem of graph K-colorability in its more general form[1] is NP-complete, but if the degree of each vertex does not exceed 3 there is a polynomial-time algorithm that solves it [Garey and Johnson, 1979].

The second technique is to go for some form of approximation, i.e., to give up the idea of finding the best solution and be happy with a "good" solution. As an example, the bin packing problem[2] is NP-complete, but we can find in polynomial time a solution which uses at most twice as much as the minimum number of bins [Garey and Johnson, 1979].

In our attempt at addressing intractability of reasoning we consider both ideas. Intuitively, adding constraints means to restrict the expressiveness of the representational language, while going for approximate answers means to give up

---

[1] **K-colorability of a graph:**
INSTANCE: Graph $G = (V, E)$, positive integer $K \leq |V|$.
QUESTION: Is G K-colorable, i.e., does there exist a function $f : V \to \{1, 2, \ldots, K\}$ such that $f(u) \neq f(v)$ whenever $\{u, v\} \in E$?

[2] **Bin packing:**
INSTANCE: Finite set U of items, a size $s(u) \in Z^+$ for each $u \in U$, a positive integer bin capacity B, and a positive integer K.
QUESTION: Is there a partition of U into disjoint sets $U_1, U_2, \ldots, U_K$ such that the sum of the sizes of items in each U_i is B or less?

soundness or completeness of reasoning. Let's see this in more detail:

Language restriction. We can **restrict** the language used for representing knowledge so that the formalization of interesting cases is still possible, but resulting tasks are computationally feasible, i.e., polynomially tractable or at least decidable. We already saw an example of this kind: going from first-order logic to propositional logic simplifies the satisfiability problem from non-recursive to NP-complete. As a further example, the satisfiability testing in the propositional case can be done in polynomial time if the formulae are restricted to be conjunction of Horn clauses [Dowling and Gallier, 1984] or conjunction of Krom clauses [Even *et al.*, 1976] (cf. Figure 1.6.)

Theory approximation. We can **approximate** a form of logic by using another one that allows weaker inferential power but is computationally feasible even with a full expressiveness in the language. As an example, propositional calculus without *modus ponens* rule admits polynomial algorithms for consistency testing [Levesque, 1984, Frisch, 1987]. The price we pay is that we loose completeness, although we still retain soundness.

This book is divided roughly into two parts, in which the above two techniques for achieving tractable reasoning are respectively addressed. We will look in a more detailed way at the contents of this book in Section 1.6. For giving a fair presentation of our work we need to define better the context of research in the field, which we shall do in the next section.

1.5   Previous studies

We are definitely not the first in the field of KR&R who propose to apply techniques of language restriction or theory approximation. Brachman and Levesque advocated in their seminal paper [1985] that it is important to analyze carefully the *tractability threshold* between polynomially tractable and intractable languages. Logic-based approximation of reasoning is also a popular idea in KR&R, and first attempts at giving a clear semantic account of a form of incomplete propositional reasoning were presented in [Levesque, 1984].

As a matter of facts, both ideas received great attention both from the theoretical and from the application-oriented community. The CLASSIC Knowledge Representation system [Borgida *et al.*, 1989, Brachman, 1992], built at AT&T and currently used in an industrial environment, uses both strategies. CLASSIC adopts a restricted language —thus avoiding some sources of intractability— but allows linguistic features that lead to intractable reasoning problems. Such "problematic" features are dealt by means of incomplete inference algorithms grounded on non-standard semantics.

For what concerns the language restriction approach, fundamental studies on

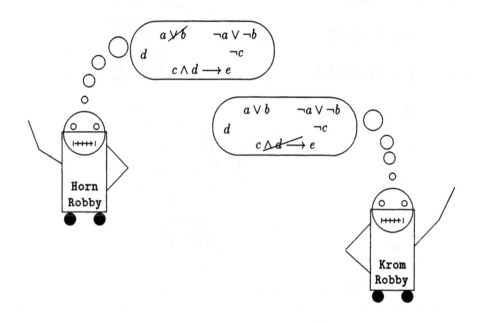

Figure 1.6: Two reasoners with limited expressiveness

the complexity of fragments of classical propositional [Schaefer, 1978] and first-order logic [Dreben and Goldfarb, 1979, Lewis, 1979] have been done in the last decades.

More recently, computational studies about several logical formalisms relevant for Knowledge Representation appeared. As a non-exhaustive list of topics we cite [Halpern and Moses, 1992] on logics for knowledge and belief, [Gottlob, 1992] on autoepistemic and default logics, [Nebel, 1991] on belief revision, [Eiter and Gottlob, 1992] on knowledge base update. Studies analyzing the tractability threshold between polynomially tractable and intractable languages are of particular practical interest. Among the most significant in this group we cite [Donini *et al.*, 1991b, Donini *et al.*, 1991a, Donini *et al.*, 1992] on concept description languages, [Kautz and Selman, 1991b, Stillman, 1990] on default logic, [Eiter and Gottlob, 1993a] on logic-based abduction, [Selman and Levesque, 1989] on path-based inheritance, [Golumbic and Shamir, 1992] on temporal reasoning, [Bylander *et al.*, 1991, Bylander, 1991] on set covering abduction, [Bäckström, 1992, Bäckström and Nebel, 1993] on planning.

Moreover it is fair to say that the limited expressiveness strategy underlies the whole Database approach. As an example, a relational Database query language

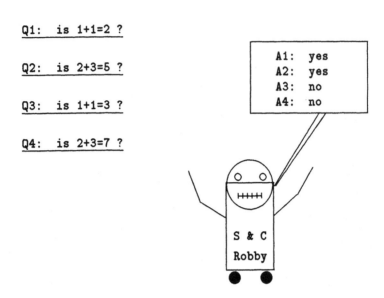

Q1:   is 1+1=2 ?

Q2:   is 2+3=5 ?

Q3:   is 1+1=3 ?

Q4:   is 2+3=7 ?

A1:   yes
A2:   yes
A3:   no
A4:   no

S & C

Robby

Figure 1.7: Sound and complete reasoner

is a fragment of first- or second-order logic, whose expressiveness goes hand in hand with its complexity [Kannelakis, 1990].

Complexity analysis is now a well-established research area in Knowledge Representation. New formal systems or techniques are frequently proposed in the literature along with their complexity analysis, and polynomial/decidable cases are typically shown.

As far as approximated forms of reasoning are concerned, it is well-known that AI has always dealt with approximation, incompleteness and heuristics. The kind of approximate reasoning we want to study in this work can be described in a nutshell as follows: we have a satisfactory logical formalization of a reasoning problem, but we don't want to implement it exactly as it is, because it is computationally too expensive; hence we look for a formalization that "looks like" our favorite one, but it is easier to compute.

In this work we are mainly interested in decision problems, as reasoning problems usually admit a boolean answer. Informally, an approximate solution to a decision problem is a "maybe" answer, equipped with reasons to believe that the "maybe" is actually a "yes" or to believe that it is actually a "no". In a form of approximate reasoning called *sound* reasoning we have two possible answers: "yes" and "maybe no". In the dual form of approximate reasoning (*complete* reasoning), the two possible answers are "no" and "maybe yes" (cf. Figs. 1.7, 1.8, 1.9.)

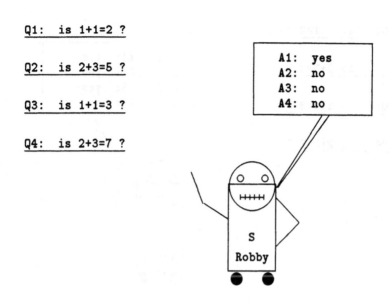

Figure 1.8: You can trust a sound reasoner on "yes" answers

When we work with approximation methods we have to face important questions like: how do we measure the accuracy of an approximate answer? How do we know an approximate answer is any better than another one? It is important to recall that in logic we have no explicit metric that gives an immediate answer to the above questions. In this respect, approximation of reasoning problems is more difficult to study than approximation of optimization problems. Approximation schemata for reasoning problems are typically justified by means of cognitive or epistemic arguments (e.g., "this is an approximate but satisfactory description of how people reason".)

Logic-based study of approximate reasoning is receiving increasing attention in the AI community. Several formalisms for approximate reasoning that are supported by a "reasonable" semantics recently appeared. To this end the most significant approaches to a formal description of partial reasoning are Levesque's [Levesque, 1984, Levesque, 1988, Levesque, 1989] architecture based on *incomplete* reasoning, Frisch's [Frisch, 1985, Frisch, 1987] *limited inference* systems, Crawford and Kuipers' [Crawford and Kuipers, 1989] *access-limited* logic, Selman and Kautz's [Selman and Kautz, 1991, Kautz and Selman, 1991a, Kautz and Selman, 1992] *Horn knowledge compilation* and Dean and Boddy's [Dean and Boddy, 1988] *anytime* algorithms, further investigated by Russell and Zilberstein in [Russell and Zilberstein, 1991] and by Ginsberg in [Ginsberg, 1991b].

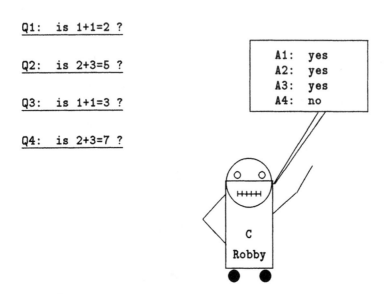

Figure 1.9: You can trust a complete reasoner on "no" answers

1.6   A closer look at the subject of this book

We have seen that the most challenging task in the "tractability via language restriction" strategy is to single out polynomially tractable languages which can be practically useful. On the other hand in the "tractability via approximation" strategy one wants to define semantically well-founded logics, justifiable from the intuitive point of view, and to provide fast algorithms for dealing with them even when using expressive languages.

We now briefly sketch the work on both fronts that is presented in this book.

1.6.1   Language restriction

As far as the language restriction technique is concerned, we focus on a specific area of KR&R, i.e., non-monotonic reasoning. More specifically, we consider the formalism of *minimal* reasoning, i.e., reasoning w.r.t. the minimal models of a formula. Minimal reasoning (also known as *circumscriptive* reasoning) is a very powerful technique developed in the AI literature as a tool for the formalization of common-sense reasoning [McCarthy, 1980, McCarthy, 1986]. Minimality has now become popular in other fields of Computer Science: for example, it is the semantical counterpart of *closed world reasoning* studied in Database Theory [Reiter, 1978, Reiter, 1984] and it is one of the semantics for the *negation as failure* rule in Logic Programming [Clark, 1978].

Several authors investigated about computational aspects of minimal reasoning —for example [Vardi, 1986b, Vardi, 1986a, Schlipf, 1988, Papalaskari and Weinstein, 1990, Kolaitis and Papadimitriou, 1990, Kolaitis and Papadimitriou, 1991, Eiter and Gottlob, 1993b, Papadimitriou, 1991]— but a thorough analysis of the tractability threshold was still missing.

The main focus of our analysis is on propositional languages, as they provide a representation language which is decidable, and in some case tractable. Our ultimate goal is to understand to what extent minimal reasoning is more difficult than classical reasoning.

More specifically, we analyze the tractability threshold of three different problems for propositional formulae:

1. *inference* w.r.t. minimal models (closed world reasoning);

2. *checking* whether a model is minimal;

3. *finding* a minimal model.

We consider several minimality criteria and we provide tractability as well as intractability results for the three problems above, plus algorithms for the tractable cases.

First-order formulae are also considered. In particular we analyze two minimality criteria for models of such formulae, providing semantical as well as computational properties of the inference problem with respect to the two criteria.

In the spirit of the language restriction strategy, we use the complexity results on minimal reasoning to define efficient methods for the solution of reasoning problems. In particular we focus on two different aspects: non-monotonic inheritance and model-based diagnosis.

In this part of the work we go in depth on a particular formal system for Knowledge Representation, trying to analyze several interesting computational problems. Complexity analysis of non-monotonic formalisms is a very active research area. A survey of the field has been compiled by ourselves and appears as [Cadoli and Schaerf, 1993b].

1.6.2 Theory approximation

As for weak reasoning, we define a method for the approximation of decision reasoning problems with the following features:

- approximate answers give semantically clear information about the problem at hand;

- approximate answers are easier to compute than answers to the original problem;

- approximate answers can be improved, and eventually they converge to the right answer (provided we have enough time and motivation);

- both sound approximations and complete ones are described.

Our method differs from the existing ones in one or more of the above points. Related proposals by other authors are compared to ours. A semantical account to our method is given in terms of multi-valued logics.

The method is flexible enough to be applied to a wide range of reasoning problems. In our research we consider approximation of several decidable problems with different worst-case complexity, involving both propositional and first-order languages. In particular we define approximation techniques for:

1. propositional logic;

2. fragments of first-order logic (concept description languages);

3. propositional default logic and circumscription;

4. modal logic.

Moreover we define an epistemic language for the representation of resource-bounded reasoners. The language provides a meta-level description of the approximate knowledge owned by an agent.

1.6.3   Linking the two techniques

Theory approximation and analysis of the tractability threshold of minimal reasoning seem to be far apart. Actually we can find interesting results relating the two studies. In particular we perform an analysis of a famous form of logic-based approximation —Selman and Kautz's Horn knowledge compilation— using techniques and results developed in our complexity analysis about minimality.

1.7   Possible critics

The area of formal computational analysis of logic-based AI is receiving increasing attention not only in the AI community, but also in Database and Theoretical Computer Science conferences. This is with no doubts due to the interdisciplinary character of logic and to the charm of AI.

Anyway it is fair to say that some of the assumptions of this book are not universally accepted in the AI community. We already mentioned that some researchers think that AI does not have necessarily to do with Knowledge Representation and Reasoning (cf. [Brooks, 1991].) Other researchers believe that —although logic is important for the purpose of AI— computational analysis of logical formalisms is not very useful [Ginsberg, 1993, Section 6.5]. More specifically, somebody's argument is that if we restrict the representational language so that polynomial-time algorithms suffice, then we are going to end up with systems that are not general enough [Doyle and Patil, 1991]. In other words, we have to give up too much expressiveness for the price of being sure that the reasoning task will be done quickly.

We already sketched arguments in favor of logic-based AI and in favor of computational analysis. We have some points in favor of the analysis of the tractability
threshold of a representational language. Generally speaking, knowing the easy
and hard cases of an intractable problem is a prerequisite to the design of any
reasonable heuristic. Analyzing the tractability threshold does not imply at all
that we cannot use heuristics for the effective solution of a problem. On the
contrary, we can expect an heuristic to be better if it is grounded on a sound
theoretical analysis.

Another common misconception about tractability analysis is that researchers
who isolate sources of intractability are also proposing that "dangerous" constructs are to be avoided. This is not necessarily the case: it is good to know
what the problematic constructs are, because —when we design an algorithm—
we know what to pay attention to. In general we know that it will be safe to limit
the usage of computationally expensive linguistic features as much as possible,
although it is not forbidden to use them.

A further consideration concerns "cultural" aspects. Generally speaking,
formal computational research in AI keeps a much slower pace than invention
of new semantics, frameworks and problems. As an example, the complexity
of the "blocks world" problem —which is probably the most well studied in
the planning literature— has been formally analyzed only recently [Chenoweth,
1991, Gupta and Nau, 1992]. This kind of delay has potential effects that can
slow down progress in research. As an example two formal systems, which may
look very different from the abstract point of view, can in fact share fundamental
computational properties such as having the same complexity and admitting
the same kinds of algorithms. Studying and understanding the computational
properties of a representational language may shed light on semantic aspects as
well.

The above set of alleged drawbacks does not apply to the "tractability via approximation" strategy, that anyway suffers from a completely orthogonal critic,
i.e., is it meaningful at all to give up soundness or completeness when dealing
with a delicate issue such as reasoning? We believe that the answer to this
question depends on the nature of the application we have in mind. Clearly if
we are implementing software for nuclear plant control it is not safe to do any
such form of approximation. Anyway if we are designing a robot whose major
feature must be promptness in decision-making then we might be happy to trade
accuracy for speed.

At this point we should say something about the major methodological assumption of the present work, i.e., that worst-case complexity, as opposed to average-
case complexity, is studied. Definitely worst-case analysis has limitations, as
worst cases may never occur in practice. Anyway the major obstacle to a serious
analysis of the average complexity for a problem is the characterization of the
real cases by means of reasonable assumptions. This holds in general for any
kind of problem, but for reasoning problems it is especially true, as probably

nobody knows how the "average Knowledge Base" should look like.

1.8   Who may be interested in reading this book?

We already mentioned that logic and computational analysis provide a ground which is common to Artificial Intelligence, Database Theory and Theoretical Computer Science. The focus of the present work is to conceal logic-based methods for treatment of information and limitation of computational resources. Therefore we believe that this book belongs to the intersection of the three disciplines.

Knowledge Representation is definitely a fascinating field, and provides plenty of clearly defined computational problems. Such problems may serve as the vehicle in which to test ideas about algorithms and complexity, developed among theoreticians.

1.8.1   Prerequisites

Although we made an effort for providing adequate definitions and motivations for each formal concept that is introduced, this book is not completely self-contained. More specifically, the reader should have basic knowledge of both logic and computational complexity. Some less-known notions and terminology about such subjects are given in an introductory section (Section 1.10.)

We point out that the logical language that is more frequently used in this book is propositional logic, for which we give syntax and semantics in Section 1.10.1. Knowledge of first-order predicate logic is necessary only for specific sections. The same is true for modal propositional logic.

As for computational aspects, we take it for granted that the reader is familiar with notions such as polynomial-time algorithm and complexity class. Anyway all complexity classes that will be cited throughout the book will be introduced in Section 1.10.3.

1.9   Structure of the book

Chapter 2 is devoted to the computational analysis of minimal reasoning. Relevant definitions are reported, then results about tractability, intractability and semantics are shown. We also describe various applications of the complexity analysis to practical reasoning problems.

In Chapter 3 we deal with approximation of logical theories. The topic is introduced by analyzing two approximation techniques defined by other authors. Such an analysis gives us inspiration for a desiderata list for a new technique. The new technique is first defined and then applied to several deductive problems. Moreover we deal with the problem of representing approximate knowledge owned by an agent with limited resources.

In Chapter 4 we analyze a technique for approximate reasoning defined by Selman and Kautz. We show that the complexity analysis performed in Chapter 2 gives us interesting computational properties of their technique.

Chapter 5 contains conclusions and open problems. Current research is also discussed.

In order to make this book more readable, all proofs of theorems as well as some technical aspects have been collected in appropriate appendices. Appendix A refers to Chapter 2, Appendix B refers to Chapter 3, Appendix C refers to Chapter 4.

Theorems, definitions and examples are numbered within each section. As an example, Theorem 2.6.1 is the first theorem of Section 2.6, and Theorem A.1.1 is the first theorem of the first section of Appendix A.

1.10 Terminology and preliminary notions

In the last section of this chapter we introduce some of the terminology used in the present work. Many other terms and concepts will be defined in specific sections.

In Subsection 1.10.1 we give a brief compendium of syntactic and semantical aspects of propositional logic. The purpose of Subsection 1.10.2 is to introduce the procedure of skolemization of a first-order formula and the notion of Herbrand interpretation of a language. In Subsection 1.10.3 we review all complexity classes that will be cited throughout the book. Finally, in Subsection 1.10.4 we define and illustrate by means of examples some classes of propositional formulae for which polynomial-time algorithms for satisfiability exist.

1.10.1 Propositional logic

For what concerns syntactic aspects of propositional logic, we use the following terminology. Given a set of propositional letters (or atoms, or variables) L, we build propositional formulae by means of the connectives $\neg$ (negation), $\wedge$ (conjunction), $\vee$ (disjunction), $\rightarrow$ (implication) and parentheses, using obvious syntactic rules. The set of propositional letters occurring in a formula T is called the alphabet of T. A literal is a propositional letter x (positive literal) or its negation $\neg x$ (negative literal.) A disjunction of literals is called clause[3]. A clause is positive when all of its literals are positive. A conjunction of clauses is called a formula in Conjunctive Normal Form (CNF). A formula obtained using only the connectives $\wedge$ and $\vee$ plus parentheses over a set of positive and negative literals is called a formula in Negation Normal Form (NNF). Each formula in CNF is also in NNF.

---

[3] In Sections 2.4 and 2.5 the term clause is used for a more general object. It will be appropriately redefined.

As an example, let $L = \{a, b, c\}$ be an alphabet, which we use for building the following propositional formulae:

$$(a \vee c) \wedge (\neg a \vee b) \wedge \neg c \qquad (1.1)$$

$$(a \wedge b \vee \neg c) \vee \neg a \vee b \qquad (1.2)$$

$$(a \wedge b \vee \neg c) \vee \neg(a \vee b) \qquad (1.3)$$

Formula (1.1) is in CNF, formula (1.2) is in NNF but not in CNF, and formula (1.3) is not in NNF.

Let's consider semantic aspects now. For us a truth assignment (also called interpretation) is a function I mapping a set of literals into the set $\{0, 1\}$. In Chapter 3 we deal with multi-valued logics, and we do not require $I(l)$ and $I(\neg l)$ to be different for each propositional letter l. Anyway, in Chapters 2 and 4 we refer to standard truth assignments, i.e., $I(l)$ is always the opposite of $I(\neg l)$ for each literal l.

In all cases, we denote with t a propositional constant such that $I(t) = 1$ for each interpretation I. Also, we denote with f a propositional constant such that $I(f) = 0$ for each interpretation I.

Considering only standard truth assignments, the ordinary semantic rules for connectives $\neg$, $\vee$, $\wedge$, $\to$ map each propositional formula into an element of the set $\{0, 1\}$. A model M of a propositional formula T is a standard truth assignment to the letters of its alphabet that maps T into 1. In symbols, this is written $M \models T$. A formula T is equivalent to a formula T' if and only if T and T' have the same models.

Each propositional formula T can be rewritten in linear time into an equivalent NNF formula T' using the following well-known rewriting rules:

$$\neg(A \wedge B) \quad \mapsto \quad \neg A \vee \neg B$$

$$\neg(A \vee B) \quad \mapsto \quad \neg A \wedge \neg B$$

$$\neg\neg(A) \quad \mapsto \quad A$$

$$(A \to B) \quad \mapsto \quad (\neg A \vee B)$$

A propositional formula is satisfiable if admits at least one model. A propositional formula T entails another formula q (written $T \models q$) if all models of T are also models of q. Note that the symbol $\models$ is overloaded. This notation is standard in logic.

1.10.2   First-order predicate logic

For what concerns first-order predicate logic, we refer the reader to source books such as [Enderton, 1972] for semantical aspects and [Loveland, 1978, Gallier, 1987] for computational aspects. Such books obviously contain comprehensive treatment of propositional logic.

For the purpose of the present work there are mainly two notions that we would like to remind: *Skolem Normal Form* of a formula and *Herbrand interpretation* of a language.

Just like in propositional logic, first-order formulae in which negation is "pushed" at the innermost level are called formulae in NNF. Each first-order formula can be rewritten in linear time into an equivalent formula in NNF using the rewriting rules mentioned in Subsection 1.10.1 plus the following rules, dealing with quantifiers:

$$\neg \forall x A \quad \mapsto \quad \exists x \neg A$$
$$\neg \exists x A \quad \mapsto \quad \forall x \neg A$$

Let Φ be a formula of first-order predicate logic in NNF. If existential quantifiers occur in Φ, it is possible to obtain in time polynomial in the length of Φ a formula Φ' with no existential quantifiers such that Φ' is satisfiable if and only if Φ is satisfiable. Φ' is called the Skolem Normal Form of Φ, and the process for obtaining it is called skolemization.

The skolemization procedure basically deletes existential quantifiers and substitutes the corresponding bounded variables with terms obtained with new constant and function symbols. For a precise definition of the skolemization procedure we refer the reader to [Gallier, 1987]. Here we illustrate it by means of some examples.

- Let's consider the formula $\Phi = \exists x P(a, x)$, where a is a constant symbol. Note that the existential quantifier does not occur in the scope of any universal quantifier. The Skolem Normal Form of Φ is the formula $P(a, c)$, where c is a new constant symbol. c is called a *Skolem constant*.

The rules about Skolem constants are the following:

  1. they must not occur in the formula to be skolemized;
  2. they must substitute all occurrences of the corresponding variable, e.g., the formula $\exists x(P(a, x) \lor R(x, b))$ is transformed into $P(a, c) \lor R(c, b)$;
  3. variables bounded by different existential quantifiers must be substituted by different Skolem constants, e.g., the Skolem Normal Form of $\exists x P(a, x) \land \exists y R(y)$ is $P(a, c) \land R(d)$.

- Now Φ is the formula $\forall x(R(x) \lor \exists y Q(y))$. Note that the existential quantifier occurs in the scope of a single universal quantifier. The Skolem Normal Form of Φ is $\forall x(R(x) \lor Q(f(x)))$, where f is a new function symbol. f is called a *Skolem function*. Note that its arity is 1, and that all terms in which it occurs are of the form $f(x)$, x being the universally quantified variable delimiting its scope.

The rules about Skolem functions are the following:

1. they must not occur in the formula to be skolemized;

2. they must substitute all occurrences of the corresponding variable, e.g., the formula $\forall y(\exists x(P(a, x) \lor R(x, b)))$ is transformed into the formula $\forall y(P(a, f(y)) \lor R(f(y), b))$;

3. variables bounded by different existential quantifiers must be substituted by different Skolem functions, e.g., the Skolem Normal Form of $\forall w(\exists x P(a, x) \land \exists y R(y))$ is $\forall w(P(a, f(w)) \land R(g(w)))$.

- When an existentially quantified variable y occurs in the scope of n universal quantifiers $\forall x_1, \ldots, \forall x_n$, all occurrences of y must be substituted by $f(x_1, \ldots, x_n)$, where f is a new function symbol of arity n.

As an example, the Skolem Normal Form of $\forall x \forall z \exists u Q(x, u)$ is the formula $\forall x \forall z Q(x, f(x, z))$.

The importance of skolemization is in that a formula in NNF is satisfiable if and only if its Skolem Normal Form is satisfiable.

The Herbrand universe U_h of a formula Φ in Skolem Normal Form is the set of terms that can be built using the constant and function symbols occurring in Φ (if no constants occur in Φ include one in U_h.) The Herbrand base B_h of Φ is the set of ground atoms built applying predicate symbols occurring in Φ to terms of the Herbrand universe.

As an example, the Herbrand universe of $\forall y(P(a, f(y)) \lor R(f(y), b))$, where a, b are constant symbols and f is a function symbol, is the infinite set:

$$\{a, b, f(a), f(b), f(f(a)), f(f(b)), \ldots\},$$

and its Herbrand base is the infinite set:

$$\{P(a, a), R(a, a), P(a, b), R(a, b), P(b, a), R(b, a), P(f(a), a), R(f(a), a), \ldots\}.$$

A Herbrand interpretation of the language $\mathcal{L}$ used in Φ is a subset of the Herbrand base B_h. The importance of Herbrand interpretations is in that (Herbrand Theorem) a first-order formula in which only universal quantifiers occur is satisfiable if and only if there exists an Herbrand interpretation satisfying it. Such an interpretation is called an Herbrand model. In Section 3.5 we will deal with Herbrand interpretations of formulae in Skolem Normal Form.

1.10.3   Complexity classes

As for complexity classes, throughout the book we refer to the standard notation in complexity theory, that can be found for example in [Garey and Johnson, 1979, Johnson, 1990, Papadimitriou, 1994]. In this subsection we give a brief review of all the complexity classes that are mentioned throughout this work.

We deal most of the times with *decision problems*, i.e., problems that admit a boolean answer. For decision problems the class P is the set of problems that can be answered by a Turing machine in polynomial time. Often we refer to computations done by non-deterministic Turing machines. The class of decision problems that can be solved by a non-deterministic Turing machine in polynomial time —where it is understood that the answer is "yes" provided *at least one* of the computations done in parallel by the machine ends in an accepting state— is denoted by NP. The class of problems whose answer is always the complement of those in NP, is denoted by co-NP. Also problems in co-NP can be solved by a non-deterministic Turing machine in polynomial time, but it is understood that the answer is "yes" provided *all* the computations done in parallel by the machine end in an accepting state. The class P is obviously contained both in NP and in co-NP.

An example of a problem in NP is testing satisfiability of a propositional formula: a formula T is satisfiable iff *at least one* truth assignment M such that $M \models T$ exists.

An example of a problem in co-NP is testing if a propositional formula T entails a propositional formula γ: $T \models \gamma$ iff *for all* truth assignments M it holds that $(M \models T) \implies (M \models \gamma)$. In fact propositional satisfiability [entailment] is an NP-*hard* [co-NP-*hard*] problem, i.e., a problem which is "at least as tough" —w.r.t. polynomial-time many-one reductions— as each problem in the class NP [co-NP]. Since satisfiability is a problem in NP and it is also NP-hard, it is an NP-*complete* problem. Analogously, propositional entailment is co-NP-complete. We recall that the best algorithms known for solving NP-complete or co-NP-complete problems require exponential time in the worst case, and that the following relations are conjectured: $P \subset NP$, $P \subset co\text{-}NP$, $NP \neq co\text{-}NP$.

We will eventually refer to a particular type of computation called computation with *oracles*. If A denotes a complexity class, then an oracle for A is an abstract entity that can solve each problem in the class A. A Turing machine can consult an oracle, which means to write a query in an appropriate tape and go into a specific state; at this point the oracle gives the answer in a single computation step. Intuitively oracles are subroutines with unit cost. As an example, an oracle for NP can solve propositional satisfiability problems in a single computation step when consulted by a machine. Given a class of decision problems C, the class P^C (NP^C) is the class of decision problems that can be solved in polynomial time by a deterministic (non-deterministic) machine that uses an oracle for the problems in C, i.e., a subroutine for any problem in C that can be called several times, spending just one time-unit for each call.

The definition of *polynomial hierarchy* is based on oracle computations. The classes Σ_k^p, Π_k^p and Δ_k^p of the polynomial hierarchy are defined by

$$\Sigma_0^p = \Pi_0^p = \Delta_0^p = P$$

and for all $k \geq 0$,

$$\Sigma_{k+1}^p = NP^{\Sigma_k^p}, \ \Pi_{k+1}^p = co\text{-}\Sigma_{k+1}^p, \ \Delta_{k+1}^p = P^{\Sigma_k^p}.$$

Note that $\Sigma_1^p = NP$, $\Pi_1^p = co\text{-}NP$, $\Delta_1^p = P$, $\Delta_2^p = P^{NP}$. The following relations have been conjectured:

$$\Delta_k^p \subset \Sigma_k^p, \ \Delta_k^p \subset \Pi_k^p, \ \Sigma_k^p \subset \Delta_{k+1}^p, \ \Pi_k^p \subset \Delta_{k+1}^p, \ \Sigma_k^p \neq \Pi_k^p$$

for all $k \geq 1$.

Two classes of the polynomial hierarchy that will have a certain importance in this book (especially in Section 3.6) are Σ_2^p (=NP^{NP}) and Π_2^p (=co-NP^{NP}.) Σ_2^p contains all problems solvable in non-deterministic polynomial time provided it is possible to use for free a subroutine for a problem in NP, for example propositional satisfiability.

In virtue of the conjectures $\Sigma_k^p \subset \Sigma_{k+1}^p$ and $\Pi_k^p \subset \Pi_{k+1}^p$, Σ_2^p-complete and Π_2^p-complete problems are considered more difficult to solve than both NP-complete and co-NP complete problems. A practical difference exists between NP-complete and Σ_2^p-complete problems. Suppose we have a good heuristic for solving an NP-complete problem (as an example propositional satisfiability testing), that normally solves the problem in an acceptable amount of time —even if exponential time is needed in the worst case. It is still not immediate how to use such a good heuristic for solving efficiently a Σ_2^p-complete problem. As a matter of fact, if the conjecture NP $\subset \Sigma_2^p$ is true, then in the worst case an exponential number of calls to an algorithm for satisfiability testing would be necessary in order to solve any Σ_2^p-complete problem. The same holds for Π_2^p-complete problems. On the other hand Δ_2^p-complete (=P^{NP}-complete) problems are "mildly" harder than NP-complete ones, since they can be solved by means of a polynomial number of calls to an algorithm for satisfiability testing.

A further class of decision problems we introduce are those polynomially solvable by a deterministic Turing machine with no more than $f(n)$ calls to a Σ_k^p oracle. Such a class is denoted by $\text{P}^{\Sigma_k^p[f(n)]}$, where $f(n)$ is a polynomial function of the size n of the problem instance. Sometimes "big o" notation is used for the function denoting the maximum number of calls to the oracle, i.e., given a polynomial function $g(n)$ of the size n of the problem instance, we deal with the class $\text{P}^{\Sigma_k^p[O(g(n))]}$. In particular we mention the class $\text{P}^{\text{NP}[O(\log n)]}$, that will be cited several times throughout the book. We note that NP $\subseteq \text{P}^{\text{NP}[O(\log n)]} \subseteq \Delta_2^p$ and that the containments are conjectured to be strict. The same properties hold for the class $\text{P}^{\text{NP}[\log n]}$.

The class of decision problems that can be solved by a deterministic Turing machine by using a polynomial amount of working space is denoted by PSPACE. Clearly $\Pi_k^p \subseteq$ PSPACE, $\Sigma_k^p \subseteq$ PSPACE for all k. Strict containment has been conjectured.

Throughout this work we assume that all the above mentioned conjectures are true.

Sometimes we refer to *search* problems, i.e., problems whose answer is more complex than just a boolean value. As an example, *finding* a satisfying truth assignment for a propositional formula is a search problem. Complexity classes for search problems are different from classes cited above, that refer to decision problems. An interesting complexity class of search problems is $\text{F}\Delta_2^p = \text{FP}^{\text{NP}}$, which is the set of problems solvable in polynomial time by a machine with access to an oracle for an NP problem. If the oracle can be accessed only a logarithmic number of times, then we have the class $FP^{NP[O(\log n)]}$.

1.10.4 Polynomial fragments of propositional logic

As we already mentioned, in this book we often deal with reasoning problems which are computationally more difficult than making inferences in plain propositional logic. For this reason, we are particularly interested in those classes of formulae for which plain propositional inference is polynomial (as mentioned in the previous subsection this problem is, for CNF propositional formulae, co-NP-complete.) The results reported in [Dowling and Gallier, 1984, Even *et al.*, 1976, Schaefer, 1978] show that this holds for the following three classes of CNF formulae: Horn (every clause contains at most one positive literal), Dual-Horn (every clause contains at most one negative literal), Krom (every clause contains at most two literals.)

In the book we refer to several subsets of such classes. A complete classification of all the classes of propositional formulae we consider is as follows:

- Horn (written HORN): at most one positive literal per clause

- Dual-Horn (DHORN): at most one negative literal per clause

- Definite (DEF): exactly one positive literal per clause

- Krom (KROM): at most two literals per clause

- HornKrom (HK): Horn and Krom

- Dual-HornKrom (DHK): Dual-Horn and Krom

- HornKrom⁻ (HK⁻): HornKrom with no negative clause having 2 literals

- 2-positive-Krom (2POSK): exactly two positive literals per clause.

Some of the above classes correspond to logical formulae which are considered in various contexts of Artificial Intelligence as well as Deductive Databases. For example, the class of Definite formulae is extensively studied in Logic Programming. The class of Horn formulae is used to model a set of Definite formulae plus a set of integrity constraints, each one specifying that a certain set of predicates have disjoint extensions. The class of Dual-Horn formulae is used to model a set of covering assertions. The class of HornKrom⁻ is used to model a set of *is-a* assertions on classes, where *A is-a B* means that every instance of *A* is also an instance of *B*. Finally, a HornKrom formula represents a set of *is-a* and *is-not* assertions, where *A is-not B* means that *A* and *B* are disjoint (see also Section 2.7.1.)

A taxonomy of all the mentioned classes is shown in Figure 1.10. Examples of clauses that it is possible to represent in each of the classes are listed in Table 1.1. The table is "incremental", in the sense that each formula that can be represented in a class C is not reported for any of the super-classes of C.

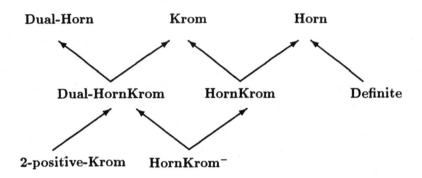

Figure 1.10: Taxonomy of some propositional classes in which inference is polynomial

Class of formulae	Example of clause
2POSK	*male* ∨ *female*
HK⁻	*man* ¬*dog* ¬*man* ∨ *person*
DHK	—
HK	¬*male* ∨ ¬*female*
DEF	*man* ¬*man* ∨ ¬*young* ∨ *boy*
DHORN	¬*person* ∨ *male* ∨ *female*
KROM	—
HORN	¬*person* ∨ ¬*very-young* ∨ ¬*worker*

Table 1.1: Clauses that each class of formulae can represent

Chapter 2 ▬▬▬▬▬▬▬▬▬▬▬▬

Language restriction: Complexity of minimal reasoning

▬▬▬▬▬▬▬▬▬▬▬▬▬▬▬▬▬▬▬▬▬▬▬▬▬▬

This chapter deals with the first strategy for achieving tractability in Knowledge Representation and Reasoning: restricting the representational language.

The framework in which we use this strategy is non-monotonic reasoning (NMR). NMR is a collection of formal systems developed in the AI community for capturing some aspects of common-sense reasoning such as reasoning with incomplete information.

In particular, we focus on a specific NMR formalism —called minimal reasoning*— which deals with models with minimal extensions.*

Our primary goal is to show the analysis of the tractability threshold for several variants of minimal reasoning.

Structure of the chapter

After a brief introduction to motivations for NMR in general (Section 2.1), we present preliminary definitions and examples in Section 2.2. We then turn to the technical part of the chapter: In Sections 2.3, 2.4 and 2.5 we show the analysis of the tractability threshold for three different problems of minimal reasoning in propositional languages, respectively

1. *inference* w.r.t. minimal models (closed world reasoning);

2. *checking* whether a model is minimal;

3. *finding* a minimal model.

First-order languages are analyzed in Section 2.6, while in Section 2.7 we describe applications of complexity results to practical reasoning problems.

2.1 Why non-monotonic reasoning?

The term "non-monotonic" refers to a peculiarity that the consequence operator of a logic may have. Let us denote with $\leadsto$ consequence in a generic logic. For non-monotonic logics the following property does not hold

$$(T \leadsto \gamma) \quad \text{implies} \quad (T \cup \delta \leadsto \gamma). \tag{2.1}$$

Non-monotonicity makes such logics very different from predicate, modal, temporal logics, for which property (2.1) is valid for each T, δ and γ.

Non-monotonic logics were born at the end of the 70s as attempts to formalize some aspects of common-sense reasoning. One of the most interesting aspects they can capture is *defeasible* reasoning, i.e., reasoning with rules that are generally valid, but may have exceptions.

In order to introduce defeasible reasoning, we show the well-known "Tweety" example (see for example [Reiter, 1980b, McCarthy, 1986, Lifschitz, 1985b, Gelfond and Przymusinska, 1986, Gelfond *et al.*, 1989]), probably the most popular in this area.

A general property of birds is to be able to fly, but exceptions to this rule definitely exist. As an example, penguins are exceptional with respect to the rule. Given a generic bird (whose name is traditionally Tweety), we would like to infer that it is able to fly, on the grounds that there is no reason to believe that it is an exception to the general rule. Clearly such a form of reasoning is non-monotonic, since if we come to know that Tweety is a penguin, then we have to retract the conclusion.

The following sentences represent in first-order syntax the general rule and the fact that Tweety is a bird

$$\forall x \; (bird(x) \wedge \neg abnormal(x) \quad \rightarrow \quad flies(x)) \tag{2.2}$$

$$bird(Tweety) \tag{2.3}$$

The purpose of $\neg abnormal(x)$ in sentence (2.2) is to avoid that the rule is applied in an unconstrained way.

The formula $\forall x \; (penguin(x) \rightarrow bird(x) \wedge abnormal(x))$ could be added to the above ones to represent that penguins are birds, and that they are exceptional (abnormal) with respect to the general rule.

Note that the disjunction $abnormal(Tweety) \vee flies(Tweety)$ is true in all the models of formulae (2.2) and (2.3), while $flies(Tweety)$ is not. Thus, plain first-order logic does not allow us to obtain exactly what we want, i.e., to have a rule that is not always true, but applies whenever there is no sufficient information to think that there is an exception.

One of the possible formalizations that have been proposed for formalizing defeasible reasoning is to reason only with a specific set of models, by using the criterion of *minimality* w.r.t. the set of true atoms. The idea behind minimality is to assume that a fact is false whenever possible. Such a criterion allows one to represent only true statements of a theory, saving the explicit representation of all false ones.

In the next section we show two non-monotonic techniques based on the idea of minimality that have been proposed in the literature in order to capture the above form of reasoning.

For fifteen years non-monotonic reasoning (NMR) has been constantly a topic of most major conferences on AI, Database Theory and Logic Programming and hundreds of papers on this subject have been written. For a general introduction to NMR we refer the reader to one of the books (e.g., [Ginsberg, 1987, Lukaszewicz, 1990, Brewka, 1991, Marek and Truszczyński, 1993]) appearing on the subject.

2.2 Minimal models, circumscription and closed world reasoning

The two formalisms of circumscription and closed world reasoning are introduced in next two subsections, respectively. Both of them are based on the notion of minimal model, which is given in the first subsection.

2.2.1 Minimal models and circumscription

The idea of McCarthy [McCarthy, 1980, McCarthy, 1986], further developed by Lifschitz in [Lifschitz, 1985b], is to define a preorder in the set of models of a first-order formula, so that models with smaller extensions for selected predicates are preferred. Referring to the above example, we prefer those models of formulae (2.2) and (2.3) in which the extension of predicate *abnormal* is as small as possible. This reflects our intuition: we would like our rule to have few exceptions.

It is important to note that we may *not* want to reduce the extension of all the predicates. As an example, we do not want to minimize the extension of the predicate *flies*, since this would be contrary to the intuitive meaning of the rule. There exists a third possibility: we do not want a predicate to be affected by our fancy form of reasoning, i.e., we want to protect it from undesired consequences. For the sake of the argument we say that *bird* is such a predicate. Intuitively, this means that the set of objects that are provably birds is the same with or without our fancy reasoning.

In Subsection 2.2.2 the intuitive meaning of the three classes of predicates will be clarified further by means of two examples.

We report now the formal definition of the preorder, as given by Lifschitz in [Lifschitz, 1985b]. The set of predicates of a first-order formula T is partitioned into three subsets $\langle P; Q; Z \rangle$. Predicates in P are those —like *abnormal*— that we want to *minimize*; predicates in Q are those —like *bird*— that we want to keep *fixed*; predicates in Z are those —like *flies*— for which we have no special attitude (they are called *varying*.) In order to be comparable, two models N and M need to have the same universe of interpretation and the same interpretation of functional symbols. Fixed predicates must also have the same extension in N and M.

Definition 2.2.1 ([Lifschitz, 1985b]) *We write $M \leq_{(P;Z)} N$ if for each predicate $p \in P$, the extension of p in M is a subset of the extension of p in N. We write $M <_{(P;Z)} N$ if $M \leq_{(P;Z)} N$ and $N \nleq_{(P;Z)} M$*

The relation $\leq_{(P;Z)}$ is clearly a preorder, hence we can talk about minimality. A model M is called $(P;Z)$-*minimal* for a formula T if there is no model N of T such that $N \leq_{(P;Z)} M$ and $M \nleq_{(P;Z)} N$. If $Q = Z = \emptyset$ then a $(P;Z)$-minimal model is called just *minimal*.

The set of $(P;Z)$-minimal models of a first-order formula can be compactly represented with a second-order formula. Lifschitz showed in [Lifschitz, 1985b] that the $(P;Z)$-minimal models of a first-order formula T are exactly the models of the second-order formula defined as follows

$$T \wedge \forall P'Z'(T[P';Z'] \rightarrow \neg(P' < P)) \qquad (2.4)$$

where $T[P';Z']$ is T with each predicate symbol r in the sets of predicates P, Z replaced by a new predicate symbol r' of the same arity. Moreover $(P' < P)$ stands for the formula

$$[\bigwedge_{1 \leq i \leq n} \forall \mathbf{x}_i(p_i'(\mathbf{x}_i) \rightarrow p_i(\mathbf{x}_i))] \wedge [\bigvee_{1 \leq i \leq n} \exists \mathbf{x}_i(\neg p_i'(\mathbf{x}_i) \wedge p_i(\mathbf{x}_i))],$$

where $\{p_1, \ldots, p_n\}$ are the predicate symbols occurring in P and $\{p_1', \ldots, p_n'\}$ are new predicate symbols of the same arity. Formula (2.4) is denoted as $CIRC(T; P; Z)$ and it is called the *circumscription* of P in T, varying the predicates in Z.

Let us clarify the above definitions with an example.

Example 2.2.1 (Tweety and circumscription) Referring to the example in Section 2.1, let T be the conjunction of the formulae (2.2) and (2.3), $P = \{abnormal\}, Q = \{bird\}, Z = \{flies\}$ and let M be the model of T whose universe of interpretation is the singleton $\{t\}$, that maps the constant symbol *Tweety* into t, and such that the extension of both *bird* and *flies* is $\{t\}$ and the extension of *abnormal* is the empty set. Clearly M is $(P;Z)$-minimal for T, hence *flies(Tweety)* is true in M. Actually it is easy to prove that *flies(Tweety)* is true in all the $(P;Z)$-minimal models of T (see [Lifschitz, 1985b].) As a consequence, $CIRC(T; P; Z) \models flies(Tweety)$ holds. $\diamond$

Definition 2.2.1 can be easily specified for propositional formulae as follows.

Definition 2.2.2 ($(P;Z)$-minimal models of a propositional formula) *Let M, N be two models of a propositional formula T and $\langle P;Q;Z \rangle$ a partition of the letters of T. We write $M \leq_{(P;Z)} N$ if M and N assign the same truth value to the letters in Q, and the set of letters of P which are mapped into 1 by M is a subset of the analogous set for N.*

In the next subsection we show examples of minimal models for propositional formulae.

The set of $(P; Z)$-minimal models of a propositional formula can be compactly represented with formula (2.4) —which is now a quantified boolean formula— where $(P' < P)$ stands for the propositional formula

$$[\bigwedge_{1 \le i \le n} p'_i \to p_i] \wedge [\bigvee_{1 \le i \le n} \neg p'_i \wedge p_i],$$

where $\{p_1, \ldots, p_n\}$ are the propositional letters occurring in P and $\{p'_1, \ldots, p'_n\}$ are new propositional letters.

Formula (2.4) is considered to be a satisfactory treatment of the idea of abnormality (even if some researchers do not agree, see for example [Etherington et al., 1991].) Many authors used such a formalization for defining deductive systems performing various tasks. As a partial list of applications of circumscription in AI we cite non-monotonic inheritance [Zadrozny, 1987, Haugh, 1988, Krishnaprasad et al., 1989], model-based diagnosis [Raiman, 1990, Besnard and Cordier, 1992] and knowledge base update [Winslett, 1989]. The idea of minimality underlying circumscription has been applied also in other areas, like data type specification [Bertossi, 1994] and Database Theory. We will go in more details about the relations between circumscription and Databases in Subsection 2.2.2. It has also been shown in [Doyle, 1985] that circumscription is able to capture several aspects of the idea of implicit definability, popular in Mathematical Logic.

$(P; Z)$-minimal models are very important also for the theory of Logic Programming and Deductive Databases, as many semantics for negation in Logic Programming originate from the idea of minimality. In particular well-founded models [Van Gelder et al., 1991], stable models [Gelfond and Lifschitz, 1988], perfect models [Przymusinski, 1988], models of the default semantics [Bidoit and Froidevaux, 1991] of a logic program Φ are $(P; Z)$-minimal models of Φ, for a suitable choice of the partition $\langle P; Q; Z \rangle$.

2.2.2 Minimal models and closed world reasoning

In this subsection we deal with the so-called *closed world reasoning*. The term closed world reasoning (CWR) refers to a collection of non-monotonic reasoning techniques commonly used for formalizing the kind of inference in which *lack* of information is important. CWR techniques originated in the area of Databases and were aimed at solving practical problems concerning information storing.

It is well known that negative information is often not explicitly stored in knowledge and data bases. In general, it is assumed that all the relevant positive information has been specified in the knowledge base, so that any positive fact not so specified is assumed to be false. Consider, for example, an information system including a flight timetable constituted by tuples collecting the relevant data on real flights. Since it is not feasible to store in the timetable every tuple not corresponding to a flight, the implicit assumption is that each tuple not occurring in the timetable does not correspond to a real flight. Note that when a person uses this assumption for inferring that a certain flight does not exist, then lack of information has a role in his reasoning.

The simplest form of closed world reasoning is the *(naive) closed world assumption* (CWA), introduced by Reiter [Reiter, 1978], which states that a negative ground fact of the form $\neg b$ is inferred from a knowledge base T just in case the corresponding positive fact b cannot be deduced from T. This represents the idea that every positive fact that is not known to be true, should be considered false. CWA is therefore adequate to represent the implicit negative information in a relational database, like the flight timetable discussed above. A semantic characterization of the CWA can be given in terms of minimal models: if a propositional formula T has a unique minimal model M, then M is the unique model of the CWA of T; if T has several minimal models, then the CWA of T is inconsistent. Inconsistency in CWA is introduced by disjunctive positive information: for example, since neither a nor b are deducible from the formula $a \vee b$, the CWA allows one to infer both $\neg a$ and $\neg b$.

Starting from the above consideration, Minker [Minker, 1982] proposed a new form of closed world reasoning, called *generalized closed world assumption* (GCWA), which states that the negative facts to be inferred from a knowledge base T, should be those which do not appear in *any* of the minimal models of T. For example, under the GCWA neither $\neg male$ nor $\neg female$ is inferred from the formula $F = male \vee female$, because there exists one minimal model of F in which $male$ is true, and one minimal model in which $female$ is true. Note, however, that both $\neg male$ and $\neg female$ are inferred from the formula $(\neg person \vee male \vee female) \wedge (\neg person \vee employed \vee unemployed)$.

Gelfond and Przymusinska [Gelfond and Przymusinska, 1986] extend the work of Minker, by allowing the generalized closed world assumption to be applied to a specified set P of (not necessarily all) predicates of the knowledge base. The resulting form of closed world reasoning, called *careful closed world assumption* (CCWA), is shown to be more expressive than the GCWA. In particular, contrary to both the CWA and the GCWA, it allows the derivation of positive facts which are not inferable from the original knowledge base. Semantically, the CCWA of T is obtained by conjoining to T the negation of all the atoms false in all the $(P; Z)$-minimal models.

The ability to infer new positive facts is a crucial feature of non-monotonic systems. Seminal papers on non-monotonic logics (see for example Reiter's default logic [Reiter, 1980b] and McCarthy's circumscription [McCarthy, 1980, McCarthy, 1986]) stress the point that a system for common-sense reasoning based on non-monotonicity should be able to infer that Tweety flies using the knowledge that Tweety is a bird and the *default* rule stating that birds generally fly (see also the discussion in the previous section.) Since we need a positive statement to represent the fact that Tweety flies, the desired conclusion can be inferred neither under the CWA nor under the GCWA, unless it is already known. On the other hand, this kind of inference can be modeled using the

CCWA, as we will see in a specific example (Example 2.2.2) later on in this subsection.

Yahya and Henschen [Yahya and Henschen, 1985] extend the work of Minker in another direction, by allowing non-atomic negated formulae to be inferred. The formalism they define is called *extended generalized closed world assumption* (EGCWA). Under the EGCWA some inferences are possible which are possible neither under the GCWA nor under the CCWA. For example we can infer $\neg male \vee \neg female$ from the formula $male \vee female$, thus changing the disjunction from inclusive to exclusive.

Gelfond, Przymusinska, and Przymusinski [Gelfond *et al.*, 1989] define the most sophisticated formalization of CWR, called *extended closed world assumption* (ECWA), that incorporates the nice features of both CCWA and EGCWA.

EGCWA and ECWA are quite satisfactory from the semantical point of view, since they are proven to be equivalent (at least for propositional theories) to circumscription. The ECWA of a propositional formula T is equivalent to formula (2.4), while its EGCWA is equivalent to (2.4) with $Q = Z = \emptyset$.

The evolution of the formalizations of CWR is reported in Figure 2.1. An edge from a formalism to another denotes an improvement, which is summarized by the label on the edge.

We give now formal definitions for all the above formalisms. A formula T together with a partition $\langle P, Q, Z \rangle$ of its letters will be denoted by $\langle T; P; Q; Z \rangle$. Moreover, given a set of letters R, we denote by R^+ (resp. R^-) the set of all positive (resp. negative) literals from R. All the forms of CWR we consider in this paper can be abstractly characterized as follows.

Definition 2.2.3 (closure of a formula) *Let T be a propositional formula, and let $\langle P; Q; Z \rangle$ be a partition of the letters of its alphabet. We define the closure of $\langle T; P; Q; Z \rangle$ with respect to the CWR-rule α as follows:*

$$\alpha(T; P; Q; Z) = T \cup \{\neg K \mid K \text{ is free for negation in } \langle T; P; Q; Z \rangle \text{ w.r.t. } \alpha\}$$

where K is a formula whose form depends on α.

As a notational convenience, we say that the formula K is α-ffn to mean that it is free for negation in $\langle T; P; Q; Z \rangle$ with respect to the CWR-rule α.

In order to precisely characterize the different forms of CWR, we now consider every CWR-rule α, specifying what it means for a formula to be free for negation with respect to α.

- The CWA-rule corresponds to the (naive) closed world assumption, defined in [Reiter, 1978]. K is CWA-ffn if K is a positive literal and $T \not\models K$.

- The GCWA-rule corresponds to the generalized closed world assumption [Minker, 1982]. K is GCWA-ffn if K is a positive literal and, for each positive clause B such that $T \not\models B$, it holds that $T \not\models B \vee K$.

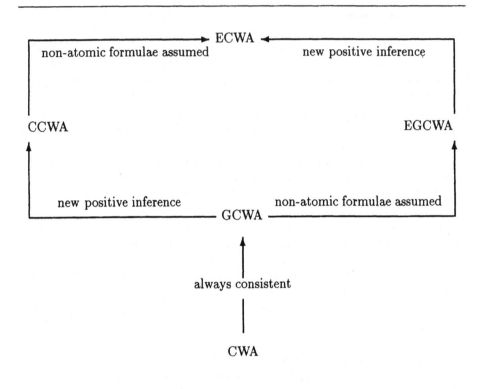

Figure 2.1: The evolution of formalisms for CWR

- The EGCWA-rule corresponds to the extended generalized closed world assumption [Yahya and Henschen, 1985]. K is EGCWA-ffn if K is a conjunction of positive literals and, for each positive clause B such that $T \not\models B$, it holds that $T \not\models B \vee K$.

- The CCWA-rule corresponds to the careful closed world assumption [Gelfond and Przymusinska, 1986]. The letters of T are partitioned into $\langle P; Q; Z \rangle$. K is CCWA-ffn if K is a positive literal from P and, for each clause B whose literals belong to $P^+ \cup Q^+ \cup Q^-$ such that $T \not\models B$, it holds that $T \not\models B \vee K$.

- The ECWA-rule corresponds to the extended closed world assumption [Gelfond *et al.*, 1989]. The letters of T are partitioned into $\langle P; Q; Z \rangle$. K is ECWA-ffn if K is an arbitrary formula not involving literals from Z and, for each clause B whose literals belong to $P^+ \cup Q^+ \cup Q^-$ such that $T \not\models B$, it holds that $T \not\models B \vee K$.

Note that in the CWA-, GCWA-, EGCWA-rules, there is no need to partition the letters into $\langle P; Q; Z \rangle$, and therefore we can simplify the notation and write $CWA(T)$, $GCWA(T)$, and $EGCWA(T)$, respectively.

We now consider two examples of applications of the CWR rules to propositional formulae. The examples are taken from the AI literature on common-sense reasoning.

Example 2.2.2 (Tweety and CWR) This is the Tweety example (cf. Example 2.2.1), that we already introduced in the previous section with formulae (2.2) and (2.3). We analyze the behavior of the CWR rules when applied to such formulae. Since we are interested in propositional languages, we consider the propositional version of formulae (2.2) and (2.3), namely

$$(\neg birdTweety \vee abnormalTweety \quad \vee \quad fliesTweety) \tag{2.5}$$

$$(birdTweety) \tag{2.6}$$

where $birdTweety$, $abnormalTweety$ and $fliesTweety$ are propositional letters that we abbreviate with b, a and f, respectively. Let T be the conjunction of clauses (2.5) and (2.6) and $P = \{a\}$, $Q = \{b\}$ and $Z = \{f\}$ be a partition of the alphabet of T. The intuitive meaning of the partition is that in the case of CCWA and ECWA we want to minimize abnormalities (letter a), while keeping fixed birds (letter b) and allowing flying things to vary (letter f.)

The free for negation formulae for each CWR rule are listed below:

$$
\begin{array}{rcl}
CWA & : & \{a, f\} \\
GCWA & : & \{\} \\
EGCWA & : & \{(a \wedge f)\} \\
CCWA & : & \{a\} \\
ECWA & : & \{a\}.
\end{array}
$$

Note that, by definition, every formula obtained by conjoining one letter to an EGCWA-ffn (resp. ECWA-ffn) formula is also an EGCWA-ffn (resp. ECWA-ffn) formula. For example, also $a \wedge b$ is an ECWA-ffn formula. However, since such formulae do not add any significant information, we did not include them in the above list.

The different closures of T are listed below:

$$
\begin{array}{rcl}
CWA(T) & = & T \wedge \neg a \wedge \neg f \\
GCWA(T) & = & T \\
EGCWA(T) & = & T \wedge \neg(a \wedge f) \\
CCWA(T; P; Q; Z) & = & T \wedge \neg a \\
ECWA(T; P; Q; Z) & = & T \wedge \neg a.
\end{array}
$$

Note that $CWA(T)$ is unsatisfiable. The following are examples of formulae inferred by means of the other CWR-rules. Note that f is a new positive fact inferable under both the CCWA and the ECWA.

$$GCWA(T) \not\models (\neg a \vee \neg f)$$
$$GCWA(T) \not\models f$$
$$EGCWA(T) \not\models f$$
$$EGCWA(T) \models (\neg a \vee \neg f)$$
$$CCWA(T; P; Q; Z) \models f$$
$$ECWA(T; P; Q; Z) \models f.$$

Both CCWA and ECWA allow us to infer that Tweety flies, and this is due to the fact we can take advantage of the partition of the letters into the three subsets. In the following example we see how ECWA allows more sophisticated forms of reasoning than CCWA. ◇

Example 2.2.3 (Nixon diamond) This is a variant of the well-known "Nixon diamond" example ([Touretzky, 1984], discussed also in [Cadoli *et al.*, 1990b].) In this case we have two general rules, saying respectively that republicans are normally hawks (2.7) and that quakers are normally doves (2.8). Moreover hawks are never doves (2.9) and both hawks and doves are politically motivated (2.10), (2.11). Nixon is both a republican and a quaker (2.12).

$$\forall x \ (republican(x) \wedge \neg abnormal_1(x) \quad \rightarrow \quad hawk(x)) \tag{2.7}$$
$$\forall x \ (quacker(x) \wedge \neg abnormal_2(x) \quad \rightarrow \quad dove(x)) \tag{2.8}$$
$$\forall x \ (hawk(x) \quad \rightarrow \quad \neg dove(x)) \tag{2.9}$$
$$\forall x \ (hawk(x) \quad \rightarrow \quad politicallyMotivated(x)) \tag{2.10}$$
$$\forall x \ (dove(x) \quad \rightarrow \quad politicallyMotivated(x)) \tag{2.11}$$
$$republican(Nixon) \quad \wedge \quad quacker(Nixon) \tag{2.12}$$

(If you can't figure out why this set of sentences is called "diamond", you can have a look at Figure 2.4 in Section 2.7.1.) In this example we do not want to infer that Nixon is definitely a hawk, neither we want to infer that he is definitely a dove. Nevertheless, on the grounds that one default rule must apply anyway, we may argue that Nixon has to be *either* a hawk *or* a dove. According to this form of reasoning by cases, Nixon is politically motivated anyway.

As in the previous example, we consider the propositional version of the above set of formulae. Let T be the conjunction of the following clauses

$$(\neg r \vee a_1 \quad \vee \quad h)$$
$$(\neg q \vee a_2 \quad \vee \quad d)$$
$$(\neg h \quad \vee \quad \neg d)$$
$$(\neg h \quad \vee \quad p)$$
$$(\neg d \quad \vee \quad p)$$
$$(r)$$
$$(q)$$

The partition of the alphabet is in this case $P = \{a_1, a_2\}$, $Q = \{r, q\}$ and $Z = \{h, d, p\}$. The intuitive meaning of the partition is that we want to minimize abnormalities (letters a_1, a_2), while keeping fixed quakers and republicans (letters r, q) and allowing everything else to vary (letters h, d, p.) We analyze the behavior of the CWR rules when applied to T.

The free for negation formulae for each CWR rule are listed below. Like in the previous example, we included only relevant EGCWA-ffn and ECWA-ffn formulae.

$$\begin{aligned}
CWA &: \{a_1, a_2, h, d, p\} \\
GCWA &: \{\} \\
EGCWA &: \{(a_1 \wedge h), (a_2 \wedge d), (d \wedge h), (a_1 \wedge a_2 \wedge p)\} \\
CCWA &: \{\} \\
ECWA &: \{(a_1 \wedge a_2)\}.
\end{aligned}$$

The different closures of T are listed below:

$$\begin{aligned}
CWA(T) &= T \wedge \neg a_1 \wedge \neg a_2 \wedge \neg h \wedge \neg d \wedge \neg p \\
GCWA(T) &= T \\
EGCWA(T) &= T \wedge \neg(a_1 \wedge h) \wedge \neg(a_2 \wedge d) \wedge \neg(d \wedge h) \wedge \\
&\quad \wedge \neg(a_1 \wedge a_2 \wedge p) \\
CCWA(T; P; Q; Z) &= T \\
ECWA(T; P; Q; Z) &= T \wedge \neg(a_1 \wedge a_2).
\end{aligned}$$

Note that $CWA(T)$ is unsatisfiable. The following are examples of formulae inferred by means of the other CWR-rules. Note that $(h \vee d)$ and p are new positive facts inferable under the ECWA.

$$\begin{aligned}
GCWA(T) &\not\models (h \vee d) \\
GCWA(T) &\not\models p \\
EGCWA(T) &\not\models (h \vee d) \\
EGCWA(T) &\not\models p \\
CCWA(T; P; Q; Z) &\not\models (h \vee d) \\
CCWA(T; P; Q; Z) &\not\models p \\
ECWA(T; P; Q; Z) &\models p \wedge (h \vee d)
\end{aligned}$$

Only the ECWA formalism allows us to perform reasoning by cases like we sketched above. ECWA let us infer that Nixon is either a hawk or a dove and that he is definitely politically motivated. This is due to the fact that we can take advantage both of the partition of the letters into the three subsets, and the non-atomicity of free for negation formulae.

We note that the results obtained do not depend on the letters r, q being in Q: the same results hold if $Q = \emptyset$ and $\{r, q\} \subset P$ or $\{r, q\} \subset Z$. On the other hand it is necessary that h, d and p belong to Z. Similar considerations hold for the previous example. $\diamond$

We now turn to the semantical characterization of CWR-rules, which is based on the notion of minimal model. By exploiting the concept of minimality and $(P; Z)$-minimality, it is possible to semantically characterize the notion of freeness for negation as follows.

- K is CWA-ffn in T iff it is a positive literal and there exists a model M of T such that $M \not\models K$ (obvious consequence of definition.)

- K is GCWA-ffn in T iff it is a positive literal and for each minimal model M of T, $M \not\models K$ (see [Minker, 1982, Theorem 2].)

- K is EGCWA-ffn in T iff it is a conjunction of positive literals and for each minimal model M of T, $M \not\models K$ (see [Yahya and Henschen, 1985, Theorem 14].)

- K is CCWA-ffn in $\langle T; P; Q; Z \rangle$ iff it is a positive literal from P and for each $(P; Z)$-minimal model M of T, $M \not\models K$ (see [Gelfond and Przymusinska, 1986, Theorem 3.6].)

- K is ECWA-ffn in $\langle T; P; Q; Z \rangle$ iff it is a formula not involving literals from Z and for each $(P; Z)$-minimal model M of T, $M \not\models K$ (see [Gelfond et al., 1989, Theorem 4.5].)

We show the minimal models of the formulae seen in the previous examples.

Example 2.2.2 (Tweety and CWR, continued) The minimal models of T are as follows (we write $M \models a_1 \wedge \cdots \wedge a_n$ to mean that the set of letters satisfied by M is exactly $\{a_1, \ldots, a_n\}$.)

$$
\begin{aligned}
M_1 &\models b \wedge a \\
M_2 &\models b \wedge f
\end{aligned}
$$

Note that M_2 is also a $(P; Z)$-minimal model. $\Diamond$

Example 2.2.3 (Nixon diamond, continued) The minimal models of T are as follows.

$$
\begin{aligned}
M_1 &\models r \wedge q \wedge a_1 \wedge a_2 \\
M_2 &\models r \wedge q \wedge a_1 \wedge d \wedge p \\
M_3 &\models r \wedge q \wedge a_2 \wedge h \wedge p
\end{aligned}
$$

Note that M_2 and M_3 are also $(P; Z)$-minimal models. $\Diamond$

From the above properties, one can easily show that for any formula F:

1. $EGCWA(T) \models F$ iff for each minimal model M of T, $M \models F$ (see [Yahya and Henschen, 1985, Theorem 14] .)

2. $ECWA(T; P; Q; Z) \models F$ iff for each $(P; Z)$-minimal model M of T, $M \models F$ (see [Gelfond *et al.*, 1989, Corollary 4.7].)

Moreover, it is shown in [Gelfond *et al.*, 1989] that for any formula F it holds that $ECWA(T; P; Q; Z) \models F$ iff $CIRC(T; P; Z) \models F$, where $CIRC(T; P; Z)$ denotes the circumscription of P in T with variables Z (see Subsection 2.2.1.)

2.3 Complexity of closed world reasoning

2.3.1 Goal of the research and related results

Our goal is to understand to what extent CWR is more difficult than monotonic inference. One can easily verify that performing inference according to some form of CWR is at least as difficult as performing monotonic inference, simply by noticing that $T \models F$ iff $ECWA(T; \emptyset; Q; Z) \models F$, hence monotonic inference can be polynomially reduced to closed world inference.

For this reason, we were particularly interested in classes of formulae for which monotonic inference is polynomial (cf. Section 1.10.4.)

Another goal we have is to analyze the efficiency of algorithms for propositional circumscription that have been proposed in the literature.

Several authors investigated about the complexity of closed world reasoning, but a detailed analysis of the tractability threshold was still missing. We now survey the main results appeared in the literature.

Apt in [Apt, 1990] proved that CWA in propositional Horn clauses is polynomial, Eiter and Gottlob in [Eiter and Gottlob, 1993b] and Schlipf in [Schlipf, 1988] studied lower bounds of CWR for unrestricted propositional formulae, Papalaskari and Weinstein [Papalaskari and Weinstein, 1990] dealt with infinite propositional languages, Vardi in [Vardi, 1986b] and Grahne in [Grahne, 1991] analyzed the complexity of CWA in relational databases, Chomicki and Subrahmanian in [Chomicki and Subrahmanian, 1990] studied GCWA in first-order logic programs, while Apt and Blair in [Apt and Blair, 1990] studied CWA in the same languages. Finally, Borgida and Etherington in [Borgida and Etherington, 1989] and Chan in [Chan, 1993] addressed other forms of CWR showing some polynomial cases for restricted propositional languages.

2.3.2 Results

We are now ready to precisely characterize the *inference problems* considered in our research. In general inference problems consist in checking if the closure of a propositional formula T according to the CWR-rule α logically entails a formula F. The decision problem we considered is specified as follows.

INF-$\alpha[c, f]$ (**CWR inference**)
INSTANCE: A CWR-rule α; a propositional formula T belonging to a class c of propositional formulae described in Figure 1.10.

f is either LIT, in which case F is a literal, or CLAUSE, in which case F is a clause.

The letters of T are partitioned into $\langle P; Q; Z \rangle$.

QUESTION: Is it the case that $\alpha(T; P; Q; Z) \models F$?

As an example, the problem INF-CCWA[HORN,CLAUSE], is the problem of deciding whether $CCWA(T; P; Q; Z) \models \gamma$, where T is a Horn formula and γ is a clause.

Whenever the problem requires one or both elements of the set $\{Q; Z\}$ to be empty, the decision problem is defined as follows.

INF-$\alpha[c,f,d]$, (**CWR inference with empty sets of letters**)

INSTANCE: Same as before, and d is either $Q = \emptyset$, or $Z = \emptyset$, or $Q = Z = \emptyset$.

QUESTION: Is it the case that $\alpha(T; P; \emptyset; Z) \models F$ (resp. $\alpha(T; P; Q; \emptyset) \models F$, or $\alpha(T; P; \emptyset; \emptyset) \models F$)?

As an example, the problem INF-ECWA[DHORN,LIT,$Q = Z = \emptyset$], is the problem of deciding whether $ECWA(T; P; \emptyset; \emptyset) \models l$, where T is a Dual-Horn formula and l is a literal.

The complexity analysis has been carried out along three directions, one concerning the form of CWR (represented by α in the above definitions), one concerning the expressive power of the language used for expressing the formula (represented by c), and one concerning the kind of formula to be inferred (represented by f.) Moreover, for those CWR-rules requiring the letters of a formula T to be partitioned into the three sets $\langle P, Q, Z \rangle$ (i.e., CCWA and ECWA), we considered two special cases, namely, $Q = \emptyset$ and $Z = \emptyset$.

The results of the analysis are summarized in four nine by eight tables; in those tables each row corresponds to a CWR formalism and each column corresponds to a propositional class. Three tables refer to problems INF-$\alpha[c,f]$ and INF-$\alpha[c,f,d]$, while one table refers to semantical properties. Here is a brief description of the four tables.

Tables 2.1, 2.2 and 2.3 summarize the complexity results for all the forms of CWR and for all the classes of propositional formulae discussed in this paper. In all these table, the symbol "–" means "non-applicable".

Table 2.1 deals with the complexity of clause inference. The symbol "P" means "polynomial", and the symbol "coNPh" means "co-NP-hard".

Table 2.2 deals with the complexity of literal inference. Obviously, each entry being a "P" in Table 2.1 is also a "P" in this table. Note that some entry being a "coNPh" in Table 2.1 is a "P" in this table.

Table 2.3 deals with the upper bound of the complexity of clause inference. The symbol "P" means membership in P, the symbol "coNP" means membership in co-NP (note that in the previous tables "coNPh" is a lower bound), whereas the symbol "P$^{NP\,log}$" means membership in $P^{NP[O(\log n)]}$.

Table 2.4 summarizes some semantical results, answering the question "is it possible to infer new positive information in a given propositional class and for a given CWR formalism?" The symbol "–" means "non-applicable". The symbol "YES" means that in some cases new positive clauses are inferable, whereas the symbol "NO" means that new positive clauses can never be inferred, with the exception of the CWA row, where the symbol "NO" means that if the CWA of a formula is consistent, then no new positive clause is inferred from the closure. Obviously, new positive clauses are derivable from an inconsistent closure.

The first three rows of each table remind the syntax of each class of formulae. For example, in the case of HornKrom (HK), the three rows indicate that the clauses have at most one positive literal and at most two literals.

Every entry in the tables contains a pointer to either a theorem proven in this work (e.g., A.1.4) or an item in the references (e.g., [Apt, 1990].) Multiple references occur for those cases that are proven by distinct results (e.g., distinct theorems proven in this work.) For each original polynomiality result a polynomial time algorithm solving the corresponding problem has been developed.

The four tables are shown in the following pages. Looking at the four tables, we observe that:

1. In the cases where new positive clauses are derivable, the inference problem is tractable only under CCWA, in particular for all classes of formulae except Dual-Horn. On the other hand, the problem is always intractable under ECWA.

2. There are cases where literal inference is easier than clause inference, in particular, for EGCWA and for ECWA with $Z = \emptyset$. Note, however, that this happens only for cases where new positive clauses are not derivable.

3. Looking at the complexity of literal and clause inference, one can verify that the CCWA is often easier than the ECWA. It seems that the characteristic of the CCWA of limiting the attention to free for negation literals rather than general formulae is a good compromise between the expressive power of the CWR technique and the computational complexity of the inference problem. However, while ECWA inference is in co-NP for all the cases considered in this paper, the upper bound we have established for CCWA is $P^{NP[O(\log n)]}$.

4. Tables 2.1 and 2.2 show that there are cases where the fact that $Q = \emptyset$ or $Z = \emptyset$ makes the inference problem easier. Although it is shown in Section 2.6 that we can always reduce in polynomial time the ECWA inference to the case where $Z = \emptyset$, and a similar reduction is shown in [de Kleer and Konolige, 1989] for $Q = \emptyset$, our complexity results confirm that such reduction does not preserve the syntactic class of formulae in which inference is performed (for example, a Horn formula with $Q \neq \emptyset$ or $Z \neq \emptyset$ is transformed into a formula with $Q = \emptyset$ or $Z = \emptyset$ which is not Horn.)

	HORN	KROM	DEF	HK	HK⁻	2POSK	DHORN	DHK
pos	≤1		1	≤1	≤1	2		
neg					≤1	0	≤1	≤1
tot		≤2		≤2	≤2	2		≤2
CWA	P a	P A.1.1	P a	P a	P a	P A.1.1	P A.1.1	P A.1.1
GCWA	P A.1.1 A.1.21 a	P A.1.9	P A.1.1 A.1.7 A.1.21 a	P A.1.1 A.1.21 A.1.9 a	P A.1.1 A.1.21 A.1.9 a	P A.1.9	coNPh A.1.2	P A.1.9
EGCWA	P A.1.1 A.1.21 a	coNPh A.1.4	P A.1.1 A.1.21 a	P A.1.1 A.1.21 a	P A.1.1 A.1.21 A.1.27 a	coNPh A.1.4	coNPh A.1.3 A.1.4	coNPh A.1.4
CCWA $Q = \emptyset$	P A.1.22	P A.1.8	P A.1.7 A.1.22	P A.1.8 A.1.22	P A.1.8 A.1.22	P A.1.8	coNPh A.1.5	P A.1.8
CCWA $Z = \emptyset$	coNPh A.1.6	P A.1.8	P A.1.7	P A.1.8	P A.1.8	P A.1.8	coNPh A.1.5	P A.1.8
CCWA	coNPh A.1.6	P A.1.8	P A.1.7	P A.1.8	P A.1.8	P A.1.8	coNPh A.1.5	P A.1.8
ECWA $Q = \emptyset$	P A.1.21	coNPh A.1.11 A.1.15	P A.1.7 A.1.21	P A.1.21	P	coNPh A.1.21 A.1.27	coNPh A.1.10 A.1.11 A.1.15	coNPh A.1.11 A.1.15
ECWA $Z = \emptyset$	coNPh A.1.12 A.1.13 A.1.16	coNPh A.1.11 A.1.16	coNPh A.1.13	coNPh A.1.16	P A.1.27	coNPh A.1.11	coNPh A.1.10 A.1.11	coNPh A.1.11
ECWA	coNPh A.1.12 A.1.13 A.1.14 A.1.16 A.1.17	coNPh A.1.11 A.1.15 A.1.16 A.1.17	coNPh A.1.13 A.1.14	coNPh A.1.16 A.1.17	P A.1.27	coNPh A.1.11 A.1.15	coNPh A.1.10 A.1.11 A.1.15	coNPh A.1.11 A.1.15

[a][Apt, 1990]

Table 2.1: Complexity of clause inference for the various syntactic classes and CWR rules (problems INF-α[c,CLAUSE] and INF-α[c,CLAUSE,d])

	HORN	KROM	DEF	HK	HK⁻	2POSK	DHORN	DHK
pos	≤1		1	≤1	≤1	2		
neg					≤1	0	≤1	≤1
tot		≤2		≤2	≤2	2		≤2
CWA	P a	P A.1.1	P a	P a	P a	P A.1.1	P A.1.1	P A.1.1
GCWA	P A.1.1 A.1.21 a	P A.1.9	P A.1.1 A.1.7 A.1.21 a	P A.1.1 A.1.21 A.1.9 a	P A.1.1 A.1.21 A.1.9 a	P A.1.9	coNPh A.1.2	P A.1.9
EGCWA	P A.1.1 A.1.21 a	P A.1.20	P A.1.1 A.1.18 A.1.21 a	P A.1.1 A.1.21 A.1.20 a	P A.1.1 A.1.21 A.1.20 A.1.27 a	P A.1.20	coNPh A.1.3	P A.1.20
CCWA $Q = \emptyset$	P A.1.22	P A.1.8	P A.1.7 A.1.22	P A.1.8 A.1.22	P A.1.8 A.1.22	P A.1.8	coNPh A.1.5	P A.1.8
CCWA $Z = \emptyset$	coNPh A.1.6	P A.1.8	P A.1.7	P A.1.8	P A.1.8	P A.1.8	coNPh A.1.5	P A.1.8
CCWA	coNPh A.1.6	P A.1.8	P A.1.7	P A.1.8	P A.1.8	P A.1.8	coNPh A.1.5	P A.1.8
ECWA $Q = \emptyset$	P A.1.21	coNPh A.1.15	P A.1.21	P A.1.21	P A.1.21 A.1.27	coNPh A.1.15	coNPh A.1.10 A.1.15	coNPh A.1.15
ECWA $Z = \emptyset$	coNPh A.1.12	P A.1.19	P A.1.18	P A.1.19	P A.1.19 A.1.27	P A.1.19	coNPh A.1.10	P A.1.19
ECWA	coNPh A.1.12 A.1.14 A.1.17	coNPh A.1.15 A.1.17	coNPh A.1.14	coNPh A.1.17	P A.1.27	coNPh A.1.15	coNPh A.1.10 A.1.15	coNPh A.1.15

[a][Apt, 1990]

Table 2.2: Complexity of literal inference for the various syntactic classes and CWR rules (problems INF-α[c,LIT] and INF-α[c,LIT,d])

	HORN	KROM	DEF	HK	HK$^-$	2POSK	DHORN	DHK
pos	≤ 1		1	≤ 1	≤ 1	2		
neg					≤ 1	0	≤ 1	≤ 1
tot		≤ 2		≤ 2	≤ 2	2		≤ 2
CWA	P a	P A.1.1	P a	P a	P a	P A.1.1	P A.1.1	P A.1.1
GCWA	P a	P A.1.8	P a	P a	P a	P A.1.8	P$^{NP\,log}$ A.2.4 b	P A.1.8
EGCWA	P a	coNP A.2.4	P a	P a	P a	coNP A.2.4	coNP A.2.4	coNP A.2.4
CCWA $Q = \emptyset$	P A.1.21	P A.1.8	P A.1.21	P A.1.8	P A.1.8	P A.1.8	P$^{NP\,log}$ A.2.4 b	P A.1.8
CCWA $Z = \emptyset$	P$^{NP\,log}$ A.2.4 b	P A.1.8	P A.1.7	P A.1.8	P A.1.8	P A.1.8	P$^{NP\,log}$ A.2.4 b	P A.1.8
CCWA	P$^{NP\,log}$ A.2.4 b	P A.1.8	P A.1.7	P A.1.8	P A.1.8	P A.1.8	P$^{NP\,log}$ A.2.4 b	P A.2.4 b
ECWA $Q = \emptyset$	P A.1.21	coNP A.2.4	P A.1.21	P A.1.21	P A.1.21	coNP A.2.4	coNP A.2.4	coNP A.2.4
ECWA $Z = \emptyset$	coNP A.2.4	coNP A.2.4	coNP A.2.4	coNP A.2.4	P A.1.27	coNP A.2.4	coNP A.2.4	coNP A.2.4
ECWA	coNP A.2.4	coNP A.2.4	coNP A.2.4	coNP A.2.4	P A.1.27	coNP A.2.4	coNP A.2.4	coNP A.2.4

^{a}[Apt, 1990]
^{b}[Eiter and Gottlob, 1993b]

Table 2.3: Upper bound of the complexity of clause inference for the various syntactic classes and CWR rules (problems INF-$\alpha[c,$CLAUSE$]$ and INF-$\alpha[c,$CLAUSE$,d]$)

	HORN	KROM	DEF	HK	HK⁻	2POSK	DHORN	DHK
pos	≤ 1		1	≤ 1	≤ 1	2		
neg					≤ 1	0	≤ 1	≤ 1
tot		≤ 2		≤ 2	≤ 2	2		≤ 2
CWA	NO	NO	NO	NO	NO	NO	NO	NO
	A.1.28	a	A.1.28	A.1.28	A.1.28	a	a	a
GCWA	NO	NO	NO	NO	NO	NO	NO	NO
	A.1.28	A.1.28	A.1.28	A.1.28	A.1.28	A.1.28	A.1.28	A.1.28
EGCWA	NO	NO	NO	NO	NO	NO	NO	NO
	A.1.28	A.1.28	A.1.28	A.1.28	A.1.28	A.1.28	A.1.28	A.1.28
CCWA $Q = \emptyset$	NO	YES	NO	NO	NO	YES	YES	YES
	A.1.30	A.1.31	A.1.30	A.1.30	A.1.30	A.1.31	A.1.31	A.1.31
CCWA $Z = \emptyset$	NO	NO	NO	NO	NO	NO	NO	NO
	A.1.29	A.1.29	A.1.29	A.1.29	A.1.29	A.1.29	A.1.29	A.1.29
	A.1.30		A.1.30	A.1.30	A.1.30			
CCWA	NO	YES	NO	NO	NO	YES	YES	YES
	A.1.30	A.1.31	A.1.30	A.1.30	A.1.30	A.1.31	A.1.31	A.1.31
ECWA $Q = \emptyset$	NO	YES	NO	NO	NO	YES	YES	YES
	A.1.30	A.1.31	A.1.30	A.1.30	A.1.30	A.1.31	A.1.31	A.1.31
ECWA $Z = \emptyset$	NO	NO	NO	NO	NO	NO	NO	NO
	A.1.29	A.1.29	A.1.29	A.1.29	A.1.29	A.1.29	A.1.29	A.1.29
	A.1.30		A.1.30	A.1.30	A.1.30			
ECWA	NO	YES	NO	NO	NO	YES	YES	YES
	A.1.30	A.1.31	A.1.30	A.1.30	A.1.30	A.1.31	A.1.31	A.1.31

a[Reiter, 1978]

Table 2.4: Can the CWR method infer new positive clauses (as opposed to only negative clauses)?

5. The presence of fixed letters (those in Q) can be a source of complexity both for CCWA and ECWA. The presence of varying letters (those in Z) is a source of complexity only for ECWA and inference of literals.

Apart from the analysis of the intrinsic complexity of the inference problem, we analyzed the complexity of two algorithms for computing inference in circumscription: the *MILO-resolution* method by Przymusinski [Przymusinski, 1989] and the *circumscriptive theorem prover* by Ginsberg [Ginsberg, 1989].) We showed syntactic classes in which the inference problem is polynomial, but it is solved by these algorithms in exponential time. In particular this holds for the class HornKrom⁻.

Proofs of theorems referred in the four tables, algorithms for the polynomial cases and the discussion of algorithms by Przymusinski and Ginsberg will be presented in the Appendix A.1.

Results of the analysis shown in this section have been published in [Cadoli and Lenzerini, 1990, Cadoli and Lenzerini, 1994].

2.4   Complexity of minimal model checking

2.4.1   Goal of the research and related results

Model checking is the problem of deciding whether a finite structure is a model of a logical formula. It is well-known that if the formula is first-order, then this problem is polynomial in the size of the finite structure.

Model checking is not only interesting from the theoretical point of view but it is also important for the AI practice. Reasoning techniques have been formalized as model checking problems since the early days of automated reasoning (see for example [Gelernter, 1959].) More recently Halpern and Vardi proposed in [Halpern and Vardi, 1991] that model checking should be used systematically for defining reasoning processes. According to these authors, one of the advantages of model checking with respect to theorem proving (i.e., checking validity in all models) is indeed in computational saving.

In the field of non-monotonic logics several authors studied computational aspects of model checking. We now survey the main results appeared in the literature

Kolaitis and Papadimitriou showed in [Kolaitis and Papadimitriou, 1990] that the model checking problem for the circumscription of a first-order formula T is:

1. polynomial when T is a logic program, i.e., is a prenex normal form universal Horn formula;

2. co-NP-complete when T belongs to the class of universal-existential first-order sentences.

The same authors left open the question [Kolaitis and Papadimitriou, 1990, Open Problem 4] whether it is possible to generalize the first case, proving that the problem is polynomial for the class of all universal first-order sentences.

Lisitsa solved the open problem, by proving in [Lisitsa, 1993] that, when the formula T is first-order, universal and not part of the input, the model checking problem is co-NP-complete.

Schlipf addressed in [Schlipf, 1988] the same problem for propositional formulae, showing that if varying letters are allowed, i.e., one wants to check $(P; Z)$-minimality, then the problem becomes intractable. Papadimitriou analyzed in [Papadimitriou, 1991] computational aspects for model checking in a form of non-monotonic reasoning defined by Selman and Kautz in [Selman and Kautz, 1990].

2.4.2   Results

We carried out a detailed analysis of the computational complexity of model checking for propositional circumscriptive formulae. Following Schaefer's approach [Schaefer, 1978], we classified propositional formulae according to the logical relations (generalized connectives) which are used to represent them.

A logical relation of arity k is a subset of the set $\{0, 1\}^k$, which denotes the truth table of the relation. If R is a logical relation of arity k and $x_1, \ldots, x_k$ are boolean variables possibly not distinct, then $R(x_1, \ldots, x_k)$ is a *clause* (we note that this term is less restrictive than the usual meaning of the word clause as a disjunction of literals, that is used throughout this book with the exception of the present section and Section 2.5.) A truth assignment to a set L of logical variables is a function $M : L \to \{0, 1\}$. A clause $R(x_1, \ldots, x_k)$ is satisfied by a truth assignment M iff $\langle M(x_1), \ldots, M(x_k) \rangle \in R$. If $S = \{R_1, \ldots, R_n\}$ is a set of logical relations, each having its own arity, then an S-formula is any conjunction of clauses built on the relations in S. The set of variables which occur in a formula is called its alphabet. An S-formula is satisfiable if and only if it has a model, i.e., a truth assignment that satisfies all of its clauses. The decision problem $SAT(S)$ consists in checking whether an S-formula T is satisfiable.

As an example, let S be the set $\{R\}$, where R is the 3-ary relation denoted by the set $\{\langle 1, 0, 0 \rangle, \langle 0, 1, 0 \rangle, \langle 0, 0, 1 \rangle\}$, i.e., the "one-in-three" relation. The conjunction $R(x, y, z) \wedge R(x, y, u) \wedge R(u, x, y)$ is a satisfiable S-formula, because it is made true by the truth assignment $\mathcal{M}$ which maps the variables x, y, z, u into the values 0,1,0,0, respectively.

Schaefer has shown in [Schaefer, 1978] that the complexity of a generic satisfiability problem $SAT(S)$ is characterized by the set of relations which are used in the formula.   He considered the following classes of formulae:

  α. every relation in S is *0-valid*, i.e., contains the tuple $\langle 0, 0, \ldots, 0 \rangle$;

  β. every relation in S is *1-valid*, i.e., contains the tuple $\langle 1, 1, \ldots, 1 \rangle$;

  γ. every relation in S is *weakly positive*, i.e., is logically equivalent to some CNF Dual-Horn formula, or every relation in S is *weakly negative*, i.e., is logically equivalent to some CNF Horn formula, or every relation in S is *bijunctive*, i.e., is logically equivalent to some CNF Krom formula, or every relation in S is *affine*, i.e., is logically equivalent to a conjunction of formulae of the form $x_1 \oplus \cdots \oplus x_n = 0$ and $x_1 \oplus \cdots \oplus x_n = 1$, where $\oplus$ denotes addition modulo 2.

An important result shown by Schaefer ("dicothomy theorem") is that $SAT(S)$ is polynomial in the classes of formulae α, β and γ just described, and it is NP-complete in all other cases.

We note that the union of the eight classes of polynomial formulae described in Section 1.10.4 is a subset of the class γ.

Formally, the decision problem of model checking for propositional circumscriptive formulae we considered is the following.

$(P; Q; Z)$-**MIN**(S)
INSTANCE: A set L of boolean variables, a partition $\langle P; Q; Z \rangle$ of L,
           an S-formula T on L and a model M of T.
QUESTION: Is M a $(P; Z)$-minimal model of T?

We referred to the representation of formulae by means of the associated logical relations in order to give a clearer picture of the tractability threshold.

We also considered three special cases of the problem, namely $Q = \emptyset, Z = \emptyset$ and $Q = Z = \emptyset$. The complexity analysis has been developed for several sets S, in particular for the three cases α, β and γ defined previously, plus the complementary case. In particular we showed that the problem $(P; \emptyset; \emptyset)$-MIN$(S)$ is co-NP-complete even for a subclass of propositional circumscriptive formulae, thus giving a negative answer to Kolaitis and Papadimitriou's question when the formula T is propositional and part of the input.

Our complexity results are summarized in a four by four table (Table 2.5.) In this table each column refers to a minimality problem, in which $Q = \emptyset$, or $Z = \emptyset$, or $Q = Z = \emptyset$, or no restriction holds. Each row refers to a condition on the set S. The first three rows correspond to cases α, β, γ, respectively, as defined previously. The fourth row corresponds to the complementary case, i.e., in which S contains at least one relation which is not 0-valid, at least one which is not 1-valid, ..., and at least one which is not affine.

Each entry of the table is "P", which means polynomiality, or "coNP", which means co-NP-completeness. Moreover, each entry contains a pointer to a theorem that proves the result (e.g., A.2.1) or to an item in the references (e.g., [Schlipf, 1988].)

We want to point out that we have provided a detailed picture of the tractability threshold of the problem. In particular the problem is polynomial for all of the eight classes of propositional formulae considered in Section 2.3.1 (cf. row γ of Table 2.5.)

	$(P;Q;Z)$-MIN(S)	$(P;\emptyset;Z)$-MIN(S)	$(P;Q;\emptyset)$-MIN(S)	$(P;\emptyset;\emptyset)$-MIN(S)
α	coNP A.2.3	P A.2.5	coNP A.2.3	P A.2.5
β	coNP A.2.1	coNP A.2.1	coNP A.2.1	coNP A.2.1
γ	P A.2.5	P A.2.5	P A.2.5	P A.2.5
compl.	coNP A.2.2 [Schlipf, 1988]	coNP A.2.2 [Schlipf, 1988]	coNP A.2.2	coNP A.2.2

Table 2.5: Complexity of the problem $(P;Q;Z)$-**MIN**(S)

Proofs of theorems referred in the table will be presented in the Appendix A.2.

Results of the analysis shown in this section have been published in [Cadoli, 1992a].

2.5   Complexity of finding a minimal model

2.5.1   Goal of the research and related results

Many AI problems are inherently *constructive*, i.e., one wants an answer that is more detailed than a simple boolean value. A typical problem of this kind is planning. In the area of non-monotonic logics, a famous constructive problem is the search of *nogoods* in truth maintenance systems (or TMSs.) A nogood is a set of literals that conjoined to a propositional formula makes it unsatisfiable (see for example in [de Kleer, 1986].) Other interesting constructive problems in non-monotonic reasoning can be found in model-based diagnosis and in knowledge base update. We will return on the practical importance of constructive problems in Section 2.7.2.

From the point of view of complexity, these problems are sometimes studied in their decisional version. For example, as opposed to analyzing the complexity of the constructive problem of finding a nogood of minimal size, Rutenburg studies in [Rutenburg, 1991] the problem of deciding whether a nogood having less than k propositional letters exists. Simplifications of this kind make sense, provided the two problems considered (decisional and constructive) are polynomial-time Turing reducible one to another.

Several attempts at a more precise characterization of the complexity of constructive problems appeared in the last few years in the field of Theoretical Computer Science (cf. for example [Krentel, 1988, Wagner, 1990, Chen and Toda, 1991].)

In the area of non-monotonic reasoning, constructive problems such as diagnosis [Reiter, 1987] and knowledge base update [Winslett, 1989] have a semantical

basis that relies on a definition of minimality. Therefore we found it interesting
to investigate about the complexity of the constructive problem of finding a
$(P; Z)$-minimal model. There are other motivations for such a kind of study. As
we recalled in Section 2.2.1, preferred models in many semantics for negation
as failure are $(P; Z)$-minimal models. Moreover there are unexpected relations
between the task of finding minimal models and some tasks in the method of
Horn knowledge compilation defined by Kautz and Selman. We will discuss this
aspect in Chapter 4.

Some authors studied computational aspects of model finding problems. We
now survey the main results appeared in the literature. The problem of finding a
$(P; Z)$-minimal model has been addressed by Papadimitriou in [Papadimitriou,
1991], where he proved that the problem is in the class FP^{NP}. The same author
showed also that the problem is doable in polynomial time when the formula
we want the minimal model of is Horn or Krom. Papadimitriou left open the
question [Papadimitriou, 1991, Section 3] whether the problem of finding a minimal model is *complete* for the class FP^{NP}. A characterization of the complexity
of the problem has been given by Chen and Toda in [Chen and Toda, 1993].
Algorithms for finding minimal models have been proposed by Ben-Eliyahu and
Dechter in [Ben-Eliyahu and Dechter, 1993]. Krentel studied in [Krentel, 1988]
the complexity of finding the lexicographically minimal model. The complexity
of finding an arbitrary model of a propositional formula has been studied by
Gottlob and Fermüller in [Gottlob and Fermüller, 1993].

2.5.2   Results

We carried out a detailed analysis of the computational complexity of finding
a $(P; Z)$-minimal model of a propositional formula. In the same way we did in
Section 2.4.2 for model checking problems, we classified propositional formulae
according to Schaefer's definition, i.e., according to the logical relations which
are used to represent them.

Formally, the constructive problem we considered is specified as follows.

$(P; Q; Z)$-**FIND**(S)
INSTANCE: A set L of boolean variables, a partition $\langle P; Q; Z \rangle$ of L,
            an S-formula T on L.
OUTPUT: A $(P; Z)$-minimal model M of T.

We considered also three special cases, namely, $Q = \emptyset$, $Z = \emptyset$, $Q = Z = \emptyset$. The
complexity analysis has been carried out for various sets S, in particular for the
three cases α, β and γ defined in Section 2.4.2, plus the general case.

The results are summarized in a four by four table (Table 2.6.) In this table
each column refers to a minimality problem, in which $Q = \emptyset$, or $Z = \emptyset$, or
$Q = Z = \emptyset$, or no restriction holds. Each row refers to a condition on the set
S. The first three rows correspond to cases α, β, γ, respectively. The fourth row
corresponds to the general case, i.e., in which we give no restriction on the set
S.

	$(P;Q;Z)$-FIND(S)	$(P;\emptyset;Z)$-FIND(S)	$(P;Q;\emptyset)$-FIND(S)	$(P;\emptyset;\emptyset)$-FIND(S)
α	P A.3.2	P A.3.2	P A.3.2	P A.3.2
β	$FP^{NP\,\log}$-h * A.3.1	$FP^{NP\,\log}$-h * A.3.1	$FP^{NP\,\log}$-h * A.3.1	$FP^{NP\,\log}$-h * A.3.1
γ	P A.3.3	P A.3.3	P A.3.3	P A.3.3
general	$FP^{NP\,\log}$-h * A.3.1	$FP^{NP\,\log}$-h * A.3.1	$FP^{NP\,\log}$-h * A.3.1	$FP^{NP\,\log}$-h * A.3.1

Table 2.6: Complexity of the problem $(P;Q;Z)$-**FIND**(S)

Each entry is either "P", which means polynomiality of the problem, or "$FP^{NP\,\log}$-h", which means that the problem is $FP^{NP[O(\log n)]}$-hard, i.e., hard with respect to the class of constructive problems solvable by a polynomial-time deterministic Turing machine with a logarithmic number of accesses to an NP oracle. The notion of polynomial-time many-one reducibility of [Megiddo and Papadimitriou, 1991] has been used. Some entries show an asterisk (*). This means that the complexity result (lower bound) holds even for the restricted case in which a model (not necessarily $(P;Z)$-minimal) of the formula is already known.

We want to point out that we have provided a detailed picture of the tractability threshold of the problem. In particular the problem is polynomial (cf. row γ of Table 2.6) for all of the eight classes of propositional formulae considered in Section 2.3.1. This generalizes the polynomial results reported in [Papadimitriou, 1991].

As for the intractable cases, we showed the lower bound $FP^{NP[O(\log n)]}$-hardness. In this way we gave a preliminary answer to Papadimitriou's question [Papadimitriou, 1991, Section 3] about completeness w.r.t. FP^{NP} of the problem of finding a minimal model.

The upper bound FP^{NP}, already shown in [Papadimitriou, 1991] for the problem $(P;\emptyset;Z)$-**FIND**(S), has been generalized to the problem $(P;Q;Z)$-**FIND**(S).

It is interesting to note that for the class of 1-valid formulae (cf. row β of Table 2.6), finding a minimal model is harder than finding an arbitrary model, which is clearly a polynomial task. On the other hand finding a minimal model can be easier than the corresponding model checking task (cf. Table 2.5 in Section 2.4.)

Proofs of theorems referred in the table and the proof for the upper bound of the problem will be presented in Appendix A.3.

Results of the analysis shown in this section have been published in [Cadoli, 1992b].

2.6   Circumscription in first-order formulae

2.6.1   Goal of the research and related results

Many researchers investigated about the possibility of simplifying formula (2.4) —that we've seen in Section 2.2.1— denoting the circumscription of a first-order formula. We report formula (2.4) for the reader's convenience.

$$T \wedge (\forall P' Z'.T[P'; Z'] \rightarrow \neg(P' < P))$$

In particular two questions have been considered :

1. what is the complexity of inferencing w.r.t. this second-order formula?

2. is it possible to eliminate fixed or varying predicates from it?

As for the first question, several researchers focused on the following aspect: is it possible to collapse this second-order formula into a first-order formula? We remark that each class of collapsible formulae corresponds to a case in which circumscriptive inference is not harder than inference in first-order logic, i.e., it is a recursively enumerable problem. Lifschitz [Lifschitz, 1985b], Rabinov [Rabinov, 1989], Kolaitis and Papadimitriou [Kolaitis and Papadimitriou, 1990] and Gabbay and Ohlbach [Gabbay and Ohlbach, 1992] showed classes of first-order formulae whose circumscription is still a first-order formula. In [Lifschitz, 1985b] it is also shown that some second-order formulae which are not collapsible to first-order ones (like the formula defining transitive closure, cf. Aho and Ullman [Aho and Ullman, 1979]) are expressible as the circumscription of a first-order formula. Krishnaprasad showed in [Krishnaprasad, 1988] that deciding collapsibility is in general undecidable.

Results about the degree of undecidability of circumscription have been found by Schlipf in [Schlipf, 1987]. In that work it is shown that the problem of inference w.r.t. all countably infinite models of formula (2.4), is complete for the class Π_2^1 of the analytical hierarchy on natural numbers. We refer the reader to the book by Rogers [Rogers, 1967] for the definition of analytical hierarchy, which must not be confused with the polynomial hierarchy (cf. Section 1.10.) Results about the degree of undecidability for the infinitary propositional case have been found by Papalaskari and Weinstein [Papalaskari and Weinstein, 1990].

For what concerns the second question, two different motivations exist: one is semantical, the other is computational. From the semantical point of view, the original definition of circumscription by McCarthy [McCarthy, 1980] did not take into account varying predicates. They have been introduced in a further version [McCarthy, 1986], after Etherington, Mercer and Reiter noted in [Etherington et al., 1985] that it is impossible to infer new positive facts (see the examples and the discussion on this aspect in Sections 2.2.1 and 2.2.2.) From the computational point of view, some algorithms for computing circumscriptive inference are defined only when varying predicates are not allowed (for example the algorithm of Bossu and Siegel [Bossu and Siegel, 1985]) while others are more efficient when the set of such predicates is empty (for example the methods by Przymusinski [Przymusinski, 1989] and Ginsberg [Ginsberg, 1989], that will be analyzed in Appendix A.1.2.)

de Kleer and Konolige [de Kleer and Konolige, 1989] showed that it is possible to translate any first-order formula T into another first-order formula T' such that the circumscription of T with fixed predicates is equivalent to the circumscription of T' without fixed predicates. Lifschitz [Lifschitz, 1985b] performed a similar transformation for the elimination of varying predicates, but introduced second-order formulae. Yuan and Wang [Yuan and Wang, 1988] defined a method for eliminating the varying predicates without introducing second-order formulae. The two major drawbacks of their method are that it is incomplete and that it yields in general an exponential-size formula.

2.6.2 Results

We addressed the following questions:

1. how hard is to inference under formula (2.4) when T is an unrestricted first-order formula?

2. is it possible to eliminate varying predicates from formula (2.4)?

We showed that the inference problem under circumscription with varying predicates is efficiently reducible to inferencing under basic circumscription, which is circumscription without fixed and varying predicates. More formally, we proved the following result.

Theorem 2.6.1 (elimination of the varying predicates) *Let T, F be first-order formulae such that all predicates in F appear in T, and let the lists P, Z partition the predicates in T. We can build in linear time a first-order formula $\Gamma(T; F; P; Z)$ such that $CIRC(T; P; Z) \models F$ if and only if $CIRC(\Gamma(T; F; P; Z)) \models \neg u$, where u is a propositional letter and all the predicates are minimized in $CIRC(\Gamma(T; F; P; Z))$.*

Fixed and varying predicates can therefore be bypassed efficiently combining the method in [de Kleer and Konolige, 1989] and the method suggested by the above theorem. An interesting practical consequence of this result is that any theorem prover or algorithm for inferencing under basic circumscription (for instance the method of Bossu and Siegel [Bossu and Siegel, 1985]) is able to handle inferencing under the general form of predicate circumscription. Moreover general algorithms that compute circumscription (for example Przymusinski's MILO-resolution [Przymusinski, 1989] and Ginsberg's circumscriptive theorem prover

[Ginsberg, 1989]) can be noticeably simplified, as they are much more efficient when varying predicates are not allowed.

This theorem extends immediately to closed world reasoning. Since circumscription is in the propositional case equivalent to ECWA (see Section 2.2.2), the transformation can be used also in this form of CWR.

Another result that we obtained concerns the complexity of inferencing under circumscription. We proved that deciding whether $CIRC(T; P; Z) \models \gamma$ holds is a task complete for second order logic. This is a negative result, since second order logic is strictly harder than first-order logic (cf. for example [van Benthem and Doets, 1983].) This result complement those of Schlipf [Schlipf, 1987], since in our case we considered standard models, not necessarily countably infinite.

Results presented in this section will be proved in the Appendix A.4. In the same appendix we also show some examples of the linear-time transformation Γ referred in the statement of Theorem 2.6.1. In particular we will see the elimination of varying predicates in the Tweety example discussed in Sections 2.2.1 and 2.2.2.

Results of the analysis shown in this section have been published in [Cadoli *et al.*, 1992].

2.7 Applications of tractable minimal reasoning to practical reasoning

In the spirit of the language restriction strategy, we wanted to use complexity results on minimal reasoning to define efficient methods for the solution of reasoning problems. In particular we focused on two different reasoning problems that we describe in this section.

The first reasoning problem is non-monotonic inheritance, that will be addressed in Subsection 2.7.1. In particular we show a simple language for the description of inheritance networks and give it a semantics in terms of circumscription of first-order formulae. Polynomial as well as intractable cases for inference will be shown.

The second reasoning problem is model-based diagnosis, that will be addressed in Subsection 2.7.2. In particular we recall the well-known Reiter's definition of diagnosis [Reiter, 1987] and show its relations with minimal reasoning. Such relations will make it possible to evaluate complexity of several diagnostic reasoning tasks.

In Subsection 2.7.3 we briefly address application of complexity results on minimal reasoning to further reasoning problems.

2.7.1   Non-monotonic inheritance

Semantic networks have been developed as a suitable knowledge representation formalism for the construction of Artificial Intelligence systems. They provide a simple language based on the concept of taxonomy, which underlies a relevant portion of human's knowledge.

In this section we deal with the problem of non-monotonic inheritance in semantic networks. In particular we focus on Inheritance Networks (IN), namely the core of semantic networks describing the hierarchical structure of classes, and supporting the inheritance of properties associated with them. The hierarchy can be viewed as a collection of containment assertions between classes, together with membership assertions between individual objects and classes.

When the containment relations are interpreted as necessary (strict assertions) we can benefit from a semantically well understood characterization of the network and the associated inference procedures (see for example [Atzeni and Parker, 1988].) However, one of the distinctive features of inheritance networks is achieved by admitting exceptions to the relationships holding among classes. In particular, it is useful to consider assertions of the form (defeasible assertions): A is generally a B, which intuitively means that we admit the possibility that there are objects belonging to the class A that are not B, and, therefore, are exceptional with respect to the general rule stating that every instance of A is also an instance of B. For example, if we represent the fact that birds generally fly, then, given that Tweety is a bird, we may infer that Tweety flies (see Section 2.1.) If we discover that Tweety is a penguin, we retract the previous conclusion about its ability to fly, without rejecting the general assertion relating birds and flying-things.

Several attempts to give a formal account of non-monotonic inheritance networks have appeared in the literature. Many of them consider the notion of path in the network as the central one, and therefore describe the set of admissible conclusions in terms of paths, relying on the original idea of implementing reasoning on such networks in terms of graph traversal procedures. Along these lines, we find for example [Horty and Thomason, 1988, Horty et al., 1990]. In other works (cf. [Brewka, 1987, Haugh, 1988, Krishnaprasad et al., 1989] for example) the net is defined as a logical formula. Computational properties of both kinds of nets are analyzed in some works (cf. for example [Selman and Levesque, 1989].)

2.7.1.1   Syntax

In our work inheritance networks have been defined as first-order formulae of limited expressiveness. We represented both strict and default assertions. This is an important aspect, since in common-sense reasoning some relations are definitely strict, and admit no exceptions: as an example, all mammals are animals. The syntactic definition of a *non-monotonic inheritance network* follows.

Definition 2.7.1 (syntax of NINs) *A Non-monotonic Inheritance Network (NIN) is a triple $\langle \Gamma, \Omega, \Sigma \rangle$, where Γ is a set of class symbols, Ω is a set of object* *symbols, and Σ is a set of assertions, each having one of the following forms (A and B are class symbols, z is an object symbol):*

1. $A(z)$

2. $\neg A(z)$

3. $(A \text{ \underline{is-a} } B)$

4. $(A \text{ \underline{is-not} } B)$

5. $(A \text{ \underline{gen} } B)$

6. $(A \text{ \underline{gen-not} } B)$

Assertions of type 1 and 2 are called *membership* assertions: an assertion of type 1 (type 2) states that the object represented by z is an instance of A (is not an instance of A.) Assertions of type 3 and 4 are called *strict*: intuitively, an assertion of type 3 (type 4) states that every instance of A is also an instance of B (is not an instance of B.) Finally, assertions of type 5 and 6 are called *defeasible*: an assertion of type 5 states that normally, an instance of A is also an instance of B; conversely, an assertion of type 6 states that normally, no object is an instance of both A and B.

A NIN $\langle \Gamma, \Omega, \Sigma \rangle$ can be represented by means of a graph whose set of nodes and edges are in one-to-one correspondence with $\Gamma \cup \Omega$ and Σ, respectively. There is a type of edge for each kind of assertion. The graphical representation of different kinds of edges is reported in Figure 2.2.

Let us see how the "Tweety" and the "Nixon" (see resp. Examples 2.2.2 and 2.2.3) scenarios that we introduced in Section 2.2 can be represented by means of NINs.

Example 2.7.1 (Tweety and NINs) Knowledge about Tweety can be represented by means of the NIN M (see also Figure 2.3):

(Bird *gen* Flies)
Bird(Tweety)   ◇

Example 2.7.2 (Nixon diamond and NINs) Knowledge about Nixon can be represented by means of the NIN N (see also Figure 2.4):

(Republican *gen* Hawk)
(Quaker *gen* Dove)
(Hawk *is-not* Dove)
(Hawk *is-a* PoliticallyMotivated)
(Dove *is-a* PoliticallyMotivated)
Republican(Nixon), Quaker(Nixon)   ◇

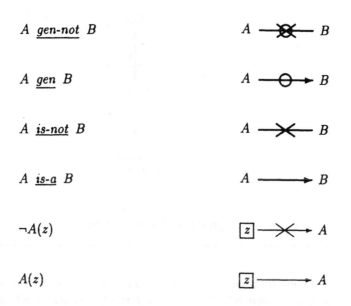

Figure 2.2: Different kinds of assertions and their representation

2.7.1.2 Semantics

In order to define the meaning of a NIN T in our approach, we first define a first-order formula T^E corresponding to T, and then we apply circumscription to such a formula. The first-order formula T^E is specified by the following definition.

Definition 2.7.2 (semantics of NINs   #1) *Let T be a NIN. The formula T^E is a first-order formula obtained from T by means of the following rules:*

- *there is one constant z for each object symbol z of T;*

- *there is one monadic predicate P for each class symbol P of T; moreover, there is one monadic predicate E_i for each defeasible assertion σ_i of T; each E_i is called an exception predicate of T^E; finally, T^E includes a distinguished binary predicate "$=$";*

- *there is one formula $A(z)$ for each membership assertion $A(z)$ of T, and one formula $\neg A(z)$ for each membership assertion $\neg A(z)$ of T.*

- *there is one formula $\forall x(A(x) \to B(x))$ for each strict assertion (A is-a B) of T, and one formula $\forall x(A(x) \to \neg B(x))$ for each strict assertion (A is-not B) of T;*

Figure 2.3: Tweety the bird

- *there is one formula $\forall x(A(x) \wedge \neg E_i(x) \rightarrow B(x))$ for each defeasible assertion $\sigma_i = (A \underline{gen} B)$ of T, and one formula $\forall x(A(x) \wedge \neg E_i(x) \rightarrow \neg B(x))$ for each defeasible assertion $\sigma_i = (A \underline{gen\text{-}not} B)$ of T;*

- *T^E includes the equality axioms and the unique name axioms; the former are used to give the predicate "$=$" the intended meaning of "equal" (see [Reiter, 1980a]), whereas the latter state that different constant symbols denote different objects (see [Reiter, 1980a].)*

The semantics of $T = \langle \Gamma, \Omega, \Sigma \rangle$ is given by the circumscription of $\{E_1, ..., E_n\}$ in T^E, with varying predicates Γ (where $E_1, ..., E_n$ are all the exception predicates of T^E), as specified by the following definition.

Definition 2.7.3 (semantics of NINs   #2) *The meaning we assign to T is represented by*

$$T^C = CIRC(T^E; \{E_1, ..., E_n\}; \Gamma)$$

where the minimized predicates are all the exception predicates of T^E, and all the other predicates of T^E belong to the set of varying predicates, except for equality.

This choice reflects the idea that we want to minimize exceptions, and, to this purpose, we accept the extensions of the classes of the network to vary.

Using the results of [Lifschitz, 1986a] it can be easily shown that T^C is satisfiable if and only if the formula obtained from T^E by eliminating all the axioms corresponding to the defeasible assertions of T is satisfiable. Therefore proving that T^C is satisfiable can be done in polynomial time (see [Lenzerini, 1988].)

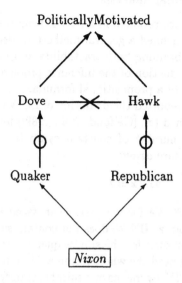

Figure 2.4: The Nixon diamond

We are mainly interested in atomic ground queries, i.e., queries of the form $T \vdash A(z)$ and $T \vdash \neg A(z)$, where A is a class, and z is an object. Using the above definition we characterize the deduction problem as follows.

Definition 2.7.4 (facts logically implied by a NIN) *A positive fact $A(z)$ is logically implied by a NIN T (written $T \vdash A(z)$) if and only if $T^C \models A(z)$. Analogously, a negative fact $\neg A(z)$ is logically implied by a NIN T (written $T \vdash \neg A(z)$) if and only if $T^C \models \neg A(z)$.*

Let us see what are the facts logically implied in the "Tweety" and in the "Nixon" cases.

Example 2.7.1 (Tweety and NINs, continued) Using forthcoming Theorem 2.7.1 and the examples seen in Section 2.2.2 (see also Example 2.2.1), we can prove that the facts logically implied by M^C are: Bird(Tweety) and Flies(Tweety). ◇

Example 2.7.2 (Nixon diamond and NINs, continued) In this case the facts logically implied by N^C are: PoliticallyMotivated(Nixon), Quaker(Nixon), and Republican(Nixon), whereas none of the following assertions are logically implied by N^C: Hawk(Nixon), Dove(Nixon), ¬Hawk(Nixon), ¬Dove(Nixon). ◇

2.7.1.3   Computational analysis

We analyzed the inference problem in a NIN T from the computational point of view. In particular we defined a general method for deciding whether $T \vdash A(z)$ and $T \vdash \neg A(z)$ hold, obtaining both tractability and intractability results. The method is based on a reduction of the inference problem in NINs to an inference problem in the ECWA of a propositional formula.

In Section 2.2.2 we reported the definition of ECWA for propositional formulae. The ECWA is defined (cf. [Gelfond *et al.*, 1989]) for function-free first-order formulae with a finite number of constant symbols $t_1, \ldots, t_n$ as long as they include the *domain closure axiom*:

$$\forall x \ (x = t_1 \vee \cdots \vee x = t_n) \ .$$

So, in order to use the ECWA for our goal, we are faced with the problem that the formula T^E coming from a NIN T, does not contain such an axiom. The above difficulty is solved as follows: for the simple queries considered in our approach, we show that we do not need the whole formula T^E, but simply the propositional formula obtained from T^E by means of a suitable transformation. It follows that, as far as our problem is concerned, we can reduce the circumscription to the ECWA, as done in [Gelfond *et al.*, 1989]. We now describe the transformation, and show that it meets the above requirement.

Let T be a NIN, T^E the corresponding first-order formula, and z a constant symbol of T^E. We define the *projection* T_z^E of T^E w.r.t. z, to be the set of formulae obtained as follows:

1. for each formula of the form $A(z)$ or $\neg A(z)$ in T^E, there is a formula of the same form in T_z^E;

2. for each universally quantified formula α corresponding to a strict or defeasible assertion of T, there is a formula in T_z^E obtained from α by eliminating the quantifier, and by substituting the variable x with z.

Theorem 2.7.1 (Reduction of circumscription to ECWA for NINs)
Let $T = \langle \Gamma, \Omega, \Sigma \rangle$ be a NIN, $A(z)$ a ground literal of T^E, $E_1, \ldots, E_n$ all the exception predicates of T^E and T_z^E the projection of T^E w.r.t. z. Then

$$CIRC(T^E; \{E_1, ..., E_n\}; \Gamma) \models A(z) \quad \text{if and only if}$$

$$ECWA(T_z^E; \{E_1, ..., E_n\}; \emptyset; \Gamma) \models A(z)$$

We now summarize the results about the complexity of inference in NINs. The above theorem reduces reasoning in NINs to CWR in a propositional formula. As a consequence some of those results have been obtained using the complexity analysis about CWR shown in Section 2.3.

The first theorem shows that the problem is intractable for NINs containing neither defeasible negative assertions nor strict positive assertions.

Theorem 2.7.2 (intractability   #1) *Let T be a NIN including only one assertion $A(z)$ of type 1, and any number of assertions of type 4 (negative strict assertions) and 5 (positive defeasible assertions.) Then, both checking whether $T \vdash B(z)$ (where B is a class symbol) and checking whether $T \vdash \neg B(z)$ are co-NP-hard problems.*

The problem is intractable also if we restrict ourselves to NINs without strict assertions, as specified by following theorem.

Theorem 2.7.3 (intractability   #2) *Let T be a NIN including only one assertion $A(z)$ of type 1, and any number of assertions of type 5 and 6 (positive and negative defeasible assertions.) Then, both checking whether $T \vdash B(z)$ (where B is a class symbol) and checking whether $T \vdash \neg B(z)$ are co-NP-hard problems.*

On the other hand, we have also found cases in which query answering is a polynomial task. The following theorem specifies a restriction which enables us to devise efficient deduction methods for our problem.

Theorem 2.7.4 (polynomiality   #1) *Let T be a NIN including no assertion of type 5 (positive defeasible.) Then, both checking whether $T \vdash B(z)$ (where B is a class symbol) and checking whether $T \vdash \neg B(z)$ are polynomial-time problems.*

We note that the language considered in the above theorem is very simple: for example it is not powerful enough to express conflicting exceptions, such as the "Nixon diamond".

On the other hand it is easy to see that, if the language allows for positive defeasible assertions and for both positive and negative membership assertions, then conflicts among exceptions may occur. The next theorem shows that the deduction problem for such a language is tractable.

Theorem 2.7.5 (polynomiality   #2) *Let T be a NIN including no assertion of type 4 (negative strict assertions), and no assertion of type 6 (negative defeasible.) Suppose that T is acyclic (i.e., no cycle exists in the graph corresponding to T, considering only edges coming from is-a and gen assertions.) Then, both checking whether $T \vdash B(z)$ (where B is a class symbol) and checking whether $T \vdash \neg B(z)$ are polynomial-time problems.*

Proofs of theorems presented in this section will be given in the Appendix A.5.

Results of the analysis shown in this section have been published in [Cadoli *et al.*, 1990b]. In that work we also addressed the problem of specificity of information, i.e., how to give more importance to information coming from more specific classes when conflicting defeasible rules are present.

2.7.2 Model-based diagnosis

The term *diagnosis* is generally used to name the process of determining the causes of a malfunction in a given system. In this process some kind of *knowledge* about the system is required. In general, different kinds of knowledge can be used to formulate a diagnostic hypothesis: heuristic knowledge, knowledge about device's structure and knowledge about previous failures are commonly used by systems performing automated diagnosis.

In the 80s several works appeared, addressing the issue of performing reasoning about the behavior of physical devices based on their structure. This kind of approach is called *model-based* diagnosis. A diagnostic problem was formulated in terms of the problem of finding a description of the device that agrees with its (unintended) behavior. One of the clearest formulations of this approach is the one by Reiter [Reiter, 1987]. Reiter's method stems on a description of the physical system as a first-order formula. The formula should take into account the possibility that every single component could be malfunctioning. As an example, a sentence like

$$andgate(g) \wedge \neg ab(g) \rightarrow out(g) = and(in_1(g), in_2(g)) \qquad (2.13)$$

(where *andgate*, *ab* and $=$ are predicate symbols, *out*, *and*, in_1 and in_2 are function symbols, and g is a constant symbol) represents the behavior of an and-gate g. The intended meaning of the above sentence is: The and-gate g functions properly —i.e., its output is the logical AND of its two inputs— unless it is in some sense *ab*normal. Another form of knowledge about the diagnostic domain is given by the observations about the system behavior. These observations should be formulated too in a logical framework. For example, the observation that the output of the component g is at the logical level 1, can be expressed as

$$out(g) = 1 \qquad (2.14)$$

The collection of all the formulae describing the system is denoted with the symbol SD. The set of all the constant symbols used to name the system's components is denoted with the symbol $COMP$. The collection of all the formulae describing the observations is denoted with the symbol OBS.

The need for a diagnosis arises when the assumption that every component is functioning properly is not consistent with the system description together with the observations. Formally, this corresponds to the fact that the formula

$$SD \cup OBS \cup \{\neg ab(c) \mid c \in COMP\}$$

is unsatisfiable. This happens, for example, if SD is formula (2.13), OBS is formula (2.14) plus $in_1(g) = 1 \wedge in_2(g) = 0$, and $COMP$ is the singleton $\{g\}$.

To obtain a description of the system which is consistent with the observations, we must formulate the hypothesis that some of the components are abnormal. Reiter's idea is that this hypothesis should be very careful, avoiding the assumption that a component is malfunctioning, if this assumption is not necessary. This idea is formalized by the following definition.

Definition 2.7.5 (Reiter [Reiter, 1987]) *A diagnosis Δ for a triple $\langle$ SD, OBS, COMP $\rangle$ is a subset of COMP such that*

1. *$SD \cup OBS \cup \{ab(c) \mid c \in \Delta\} \cup \{\neg ab(c) \mid c \in COMP \setminus \Delta\}$ is satisfiable;*

2. *there exists no Δ' such that $\Delta' \subset \Delta$ and $SD \cup OBS \cup \{ab(c) \mid c \in \Delta'\} \cup \{\neg ab(c) \mid c \in COMP \setminus \Delta'\}$ is satisfiable.*

We note that, for a given triple $\langle SD, OBS, COMP \rangle$, zero, one or many diagnosis may exist.

Reiter provides an interesting result concerning the relationships between the above definition of diagnosis and non-monotonic reasoning (more specifically, with *default logic*, that we will see in detail in Section 3.6.1), thus stressing the strong non-monotonic character of the formulation of diagnostic hypotheses. In particular he shows a correspondence between diagnosis and extensions of a suitable default theory (see [Reiter, 1980b].)

The following questions are obviously interesting for a system performing automated diagnosis according to Reiter's definition:

Q1 given $\langle SD, OBS, COMP \rangle$, find a diagnosis;

Q2 given $\langle SD, OBS, COMP \rangle$ and a set $\Delta \subset COMP$ of components, is Δ a diagnosis?

Q3 given $\langle SD, OBS, COMP \rangle$ and a formula γ, is γ true in all possible diagnosis?

We studied the above questions from the computational point of view, focusing on propositional logic, i.e., $SD \cup OBS$ are propositional formulae. The expressiveness of propositional logic is sufficient to describe most of the diagnostic problems discussed in the literature, in particular the classic examples on digital circuits. Formulae (2.13) and (2.14) don't look propositional, but can be transformed using a projection similar to that described by Theorem 2.7.1 of Section 2.7.1. Basically each ground atom of $SD \cup OBS$ corresponds to a different propositional letter. We define the following partition of the propositional letters occurring in $SD \cup OBS$: all letters obtained by instantiating the ab predicate belong to the set P of letters to be minimized; all other letters are varying, i.e., belong to the set Z, while the set Q of fixed letters is empty.

We showed that the relationships between diagnosis and non-monotonic reasoning extend to circumscription.

Theorem 2.7.6 (diagnosis and $(P; Z)$-minimal models) *The following facts hold:*

1. *for every diagnosis Δ for $\langle SD, OBS, COMP \rangle$ there is a $(P; Z)$-minimal model M of $SD \cup OBS$ such that $\Delta = \{c \in COMP \mid M \models ab(c)\}$;*

   2. for every $(P; Z)$-minimal model M of $SD \cup OBS$ there is a diagnosis Δ
   for $\langle SD, OBS, COMP \rangle$ such that $\Delta = \{c \in COMP \mid M \models ab(c)\}$.

The above theorem is quite intuitive, since expresses in a clear way the fact that every diagnosis is a minimal set of abnormalities. The theorem states also a correspondence between the two non-monotonic logics of default logic and circumscription. Similar correspondences are shown in [Etherington, 1987, Imielinski, 1987b, Lobo and Subrahmanian, 1992].

Theorem 2.7.6 has a clear computational meaning. As an example, the first fact states that the problem of finding a diagnosis is at least as hard as the problem of finding a minimal model of a formula. Dually, the second fact states that the problem of finding a $(P; Z)$-minimal model is at least as hard as the problem of finding a diagnosis. In other words the theorem says that the problems **Q1**, **Q2** and **Q3** are basically the same as the problems of finding a $(P; Z)$-minimal model of a propositional formula, of checking whether a model of a formula is $(P; Z)$-minimal and of testing the validity of γ w.r.t. all $(P; Z)$-minimal models of a propositional formula, respectively. In this way all the results presented in Sections 2.3, 2.4 and 2.5 can be used for determining the complexity of diagnostic reasoning for various classes of formulae used for representing the system and the observations, i.e., the formula $SD \cup OBS$.

   As an example we can say that finding a diagnosis is a constructive problem which is hard w.r.t. the class $FP^{NP[O(\log n)]}$, while deciding whether a subset of $COMP$ corresponds to a diagnosis is a co-NP-complete problem, and that both problems are polynomial if the formula $SD \cup OBS$ is Horn.

The proof of Theorem 2.7.6 is shown in Appendix A.5.

Results of the analysis shown in this section have been published in [Cadoli, 1990]. In that work we also addressed the problem of formalizing diagnosis using heuristic knowledge, such as the knowledge that a component is more likely to be faulty than another one.

2.7.3   Other applications

In [Cadoli *et al.*, 1990a] we applied results about complexity of minimal reasoning to concept description languages for knowledge representation. Concept description languages are studied also in Section 3.5 of this work. In [Cadoli *et al.*, 1990a] we defined a technique for using minimal reasoning in such languages. The technique consists in applying circumscription to a first-order formula representing a terminological knowledge base. Such technique can be analyzed from the computational point of view using results shown in this chapter. The fundamental aspects of an analysis of this kind have already been shown in Subsection 2.7.2

Minimal reasoning is closely related to other forms of non-monotonic reasoning. In particular various reductions from circumscription to default logic, autoepistemic logic and the other way around have been shown in the literature (see for example [Grosof, 1984, Etherington, 1987, Imielinski, 1987b, Konolige, 1988, Lobo and Subrahmanian, 1992] and also Theorem 2.7.6.) Using such reductions and the analysis carried out in this chapter it is possible to obtain complexity results (both lower and upper bounds) for various forms of non-monotonic reasoning.

We showed results of this kind in [Cadoli and Lenzerini, 1994, Cadoli and Schaerf, 1993b].

Chapter 3

Approximation of a logical theory

*In the previous chapter we dealt with the "tractability via language restriction"
approach, i.e, the first strategy for achieving computationally feasible reasoning
in AI problems we study in this book.*

*In this chapter we deal with the approximation of a logical theory, which is
the second strategy for tractable reasoning we are interested in.*

*After defining precisely what we mean by approximation, we show how the
method works in several logical languages for Knowledge Representation and
Reasoning.*

Structure of the chapter

As we noted in the introductory chapter, there are several important aspects one
has to take into account when designing a method for performing approximate
reasoning. In order to understand what these aspects are, we introduce the topic
of logic-based approximation in Section 3.1 by showing two methods that have
been defined in the literature by other authors. The analysis of those methods
motivates the list of desiderata for a theory of approximation that we give in
Section 3.2. In Section 3.3 we formalize our technique and we illustrate it for
propositional logic, the simplest of all languages for knowledge representation.
In Section 3.4 we address the issue of representing in a modal language the approximate knowledge owned by a resource-limited reasoner. In Sections 3.5, 3.6
and 3.7 we apply the approximation technique to intractable tasks in fragments
of first-order logic, non-monotonic logics and propositional modal logics, respectively.

3.1   Logic-based methods for approximation: existing techniques

The goal of this section is to introduce the topic of logic-based approximation. Several proposals in this field recently appeared in the literature. In order to give the flavor of what is going on in the field, we survey two different techniques. The first one is a "classic" method for incomplete reasoning, which has been introduced several years ago by Levesque and further analyzed by other authors. The second is a more recent —but already popular— method, proposed by Selman and Kautz. The two methods will be briefly compared at the end of the section.

3.1.1   Levesque's limited inference

The first method has been introduced by Levesque in several works [Levesque, 1984, Levesque, 1988, Levesque, 1989] and it is based on the idea of *limited inference*. Independently, Frisch [Frisch, 1985, Frisch, 1987] developed similar formalizations.

The initial idea of Levesque is that if we are to model the mental activity of an agent, it is not reasonable to assume that he always answers queries by using a method that needs an exponential amount of time. It is more realistic to assume that, when faced with normal problems, the agent only applies simple inference rules. On the other hand, when the agent is faced with extremely important or tricky questions, he moves to what Levesque calls a "puzzle mode" and uses more complex inference procedures. In particular, a knowledge representation and reasoning system should be able to distinguish between what is explicit or evident in what he knows, and what is implicit and can be inferred given enough time and motivation. Since ordinary logic does not make any distinction of this kind, it is necessary to make appropriate formal steps in this direction.

Levesque notes that a good deal of ordinary reasoning is based on detecting that a sentence and its negation are contradictory. As an example —taken from [Levesque, 1986, Section 10]— starting from $(p \vee q) \wedge (\neg q \vee r)$, we infer that $(p \vee r)$ because q and $\neg q$ are contradictory. On the other hand we can think about a *shallow* reading of sentences, where the contradiction between a sentence and its negation is not observed. In particular reasoning like in the above example is not possible in the shallow reading.

Levesque gives in [Levesque, 1984] and refines in [Levesque, 1989] a formal definition —based on multi-valued logics— of the notion of shallow reading of sentences. L denotes a set of propositional letters. A literal is a letter l of L or its negation $\neg l$. L^* denotes the set of all literals associated with the letters of L. A truth assignment is a function mapping the set of literals L^* into the set $\{0, 1\}$.

Definition 3.1.1 (Levesque [Levesque, 1989]) [1] *A 3-interpretation of L^**

---

[1] The term *3-interpretation*, as well as the term *3-entailment* and the symbol $\models^3$ used in the following are not the same originally used by Levesque. The terminology has been chosen in order to be coherent with definitions that will be given in Section 3.3

is a truth assignment which does not map both a letter l of L and its negation $\neg l$ into 0.

According to this definition, for each propositional letter l and each 3-interpretation I there are three possibilities (hence the name 3-interpretation):

1. $I(l) = 1$, $I(\neg l) = 0$;

2. $I(l) = 0$, $I(\neg l) = 1$;

3. $I(l) = 1$, $I(\neg l) = 1$.

Standard (2-valued) interpretations admit only the first two possibilities, and l is respectively, *true* or *false*. The third possibility can be regarded as the logical value *contradiction*.

The notion of 3-interpretation is extended to formulae in Conjunctive Normal Form (CNF) in the following way: a 3-interpretation I *satisfies* a clause iff it maps one of its literals into 1; I satisfies a CNF formula iff it satisfies all of its clauses. In Section 3.3 we show how to define the 3-interpretation of an arbitrary formula.

The relation of 3-entailment can be immediately defined in the intuitive way: T *3-entails* γ (written $T \models^3 \gamma$) iff every 3-interpretation mapping T into 1 also maps γ into 1. Levesque notes that 3-entailment has interesting properties:

soundness for each T, γ it holds that $(T \models^3 \gamma)$ implies $(T \models \gamma)$;

polynomiality if both T and γ are in CNF, then $T \models^3 \gamma$ can be tested in $O(|T| \cdot |\gamma|)$ time.

Another independent motivation for $\models^3$ is that $(T \models^3 \gamma)$ holds iff either γ is a tautology or T tautologically entails γ in the system of Relevance Logic of Anderson and Belnap [Anderson and Belnap, 1975] and Dunn [Dunn, 1976] (see [Levesque, 1986, Theorem 6].) Moreover $\models^3$ can be modeled in terms of the proof theory of propositional calculus without the *modus ponens* inference rule (see also [Frisch, 1985, Frisch, 1987].)

Example 3.1.1 (*modus ponens* **does not hold for 3-entailment**) Let L be the set $\{a, b\}$, and T be $\{a, \neg a \vee b\}$. Clearly both $T \models^3 a$ and $T \models^3 \neg a \vee b$ hold, hence 3-entailment captures explicit knowledge. On the other hand $T \models b$ holds, but $T \models^3 b$ does not hold: the truth assignment which maps $a, \neg a$ and $\neg b$ into 1 and b into 0 is a 3-interpretation satisfying T. $\diamondsuit$

Levesque's conclusion is that $\models^3$ can model the kind of quick surface reasoning that the agent should always do prior to any form of deep logical analysis or problem solving, i.e., before entering into the "puzzle mode".

3.1.2   Selman and Kautz's Horn knowledge compilation

The second method we survey has been introduced by Selman and Kautz in [Selman and Kautz, 1991, Kautz and Selman, 1991a, Kautz and Selman, 1992] and further explored by Greiner and Schuurmans in [Greiner and Schuurmans, 1992] and by Roth in [Roth, 1993]. The method is based on the idea of *knowledge compilation*.

The starting point of this technique stems from the fact that inference for general propositional formulae is co-NP-complete —hence polynomially unfeasible— while it is doable in polynomial time when Σ is a Horn formula. The fascinating question Selman and Kautz address is the following: is it possible to *compile* a propositional formula Σ into a Horn one Σ' so that a significant amount of the inferences that are performed under Σ can be performed under Σ' in polynomial time?

Selman and Kautz note that there exist two different ways of doing such a compilation. In the first case the compiled formula satisfies the relation $\Sigma' \models \Sigma$, or equivalently $\mathcal{M}(\Sigma') \subseteq \mathcal{M}(\Sigma)$ —where $\mathcal{M}(\Phi)$ denotes the set of models of the formula Φ. For this reason Σ' is called a *Horn lower bound* —or LB— of Σ. As an example —taken from [Selman and Kautz, 1991]— let Φ be the formula

$$(man \rightarrow person) \land (woman \rightarrow person) \land (man \lor woman)$$

The formula $\Phi_{lb} = man \land woman \land person$ is a Horn LB of Φ.

The second form of compilation is dual. The compiled version of Σ is a Horn formula Σ' that satisfies the relation $\Sigma \models \Sigma'$, or equivalently $\mathcal{M}(\Sigma) \subseteq \mathcal{M}(\Sigma')$. Σ' is called a *Horn upper bound* —or UB— of Σ. Returning to the previous example, the formula $\Phi_{ub} = (man \rightarrow person) \land (woman \rightarrow person)$ is a Horn UB of Φ.

The importance of having compiled forms of a Knowledge Base is in that sometimes we can use them for providing a quick answer to an inference problem. As an example, if we are faced with the problem of checking $\Sigma \models \alpha$, we may benefit from the fact that for any Horn LB Σ_{lb} of Σ, $\Sigma_{lb} \not\models \alpha$ implies $\Sigma \not\models \alpha$. Σ_{lb} is therefore a *complete approximation* of Σ. Dually, a Horn UB Σ_{ub} is a *sound approximation* of Σ, since $\Sigma_{ub} \models \alpha$ implies $\Sigma \models \alpha$.

Selman and Kautz note that some complete approximations are better than others. In the previous example, both $\Phi_{lb1} = man \land woman \land person$ and $\Phi_{lb2} = man \land person$ are Horn LBs of Φ. Φ_{lb2} seems to be a better approximation than Φ_{lb1}, since $\mathcal{M}(\Phi_{lb1}) \subset \mathcal{M}(\Phi_{lb2}) \subset \mathcal{M}(\Phi)$, hence the former is in some precise sense "closer" to Φ than the latter. This consideration leads to the notion of *Horn greatest lower bound* —or GLB— of a formula Σ, which is a Horn formula Σ_{glb} such that $\mathcal{M}(\Sigma_{glb}) \subseteq \mathcal{M}(\Sigma)$ and for no Horn formula Σ' it holds that $\mathcal{M}(\Sigma_{glb}) \subset \mathcal{M}(\Sigma') \subseteq \mathcal{M}(\Sigma)$. In the previous example Φ_{lb2} is a Horn GLB of Φ.

The same argument can be done for Horn upper bounds: in our example both $\Phi_{ub1} = (man \rightarrow person) \land (woman \rightarrow person)$ and $\Phi_{ub2} = person$ are Horn UBs of Φ, but $\mathcal{M}(\Phi) \subset \mathcal{M}(\Phi_{ub2}) \subset \mathcal{M}(\Phi_{ub1})$, hence Φ_{ub2} is a better approximation of Φ. A *Horn least upper bound* —or LUB— of a formula Σ is a

	INFERENCE	SIZE	NUMBER	COMPLEXITY
Σ_{glb}	complete unsound	linear	many	NP-hard
Σ_{lub}	sound incomplete	in general exponential	one	NP-hard

Table 3.1: Some properties of Horn GLBs and LUBs

Horn formula Σ_{lub} such that $\mathcal{M}(\Sigma) \subseteq \mathcal{M}(\Sigma_{lub})$ and for no Horn formula Σ' it holds that $\mathcal{M}(\Sigma) \subseteq \mathcal{M}(\Sigma') \subset \mathcal{M}(\Sigma_{lub})$. Φ_{ub2} is a Horn LUB of Φ.

Selman and Kautz's proposal is to approximate inference w.r.t. a propositional formula Σ by using its Horn GLBs and LUBs. In this way inference could be unsound or incomplete, but it is anyway possible to spend more time and use a general inference procedure to determine the answer directly from the original formula. The general inference procedure could still use the approximations to prune its search space (see [Selman and Kautz, 1991, page 905].) It is also important to note that Horn GLBs and LUBs can be computed off-line and can be used for giving several approximate answers. This form of approximate reasoning is therefore a *compilation*.

Table 3.1 summarizes the major properties of Horn GLBs and LUBs stated in [Selman and Kautz, 1991, Kautz and Selman, 1992]. The four columns refer respectively to:

- logical relation w.r.t. Σ (i.e., what kind of inference can be performed using this approximation?);

- size of the formula w.r.t. the size $|\Sigma|$ of Σ;

- number of possible approximations of this kind;

- computational complexity of the search problem of finding the approximation.

Relations between Horn compilation and non-monotonic reasoning as well as several computational properties of Horn GLBs and LUBs will be shown in Chapter 4 of this book.

3.1.3   Comparison between the two approaches

Levesque's approach is characterized by philosophical motivations and aims at building inference systems justifiable from the intuitive point of view. Semantics is important for Levesque, as well as a comparison to techniques for the formalization of limited reasoning developed in different fields (e.g., Relevance

Logic [Anderson and Belnap, 1975].) Selman and Kautz's method is motivated with strictly computational arguments, and semantics of approximate answers is given in terms of the syntactic notion of Horn clause.

3-entailment can be tested in polynomial time. Both kinds of Horn compilation are polynomially intractable and the Horn LUB needs exponential space to be represented explicitly (see [Kautz and Selman, 1992] for further details.) Anyway it is worth noticing that a Horn LUB or GLB can be computed off-line, i.e., not necessarily when the query to the knowledge base is issued. Moreover the compilations can be used for giving approximate answers to many different queries.

Both methods are characterized by being "one-shot": if we know that the approximate solution may be wrong, the only thing to do is to resort on general purpose theorem-proving procedures. In other words the quality of approximate solutions cannot be improved. The methods do not allow to spend more resources in order to give better quality answers which are still approximate.

Horn knowledge compilation supports sound inferences as well as complete ones. Levesque's method is only sound.

Levesque's idea has been generalized to the solution of other reasoning problems, like epistemic reasoning [Levesque, 1984, Lakemeyer, 1987] and reasoning in terminological languages [Patel-Schneider, 1989, Patel-Schneider, 1990].

3.2   Guidelines of a new method for approximation

Here is our desiderata list for a theory of approximate reasoning. We would like a method that is:

semantically well-founded: approximate answers should give semantically clear information about the problem at hand;

computationally attractive: approximate answers should be easier to compute than answers to the original problem;

improvable: approximate answers can be improved, and eventually they converge to the right answer (provided we have enough time and motivation);

dual: both sound approximations and complete ones should be described;

flexible: the approximation schema should be general enough to be applied to a wide range of reasoning problems.

We found in Levesque's approach inspiration for developing a method that fulfills all the above desiderata. Loosely speaking we added to Levesque's method duality and improvability, keeping its nice computational features and its semantical flavor coming from a clear formulation in multi-valued logics. We give now an abstract description of our technique.

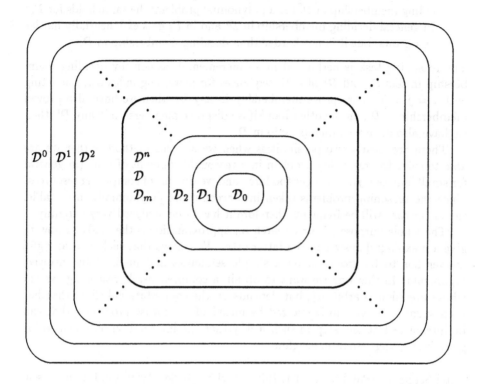

Figure 3.1: Approximation of a set of logical formulae

We model a reasoning task as the problem of deciding whether a string x belongs to a set $\mathcal{D}$ (e.g., the set of satisfiable propositional formulae) or not. The method we defined for approximating a reasoning problem, or equivalently the corresponding set $\mathcal{D}$, relies on the definition of two sequences of sets $\langle \mathcal{D}_0, \mathcal{D}_1, \ldots, \mathcal{D}_m \rangle$ and $\langle \mathcal{D}^0, \mathcal{D}^1, \ldots, \mathcal{D}^n \rangle$ such that

$$\mathcal{D}_0 \subseteq \mathcal{D}_1 \subseteq \cdots \subseteq \mathcal{D}_m = \mathcal{D} = \mathcal{D}^n \subseteq \mathcal{D}^{n-1} \subseteq \cdots \subseteq \mathcal{D}^0 \qquad (3.1)$$

(cf. Figure 3.1.)

The sequences have the following properties:

- the length n, m of the sequences is polynomial with respect to the input x of the problem;

- the elements of both sequences are defined by means of a semantics closely related to that of $\mathcal{D}$;

- deciding whether the input string x belongs to $\mathcal{D}^0$ or not (or loosely, deciding membership in $\mathcal{D}^0$) is a polynomial problem; the same holds for $\mathcal{D}_0$. In general deciding membership in $\mathcal{D}^i$ and in $\mathcal{D}_i$ gets exponentially harder as i grows, but it is not harder than deciding membership in $\mathcal{D}$.

The reasoning task is performed in an incremental fashion, by deciding membership in sets $\mathcal{D}_i$ and $\mathcal{D}^j$ of both sequences for increasing indexes i, j, starting with $i = j = 0$. If we prove membership in any $\mathcal{D}_i$, then we have also proved membership in $\mathcal{D}$; on the other hand if we disprove membership in any $\mathcal{D}^i$, then we have also disproved membership in $\mathcal{D}$.

There are clearly two possibilities when we use this method: either we are able to solve the reasoning problem in a reasonable amount of time (in general for small indices i, j), or i, j get too large and we run out of computing resources. Since the reasoning problems taken into account are polynomially intractable, the latter case will be frequent, therefore it has to be analyzed very carefully.

The whole purpose of our research on approximation is the study of how to give a meaningful answer in the latter case. We believe that such a meaningful answer has to be grounded on a simple semantics and justified by intuitive arguments. In this way we want to obtain a comprehensible reasoning system whose precision is arbitrary, but depends on the computational effort that has been spent. The system is realized by means of a stepwise procedure that can be interrupted at any step in such a way that the information obtained so far gives interesting semantic insights.

Patel-Schneider [Patel-Schneider, 1989, Patel-Schneider, 1990] and Frisch [Frisch, 1987] pointed out that Levesque's system successfully managed to lower the complexity of the inference tasks, but it is far too weak in sanctioning conclusions to be useful in many situations (see Example 3.1.1) in the previous section.) They also argued that Levesque's weak semantics is the building block on top of which more inferential capabilities should be added, without losing tractability. This is exactly the direction of research we pursue in our work. What we will show is that

- a very weak semantics can be used as the starting step of high complexity decision problems;

- on top of this we can define sound and increasingly more complete procedures that are based on stronger semantics.

In the following we also present a dual semantics being stronger than the classical one, that will be used as a basis for complete and increasingly more sound reasoning procedures. What we gain with our approach is the ability to characterize with a precise semantics a wide class of incomplete or unsound inference procedures.

We proved the flexibility of the method applying it to several reasoning problems very popular in Knowledge Representation. In particular we defined approximation methods for:

1. propositional logic;

2. fragments of first-order logic (concept description languages);

3. propositional default logic and circumscription;

4. modal logics.

Moreover we defined an epistemic language for the representation of resource-bounded reasoners. The language provides for a meta-level description of the approximate knowledge owned by an agent. In the rest of this chapter we show all such applications.

Our method depends on the complexity of the reasoning task only to some extent. The complexity of the reasoning problems addressed ranges from NP-complete to PSPACE-complete.

3.3 Approximation of propositional logic

In this section we illustrate our approximation technique for entailment in propositional logic. In particular we define a method for approximating the set

$$\{\langle T; \gamma \rangle \mid T, \gamma \text{ are propositional formulae and } T \models \gamma\}.$$

In Subsection 3.3.1 we define the semantics of the approximation. In Subsection 3.3.2 we address computational aspects and in Subsection 3.3.3 we present some examples and discuss the method.

3.3.1 Semantics

As we said in the previous section, we are interested both in sound and in complete approximations. We first show the sound approximation, which is a generalization of Levesque's shallow reading of sentences (cf. Definition 3.1.1.) Throughout this section we assume that there is an underlying finite language L used for building all the sentences. Symbols t and f are used for denoting special propositional letters, which are always mapped into 1 and 0, respectively. In the following we denote with S a subset —possibly not proper— of L.

Definition 3.3.1 (S-3-interpretation) *An S-3-interpretation of L is a truth assignment which maps every letter l of S and its negation $\neg l$ into opposite values. Moreover, it does not map both a letter l of $L \setminus S$ and its negation $\neg l$ into 0.*

According to this definition, for each propositional letter l and each S-3-interpretation I there are the following possibilities:

1. $I(l) = 1$, $I(\neg l) = 0$;

2. $I(l) = 0$, $I(\neg l) = 1$;

3. $I(l) = 1$, $I(\neg l) = 1$ [only if $l \in L \setminus S$].

S-3-interpretations are therefore "something in between" standard 2-valued interpretations and Levesque's 3-interpretations. Often we refer to standard 2-valued interpretations using the term *2-interpretations*. Both 2-interpretations and 3-interpretations are generalized by S-3-interpretations, since a 2-interpretation is an S-3-interpretation with $S = L$, while a 3-interpretation is an S-3-interpretation with $S = \emptyset$. We can say that in S-3-interpretations the truth value *contradiction* is possible only for those letters that do not belong to S.

Interpretations (standard 2-valued interpretations as well as 3-interpretations or S-3-interpretation) assign a truth value to an arbitrary formula by means of simple rules. First-of all, we put formulae in Negation Normal Form (NNF) using the rewriting rules shown in Section 1.10. Now negation occurs in a formula only at the literal level. Rules for assigning truth values to NNF formulae are the following:

∨-**rule** $I \models \alpha \vee \beta$ iff $I \models \alpha$ or $I \models \beta$;

∧-**rule** $I \models \alpha \wedge .\beta$ iff $I \models \alpha$ and $I \models \beta$.

A formula is *S-3-satisfiable* if an S-3-interpretation I exists such that I satisfies it, i.e., I maps it into 1. Entailment is defined in the standard way for S-3-entailment: we say that T *S-3-entails* γ (written $T \models_S^3 \gamma$) iff every S-3-interpretation satisfying T also satisfies γ.

Example 3.1.1 of Section 3.1.1 showed that *modus ponens* rule does not hold for 3-entailment. Let us continue that example considering the definitions we just gave.

Example 3.3.1 (sometimes *modus ponens* holds for S-3-entailment ...)
Let L be the set $\{a, b\}$, and T be $\{a, \neg a \vee b\}$. $T \models b$ holds and $T \models^3 b$ does not hold. If $S = \{a\}$ then $T \models_S^3 b$, since every S-3-interpretation satisfying T maps a and b into 1, and $\neg a$ into 0.

(...and sometimes it doesn't.)
Let L be the set $\{a, b, c\}$, $S = \{a\}$ and T be $\{a, \neg a \vee b, \neg b \vee c\}$. $T \models c$ holds, but $T \models_S^3 c$ does not hold. ◇

In the above example the relation $\models_S^3$ is *sound* and not complete w.r.t. $\models$. We will see in the following that this is a general characteristic of $\models_S^3$ and we will return later on the possibility of using $\models_S^3$ as an approximation of $\models$. Now we want to deal with *complete and unsound* approximations of $\models$. Such a form of entailment is based on the following definition.

Definition 3.3.2 (S-1-interpretation) *An S-1-interpretation of L is a truth assignment which maps every letter l of S and its negation $\neg l$ into opposite values. Moreover, it maps every letter l of $L \setminus S$ and its negation $\neg l$ into 0.*

2	INTERPRETATION				LITERAL		TRUTH VALUE
	S-1	S-3	S-1	S-3	l	$\neg l$	
	$l \in S$		$l \in L \setminus S$				
√	√	√		√	1	0	true
√	√	√		√	0	1	false
				√	1	1	contradiction
			√		0	0	undefined

Table 3.2: Various forms of interpretation of a propositional letter

According to this definition, for each propositional letter $l \in L \setminus S$ and each S-1-interpretation I there are the following possibilities:

1. $I(l) = 1$, $I(\neg l) = 0$;

2. $I(l) = 0$, $I(\neg l) = 1$;

3. $I(l) = 0$, $I(\neg l) = 0$ [if and only if $l \in L \setminus S$].

The name S-1-interpretation originates from the fact that for each letter $l \in L \setminus S$ there is exactly one possibility. Intuitively, letters in $l \in L \setminus S$ are mapped into a truth value which is different from those already seen (*true, false, contradiction*), that we might call *undefined.* Truth assignment for arbitrary formulae is defined in the same way we did for S-3-interpretations. A formula is S-1-*satisfiable* if an S-1-interpretation I exists such that I satisfies it, i.e., I maps it into 1. Analogously, S-1-entailment (denoted by $\models^1_S$) directly follows from that of S-1-interpretation using the same rule. We note that 2-interpretations are not S-1-interpretations and vice-versa, unless $S = L$. In the following we show an example in which the notions of S-1-interpretation and S-1-entailment are used.

Table 3.2 summarizes the four different possibilities that may occur for a generic letter l and its negation $\neg l$ in the various forms of interpretation introduced in the above definitions. The table shows that for 2-interpretations only two possibilities exist, since a letter l and its negation $\neg l$ are always mapped into opposite values. Exactly the same possibilities exist for S-1- and S-3-interpretations when the letter l belongs to S. When l belongs to $L \setminus S$, in S-3-interpretations a third possibility exists, since both a letter l and its negation $\neg l$ might be mapped into 1. When l belongs to $L \setminus S$, in S-1-interpretations there is only one possibility —which is different from all the previous ones— since both a letter l and its negation $\neg l$ must be mapped into 0.

3.3.2 Computational aspects

In this subsection we show some properties of S-3- and S-1-entailment that are important from the computational point of view. We denote with T a generic propositional CNF formula and with γ a generic propositional clause not containing both a letter l and its negation $\neg l$.

Theorem 3.3.1 (monotonicity) *For any S, S' such that $S \subseteq S' \subseteq L$, if $T \not\models^1_S$ γ, then $T \not\models^1_{S'} \gamma$ (hence $T \not\models \gamma$.) Moreover if $T \models^3_S \gamma$, then $T \models^3_{S'} \gamma$ (hence $T \models \gamma$.)*

Observation 3.3.2 (convergence) *If $T \models \gamma$ then there exists an $S \subseteq L$ such that $T \models^3_S \gamma$. If $T \not\models \gamma$ then there exists an $S \subseteq L$ such that $T \not\models^1_S \gamma$.*

Theorem 3.3.3 (uniform complexity) *There exists an algorithm for deciding if $T \models^3_S \gamma$ and deciding if $T \models^1_S \gamma$ which runs in $O(|T| \cdot |\gamma| \cdot 2^{|S|})$ time.*

We note that Observation 3.3.2 directly follows from the previous definitions. A set S that trivially satisfies its statement is L itself, but we are interested in sets S of smaller size. Theorem 3.3.1 and Observation 3.3.2 show that the co-NP-complete problem of deciding whether $T \models \gamma$ holds can be computed in a stepwise fashion by proving or disproving $T \models^1_S \gamma$ and $T \models^3_S \gamma$ for increasing sets S, starting with $S = \emptyset$ and stopping for the least $S \subseteq L$ such that either $T \not\models^1_S \gamma$ or $T \models^3_S \gamma$ hold.

Referring to the terminology introduced in Section 3.2 (cf. formula (3.1) and Figure 3.1), we are approximating the set

$$\mathcal{D} = \{\langle T; \gamma \rangle \mid T \models \gamma\}$$

by means of the two collections of sets

$$\mathcal{D}_i = \{\langle T; \gamma \rangle \mid T \models^3_{S_i} \gamma\}$$

and

$$\mathcal{D}^j = \{\langle T; \gamma \rangle \mid T \models^1_{S^j} \gamma\}$$

In particular an approximation is defined by two increasing sequences of sets

$$\langle S_0 = \emptyset \subset \cdots \subset S_i \subset \cdots \subset S_m = L \rangle$$

and

$$\langle S^0 = \emptyset \subset \cdots \subset S^j \subset \cdots \subset S^n = L \rangle$$

The above results do not tell us for which set S we are going to have a definite answer to the query $T \models \gamma$. Theorem 3.3.3 tells us that, even in the worst case (i.e., when we prove or disprove $T \models \gamma$ for $S = L$), the complexity of the method is $O(|T| \cdot |\gamma| \cdot 2^{|L|})$, hence similar to the best known algorithms for deciding $T \models \gamma$.

The method for deciding propositional entailment can be stopped for any $S \subset L$, and in this case the time spent in the computation has provided clear semantical information. Propositional entailment is computed in a step-wise fashion, and the parameter S controls the quality of the inference. The precision of the inference is arbitrary and depends on the computational effort that has been spent. If $|S|$ is limited by a logarithmic function, then the resulting inference is polynomial. This is a typical *approximation* process, since every intermediate step provides a partial solution whose relation to the final solution (the *error*) is clearly identified.

We have therefore reached our goal of defining a method for approximation of the consequence relation in propositional logic such that:

- it is semantically founded;

- approximate answers are easier to compute than the answers to the original inference problem;

- approximate answers can be improved, and converge to the right answer (provided we have enough resources and motivation);

- both only sound and only complete approximations are provided.

In the following sections we show methods for approximating other reasoning tasks. All such methods are supported by results analogous to Theorems 3.3.1, 3.3.2 and 3.3.3.

All the results just shown (and in particular Theorem 3.3.3) hold even if T is a NNF formula and γ is a generic formula in CNF. This aspect has been analyzed in [Cadoli and Schaerf, 1993a], where we showed other normal forms for which the uniform complexity result holds.

Results analogous to Theorems 3.3.1, 3.3.2 and 3.3.3 hold for S-1- and S-3-satisfiability problems. In particular the following result holds:

Theorem 3.3.4 (monotonicity for S-satisfiability) *For any S, S' such that $S \subseteq S' \subseteq L$, if T is S-1-satisfiable, then T is S'-1-satisfiable (hence satisfiable.) Moreover if T is S-3-unsatisfiable, then T is S'-3-unsatisfiable (hence unsatisfiable.)*

In Appendix B.1 we show that the problem of testing S-3-entailment [S-1-entailment] can be reduced to the problem of deciding S-3-unsatisfiability [S-1-unsatisfiability] of a suitable formula. This extends the well-known relation existing between classical entailment and satisfiability, namely $T \models \gamma$ iff $T \wedge \neg\gamma$ is unsatisfiable. The importance of such a result is in that S-3-satisfiability [S-1-satisfiability] of a CNF formula T can be tested in the following way:

1. replace by t [f] all occurrences (both positive and negative) in T of letters which belong to $L \setminus S$, thus obtaining the formula T_S^3 [T_S^1];

2. test standard (2-valued) satisfiability of T_S^3 $[T_S^1]$.

The transformation shown in point 1. preserves S-3- and S-1- satisfiability for NNF formulae as well (see [Cadoli and Schaerf, 1993a].) We note that only letters which belong to S occur in T_S^3 and T_S^1. As a consequence simple algorithms for deciding S-1- and S-3-satisfiability and running in time $O(|T| \cdot 2^{|S|})$ can be obtained as variants of classic algorithms for satisfiability like Davis and Putnam's [Davis and Putnam, 1960] or Robinson's [Robinson, 1965]. Nevertheless very specialized algorithms for propositional satisfiability (e. g. Van Gelder's [Van Gelder, 1988]) can be used without loss of efficiency for computing S-1- or S-3-satisfiability.

We want to stress that we are not proposing a new algorithm or heuristic for the satisfiability problem, but we are instead interested in a semantic description of *partial* reasoning. We claim that many heuristics commonly used for the satisfiability problem can be applied in our method as well, since we are able to reduce the relations for approximate entailment to ordinary (2-valued) satisfiability of a smaller formula.

In Appendix B.1 we also show detailed algorithms for deciding S-1- and S-3-entailment relations as well as custom algorithms for deciding S-1- and S-3-satisfiability.

3.3.3 Discussion and examples

In this subsection we perform some informal considerations on the meaning of the entailment relations we defined. From the intuitive point of view, both S-3-interpretation and S-1-interpretation correspond to a representation in which only some of the propositional letters are "taken seriously", while others are ignored. This leads to an entailment relation that models a way of reasoning in which part of the knowledge (the knowledge represented by letters not in the set S) is ignored on purpose. S-3- and S-1-entailment are therefore mechanisms for creating partial *views* of the knowledge base.

S-3-entailment and S-1-entailment differ with respect to the treatment of the letters that are ignored. In particular in S-3-entailment we don't care if ignoring letters leads to contradictions, i.e., a knowledge base T may have plausible states (S-3-models) that do not correspond to ordinary models. This proliferation of admissible states makes it "harder" (logically, not computationally) to prove entailment, i.e., S-3-entailment is sound and not complete with respect to classical entailment.

We claim that S-3-entailment models a deductive strategy that is sometimes applied in reality. Let us see this with an example. We are consulting an encyclopedia about animals, looking for a particular information, let's say whether cows have molar teeth or not. It is natural to start our research from the paragraph about cows, then to broaden the scope more and more, taking into account the section on herbivores, the chapter on mammals, the volume on vertebrates, … During this process it may happen that we find a term that we do not understand, because it is defined in a part that we did not read. Anyway we continue until we are able to answer the question or we run out of resources (time, motivation, ...) We are performing two different forms of local reasoning: 1) only a part of the knowledge base is taken into account and 2) only a part of the language is taken into account. While performing this research, we assume that the information not yet considered can be ignored, in the sense that if we prove that cows actually have molar teeth by considering only little information or a small part of the language, then such an answer is definitely exact. Ignoring a part of the knowledge base (i.e., the first aspect of local reasoning) can be trivially modeled. On the other hand S-3-entailment models the second aspect of local reasoning: the set S represents the terms that "make sense" to us. Broadening the scope of our research is modeled by making the set S larger and larger.

As far as the S-1-entailment relation is concerned, dual considerations hold. Also in this case we deal with a form of local reasoning, but the information which is ignored is considered in a pessimistic way. In other words we think that the information we are currently holding is useful only for disproving, and not for proving. This leads to dramatic reduction of the admissible states of a knowledge base (i.e., its S-1-models), hence it is possible to accept as a consequence what is not really a consequence (S-1-entailment is complete and unsound w.r.t. 2-entailment.)

Summing up, both relations for approximate entailment can model agents with limited resources. The difference is in that they have different attitudes with respect to what is outside the scope of the agents' competence.

We now show two examples that will be useful for further discussion.

Example 3.3.2 (proving a consequence) We assume that the following CNF formula T is part of a very large knowledge base containing information about animals and their properties. T uses a small alphabet L, which we assume to be part of a larger dictionary. The large knowledge base contains a taxonomy of classes, which is partially present in T.

$L = \{cow, dog, grass\text{-}eater, carnivore, mammal, has\text{-}canine\text{-}teeth,$
$\qquad has\text{-}molar\text{-}teeth, vertebrate, animal\}$
$T = (\neg cow \lor grass\text{-}eater),$
$\qquad (\neg dog \lor carnivore),$
$\qquad (\neg grass\text{-}eater \lor \neg has\text{-}canine\text{-}teeth),$
$\qquad (\neg grass\text{-}eater \lor mammal),$
$\qquad (\neg carnivore \lor mammal),$
$\qquad (\neg mammal \lor has\text{-}canine\text{-}teeth \lor has\text{-}molar\text{-}teeth),$
$\qquad (\neg mammal \lor vertebrate),$
$\qquad (\neg vertebrate \lor animal).$

Note that T is not a Horn formula. We want to prove that $T \models (\neg cow \lor has\text{-}molar\text{-}teeth)$ holds. Since $T \not\models^3 (\neg cow \lor has\text{-}molar\text{-}teeth)$, we try to determine a subset S of L such that $T \models_S^3 (\neg cow \lor has\text{-}molar\text{-}teeth)$ holds. By Theorem 3.3.1

this is sufficient for our goal. In fact, this happens when $S = \{cow, grass\text{-}eater, mammal, has\text{-}canine\text{-}teeth, has\text{-}molar\text{-}teeth\}$, which is a small subset of the whole dictionary. ◇

Example 3.3.3 (disproving a consequence)

$L = \{person, child, youngster, adult, senior, student, pensioner,$
$\quad\quad worker, unemployed\}$
$T = (\neg person \vee child \vee youngster \vee adult \vee senior),$
$\quad\quad (\neg youngster \vee student \vee worker),$
$\quad\quad (\neg adult \vee student \vee worker \vee unemployed),$
$\quad\quad (\neg senior \vee pensioner \vee worker),$
$\quad\quad (\neg student \vee child \vee youngster \vee adult),$
$\quad\quad (\neg pensioner \vee senior),$
$\quad\quad (\neg pensioner \vee \neg student),$
$\quad\quad (\neg pensioner \vee \neg worker).$

We want to prove that $T \not\models (\neg child \vee pensioner)$. By Theorem 3.3.1 we try to determine a subset S of L such that $T \not\models^1_S (\neg child \vee pensioner)$. In fact this happens when $S = \{child, worker, pensioner\}$ since the S-1-interpretation mapping $child, worker, \neg pensioner$ into 1 and all the other literals into 0 satisfies T but not $(\neg child \vee pensioner)$. ◇

Let us give a qualitative analysis of the above examples. In the first example, in which taxonomic knowledge is present, it seems that in order to reach an exact solution it is useful to include in the set S concepts of the taxonomy which are super-classes of the concepts occurring in the query. As for the second example, in which the knowledge is spread over several indefinite clauses, an useful strategy seems to be that of extending S with classes with several properties, such as *pensioner*, or properties shared by several classes, such as *worker*.

The above examples show that an exact solution to an entailment problem can be reached with a small S, but we do not expect the choice of the minimal set S having this property to be easy in general. We note that if we knew the minimum size of a set S for which $T \models^3_S \gamma$ or $T \not\models^1_S \gamma$ holds, then we would know that an upper bound for the entailment problem is $O(|T| \cdot |\gamma| \cdot 2^{|S|})$.

A natural question is therefore the following: is approximation of propositional entailment only a theoretical method, or do we have a technique for choosing a set S of letters for which we have high expectation of having correct answers? Moreover, how much can we trust an approximate answer? What kind of "degree of belief" can we associate to it?

There are several ways to give answers to this kind of questions. For example we could look for "good" sets S using purely syntactic techniques, like using topological criteria in suitable representations of the formula as a graph. Another possibility relying on syntactic methods is to use parameters such as the number of occurrences of a single literal in the formula. Techniques of this kind have actually been used by several researchers for providing smart methods for solving computationally hard problems (see for example [Dechter and Pearl, 1988] in the area of constraint propagation.) Moreover several heuristics for an intelligent choice of the letters to be used in resolution algorithms (see for example [Loveland, 1978]) or in Davis-Putnam's procedure for propositional satisfiability (see for example [Jeroslow and Wang, 1990]) have been developed. Another possibility is to use numerical parameters for the attribution of a degree of confidence to an approximate answer.

In our work we preferred to use a logical language for addressing the questions reported above. We deal with this aspects in Section 3.4, where preliminary answers have been given in the framework of epistemic logic. Our goal has been to provide a meta-level language for the representation of approximate knowledge, as specified by the logical relations presented in this section. This meta-level knowledge can be used for a smart choice of the set S.

Some techniques defined by other authors —apart from those addressed in Section 3.1— share ideas with our method. For example Giunchiglia and Walsh's *abstract proofs* method [Giunchiglia and Walsh, 1992] give logical description of only sound as well as only complete forms of approximate reasoning. Related ideas can also be found in Imielinski's work on *domain abstraction* [Imielinski, 1987a] and in general in the area of *abstract interpretation*, born in the programming languages community [Cousot and Cousot, 1977]. Gallo and Scutellà's method [Gallo and Scutellà, 1988], modified by Dalal and Etherington in [Dalal and Etherington, 1992], defines classes of propositional formulae whose associated satisfiability problem is more and more computationally demanding. Dalal's *k-consistency* [Dalal, 1992] is similar to this respect.

Our method differs significantly from all the above techniques.

All the results presented in this section will be proved in Appendix B.1. The appendix also shows algorithms for testing S-3- and S-1-satisfiability as well as other computational aspects of approximate entailment.

The ideas shown in this section have been presented in a preliminary form in [Cadoli and Schaerf, 1991] and will appear as [Schaerf and Cadoli, 1995].

3.4   Approximate reasoning and non-omniscient agents

In the previous section we showed how to represent approximations of the consequence relation in propositional logic. Our goal in this section is to define a very general system, where "approximate" knowledge owned by an agent can be explicitly represented and used.

Modal logics are probably the most widely used formalism to represent propositional attitudes —such as *knowledge* and *belief*— held by agents. For a detailed account of this usage of modal logics we refer to Hintikka's work [Hintikka, 1962].

One of the shortcomings of this representation is that agents represented through modal theories are ascribed the capability to infer any logical consequence of their knowledge (or belief.) In other words, we make the unrealistic assumption that agents are capable of performing extremely complex inferences. This drawback is known as the *logical omniscience problem* (see [Hintikka, 1962].)

Technically, logical omniscience is a consequence of the *possible-worlds* semantics commonly used [Kripke, 1963, Hintikka, 1962] as the semantics for logics of knowledge and belief. Generalizations of the possible-worlds semantics have been proposed to overcome the logical omniscience problem (see [Scott, 1970] for an example; for a detailed survey see [Halpern, 1991].)

We remind that modal systems can be characterized either by a set of axiom schemata or by the corresponding constraints on the accessibility relation. A detailed description of the various modal systems can be found for example in the book by Chellas [Chellas, 1980].

In this section we define a modal system for representing approximate knowledge owned by a non-omniscient agent. In Subsection 3.4.1 we define formally the system. In Subsection 3.4.2 we show some properties and applications and we compare the system with some of the formalisms presented in the literature.

3.4.1 Syntax and semantics

The main idea underlying the system consists in providing language constructs for representing the kind of approximation given by the entailment relations $\models_S^3$ and $\models_S^1$ defined in Section 3.3. The system consists of two collections of modal operators related to the notion of S-interpretation. The elements of the first collection are denoted as $\Box_S^3$ and the elements of the second collection as $\Box_S^1$. Formulae are built using the usual connectives and the two sets of modal operators $\Box_S^3$ and $\Box_S^1$ for any $S \subseteq L$.

Formulae of the language are built over a set of positive and negative literals L^* using the binary connectives $\wedge$, $\vee$ and $\rightarrow$, the modal operators $\Box_S^3$ and $\Box_S^1$, their negation $\neg\Box_S^3$ and $\neg\Box_S^1$ plus parentheses. In the following, we refer to formulae in this form as *Modal Negation Normal Form* (MNNF). This restriction does not cause any loss of generality since any modal formula can be transformed into an equivalent one in MNNF by substituting implication $\rightarrow$ and by pushing negation inside the formulae, i.e., by using the following rules.

$$
\begin{aligned}
(\alpha \rightarrow \beta)^* &\mapsto (\neg\alpha)^* \vee \beta^* \\
(\neg(\alpha \vee \beta))^* &\mapsto (\neg\alpha)^* \wedge (\neg\beta)^* \\
(\neg(\alpha \wedge \beta))^* &\mapsto (\neg\alpha)^* \vee (\neg\beta)^*
\end{aligned}
$$

$$(\neg\neg\alpha)^* \mapsto \alpha^*$$
$$(\Box\alpha)^* \mapsto \Box\alpha^*$$
$$(\neg\Box\alpha)^* \mapsto \neg\Box\alpha^*$$

When we discuss the semantics of general formulae we implicitly refer to their MNNF equivalent formula. Formulae not containing the modal operator are called simply propositional.

The semantics is a generalization of the classical possible-worlds semantics. A model is a triple $M = (Sit, R, V)$, where Sit is a set of situations, R is an accessibility relation, and V a (4-valued) valuation, which maps any situation into a truth assignment $(V : Sit \rightarrow (L^* \rightarrow \{0,1\})$.) We denote with $\mathcal{W}(Sit)$ the set of situations $s \in Sit$ such that s is also a possible world, i.e., $V(s)$ is a 2-interpretation. Similarly, we denote with $S\text{-}3(Sit)$ and $S\text{-}1(Sit)$ the sets of situations that can be interpreted as S-3- and S-1-interpretations, respectively. The semantics of the modal language is given by the following definition.

Definition 3.4.1 (Semantics of $\Box_S^3$ and $\Box_S^1$) *Let γ be a propositional formula:*

- $\mathcal{M}, s \models \gamma$ *iff* $V(s)(\gamma) = 1$;

- $\mathcal{M}, s \models \Box_S^3\alpha$ *iff* $\forall t \in S\text{-}3(Sit)sRt$ *implies* $\mathcal{M}, t \models \alpha$;

- $\mathcal{M}, s \models \neg\Box_S^3\alpha$ *iff* $\exists t \in S\text{-}3(Sit)sRt$ *and* $\mathcal{M}, t \not\models \alpha$;

- $\mathcal{M}, s \models \Box_S^1\alpha$ *iff* $\forall t \in S\text{-}1(Sit)sRt$ *implies* $\mathcal{M}, t \models \alpha$;

- $\mathcal{M}, s \models \neg\Box_S^1\alpha$ *iff* $\exists t \in S\text{-}1(Sit)sRt$ *and* $\mathcal{M}, t \not\models \alpha$.

A formula α is valid, written $\models \alpha$, if α is true at every possible world $w \in \mathcal{W}(Sit)$ of every model $\mathcal{M} = (Sit, R, V)$. A formula α is satisfiable if there is a model $\mathcal{M} = (Sit, R, V)$ and a possible world $w \in \mathcal{W}(Sit)$ s.t. $\mathcal{M}, w \models \alpha$.

3.4.2 Properties and applications

A minimal requirement for the system is its ability to represent the entailment relations $\models_S^1$ and $\models_S^3$ via the modal operators $\Box_S^1$ and $\Box_S^3$. This is in fact possible, as proven by the following result (α and γ are propositional formulae.)

Theorem 3.4.1 (modal validity and S-3-entailment) *($\models \Box_S^3\alpha \rightarrow \Box_S^3\gamma$) iff ($\Box_S^3\alpha \wedge \neg\Box_S^3\gamma$ is unsatisfiable) iff ($\alpha \models_S^3 \gamma$.)*

Theorem 3.4.2 (modal validity and S-1-entailment) *($\models \Box_S^1\alpha \rightarrow \Box_S^1\gamma$) iff ($\Box_S^1\alpha \wedge \neg\Box_S^1\gamma$ is unsatisfiable) iff ($\alpha \models_S^1 \gamma$.)*

Hence, the proposed language can represent the approximate entailment relations.

In order to make our system comparable with the modal system $S5$ (see [Chellas, 1980]), which is generally considered as an appropriate formalization of the notion of knowledge (see [Hintikka, 1962]), in the following we assume that the accessibility relation R is reflexive, transitive and euclidean.

It is now interesting to check whether the schemata defining the system $S5$ are valid for these new operators, in order to show their adequacy to represent resource-bounded agents.

The system $S5$ is characterized by the usual rules and axiom schemata of the propositional calculus plus the inference rule (necessitation):

Nec : $\models \alpha$ implies $\models \mathbf{K}\alpha$

and the axiom schemata:

K : $\mathbf{K}(\alpha \to \beta) \to (\mathbf{K}\alpha \to \mathbf{K}\beta)$

T : $\mathbf{K}\alpha \to \alpha$

4 : $\mathbf{K}\alpha \to \mathbf{K}\mathbf{K}\alpha$

5 : $\neg\mathbf{K}\alpha \to \mathbf{K}\neg\mathbf{K}\alpha$

We now analyze which of these schemata are valid in our semantics when we replace $\mathbf{K}$ with $\square_S^1$. The result is the following.

Proposition 3.4.3 (Axiom schemata and rules valid for $\square_S^1$) *The following relations hold:*

Nec : $\models \alpha$ *does not imply* $\models \square_S^1\alpha$

K : $\models \square_S^1(\alpha \to \beta) \to (\square_S^1\alpha \to \square_S^1\beta)$

T : $\not\models \square_S^1\alpha \to \alpha$

4 : $\models \square_S^1\alpha \to \square_S^1\square_S^1\alpha$

5 : $\models \neg\square_S^1\alpha \to \square_S^1\neg\square_S^1\alpha$

Both the rule of necessitation and the axiom schema T do not hold in general. As a consequence we can use $\square_S^1$ to model an agent capable of performing *at least* every sound inference, because its knowledge is closed under *modus ponens* (the K schema), nevertheless, the agent can do some inference which is not sound, in fact the T schema does not hold. Since both schemata 4 and 5 are valid, it follows that agents modeled in our system are fully introspective. Even if the necessitation rule and the T schema do not hold in general they are valid whenever all the letters of α occur also in S, so they still hold for a subset of the language.

We now analyze which schemata are valid in our semantics when we replace **K** with $\square_S^3$.

Proposition 3.4.4 (Axiom schemata and rules valid for $\square_S^3$) *The following relations hold:*

$Nec\ :\ \models \alpha\ implies\ \models \square_S^3\alpha$

$K\ :\ \not\models \square_S^3(\alpha \to \beta) \to (\square_S^3\alpha \to \square_S^3\beta)$

$T\ :\ \models \square_S^3\alpha \to \alpha$

$4\ :\ \models \square_S^3\alpha \to \square_S^3\square_S^3\alpha$

$5\ :\ \models \neg\square_S^3\alpha \to \square_S^3\neg\square_S^3\alpha$

Even this set of modal operators does not satisfy all the rules and axiom schemata of $S5$. In this case the only property which is not satisfied is property K, that is the closure of the knowledge under *modus ponens*. This implies that an agent modeled with these operators is not committed to full logical omniscience. Its deductive capabilities are limited, but its inferences are always sound, as witnessed by the validity of the T schema. Again properties 4 and 5 continue to hold thus providing the agent with perfect introspection. Since $\square_S^3$ is an approximation of **K**, it is clear that whenever the set S is equal to L the two operators coincide and therefore $\square_L^3$ will satisfy exactly the same properties of **K**, including the K schema. This schema is also satisfied under weaker conditions. For example if α is a propositional formula we have that $\square_S^3(\alpha \to \beta) \to (\square_S^3\alpha \to \square_S^3\beta)$ is valid if and only if $\alpha \wedge \neg\alpha$ is S-3-unsatisfiable.

Other interesting properties involve different sets S. An example is stated in the following proposition.

Proposition 3.4.5 (monotonicity for $\square_S^3$) *Let* $S \subseteq S' \subseteq L$. $\models (\square_S^3\alpha \to \square_{S'}^3\alpha)$.

We claim that the two sets of operators $\square_S^3$ and $\square_S^1$ account for a non-ideal reasoner with a limited amount of resources. The first set of operators accounts for a skeptical reasoner, i.e., not willing to believe validity of facts, while the second set accounts for a credulous one.

Using the two different operators we can model an agent's reasoning capabilities avoiding the logical omniscience assumption and providing a set of semantically motivated restrictions to its deductive capabilities. In particular our system can be used for modeling the interaction of several non-ideal agents, each having its own attitude —either credulous or skeptical— and competence, characterized by the set S.

We would like to use the epistemic language introduced above for driving the search of a "good" set S in approximate inference (cf. end of Section 3.3.) We just sketch some preliminary ideas.

It is commonplace that knowledge about the structure of a knowledge base can be very useful in the choice of an efficient query-answering strategy. In general, the knowledge engineer who creates a knowledge base has some knowledge about its structure. If we can design a language well suited to represent this kind of knowledge, then we can take advantage of it when the system is asked to answer queries. While the importance to represent this information is generally acknowledged, very little has been done in practice in order to achieve this goal.

We show how the proposed language can be (sometimes) useful to represent information about the knowledge base. As an example, the knowledge engineer of the knowledge base T, which contains knowledge about animals, may know that, in order to decide whether cows have molar teeth, it is sufficient to take into account only the properties of herbivores. This information can be modeled by a formula like:

$$[T \rightarrow (cow \rightarrow has\text{-}molar\text{-}teeth)] \rightarrow [\Box_S^3 T \rightarrow \Box_S^3 (cow \rightarrow has\text{-}molar\text{-}teeth)]$$

for a suitable set S of propositional letters, for example all letters expressing properties of the herbivores (cf. Example 3.3.2.) The intuitive reading of the above formula is: if it holds that cows have molar teeth, then we can prove it using only S-3-entailment, for a fixed S. In the query-answering process this meta-knowledge should be automatically used to perform an intelligent choice of the set S which guarantees an approximate answer with a high degree of confidence.

Several other systems capable of representing non-omniscient agents have been presented in the literature. We now briefly compare our system with some of the best known formal systems.

In Levesque's system [Levesque, 1984] the semantics of the modal operator of implicit belief **L** is defined in terms of possible worlds. Conversely, the modal operator of explicit belief **B** is defined in terms of situations. The intuitive meaning of **L**α is "α is known implicitly", i.e., we need a significant effort to know it. On the other hand **B**α intuitively means "α is known explicitly", i.e., we need little or no effort to know it. Both operators can be represented in our semantics and with our operators, in fact, **L** is equivalent to $\Box_S^3$ or $\Box_S^1$ when $S = L$ and **B** is equivalent to $\Box_S^3$ when $S = \emptyset$. Hence, $\Box_S^3 \alpha$ has the intuitive reading of "α can be made explicit by reasoning only on letters in S", i.e., with an effort that is parameterized by S.

Lakemeyer [Lakemeyer, 1987] has extended Levesque's system, allowing a restricted form of nesting of operators. However his semantics, which relies on two distinct accessibility relations R and $\overline{R}$ for interpreting negated formulae, is very different from ours, thus making difficult any comparison.

A very interesting proposal has been presented by Fagin and Halpern in [Fagin and Halpern, 1988]. In that paper they introduce a new propositional attitude, in addition to knowledge and belief: the attitude of awareness. This new modality should act as a kind of filter on the consequences that can be drawn. In their system, truth in a world is defined in terms of the relation $\models^\Psi$, where $\Psi \subseteq L$ is a set of propositional letters and the agent is aware only of them. The intended meaning of $\models^\Psi$ is to restrict the attention only to letters in Ψ, while letters in $L \setminus \Psi$ are ignored. Our notion of S-1-interpretation is exactly in the same spirit. However, in Fagin and Halpern's system there is nothing close in spirit to the notion of S-3-interpretation.

In a more recent work [Fagin et al., 1990], Fagin, Halpern and Vardi present a different system which does not commit to the logical omniscience assumption. The presented system clarifies the reason why most of the non-classical semantics are not committed to logical omniscience. The main reasons are the impossibility of distinguishing either between coherent and incoherent worlds or between complete and incomplete ones. It is exactly the possibility of discerning between the various degrees of incoherence and incompleteness which has led us to the definition of our system. For example, the effect of the operator $\Box^3_S$ is exactly to select only complete situations which can be only partially incoherent, i.e., can use the truth value *contradiction* only in the interpretation of the propositions in $L \setminus S$. The effect of $\Box^1_S$ —which selects only coherent situations being partially incomplete— is analogous.

All the above formalizations of knowledge propose solutions to the logical omniscience problem by modifying the possible-worlds semantics. In fact different approaches have been attempted: As an example Weyhrauch, the present author and Talcott propose in [Weyhrauch et al., 1993] a formalization of knowledge that involves the use of abstract resources to control the use of logic. In that work the notion of resource is used to describe several principles of reasoning that can be used for ascribing knowledge to agents. Resources are abstract objects, having features suggestive of many diverse things: memory; computing time; knowing an algorithm or an heuristic.

All the results presented in this section will be proved in Appendix B.2.

The results of this section have been published in a preliminary form in [Cadoli and Schaerf, 1992b].

3.5 Approximation of concept description languages

In this section we generalize the technique introduced in Section 3.3 to deal with (fragments of) first-order logic. In particular, we take into account the so-called *concept description logics*, also known as terminological logics, that are abstractions for several languages in Computer Science and Artificial Intelligence. The first of those languages is the famous KL-ONE, described for example in [Brachman and Schmolze, 1985]. The importance of concept languages in data modeling [Brachman and Schmolze, 1985], object oriented data bases [Beeri, 1988] and Logic Programming [Aït-Kaci and Nasr, 1986] has been stressed by several authors.

The computational complexity of concept languages has been extensively studied by many researchers (cf. [Brachman and Levesque, 1984, Donini *et al.*, 1992, Donini *et al.*, 1991a, Donini *et al.*, 1991b, Schmidt-Schauß and Smolka, 1991, Nebel, 1988, Nebel, 1990, Nebel and Smolka, 1990].) In particular, it has been shown that reasoning is polynomially intractable in many interesting cases, and that tractability depends on small variations of the expressiveness of the language. A big effort has been spent in the design of "maximally polynomial languages", i.e., polynomial languages such that no expressiveness can be added without losing tractability.

Other researchers (see [MacGregor, 1991, Patel-Schneider, 1989]) proposed incomplete or unsound reasoning systems based on non-standard semantics in order to simplify reasoning tasks for concept languages. Patel-Schneider in [Patel-Schneider, 1989] presented a polynomially tractable terminological logic based on a 4-valued semantics. Kautz and Selman proposed in [Kautz and Selman, 1991a] a syntactic simplification of concepts in order to make inference computationally more easy. They defined sound as well as complete approximations.

In this section we focus our attention on the languages belonging to the $\mathcal{AL}$-family (see [Schmidt-Schauß and Smolka, 1991] for an overview on the family) and in particular on $\mathcal{ALE}$ and $\mathcal{ALC}$. As shown in [Donini *et al.*, 1991a], these languages are representative of a wide class of concept languages.

The structure of this section is as follows: in the following subsection we recall the basic notions on concept languages, while in Subsection 3.5.2 we introduce multi-valued logics for approximation in first-order languages. In Subsections 3.5.3 and 3.5.4 we demonstrate our approximation method for the two languages $\mathcal{ALE}$ and $\mathcal{ALC}$, respectively.

3.5.1   Concept Languages

In this subsection we briefly summarize the syntax and semantics of concept description languages.

Concept languages are decidable sub-languages of predicate logic, designed for dealing with *concepts*. A concept is a monadic predicate that can be built up of two kinds of symbols, primitive concepts and roles. Primitive entities can be combined by various language constructors yielding complex concepts. A primitive concept is simply a symbol, like female, that is used to represent a class of individuals all having a common property, like being female. A primitive role is a symbol, like friend, that is used to represent a binary relation among individuals, like friendship. A typical example of language constructor is the universal quantification ∀. The symbol ∀friend.female is a composite concept that represents the set of individuals having all the friends being female. Other typical language constructors are the existential quantification $\exists$ and the boolean connectives $\sqcap$, $\sqcup$, $\neg$. Another example of composite concept is $\exists$friend.$\neg$female, that represents the set of individuals having at least one friend being not female.

Throughout this section we denote primitive concepts with the letters A, B, concepts (either primitive or composite) with the letters C, D and primitive roles with the letter R.

The syntax of the language $\mathcal{ALC}$ is the following:

$$C, D \longrightarrow \top \mid \bot \mid A \mid \neg A \mid C \sqcap D \mid C \sqcup D \mid \forall R.C \mid \exists R.C$$

The special symbols $\top$ and $\bot$ stand for the universal concept and the empty concept, respectively. All the individuals belong to $\top$, while no individual belongs to $\bot$. Although the standard syntax of $\mathcal{ALC}$ (cf. [Schmidt-Schauß and Smolka, 1991]) allows negation in front of any concept, due to the presence of disjunction we don't lose any generality by allowing negation only in front of primitive concepts. Examples of well-formed $\mathcal{ALC}$ concepts are:

$$(\exists R.A) \sqcap (\exists R.(\neg A \sqcap \forall R.\exists R.A))$$

and

$$\exists R.\exists R.\forall R.(A \sqcup B).$$

$\mathcal{ALE}$ is another interesting language, whose syntax is a restriction of that of $\mathcal{ALC}$. In particular the construct $C \sqcup D$ is not allowed in $\mathcal{ALE}$, therefore the first of the two $\mathcal{ALC}$ concepts above is also an $\mathcal{ALE}$ concept, while the second one is not.

The semantics of concept languages is usually given by defining a domain of interpretation U, by assigning to every primitive concept a subset of U and to every primitive role a subset of $U \times U$ and by defining a rule for each constructor (see Appendix B.3.) For the purpose of our work we prefer to define the semantics of a generic concept C of $\mathcal{ALE}$ or $\mathcal{ALC}$ in the following way:

1. we translate C into a first-order sentence $\Gamma(C)$;

2. we interpret $\Gamma(C)$ with the classical semantics of first-order logic.

As an example, the $\mathcal{ALC}$ concept $D \equiv (B \sqcap \forall R.A) \sqcup \exists R.\neg B$ is translated into the first-order formula $\Gamma(D)$:

$$(B(a) \wedge \forall x R(a, x) \rightarrow A(x)) \vee (\exists y R(a, y) \wedge \neg B(y))$$

where a is a constant symbol. In general the translation from a concept C into the corresponding first order formula is obtained by applying the following rewriting rules to C:

$$\Gamma(C) \mapsto \Phi(C, a)$$
$$\Phi(\top, x) \mapsto t$$

$$\begin{aligned}
\Phi(\bot, x) &\mapsto f \\
\Phi(A, x) &\mapsto A(x) \\
\Phi(\neg A, x) &\mapsto \neg A(x) \\
\Phi(C \sqcap D, x) &\mapsto \Phi(C, x) \wedge \Phi(D, x) \\
\Phi(C \sqcup D, x) &\mapsto \Phi(C, x) \vee \Phi(D, x) \\
\Phi(\forall R.C, x) &\mapsto \forall y R(x, y) \rightarrow \Phi(C, y) \\
\Phi(\exists R.C, x) &\mapsto \exists y R(x, y) \wedge \Phi(C, y)
\end{aligned}$$

where a is a constant symbol, y is a variable symbol and x is either the constant symbol a or a variable symbol. We assume that the new variables introduced by the last two rules are fresh. Note that the first-order sentence we end up with is always in NNF. A concept C is *satisfiable* iff its translation $\Gamma(C)$ is a satisfiable sentence, *unsatisfiable* otherwise. As an example, the concept $\forall R.A$ is satisfiable, while the concept $(\forall R.A) \sqcap \exists R.\neg A$ is unsatisfiable. It is immediate to show that —as far as satisfiability is concerned— this semantics is equivalent to the more standard semantics for concept languages as found for example in [Schmidt-Schauß and Smolka, 1991] and reported in Appendix B.3.

In this section we are interested in analyzing satisfiability problems. The complexity analysis has shown that satisfiability checking is PSPACE-complete for $\mathcal{ALC}$ [Schmidt-Schauß and Smolka, 1991] and co-NP-complete for $\mathcal{ALE}$ [Donini *et al.*, 1992]. The computational complexity of other reasoning tasks like subsumption and instance checking has also been studied in the literature.

3.5.2   First-order generalization of S-interpretations

In this subsection we define a generalized notion of interpretation of first-order formulae. In particular we extend to a first-order semantics the definitions of S-3- and S-1-interpretations introduced in Section 3.3 for propositional formulae. This new notion will be used in the following for defining approximations methods for satisfiability of $\mathcal{ALE}$ and $\mathcal{ALC}$ concepts.

In order to simplify our definitions, we consider fixed domains of interpretation for the models. In particular we only consider Herbrand models. To this end, we assume that the sentences built on $\mathcal{L}$ are in Skolem Normal Form (cf. Section 1.10.2.) Since we are interested only in studying the satisfiability of sentences, the Herbrand theorem ensures that we are not losing any generality.

We assume that the formulae are built over a language $\mathcal{L}$. We recall that a Herbrand interpretation of the language $\mathcal{L}$ is a subset of the Herbrand base B_h. Equivalently, we can say that a Herbrand interpretation is a pair $I = <I^+, I^->$ of subsets of B_h which partition B_h. In other words I is built using two rules:

Rule 1 $I^+ \cup I^- = B_h$;

Rule 2 $I^+ \cap I^- = \emptyset$.

The subset I^+ represents the set of atoms α of B_h which are true in I, while I^- represents the set of atoms α of B_h whose negation is true in I. Since there are only two possibilities for an atom, namely it may belong either to I^+ or to I^-, we are entitled to call the partition I a *2-interpretation* of $\mathcal{L}$. A 2-interpretation I satisfies an atom α (written $I \models \alpha$) iff $\alpha \in I^+$ and satisfies a negated atom $\neg\alpha$ (written $I \models \neg\alpha$) iff $\alpha \in I^-$. The satisfaction of complex sentences is defined using the standard rules for disjunction, conjunction and universal quantification:

∨-**rule** $I \models \alpha \vee \beta$ iff $I \models \alpha$ or $I \models \beta$;

∧-**rule** $I \models \alpha \wedge \beta$ iff $I \models \alpha$ and $I \models \beta$;

∀-**rule** $I \models \forall x \ \gamma(x)$ iff $I \models \gamma(t)$ for all $t \in U_h$.

We are not interested in rules for the interpretation of complex negated formulae, since it is always possible to "push" the negation in front of atoms using a variant of the rewriting rules presented in Section 1.10. The notions of satisfiability and entailment are defined as in the propositional case.

The main idea of our semantic notion of approximation is to define interpretation of formulae without using one of **Rule 1**, **Rule 2**. This idea is a generalization of the idea presented in Section 3.3. In fact, loosely speaking, the Herbrand base of a propositional formula is the set of the boolean variables occurring in it. From this point of view Definition 3.1.1 of 3-interpretation given by Levesque (see Section 3.1.1) corresponds to keep **Rule 1** but not **Rule 2**.

For a first-order language, we define a *3-interpretation* of $\mathcal{L}$ in the following way.

Definition 3.5.1 (3-interpretation of first-order formulae) *A 3-interpretation of $\mathcal{L}$ is a pair $I =< I^+, I^- >$ where both I^+ and I^- are subsets of B_h, such that* **Rule 1** *holds.*

In other words it is possible that both an atom and its negation are satisfied by I, hence a formula like $\alpha \wedge \neg\alpha$ could be satisfied by a 3-interpretation. The term 3-interpretation is justified by the fact that there are three possibilities for each atom α of B_h:

1. $\alpha \in I^+$, $\alpha \notin I^-$;

2. $\alpha \notin I^+$, $\alpha \in I^-$;

3. $\alpha \in I^+$, $\alpha \in I^-$.

Interpretation of literals is the same as before, namely $I \models \alpha$ iff $\alpha \in I^+$ and $I \models \neg\alpha$ iff $\alpha \in I^-$. Interpretation of complex formulae is defined by means of ∨-**rule**, ∧-**rule**, ∀-**rule**.

Definition 3.3.1 of S-3-interpretation we presented in Section 3.3 makes use of **Rule 2** in a restricted way. We now give a definition that applies to first-order formulae. Let S be a subset —possibly not proper— of the Herbrand base B_h.

Definition 3.5.2 (*S-3-interpretation of first-order formulae*) *An S-3-interpretation of $\mathcal{L}$ is a pair $I = <I^+, I^->$ where both I^+ and I^- are subsets of B_h, such that the following rules hold:*

Rule 1 $I^+ \cup I^- = B_h$;

Rule 2' $I^+ \cap I^- \cap S = \emptyset$.

Intuitively, an S-3-interpretation is a 2-interpretation of the atoms of S, while it is a 3-interpretation of the remaining atoms. The three possibilities for each atom α of B_h are the following:

1. $\alpha \in I^+$, $\alpha \notin I^-$;

2. $\alpha \notin I^+$, $\alpha \in I^-$;

3. $\alpha \in I^+$, $\alpha \in I^-$ [only if $\alpha \in L \setminus S$].

Note that, for any S, a 2-interpretation is always an S-3-interpretation, while the latter is always a 3-interpretation. Satisfaction of complex sentences is defined by means of $\vee$-**rule**, $\wedge$-**rule**, $\forall$-**rule**. Note also that if $S \subseteq S' \subseteq B_h$, then S-3-unsatisfiability of a formula always implies its S'-3-unsatisfiability, hence its 2-unsatisfiability.

Using this characteristic of S-3-satisfiability we can approximate the satisfiability problem for a formula by means of a sequence $\langle S_0 \subset S_1 \subset \ldots \subset S_n = B_h \rangle$ of sets. In the following we show actual examples of the choice of this kind of sequences in the context of the languages $\mathcal{ALE}$ and $\mathcal{ALC}$.

We now introduce the definition of S-1-interpretation of first-order formulae, which is dual to S-3-interpretation and modifies **Rule 1** while keeping **Rule 2**.

Definition 3.5.3 (*S-1-interpretation of first-order formulae*) *An S-1-interpretation of $\mathcal{L}$ is a pair $I = <I^+, I^->$ where both I^+ and I^- are subsets of B_h, such that the following rules hold:*

Rule 1' $I^+ \cup I^- = S$;

Rule 2 $I^+ \cap I^- = \emptyset$.

An S-1-interpretation is a 2-interpretation as long as the atoms of S are concerned, while for all the atoms α not in S it holds that $\alpha \notin I^+$, $\alpha \notin I^-$.

We define $Terms(S)$ to be the set of all the terms that can be generated by using the functions and constants which occur in atoms of S. Note that this is in general a subset of the Herbrand universe. We define S-1-interpretation by means of $\vee$-**rule**, $\wedge$-**rule**, and the following rule:

$\forall'$-**rule** $I \models \forall x\; \gamma(x)$ iff $I \models \gamma(t)$ for all $t \in Terms(S)$.

As we show in the following subsections, we are not interested in sets S containing all the ground instances of a predicate symbol. S-1-interpretation with the ∀-**rule** would therefore be trivial, since no sentence can be satisfied. The intuition behind the ∀'-**rule** is that we are ignoring objects that are not in the intended domain of interpretation.

3.5.3 Approximation of $\mathcal{ALE}$

We now define a method for approximating the task of deciding satisfiability of an $\mathcal{ALE}$ concept. The method is based on a syntactic manipulation of concepts that simplifies the task of checking their satisfiability. The syntactic manipulation is given a precise semantics in terms of S-1- and S-3-interpretations.

The method we are going to present is based on the idea of approximating an $\mathcal{ALE}$ concept by means of two sequences of "simpler" $\mathcal{ALE}$ concepts. There are two ways in which a concept can be simpler than another one: a concept can be approximated either by a *weaker* concept or by a *stronger* one. A concept D is weaker than C if it represents a class with weaker properties, i.e., a less specific class. On the other hand, stronger concepts represent more specific classes. Both kinds of approximated concepts carry interesting information. In fact, if we can prove that a weaker concept is unsatisfiable, then the unsatisfiability of C is also proved. Proving the satisfiability of a stronger concept implies the satisfiability of C. One of the two sequences defining the approximation contains only weaker concepts. It starts with a very rough approximation and is improved in a stepwise process, giving "stronger and stronger" approximations and eventually converging to the original concept. The second sequence is dual, and contains only stronger concepts.

As an example, let's consider an unsatisfiable $\mathcal{ALE}$ concept, called *dummy* in the following

$$(\exists \mathsf{friend.tall}) \sqcap \forall \mathsf{friend.}((\forall \mathsf{friend.doctor}) \sqcap \exists \mathsf{friend.}\neg \mathsf{doctor}).$$

It denotes the (empty) set of the individuals having at least one friend tall and all the friends having both all the friends doctor and at least one friend who is not a doctor.

For obtaining concepts approximating *dummy* we syntactically simplify it by substituting complex sub-concepts with simpler ones, where a subconcept D of an $\mathcal{ALE}$ concept C is a substring of C being an $\mathcal{ALE}$ concept. The *depth* of D is the number of universal quantifiers occurring in C and having D in their scope. For example, the depth of the subconcept $\exists \mathsf{friend.}\neg \mathsf{doctor}$ of *dummy* is 1, while the depth of $\exists \mathsf{friend.tall}$ is 0. We define the depth of a concept to be the maximum depth of its existentially quantified sub-concepts. The depth of *dummy* is 1.

Using the notion of depth we define the sequence of weaker approximated concepts. The i-th weaker concept is obtained by replacing every existentially quantified subconcept of depth greater or equal than i with the primitive concept ⊤. As an example, taking into account *dummy* we obtain the sequence of concepts:

- $\top \sqcap \forall \mathsf{friend}.((\forall \mathsf{friend}.\mathsf{doctor}) \sqcap \top)$
- $(\exists \mathsf{friend}.\mathsf{tall}) \sqcap \forall \mathsf{friend}.((\forall \mathsf{friend}.\mathsf{doctor}) \sqcap \top)$
- *dummy.*

The elements of the sequence are denoted as $dummy_0^\top$, $dummy_1^\top$, $dummy_2^\top$, respectively. Note that the first two concepts are both satisfiable, while the third one is unsatisfiable. The sequence of the stronger concepts is obtained by substituting $\bot$ instead of $\top$. Its elements are denoted as $dummy_0^\bot$, $dummy_1^\bot$, $dummy_2^\bot$, respectively, and are all unsatisfiable.

In general we refer to the following definition.

Definition 3.5.4 (syntactic approximations of an $\mathcal{ALE}$ concept) *We associate to an $\mathcal{ALE}$ concept C of depth n two distinct sequences $\sigma^\top = C_0^\top, \ldots,$ $C_{n+1}^\top$ and $\sigma^\bot = C_0^\bot, \ldots, C_{n+1}^\bot$ of $\mathcal{ALE}$ concepts. For each i $(0 \le i \le n)$, every concept $C_i^\top$ $[C_i^\bot]$ of the sequence $\sigma^\top$ $[\sigma^\bot]$ is obtained from C by substituting every existentially quantified subconcept of C which is in the scope of at least i universal quantifiers with the concept $\top$ $[\bot]$. Moreover $C_{n+1}^\top = C_{n+1}^\bot = C$.*

We note that, for each i $(1 \le i \le n+1)$ the depth of both $C_i^\top$ and $C_i^\bot$ is strictly less than i.

The semantics of the approximation will be addressed later on, but at this point we would like to make some intuitive considerations on the simplified concepts. As we noted in Subsection 3.5.1, proving the satisfiability of a concept C is equivalent to proving the existence of an object a having the property represented by the first-order formula $\Gamma(C)$. If existentially quantified sub-concepts of depth 0 occur in C, then it is necessary to consider objects related to a. As an example, when we deal with the concept *dummy* we need to consider the existence of a friend of a being tall, because of the subconcept $\exists \mathsf{friend}.\mathsf{tall}$ of C. Let's call c this friend. Deeper existentially quantified sub-concepts may also contribute to the generation of objects that have to be considered. Continuing our example, the subconcept $\exists \mathsf{friend}.\neg\mathsf{doctor}$ of *dummy* makes it necessary to take into account the existence of a friend of c —let's call it $f(c)$— not being a doctor. Intuitively, focusing on simplified concepts means ignoring the properties of objects which are "far away" from a. As an example, considering $dummy_1^\top$ frees us from taking into account the object $f(c)$, while when we consider $dummy_0^\top$ we don't even have to deal with the object c. This intuition will be clarified when we will analyze the semantics of the concepts in the approximating sequences.

We give now a couple of important properties of the sequences $\sigma^\top$ and $\sigma^\bot$, that are useful for defining our approximation schema.

Theorem 3.5.1 (monotonicity of the syntactic approximations) *For each i $(0 \le i \le n+1)$, if $C_i^\top$ is unsatisfiable then $C_j^\top$ is unsatisfiable for all $j \ge i$, hence C is unsatisfiable.*

For each i ($0 \leq i \leq n+1$), if $C_i^{\perp}$ is satisfiable then $C_j^{\perp}$ is satisfiable for all $j \geq i$, hence C is satisfiable.

Observation 3.5.2 (convergence of the syntactic approximations) *If C is unsatisfiable then there exists an i ($0 \leq i \leq n+1$) such that $C_i^{\top}$ is unsatisfiable. If C is satisfiable then there exists an i ($0 \leq i \leq n+1$) such that $C_i^{\perp}$ is satisfiable.*

We note that these results correspond to Theorem 3.3.1 and Observation 3.3.2 shown in Section 3.3. Theorem 3.5.1 and Observation 3.5.2 suggest a method for deciding in an incremental fashion the satisfiability of an $\mathcal{ALE}$ concept C. We may start by deciding the satisfiability of $C_0^{\top}$; if $C_0^{\top}$ is unsatisfiable, then by Theorem 3.5.1 we are guaranteed that C is unsatisfiable as well. Analogously, if $C_0^{\perp}$ is satisfiable, then we know that C is satisfiable. If neither of the two cases happens, then we decide the satisfiability of $C_1^{\top}$ and $C_1^{\perp}$, and so on. Clearly we have a definite answer as soon as we prove either unsatisfiability of some $C_i^{\top}$ or satisfiability of some $C_i^{\perp}$. Referring to the notation defined in Section 3.2, we approximate the set $\mathcal{D}$ of satisfiable $\mathcal{ALE}$ concepts of depth n by means of two sequences of sets $\langle \mathcal{D}_0, \mathcal{D}_1, \ldots, \mathcal{D}_{n+1} \rangle$ and $\langle \mathcal{D}^0, \mathcal{D}^1, \ldots, \mathcal{D}^{n+1} \rangle$, where $\mathcal{D}_i$ [$\mathcal{D}^i$] is the set of $\mathcal{ALE}$ concepts C whose stronger [weaker] form $C_i^{\perp}$ [$C_i^{\top}$] is satisfiable.

We make now some considerations on the computational cost of deciding satisfiability of an $\mathcal{ALE}$ concept in such an incremental fashion. Donini et al. show in [Donini *et al.*, 1992] that the problem of checking the satisfiability of an $\mathcal{ALE}$ concept whose depth is linear in its length is co-NP-complete. In the same paper it is shown that the satisfiability of any $\mathcal{ALE}$ concept having depth m can be checked in time proportional to $l \cdot 2^m$, where l is the length of the concept. In other words, the nesting of existential and universal quantifiers is the crucial measure of the complexity of satisfiability checking. This observation has the same importance of Theorem 3.3.3 presented in Section 3.3 for the propositional case.

Our method for checking satisfiability of an $\mathcal{ALE}$ concept C considers simplified versions of C of increasing depth and may use existing algorithms for checking their satisfiability. The complexity of the whole method is $O(l^2 \cdot 2^m)$ even if satisfiability cannot be decided until the unsimplified concept C is taken into account. In the worst case the complexity of our method is therefore comparable to that of the existing algorithms.

We are now interested in giving a clear semantics to our approximation schema. This is particularly important, since as we stressed earlier it is not always possible to obtain in a reasonable amount of time a definite answer to the problem of checking the satisfiability of an $\mathcal{ALE}$ concept. Therefore the meaning of each step of the approximation should be very clear, since in general we can afford only an approximate solution.

In order to give a semantic account to the approximations of $\mathcal{ALE}$ concepts, we are now going to use the notions of S-3- and S-1-interpretation introduced in Subsection 3.5.2. As we noted earlier, S-3-interpretations lead to a complete (and in general unsound) definition of satisfiability. Analogously, Theorem 3.5.1 shows that satisfiability of the concepts of the sequence $\sigma^{\top}$ is complete and unsound w.r.t. the satisfiability of the original concept C. Our goal is to show that 2-satisfiability (or simply, satisfiability) of each concept $C_i^{\top}$ is equivalent to S_i-3-satisfiability of C for a suitable subset S_i of the Herbrand base of the Skolem Normal Form $SNF(\Gamma(C))$ of $\Gamma(C)$. An analogous result will be obtained for a concept $C_i^{\perp}$ and S_i-1-satisfiability of C.

As we said in Subsection 3.5.1, the semantics of an $\mathcal{ALE}$ concept C can be defined in terms of a first-order formula $\Gamma(C)$. Since we are only interested in satisfiability properties, we take into account the Skolem Normal Form $SNF(\Gamma(C))$ of $\Gamma(C)$. The Herbrand universe of $SNF(\Gamma(C))$ can be stratified in a very simple way by taking into account the increasing complexity of its terms. This stratification delivers another simple stratification on the Herbrand base. More precisely, let U_h be the Herbrand universe of $SNF(\Gamma(C))$. This universe can be stratified with the following rule: Let U_0 be $\{a\}$ and U_i be the set of all the terms which can be formed using a, Skolem constants of U_h and functions of U_h of arity strictly less than i. Clearly it holds that $U_0 \subseteq U_1 \subseteq \ldots \subseteq U_{n+1} = U_h$. Note that a function of arity i comes from the skolemization of an existential quantifier of depth i. This stratification of the Herbrand universe of $SNF(\Gamma(C))$ induces a stratification $S_0 \subseteq S_1 \subseteq \ldots \subseteq S_{n+1} = B_h$ on its Herbrand base H_b defined in the following way:

$$S_i = \{A(t) \mid A \text{ is a primitive concept and } t \in U_i\}$$
$$\cup \{R(t_1, t_2) \mid R \text{ is a role and } t_1, t_2 \in U_i\}.$$

A clarifying example is in order. Let's consider again the concept *dummy*

$$(\exists \text{friend.tall}) \sqcap \forall \text{friend.}((\forall \text{friend.doctor}) \sqcap \exists \text{friend.}\neg \text{doctor})$$

and the related first-order formula $\Gamma(dummy)$, in which we use obvious abbreviations for the predicate symbols:

$$(\exists x F(a, x) \wedge T(x)) \wedge \forall y F(a, y) \rightarrow$$
$$(\forall z (F(y, z) \rightarrow D(z)) \wedge (\exists u F(y, u) \wedge \neg D(u)))$$

The following formula is the Skolem Normal Form $SNF(\Gamma(dummy))$ of the formula $\Gamma(dummy)$:

$$F(a, c) \wedge T(c) \wedge \forall y (F(a, y) \rightarrow$$
$$(\forall z (F(y, z) \rightarrow D(z)) \wedge F(y, f(y)) \wedge \neg D(f(y))))$$

In $SNF(\Gamma(dummy))$, c is a new constant symbol that replaces the variable x, while $f()$ is a new function symbol —having arity 1— replacing the variable u. The Herbrand universe U_h of $SNF(\Gamma(dummy))$ is the set of all the terms that can be obtained from a, c and $f()$. The universe U_h is stratified into the three sets $U_0 = \{a\}, U_1 = \{a, c\}, U_2 = \{a, c, f(a), f(c), f(f(a)), \ldots\}$.

Note that the S_i turns out to be equal (up to Skolem functions and constants renaming) to the Herbrand base of $SNF(\Gamma(C_i^\top))$.

As we saw before the concept *dummy* is unsatisfiable. We noted informally that its unsatisfiability can only be proven by taking into account the properties of the friends of the friends of a: All the members of this class should be doctors, while one of them is not a doctor. As a consequence, *dummy* is unsatisfiable, but its simplified versions $dummy_0^\top$ and $dummy_1^\top$ are both satisfiable. As a semantic counterpart, we note that $SNF(\Gamma(dummy))$ is unsatisfiable and this follows from the existence of a term of the form $f(c)$ which denotes the friend of the friend c of a. Actually $SNF(\Gamma(dummy))$ is both S_0-3- and S_1-3- satisfiable, where a concept C is S_i-3-satisfiable if $SNF(\Gamma(C))$ is S-3-satisfiable with $S = S_i$. This can be easily shown by noticing that the atom $D(f(c))$ does not belong to S_1, hence it is possible to define a S_1-3-interpretation $I = \langle I^+, I^- \rangle$ such that $D(f(c)) \in I^+, D(f(c)) \in I^-$. This kind of interpretation "hides" the reason of inconsistency of the concept *dummy*, which is therefore S_1-3-satisfiable. This argument obviously holds also for the stratum S_0.

The above example shows that it is possible to relate S_i-3-satisfiability of a concept C of $\mathcal{ALE}$ to satisfiability of the i-th element $C_i^\top$ of the sequence $\sigma^\top$. The following theorem formalizes this result.

Theorem 3.5.3 (semantics of the syntactic approximation $\sigma^\top$) *For all i* $(0 \le i \le n + 1)$ C *is S_i-3-satisfiable iff $C_i^\top$ is satisfiable.*

What this theorem says is that our approximation schema based on the analysis of syntactically simplified concepts readily corresponds to the semantic idea of focusing on subsets of the Herbrand base which are defined by a simpler universe. This characterization of the approximation process could not be obtained if we were to use the more standard semantics for $\mathcal{AL}$-languages based on extension functions, since we could not introduce the notion of complexity of terms.

The above correspondence between S_i-3-satisfiability of a concept C of $\mathcal{ALE}$ and satisfiability of the i-th element $C_i^\top$ of the sequence $\sigma^\top$ can be easily extended to the dual case of S_i-1-satisfiability. A concept C is S_i-1-satisfiable if $SNF(\Gamma(C))$ is S-1-satisfiable with $S = S_i$. Similarly to the previous case, it is possible to show that the approximation of the satisfiability of a concept C through the sequence $\sigma^\perp$ can be interpreted as S_i-1-satisfiability of the translated concept $SNF(\Gamma(C))$. This follows from the equivalence of the Herbrand base of $SNF(\Gamma(C_i^\perp))$ and the Herbrand base of $SNF(\Gamma(C_i^\top))$.

Theorem 3.5.4 (semantics of the syntactic approximation $\sigma^\perp$) *For all i* $(0 \le i \le n + 1)$ C *is S_i-1-satisfiable iff $C_i^\perp$ is satisfiable.*

Note that the difference between S_i-1- and S_i-3-interpretations relies on the interpretation of atoms not belonging to the stratum S_i. As an example, in each S_1-1-interpretations I of the concept *dummy* it holds $D(f(c)) \notin I^+, D(f(c)) \notin I^-$.

We conclude this section by making some considerations about the choice of the subsets S_i of the Herbrand base of $SNF(\Gamma(C_i^{\top}))$ defining our approximation schema. Donini et al. show in [Donini *et al.*, 1992] that the number of primitive concepts and roles used is not a source of complexity in $\mathcal{ALE}$. More precisely, deciding the satisfiability of an $\mathcal{ALE}$ concept C is a co-NP-complete problem even if a single primitive role and no primitive concepts but $\top$ occur in C.

This fact has an important impact in the choice of an approximation schema for $\mathcal{ALE}$ concepts. In particular it shows that, if the subset S of the Herbrand base contains all the ground instances of a single atomic role, then deciding S-3-satisfiability of an $\mathcal{ALE}$ concept is still co-NP-complete. Therefore the sets S defining the approximation schema must be designed so that the real source of complexity —which is the depth of concepts— is addressed.

3.5.4   Approximation of $\mathcal{ALC}$

In this subsection we define a method for approximating the task of deciding satisfiability of an $\mathcal{ALC}$ concept. Similarly to the method illustrated in the previous subsection, also this one is based on a syntactic manipulation of concepts that is interpreted in terms of S-1- and S-3-satisfiability.

A first obvious question is: can we plainly use the method introduced in Subsection 3.5.3 for the purpose of approximating $\mathcal{ALC}$ concepts? We note that $\mathcal{ALC}$ without existential quantifiers has at least the expressiveness of propositional calculus. As a consequence deciding satisfiability of $\mathcal{ALC}$ concepts without existential quantifiers is an NP-hard problem. This implies that the method defined for the approximation of an $\mathcal{ALE}$ concept leads —when used for $\mathcal{ALC}$ concepts— to polynomially intractable problems at the very first step of the approximation.

In fact an effective method for the approximation of $\mathcal{ALC}$ should address both sources of complexity of this language (see [Donini *et al.*, 1991a]): the complexity of existentials, also present in $\mathcal{ALE}$, and that of disjunction, present in the existential-free fragment of $\mathcal{ALC}$.

The source of complexity of disjunction is also present in the propositional calculus. The method presented in Section 3.3 for approximating propositional satisfiability relies on the use of S-1- and S-3-satisfiability in which sets S containing more and more boolean variables are taken into account. This corresponds to a stratification $S_0 \subseteq S_1 \subseteq \ldots \subseteq S_{n+1} = B_h$ of the Herbrand base B_h, in which each stratum contains all the ground instances of a predicate symbol. As we noted at the end of Subsection 3.5.3, such a stratification cannot be used for the approximation of $\mathcal{ALE}$, which must instead be based on the complexity of the terms of the Herbrand universe. It is therefore natural to combine both ideas for the approximation of $\mathcal{ALC}$. In the method we are going to present the concepts of the approximating sequences have both a fixed depth and interpret classically only a subset of the primitive concepts.

Let's start again with a concrete example and consider the following $\mathcal{ALC}$ concept:

$$D \equiv (A \sqcap \neg A) \sqcup ((\forall R.A) \sqcap \exists R.\neg A)$$

D is unsatisfiable, because it is the union of two unsatisfiable $\mathcal{ALE}$ concepts. D can be approximated either by substituting the existentially quantified sub-concept $\exists R.\neg A$ with $\top$ or by replacing both the primitive concept A and its negation $\neg A$ with $\top$. Moreover both methods can be combined. Each of the following $\mathcal{ALC}$ concepts is weaker than D and satisfiable:

$$
\begin{aligned}
D_{\emptyset,0}^{\top} &\equiv (\top \sqcap \top) \sqcup (\forall R.\top \sqcap \top) \\
D_{\{A\},0}^{\top} &\equiv (A \sqcap \neg A) \sqcup (\forall R.A \sqcap \top) \\
D_{\emptyset,1}^{\top} &\equiv (\top \sqcap \top) \sqcup (\forall R.\top \sqcap \exists R.\top)
\end{aligned}
$$

The first subscript denotes the set of primitive concepts that are not substituted by $\top$, while the second one denotes the depth of the approximation.

In general we refer to the following definition.

Definition 3.5.5 (syntactic approximations of an $\mathcal{ALC}$ concept) *Let C be an $\mathcal{ALC}$ concept of depth n built on the set A of primitive concepts, a set $P \subseteq A$ and an index $0 \le i \le n + 1$, we denote with the symbol $C_{P,i}^{\top}$ the $\mathcal{ALC}$ concept obtained from C by means of the following rules:*

1. *substitute each (positive or negative) occurrence of a primitive concept not in P with the concept $\top$, thus obtaining the concept C';*

2. *substitute every existentially quantified subconcept of C' which is in the scope of at least i universal quantifiers with the concept $\top$.*

The concept $C_{P,i}^{\perp}$ is obtained by substituting $\perp$ instead of $\top$.

Let P_1, P_2 be two subsets of A and let i_1, i_2 be two indexes such that $0 \le i_1, i_2 \le n + 1$. Let C be an $\mathcal{ALC}$ concept and $C_1 \equiv C_{P_1,i_1}^{\top}$, $C_2 \equiv C_{P_2,i_2}^{\top}$ two approximations of C. We say that $C_1 \preceq C_2$ holds iff both $P_1 \subseteq P_2$ and $i_1 \le i_2$ hold. We define the relation $\preceq$ only between pairs of weaker approximations and pairs of stronger ones. This relation is a partial order in the set of the approximations of an $\mathcal{ALC}$ concept. The following are two interesting properties of this relation:

Theorem 3.5.5 (monotonicity of the syntactic approximations) *Let P be a subset of A and i be an index such that $0 \le i \le n+1$. If $C_{P,i}^{\top}$ is unsatisfiable then any subconcept D of C such that $C_{P,i}^{\top} \preceq D$ is unsatisfiable. If $C_{P,i}^{\perp}$ is satisfiable then any subconcept D of C such that $C_{P,i}^{\perp} \preceq D$ is satisfiable.*

Observation 3.5.6 (convergence of the syntactic approximations) *If C is unsatisfiable, then there exists a subset P of A and an index i $(0 \le i \le n+1)$ such that $C_{P,i}^{\top}$ is unsatisfiable. If C is satisfiable, then there exists a subset P of A and an index i $(0 \le i \le n+1)$ such that $C_{P,i}^{\perp}$ is satisfiable.*

The above properties are analogous to Theorem 3.5.1 and Observation 3.5.2 for $\mathcal{ALE}$. Along the same lines of Subsection 3.5.3, we say that any $\mathcal{ALC}$ concept C can be approximated by means of an increasing (w.r.t. $\preceq$) sequence of weaker concepts $C_{P,i}^{\top}$. This corresponds to a weak approximation of C. A strong approximation can be obtained by considering an increasing sequence of concepts $C_{P,i}^{\perp}$.

It can be shown that satisfiability checking of a subconcept $C_{P,i}^{\top}$ or $C_{P,i}^{\perp}$ can be done in time proportional to $2^{|P| \cdot i}$. This property entitles us to perform an argument similar to that of Subsection 3.5.3, in order to show that our method for checking satisfiability of $\mathcal{ALC}$ concepts in an incremental fashion has a complexity comparable to the standard algorithms (see [Schmidt-Schauß and Smolka, 1991].)

From the semantical point of view it is possible to characterize this form of approximation in terms of S-3- and S-1-interpretations. Let C be an $\mathcal{ALC}$ concept and n be its depth —defined exactly as in the case of $\mathcal{ALE}$ concepts. The stratification $U_0 \subseteq U_1 \subseteq \ldots \subseteq U_{n+1} = U_h$ of the Herbrand universe U_h of $SNF(\Gamma(C))$ is defined as in Subsection 3.5.3. We define the subset $S_{P,i}$ of the Herbrand base H_b of $SNF(\Gamma(C))$ to be the following set:

$$\{A(t) \mid A \text{ is a primitive concept in } P \text{ and } t \in U_i\}$$
$$\cup \{R(t_1, t_2) \mid R \text{ is a role and } t_1, t_2 \in U_i\}$$

We say that C is $S_{P,i}$-3-satisfiable iff it is S-3-satisfiable for $S = S_{P,i}$. The intuition behind this definition is that we are confining our attention only to a subset of the set S_i defined in Subsection 3.5.3. In particular we want a unary atom $A(t)$ to be in $S_{P,i}$ only if the concept A belongs to the set of privileged primitive concepts P. In this way we are limiting both sources of potential complexity: disjunction and existential quantification. Contradiction cannot arise from roles, since $\mathcal{ALC}$ does not support negation on roles. In an analogous way we define $S_{P,i}$-1-satisfiability. The following properties formalize the relations between syntax and semantics:

Theorem 3.5.7 (semantics of the $\top$ syntactic approximation) *For all i ($0 \leq i \leq n+1$) and $P \subseteq A$ the concept C is $S_{P,i}$-3-satisfiable iff $C_{P,i}^{\top}$ is satisfiable.*

Theorem 3.5.8 (semantics of the $\perp$ syntactic approximation) *For all i ($0 \leq i \leq n+1$) and $P \subseteq A$ the concept C is $S_{P,i}$-1-satisfiable iff $C_{P,i}^{\perp}$ is satisfiable.*

We conclude this section by noticing that the method we propose for the approximation of $\mathcal{ALC}$ concepts is in some sense under-specified, since we gave no criteria for choosing subsets P of the set of primitive concepts. The same considerations developed in Sections 3.3 and 3.4 for the propositional calculus apply to this case as well.

All the results presented in this section will be proved in Appendix B.3.

The results of this section have been published in [Cadoli and Schaerf, 1992c].

3.6 Approximation of non-monotonic logics

In this section we propose a further application of the approximate reasoning technique. We deal with inference in two propositional non-monotonic logics: circumscription (that we already dealt with in Chapter 2) and default logic, defined by Reiter in [Reiter, 1980b] (the we already met in Section 2.7.2.) Circumscription and default logic are the most interesting and well-studied formalisms for the description of non-monotonic reasoning. As for the relevance of non-monotonic reasoning in AI, we refer to the preliminary motivations shown in Section 2.1.

In Chapter 2 we showed that non-monotonic formal systems suffer from a high computational complexity, which is generally higher than that of the monotonic case. In particular, the problems of testing entailment in propositional default logic and circumscription are complete with respect to the class Π_2^p of the polynomial hierarchy [Eiter and Gottlob, 1993b, Gottlob, 1992, Stillman, 1992, Papadimitriou and Sideri, 1992]. In fact these forms of non-monotonic reasoning have two distinct sources of complexity. For example in circumscriptive entailment we have to test validity in *all* minimal models —which can be exponentially many— and checking whether a model is minimal is itself polynomially intractable (cf. Section 2.4.) As a consequence it is not possible to collapse approximation of non-monotonic reasoning into approximation of propositional calculus.

In this section we define a method for approximating inference in non-monotonic formalisms that attacks both sources of complexity. In the spirit of our research paradigm, we give the method a semantics in terms of S-1- and S-3-interpretations, we define sound as well as complete approximations, proving monotonicity, convergence and uniform complexity results. We also show how existing algorithms for propositional circumscription [Przymusinski, 1989] and default logic [Reiter, 1980b] can be easily adapted to work with our definitions.

This is not the first approach to non-monotonic reasoning based on multi-valued logic (see for example the work of Doherty and Lukaszewicz in [Doherty and Lukaszewicz, 1992].) The focus of our research —namely the exploitation of the computational properties of a particular multi-valued logic— is nevertheless novel. The use of non-standard forms of logic for building non-monotonic reasoning systems having nice computational properties has been attempted also by Etherington and Crawford in [Etherington and Crawford, 1992] and by Ginsberg in [Ginsberg, 1991a]. These authors are especially interested in preserving the plausibility of the mechanism as a model of human reasoning.

This section has two subsections, devoted respectively to approximation of default logic and circumscription.

3.6.1   Approximation of default logic

In this subsection we deal with approximation for propositional default logic.
Definition of propositional default logic is summarized in the first part and a
method for approximate inference is presented in the second part.

3.6.1.1   Preliminaries

A propositional default theory has been defined by Reiter in [Reiter, 1980b]
as a pair $\langle D, W \rangle$, where D is a set of *defaults* of the form $(\alpha : \beta_1, \ldots, \beta_n)/\gamma$
and $\alpha, \beta_1, \ldots, \beta_n, \gamma$ are propositional formulae and W is a set of propositional
formulae. The intuitive reading of a default $(\alpha : \beta_1, \ldots, \beta_n)/\gamma$ is: If it is the case
that α is derivable and $\beta_1, \ldots, \beta_n$ can be consistently assumed, then infer γ.

Given a default $d = (\alpha : \beta_1, \ldots, \beta_n)/\gamma$ α is called the prerequisite of d
$(PREREQ(d))$, $\beta_1, \ldots, \beta_n$ are the justifications $(JUSTIF(d))$ and γ is the consequence $(CONSEQ(d))$. A default theory is *normal* iff all the defaults in D
are of the form $(\alpha : \beta)/\beta$. The semantics of a default theory is based on the
notion of *extension*.

Definition 3.6.1 (Reiter [Reiter, 1980b]) *Let* $\langle D, W \rangle$ *be a default theory.*
For any set A of formulae let $\Gamma(A)$ be the smallest set such that:

1. $W \subseteq \Gamma(A)$;

2. $\Gamma(A) = \{\epsilon | \Gamma(A) \models \epsilon\}$;

3. *if* $(\alpha : \beta_1, \ldots, \beta_n)/\gamma \in D$, $\alpha \in \Gamma(A)$ *and* $\forall_{j=1}^n (A \cup \{\beta_j\})$ *is satisfiable, then*
   $\gamma \in \Gamma(A)$.

A set of formulae E is an extension of $\langle D, W \rangle$ if and only if it is a fixed point
of the operator Γ, i.e., $\Gamma(E) = E$.

Although extensions are infinite sets, they can be compactly represented by their
associated set of generating defaults.

Definition 3.6.2 (Reiter [Reiter, 1980b]) *The set of generating defaults for*
an extension E w.r.t. a default theory $\langle D, W \rangle$ is the set:
   $GD(E, D, W) = \{(\alpha : \beta_1, \ldots, \beta_n)/\gamma \in D | \alpha \in E$ *and* $\forall_{j=1}^n \neg\beta_j \notin E\}$.

Credulous default reasoning [Reiter, 1980b] is an interesting form of inference
which can be performed in default logic: all the formulae α which belong to at
least one extension E of $\langle D, W \rangle$ are inferred.

In the sequel we only deal with credulous reasoning in normal default theories.
While normal default theories are less expressive than general default theories,

it has been proven [Gottlob, 1992, Stillman, 1992] that credulous reasoning in the two cases has exactly the same computational complexity i.e., both problems are complete with respect to the class Σ_2^p of the polynomial hierarchy.

In this work we are only interested in default theories in clausal form, in which W and each of the α, β and γ are CNF formulae. Moreover we are only interested in inference of clauses. With this restriction the formulae ϵ occurring in point 2 of Definition 3.6.1 can be assumed to be clauses without any loss of generality. This property will be used in the sequel.

Few algorithms have been presented in the literature for default logic. We refer here to the algorithm presented by Reiter in [Reiter, 1980b] for credulous reasoning with normal defaults. Very briefly, the algorithm is based on the following idea: Use linear resolution to find a proof of the goal α from $W \cup CONSEQ(D)$. Collect all the defaults whose consequences have been used in the proof in a set D_1. If this set is empty then return true otherwise iterate the process by looking for a proof of the prerequisites of the defaults in D_1 until a proof not using defaults is found or all proofs have been explored. If we assume that the cost of deciding whether $T \models \gamma$ holds is $O(|T| \cdot |\gamma| \cdot 2^{|L|})$ —where T, γ are propositional formulae and L is the propositional alphabet— then Reiter's algorithm has a worst-case time complexity of $O(|\langle D, W \rangle| \cdot |D|^2 \cdot |\gamma| \cdot |L| \cdot 2^{|L|} \cdot 2^{|D|})$.

We want to spend few words on the above complexity estimate. First of all we note that the cost function has two exponential factors. Actually it is well known that credulous default reasoning has two distinct sources of complexity. Roughly speaking one source is caused by the non-determinism in the choice of an appropriate set of generating defaults, while the second is caused by the consistency checking explicit in Definition 3.6.1. These two sources of complexity are indeed independent, since credulous default reasoning is a Σ_2^p-complete problem. Two exponential factors seem therefore to be not avoidable, and we don't expect any algorithm to be significantly more efficient than Reiter's in the worst case.

This considerations will play a major role in the method for approximate credulous reasoning we are going to present in the following. The method works simultaneously on both sources of complexity, diminishing both the search space of the possible extensions and the cost of the consistency checking.

3.6.1.2 Approximation method

We are now ready to describe a method for the approximation of credulous default reasoning in normal default theories. Since we want to apply the techniques developed in Section 3.3 to the inference problems of propositional default reasoning, the most intuitive approach seems the following one: find a mapping from the credulous default reasoning into the propositional calculus and then apply those techniques to the formulae we end up with. For what concerns "translations" from default logic into propositional logic, a first step has been done by Ben-Eliyahu and Dechter in [Ben-Eliyahu and Dechter, 1991]. In that work they show a polynomial translation from a default theory $\langle D, W \rangle$ into a propositional formula T, such that there is a correspondence between the extensions of $\langle D, W \rangle$ and the models of T. This mapping works for a restricted class of default theories (namely disjunction-free semi-normal defaults) and it has been extended by the same authors in [Ben-Eliyahu and Dechter, 1992] for any default theory, but requires exponential time and space. Due to the Σ_2^p-completeness of the problem of deciding the existence of an extension (see [Gottlob, 1992, Stillman, 1992]) this is not surprising. Since we want our method for approximate default reasoning to be "uniformly" complex (i.e., having a complexity proportional to the quality of the inference), this shows that approximation of credulous default reasoning cannot be collapsed into approximation of propositional reasoning.

The approximation schema we present uses a technique that is specific to default reasoning. This approach has the advantage of providing approximate solutions whose semantics is closer in spirit to the semantics of default logic. In Reiter's original paper [Reiter, 1980b] extensions are defined on top of a classical consequence relation, but this notion can be easily generalized by using arbitrary consequence relations. In the following we restrict our attention to CNF normal default theories and inference of clauses δ, where a normal default theory is in CNF if W is a set of CNF formulae and for each default $(\alpha : \gamma/\gamma)$ in D it holds that α, γ are CNF formulae. Furthermore, we assume that tautological clauses (i.e., clauses containing both a literal and its negation) do not appear in D, in W or in δ. While the first restriction is necessary to ensure some of the following results, the second restriction is only required to simplify the statements and the proofs of the theorems.

We will provide two methods for approximation, the first one being correct and the second one being complete w.r.t. credulous default reasoning. The sound method relies on the following definition.

Definition 3.6.3 (S-3-extensions) *Let $\langle D, W \rangle$ be a normal default theory. For any set A of formulae let $\Gamma_S^3(A)$ be the smallest set such that:*

1. *$W \subseteq \Gamma_S^3(A)$;*

2. *$\Gamma_S^3(A) = \{\epsilon | \; \epsilon \text{ is a non-tautological clause and } \Gamma_S^3(A) \models_S^3 \epsilon\}$;*

3. *if $(\alpha : \gamma/\gamma) \in D$, $\alpha \in \Gamma_S^3(A)$ and $(A \cup \{\gamma\})$ is S-1-satisfiable, then $\gamma \in \Gamma_S^3(A)$.*

A set of formulae E is an S-3-extension of $\langle D, W \rangle$ if and only if it is a fixed point of the operator Γ_S^3, i.e., $\Gamma_S^3(E) = E$.

Examples illustrating this and the following definitions can be found at the end of this subsection.

Note that both notions of S-1- and S-3-interpretation of a propositional formula are used in this definition. Comparing this definition to Definition 3.6.1 of extension, we can say that we are "weakening" both points 2. and 3., since

S-3-entailment implies classical entailment (see Theorem 3.3.1 in Section 3.3), while S-1-satisfiability implies classical satisfiability (see Theorem 3.3.4.) Like extensions, S-3-extensions also support a compact representation, since in the same style of Reiter [Reiter, 1980b] we can associate to any S-3-extension E a set of generating defaults $GD_S^3(E, D, W) \subseteq D$. This set contains all the defaults that have been applied in order to generate E. The following result clarifies what happens to S-3-extensions when bigger sets S are taken into account.

Lemma 3.6.1 (monotonicity of S-3-extensions) *Let $S \subseteq S' \subseteq L$, $\langle D, W \rangle$ be a normal default theory and E be one of its S-3-extensions. There exists an E' s.t. $E' \supseteq E$ and E' is an S'-3-extension of $\langle D, W \rangle$.*

Note that the above lemma implies that each S-3-extension is a subset of some (classical) extension.

The definition dual to S-3-extension is that of S-1-extension. This definition rules the complete approximation.

Definition 3.6.4 (S-1-extensions) *Let $\langle D, W \rangle$ be a normal default theory. For any set A of formulae let $\Gamma_S^1(A)$ be the smallest set such that:*

1. $W \subseteq \Gamma_S^1(A)$;

2. $\Gamma_S^1(A) = \{\epsilon | \ \epsilon$ *is a non-tautological clause and* $\Gamma_S^1(A) \models_S^1 \epsilon\}$;

3. *if* $(\alpha : \gamma/\gamma) \in D$, $\alpha \in \Gamma_S^1(A)$ *and* $(A \cup \{\gamma\})$ *is S-3-satisfiable, then* $\gamma \in \Gamma_S^1(A)$.

A set of formulae E is an S-1-extension of $\langle D, W \rangle$ if and only if it is a fixed point of the operator Γ_S^1, i.e., $\Gamma_S^1(E) = E$.

Note that in the above definition the notions of S-1- and S-3-interpretation are used for "strengthening" both points 2. and 3. of Definition 3.6.1 of extension. Also in this case we can associate to any S-1-extension E a set of generating defaults $GD_S^1(E, D, W) \subseteq D$. This set contains all the defaults that have been applied in order to generate the S-1-extension E. The following result clarifies what happens to S-1-extensions when smaller sets S are taken into account.

Lemma 3.6.2 (monotonicity of S-1-extensions) *Let $S \subseteq S' \subseteq L$ and $\langle D, W \rangle$ be a normal default theory. For all E' being an S'-1-extension there exists an E being an S-1-extension s.t. $E' \subseteq E$.*

Note that the above lemma implies that each (classical) extension is a subset of some S-1-extension.

Most of the properties of the extensions as defined by Reiter are enjoyed by S-3-extensions as well as S-1-extensions. A result which is worth showing is the following.

Theorem 3.6.3 (S-satisfiability of S-extensions) *Let $\langle D, W \rangle$ be a normal default theory and $S \subseteq L$ be a non empty set of letters. If W is S-3-satisfiable then all the S-3-extensions of $\langle D, W \rangle$ are also S-3-satisfiable. If W is S-1-satisfiable then all the S-1-extensions of $\langle D, W \rangle$ are also S-1-satisfiable.*

We use the following notations for representing approximate credulous default reasoning.

Definition 3.6.5 (approximate credulous default reasoning) *We write $\langle D, W \rangle_S^3 \vdash \delta$ to denote that the wff δ belongs to at least one S-3-extension of the default theory $\langle D, W \rangle$. Similarly, $\langle D, W \rangle_S^{\frac{1}{2}} \vdash \delta$ denotes that δ belongs to at least one S-1-extension of $\langle D, W \rangle$, while $\langle D, W \rangle \vdash \delta$ denotes that δ belongs to at least one (classical) extension of $\langle D, W \rangle$.*

As discussed in Section 3.3, we require an approximation schema to have the three properties of monotonicity, convergence and uniform complexity. The first property easily follows from Lemmata 3.6.2 and 3.6.1.

Theorem 3.6.4 (monotonicity of approximate credulous default reasoning) *Let $S \subseteq S' \subseteq L$ and $\langle D, W \rangle$ be a normal default theory. $\langle D, W \rangle_S^3 \vdash \delta$ implies $\langle D, W \rangle_{S'}^3 \vdash \delta$ (hence $\langle D, W \rangle \vdash \delta$). $\langle D, W \rangle_S^{\frac{1}{2}} \not\vdash \delta$ implies $\langle D, W \rangle_{S'}^{\frac{1}{2}} \not\vdash \delta$ (hence $\langle D, W \rangle \not\vdash \delta$).*

The second property follows from the definitions.

Observation 3.6.5 (convergence of approximate credulous default reasoning) *If $\langle D, W \rangle \vdash \delta$ then there exists an $S \subseteq L$ s.t. $\langle D, W \rangle_S^3 \vdash \delta$. Moreover, if $\langle D, W \rangle \not\vdash \delta$ then there exists an $S \subseteq L$ s.t. $\langle D, W \rangle_S^{\frac{1}{2}} \not\vdash \delta$.*

As we already noted for propositional logic and for concept languages, the results presented readily account for a stepwise procedure for approximate propositional credulous default reasoning. Now we have to deal with the computational aspects.

As we have recalled previously in this subsection, there are two sources of complexity in credulous default reasoning, that are nondeterminism in the choice of an appropriate set of generating defaults and the satisfiability checks. These sources show up in the exponential factors in the time complexity of Reiter's algorithm. What we want to show is that in our approximated relations both sources of complexity are bounded by the size of the parameter S. We first show that the number of S-3- and S-1-extensions is bound by $2^{|S|}$.

Lemma 3.6.6 (number of S-extensions) *Any normal default theory $\langle D, W \rangle$ has at most $2^{|S|}$ S-3-extensions. The same bound holds for the number of S-1-extensions.*

We now show that the computational cost of deciding whether a set of formulae is an extension is also bound by the size of the parameter S.

Lemma 3.6.7 (complexity of checking S-extensions) *Let $\langle D, W \rangle$ be a normal default theory and $D' \subseteq D$ a set of defaults. Deciding whether $E = W \cup CONSEQ(D')$ is an S-3 or S-1-extension of $\langle D, W \rangle$ can be done in $O(|D|^3 \cdot |E| \cdot 2^{|S|})$ time.*

Using the two lemmata above, we can give a precise estimate of the computational cost of deciding $\langle D, W \rangle_S^1 \vdash \delta$ and $\langle D, W \rangle_S^3 \vdash \delta$.

Theorem 3.6.8 (uniform complexity of approximate credulous default reasoning) *Let $\langle D, W \rangle$ be a normal default theory and δ a CNF formula (we assume that $|\delta| \leq |\langle D, W \rangle|$.) Both $\langle D, W \rangle_S^3 \vdash \delta$ and $\langle D, W \rangle_S^1 \vdash \delta$ can be decided in $O(|\langle D, W \rangle| \cdot |D|^3 \cdot 2^{|S|} \cdot 2^{|S|})$ time.*

We note that the above complexity result is just the worst-case upper bound of an enumeration algorithm. While we consider the worst-case analysis important, nevertheless we do not claim that the "brute-force" method is the most feasible one. Actually we argue that we can use heuristics and ideas of other algorithms for computing the approximate relations.

As an example, we now show how Reiter's algorithm can be modified in order to decide the relation $\langle D, W \rangle \vdash_S^3 \delta$. Reiter's algorithm is based on the use of a linear resolution theorem prover to choose a set of defaults which, if applicable, would prove the goal. This process is iterated by setting as new goal the preconditions of the defaults used and verifying the global consistency of the defaults applied. Reiter claims that linear resolution is the most suitable form of resolution for achieving this task. If we are to decide $\langle D, W \rangle \vdash_S^3 \delta$ we can use the same algorithm with two changes: The linear resolution theorem prover can only resolve upon letters in S and the global satisfiability check is done by using an algorithm for S-1-satisfiability (see Appendix B.1.)

We have shown how our approximation schema can successfully help keeping under control the computational complexity of default reasoning by replacing two computationally expensive tasks —namely choosing the right set of defaults and checking consistency— with simpler ones. This obviously introduces some incompleteness or unsoundness, but in a controlled manner.

Along the same lines is also the work by Etherington and Crawford [Etherington and Crawford, 1992] where they control the sources of complexity by using fast and sound (though incomplete) consistency tests and a mechanism for restricting the attention to small contexts, without having to deal with large knowledge bases. The main difference between the two approaches is that we aim at precisely characterizing the error introduced by the approximation method, while Etherington and Crawford are more interested in preserving the plausibility of the mechanism as a model of human default reasoning.

We close this section giving a couple of examples, one for $\langle D, W \rangle \vdash_S^3$ and the other for $\langle D, W \rangle \vdash_S^1$, showing how our approximate forms of default reasoning work.

Example 3.6.1 (proving a consequence) We show a default theory $\langle D, W \rangle$ on the alphabet L, a set $S \subset L$ and a formula δ on L such that $\langle D, W \rangle_S^3 \vdash \delta$. By Theorem 3.6.4 this implies $\langle D, W \rangle \vdash \delta$.

$$
\begin{aligned}
L &\doteq \{flies, wings, walks, runs, light, legs\} \\
S &\doteq \{flies, wings, walks, legs\} \\
\delta &\doteq legs \\
W &\doteq (walks \vee flies) \wedge (\neg flies \vee wings) \\
D &\doteq \{(runs \vee walks : legs/legs), (: \neg flies/\neg flies), (flies : light/light)\}
\end{aligned}
$$

We must show that there exists an S-3-extension containing $legs$. To this end we prove that an S-3-extension can be generated by firing both the first and the second default. In particular, we show that the set $E = \{\epsilon | \epsilon$ is a non-tautological clause and $W \cup \{\neg flies, legs\} \models_S^3 \epsilon\} = \{\epsilon | \epsilon$ is a non-tautological clause and $W \cup \{walks, \neg flies, legs\} \models_S^3 \epsilon\}$ satisfies the property $E = \Gamma_S^3(E)$ (cf. Definition 3.6.3.) Note first of all that in each of the clauses of E at least one literal in $\{walks, \neg flies, legs\}$ occurs. Therefore, E is S-1-satisfiable, since the S-1-interpretation mapping $walks$, $\neg flies$, $\neg wings$ and $legs$ into 1 and every other literal into 0 satisfies E. Moreover, the first and second defaults are clearly applicable w.r.t. E according to the point 3 of Definition 3.6.3, while on the other hand the third default is not applicable because $E \cup \{flies\}$ is S-1-unsatisfiable. Since $legs \in E$ it follows that $\langle D, W \rangle_S^3 \vdash \delta$. $\diamond$

Example 3.6.2 (disproving a consequence) We show a default theory $\langle D, W \rangle$ on the alphabet L, a set $S \subset L$ and a formula δ on L such that $\langle D, W \rangle_S^1 \nvdash \delta$. By Theorem 3.6.4 this implies $\langle D, W \rangle \nvdash \delta$.

$$
\begin{aligned}
L &\doteq \{wings, flies, walks, bird, light, plane\} \\
S &\doteq \{wings, flies, walks\} \\
\delta &\doteq light \\
W &\doteq (\neg flies \vee wings) \wedge (flies \vee walks) \wedge (\neg wings \vee bird \vee plane) \wedge \\
  &\qquad \neg wings \\
D &\doteq \{(flies : light/light), (wings : flies/flies), (: \neg flies/\neg flies)\}
\end{aligned}
$$

We must show that it does not exist any S-1-extension E containing *light*. First of all, note that W is S-1-satisfiable since the S-1-interpretation M mapping *walks*, $\neg wings$ and $\neg flies$ into 1 and everything else into 0 satisfies it.

Using Theorem 3.6.3, all the S-1-extensions are also S-1-satisfiable. As a consequence, the second default can never be fired, because its consequence *flies* added to W makes it S-1-unsatisfiable. The first default cannot be fired either, because the *negation* of its prerequisite *flies* is S-1-entailed by W, hence *flies* can be S-1-entailed by a superset of W iff such a superset is S-1-unsatisfiable. But this is not possible, because S-1-extensions are S-1-satisfiable. As a consequence, the only S-1-extension is $E = \{\epsilon | \epsilon$ is a non-tautological clause and $W \cup \{\neg flies\} \models_S^1 \epsilon\}$ where only the third default is fired. Since $light \notin E$ then it follows that $\langle D, W \rangle_S^1 \not\models \delta$. $\diamond$

3.6.2 Approximation of circumscription

In this subsection we define a method for approximating propositional circumscription. Relevant definitions are summarized in the first part, the method itself is presented in the second part.

3.6.2.1 Preliminaries

We are concerned with the approximation of the inference problem under propositional circumscription (we refer to Section 2.2.1 for the definition of circumscription.) More precisely, we will approximate the problem of deciding whether $CIRC(T) \models \neg u$ holds, where $CIRC(T)$ denotes the circumscription of T in which all the letters are minimized, and $\neg u$ is a negative literal. We are taking into account neither inference of more complex formulae, nor the presence of varying and/or fixed letters, because as shown by Theorem 2.6.1 in Section 2.6 any inference problem under propositional circumscription can be reduced in polynomial time to the above problem.

In [Gelfond *et al.*, 1989] it is shown that $CIRC(T) \models \neg u$ holds iff for each positive clause B,

$$(T \not\models B) \implies (T \not\models B \vee u). \tag{3.2}$$

This relation can be used for building a straightforward algorithm for inferring under circumscription. Actually the *MILO-resolution* algorithm defined by Przymusinski in [Przymusinski, 1989] is based exactly on the idea of finding — by resolution— a clause B such that $T \models B \vee u$, and successively proving that $T \not\models B$ (Przymusinski's method is analyzed in Appendix A.1.2.) Such a clause is a "witness" of the fact that $CIRC(T) \not\models \neg u$.

This algorithm has a worst-case time complexity of $O(|T| \cdot |L| \cdot 2^{|L|} \cdot 2^{|L|})$, which is again a function with two exponential terms. The two sources of complexity of circumscriptive reasoning are clear also in this case: non-determinism in the choice of B and cost of the entailment relation occurring in formula (3.2). The problem of deciding if $CIRC(T) \models \neg u$ holds is complete with respect to the class Π_2^p of the polynomial hierarchy (see [Eiter and Gottlob, 1993b]), therefore we don't expect any algorithm to be more efficient than this one in the worst case.

The method for approximate inference under circumscription that we are going to present works indeed on both sources of complexity. In particular both the search space of the relevant clauses B and the cost of the entailment checking are decreased.

3.6.2.2 Approximation method

Our goal is to approximate the decision problem $CIRC(T) \models \neg u$, where T is any propositional formula and $\neg u$ is a negative literal. The considerations we made at the beginning of Subsection 3.6.1.2 on the feasibility of mapping credulous default reasoning into propositional calculus apply to this problem as well, since it is Π_2^p-complete.

   We provide two methods for the approximation of circumscriptive reasoning, one being correct and the other being complete. The sound method is based on the following definition.

Definition 3.6.6 (approximate circumscription $\mathbf{CIRC_S^3(T)}$) *We write* $CIRC_S^3(T) \vdash \neg u$ *iff for each positive clause B (possibly empty), $(T \not\models_S^3 B) \Longrightarrow (T \not\models_S^1 B \vee u)$.*

Comparing Definition 3.6.6 with formula (3.2), we note that the antecedent of the implication is weakened, while the consequent is strengthened. The relation $CIRC_S^3(T) \not\vdash \neg u$ holds whenever a clause B exists such that $T \not\models_S^3 B$ and $T \models_S^1 B \vee u$. Such a clause B *could be* a witness that $CIRC(T) \not\models \neg u$, hence we have just defined a form of circumscription that is intuitively very cautious. Now we define a brave form of circumscription, with the opposite intuition.

Definition 3.6.7 (approximate circumscription $\mathbf{CIRC_S^1(T)}$) *We write* $CIRC_S^1(T) \vdash \neg u$ *iff for each positive clause B (possibly empty), $(T \not\models_S^1 B) \Longrightarrow (T \not\models_S^3 B \vee u)$.*

The following properties formalize the intuition about the new definitions.

Theorem 3.6.9 (monotonicity of approximate circumscription) *For any* S, S' *such that* $S \subseteq S' \subseteq L$, $CIRC_S^3(T) \vdash \neg u$ *implies* $CIRC_{S'}^3(T) \vdash \neg u$ *(hence* $CIRC(T) \models \neg u$*). Moreover* $CIRC_S^1(T) \not\vdash \neg u$ *implies* $CIRC_{S'}^1(T) \not\vdash \neg u$ *(hence* $CIRC(T) \not\models \neg u$*).*

Observation 3.6.10 (convergence of approximate circumscription) *If* $CIRC(T) \models \neg u$, *then there exists an* $S \subseteq L$ *such that* $CIRC_S^3(T) \vdash \neg u$. *Moreover, if* $CIRC(T) \not\models \neg u$, *then there exists an* $S \subseteq L$ *such that* $CIRC_S^1(T) \not\vdash \neg u$.

The above facts account for a stepwise procedure for inferring under propositional circumscription. They are to be compared to Theorems 3.3.1 and 3.3.2 for the propositional case and to Theorems 3.6.4 and 3.6.5 for credulous default reasoning. We now have to understand the computational properties of such a stepwise procedure.

First of all we focus on inference under $CIRC_S^3(T)$ and we propose a simple algorithm based on enumeration that looks for a clause B such that $T \not\models_S^3 B$ and $T \models_S^1 B \vee u$. The following lemma is useful to reduce the search space of the relevant clauses B.

Lemma 3.6.11 $CIRC_S^3(T) \vdash \neg u$ iff for all the positive clauses B whose letters belong to S it holds $(T \not\models_S^3 B) \Longrightarrow (T \not\models_S^1 B \vee u)$.

The above lemma states that for the enumeration algorithm it is sufficient to look through all of the $2^{|S|}$ positive clauses made out of literals from S. Using Theorem 3.3.3 shown in Section 3.3, we can now easily compute the complexity of such an algorithm.

Corollary 3.6.12 (uniform complexity of CIRC$_S^3$(T)) $CIRC_S^3(T) \vdash \neg u$ can be decided in $O(|T| \cdot |S| \cdot 2^{|S|} \cdot 2^{|S|})$ time.

Turning now to inference under $CIRC_S^1(T)$, we now prove a lemma that, similarly to Lemma 3.6.11, is useful for reducing the search space of an enumeration algorithm that looks for a clause B such that $T \not\models_S^1 B$ and $T \models_S^3 B \vee u$.

Lemma 3.6.13 $CIRC_S^1(T) \not\vdash \neg u$ iff there exists a positive clause B whose letters belong to S such that $(T \not\models_S^1 B) \wedge (T \models_S^3 B \vee u \vee \delta)$, where $\delta = \bigvee_{p \in L \setminus S} p$.

The above lemma states that for the enumeration algorithm that decides the validity of $CIRC_S^1(T) \vdash \neg u$ it is sufficient to look through all of the $2^{|S|}$ positive clauses made out of literals from S. The complexity of the algorithm can now be easily computed.

Corollary 3.6.14 (uniform complexity of CIRC$_S^1$(T)) $CIRC_S^1(T) \vdash \neg u$ can be decided in $O(|T| \cdot |S| \cdot 2^{|S|} \cdot 2^{|S|})$ time.

Apart from worst-case analysis, we can show how ideas and heuristics used in sound and complete algorithms for circumscription can be used also for the approximate inference. As an example, in order to prove that $CIRC_S^1(T) \not\vdash \neg u$ holds, i.e., that a clause B exists such that $T \not\models_S^1 B$ and $T \not\models_S^3 B \vee u$, we can easily modify Przymusinski's algorithm, that we briefly recalled above and that will be further analyzed in Appendix A.1.2. First of all we use resolution only on the literals of S for computing all the minimal clauses B such that $T \models_S^3 B \vee u$;

then we try to prove that $T \models_S^1 B$ for at least one of those B's. Similarly to Przymusinski's algorithm, only a subset of the possible clauses (the minimal ones) is generated in this way.

We close the section giving a couple of examples, one for $CIRC_S^3(T)$ and one for $CIRC_S^1(T)$, showing how our approximate circumscriptive relations work.

Example 3.6.3 (proving a consequence) We show a formula T on the alphabet L, a set $S \subset L$ and a letter $whale \in L$ such that $CIRC_S^3(T) \vdash \neg whale$. By Theorem 3.6.9 this implies $CIRC(T) \models \neg whale$.

$$
\begin{aligned}
L \;\; &= \;\; \{big, animal, whale, elephant, sequoia\} \\
S \;\; &= \;\; \{big, animal, whale\} \\
T \;\; &= \;\; animal \;\wedge \\
&\quad\;\; (\neg elephant \vee \neg whale) \;\wedge \\
&\quad\;\; (\neg big \vee sequoia \vee elephant \vee whale) \;\wedge \\
&\quad\;\; (\neg big \vee \neg animal \vee elephant \vee whale)
\end{aligned}
$$

By Lemma 3.6.11 we must prove that for each positive clause B whose letters belong to S it holds $(T \not\models_S^3 B) \Longrightarrow (T \not\models_S^1 B \vee whale)$.

   Since $T \models_S^3 animal$, we have to consider only the three clauses $whale$, big, $(whale \vee big)$. Since there is an S-1-interpretation of T satisfying it that maps $animal$ into 1 and both $whale$ and big into 0, it holds that $(T \not\models_S^1 big \vee whale)$ and $(T \not\models_S^1 whale)$. This proves that $CIRC_S^3(T) \vdash \neg whale$. ◇

Example 3.6.4 (disproving a consequence) We show a formula T on the alphabet L, a set $S \subset L$ and a letter $indian \in L$ such that $CIRC_S^1(T) \not\vdash \neg indian$. By Theorem 3.6.9 this implies $CIRC(T) \not\models \neg indian$.

$$
\begin{aligned}
L \;\; &= \;\; \{big, sequoia, elephant, african, indian\} \\
S \;\; &= \;\; \{big, elephant, indian\} \\
T \;\; &\doteq \;\; big \;\wedge \\
&\quad\;\; (\neg big \vee sequoia \vee elephant) \;\wedge \\
&\quad\;\; (\neg elephant \vee african \vee indian)
\end{aligned}
$$

By Lemma 3.6.13 we must show a positive clause B whose letters belong to S such that $(T \not\models_S^1 B) \wedge (T \models_S^3 B \vee indian \vee \delta)$, where $\delta = sequoia \vee african$.

   It is easy to prove that the empty clause $\square$ satisfies all these conditions: by performing two *modus ponens* steps on big and $elephant$ (both letters belong to S) we prove that $(T \models_S^3 sequoia \vee indian \vee african)$. Moreover the S-1-interpretation that maps big, $elephant$ and $indian$ into 1 satisfies T and does not satisfy the empty clause, hence $T \not\models^1_S \square$ holds. This proves that $CIRC^1_S(T) \not\vdash \neg indian$. $\diamond$

All the results presented in this section will be proved in Appendix B.4.

The results of this section have been published in [Cadoli and Schaerf, 1992a].

3.7 Approximation of propositional modal logics

In this section we show the last application of our approximation method, which is in the fields of modal logics. In particular we show how it is possible to approximate satisfiability in the most widely used modal logics for knowledge and belief, namely $\mathcal{S}5$, $\mathcal{K}$, $\mathcal{T}$ and $\mathcal{S}4$. In Section 3.4 we already stressed the importance of modal languages for the purpose of Knowledge Representation.

A detailed analysis of the computational complexity of satisfiability problems in several propositional modal systems has been done by Ladner [Ladner, 1977]. He showed that the problem of checking satisfiability of a formula in the systems $\mathcal{K}$, $\mathcal{T}$ and $\mathcal{S}4$ is PSPACE-complete, while the same problem is NP-complete in the system $\mathcal{S}5$. Therefore most of the modal logics frequently used for modeling knowledge and belief (see [Hintikka, 1962]) lead to computationally intractable reasoning problems.

In this section we focus on the problem of applying approximation techniques to such propositional modal systems. The main idea is to extend the method defined for propositional logic by defining two classes of interpretations which are approximations of the standard Kripke semantics.

In the first subsection we introduce semantics of approximation. In the second one we show several computational properties.

3.7.1 Semantics

In the following we refer to modal formulae which are built on a set L^* of literals by means of the usual connectives $\vee$ and $\wedge$, the modal operator $\mathbf{K}$, the negation $\neg\mathbf{K}$ of the modal operator, plus parentheses. Using the terminology introduced in Section 3.4, we call formulae of this kind modal negation normal form (MNNF) formulae. Formulae not containing the modal operator are called simply propositional.

We remind the definition of a Kripke model.

Definition 3.7.1 (Kripke [Kripke, 1963]) *A Kripke model is a triple $\mathcal{M} = \langle W, R, V \rangle$ where W is a set of worlds, R an accessibility relation among worlds and V a mapping $W \to \tau$, where τ is the set of all the truth assignments of L^*.*

In a standard Kripke model $V(w)$ is a 2-interpretation for every world $w \in W$. We refer to standard Kripke models as 2-*Kripke interpretations*. In this section we want to consider also other forms of interpretations, defined as follows.

Definition 3.7.2 (S-1-Kripke interpretation) *An S-1-Kripke interpretation is a Kripke model such that $V(w)$ is an S-1-interpretation for every world $w \in W$ (cf. Definition 3.3.2 in Section 3.3.)*

Definition 3.7.3 (S-3-Kripke interpretation) *An S-3-Kripke interpretation is a Kripke model such that $V(w)$ is an S-3-interpretation for every world $w \in W$ (cf. Definition 3.3.1 in Section 3.3.)*

The evaluation of a propositional formula γ in any world $w \in W$ of an S-1-Kripke interpretation $\mathcal{M} = \langle W, R, V \rangle$ is defined as in Section 3.4. In particular we write $\mathcal{M}, w \models_S^1 \gamma$ iff $V(w)(\gamma) = 1$, that is $V(w)$ maps γ into 1. The value assigned by $\mathcal{M}$ to a MNNF formula α in a world $w \in W$ is defined by using the rule for propositional formulae and recursively the following rules:

- $\mathcal{M}, w \models_S^1 \mathbf{K}\beta$ iff $\forall t \in W \ wRt$ implies $\mathcal{M}, t \models_S^1 \beta$;

- $\mathcal{M}, w \models_S^1 \neg\mathbf{K}\beta$ iff $\exists t \in W \ wRt$ and $\mathcal{M}, t \models_S^1 \neg\beta$.

Note that β may not be in MNNF, in this case we need to transform it into its MNNF equivalent. A modal formula α is S-1-*Kripke satisfiable* iff there exists an S-1-Kripke interpretation $\mathcal{M} = \langle W, R, V \rangle$ and a $w \in W$ s.t. $\mathcal{M}, w \models_S^1 \alpha$.

The corresponding definition for S-3-Kripke interpretations are straightforward. We refer to standard satisfiability of a modal formula as 2-*Kripke satisfiability*.

Some remarks are in order here to make clear the differences and the analogies with the modal system introduced in Section 3.4. Note, first of all, that the language introduced in Section 3.4 is an extension of the classical modal language with one modal operator, in fact we have two collections of modal operators, i.e., $\Box_S^3$ and $\Box_S^1$, which are used as meta-descriptors of the entailment relations $\models_S^3$ and $\models_S^1$. Here, on the other hand, we are dealing with a simple modal language. Furthermore, here our main concern is the computational behavior of the problems of satisfiability testing, while in Section 3.4 we were mainly interested in the expressiveness of the language as a representational tool for approximate inference.

This difference in the emphasis leads to two different semantic definitions for negation in front of modal operators. To be more concrete, let α be a propositional formula, it is always the case that $\Box_S^3 \alpha \wedge \neg\Box_S^3 \alpha$ is unsatisfiable while $\mathbf{K}\alpha \wedge \neg\mathbf{K}\alpha$ is S-3-Kripke satisfiable whenever $\alpha \wedge \neg\alpha$ is S-3-satisfiable. This is an immediate consequence of the two different definitions for negation. In fact here $\mathcal{M}, w \models_S^3 \neg\mathbf{K}\beta$ holds iff we can find a world connected to w which makes

β false, while $\mathcal{M}, w \models \neg\Box_S^3\alpha$ holds iff we can find an S-3-situation connected to w which does not make α true, i.e., $\mathcal{M}, w \not\models \Box_S^3\alpha$.

We want to point out that, if we were to choose the second definition for S-3-Kripke satisfiability then the results proven in the sequel on uniform complexity would no longer hold. On the other side, if we were to define satisfiability of negated modal formulae in Section 3.4 referring to the rule used here, the resulting language would not be expressive enough to be able to represent the approximate entailment relations.

We now demonstrate our definitions by means of two examples.

Example 3.7.1 (proving S-3-Kripke unsatisfiability) We show a set of letters L, a modal formula σ on L and a subset S of L such that σ is S-3-Kripke unsatisfiable.

Let L be $\{a, b, c\}$, S be $\{a, b\}$ and σ be $(\mathbf{K}a \wedge \mathbf{K}(\neg a \vee b) \wedge \mathbf{K}\neg b \wedge \neg \mathbf{K}c)$. Let us assume that σ is S-3-Kripke satisfiable. By the above definition this implies that there exists an S-3-Kripke-interpretation $\mathcal{M} = \langle W, R, V \rangle$ and a $w \in W$ such that all the following conditions hold:

- $\mathcal{M}, w \models_S^3 \mathbf{K}a$;
- $\mathcal{M}, w \models_S^3 \mathbf{K}(\neg a \vee b)$;
- $\mathcal{M}, w \models_S^3 \mathbf{K}\neg b$;
- $\mathcal{M}, w \models_S^3 \neg\mathbf{K}c$.

The above conditions are equivalent to the following ones:

- $\forall t \in W\ wRt$ implies $\mathcal{M}, t \models_S^3 a$;
- $\forall t \in W\ wRt$ implies $\mathcal{M}, t \models_S^3 (\neg a \vee b)$;
- $\forall t \in W\ wRt$ implies $\mathcal{M}, t \models_S^3 \neg b$;
- $\exists t \in W\ wRt$ and $\mathcal{M}, t \models_S^3 \neg c$.

Let t_0 be the world whose existence is implied by the last condition, that is let $t_0 \in W$, wRt_0 and $V(t_0)(\neg c) = 1$. According to the other conditions, the truth assignment $V(t_0)$ must satisfy the propositional formula $(a \wedge (\neg a \vee b) \wedge \neg b)$. Taking into account that $V(t_0)$ is an S-3-interpretation of L^* and that $S = \{a, b\}$, $V(t_0)$ satisfies $(a \wedge \neg b)$ if and only if it maps a into 1, $\neg a$ into 0, b into 0 and $\neg b$ into 1. Therefore $V(t_0)$ maps $(\neg a \vee b)$ into 0, hence it does not satisfy $(a \wedge (\neg a \vee b) \wedge \neg b)$. This contradiction proves that σ is S-3-Kripke unsatisfiable.

Note that σ is S'-3-Kripke satisfiable, where $S' = \{a\}$. $\diamond$

Example 3.7.2 (proving S-1-Kripke satisfiability) We show an alphabet L, a modal formula τ on L and a subset S of L such that τ is S-1-Kripke satisfiable.

Let L be $\{a, b\}$, S be $\{b\}$ and τ be $(\neg b \wedge \mathbf{K}a \wedge \mathbf{K}(\neg a \vee b))$. By the above definition, τ is S-1-Kripke satisfiable if and only if there exists an S-1-Kripke-interpretation $\mathcal{M} = \langle W, R, V \rangle$ and a $w \in W$ such that all the following conditions hold:

- $\mathcal{M}, w \models_S^1 \neg b$;

- $\forall t \in W$ wRt implies $\mathcal{M}, t \models_S^1 a$;

- $\forall t \in W$ wRt implies $\mathcal{M}, t \models_S^1 (\neg a \vee b)$.

Let W be the singleton $\{w\}$, R be the empty set and the S-1-interpretation $V(w)$ of L^* be such that $V(w)(a) = V(w)(\neg a) = V(w)(b) = 0$ and $V(w)(\neg b) = 1$. It is easy to see that $\mathcal{M}, w \models_S^1 \tau$ holds, where $\mathcal{M} = \langle W, R, V \rangle$. Therefore τ is S-1-Kripke satisfiable. $\Diamond$

3.7.2 Properties

We start showing two straightforward consequences of the definitions of S-1 and S-3-Kripke satisfiability (α is a MNNF formula.)

Theorem 3.7.1 (monotonicity of S-Kripke satisfiability) *For any S, S' such that $S \subseteq S' \subseteq L$, if α is S-1-Kripke satisfiable, then α is S'-1-Kripke satisfiable (hence 2-Kripke satisfiable.) Moreover if α is S-3-Kripke unsatisfiable, then α is S'-3-Kripke unsatisfiable (hence 2-Kripke unsatisfiable.)*

Observation 3.7.2 (convergence of S-Kripke satisfiability) *If α is 2-Kripke satisfiable, then there exists an $S \subseteq L$ such that α is S-1-Kripke satisfiable. If α is 2-Kripke unsatisfiable, then there exists an $S \subseteq L$ such that α is S-3-Kripke unsatisfiable.*

The above properties account for a stepwise procedure for deciding 2-Kripke satisfiability of a modal formula, which is analogous to those defined in the previous sections for propositional logic, concept languages and non-monotonic logics. As a consequence of Theorem 3.7.1 we have that the formula σ of Example 3.7.1 is 2-Kripke-unsatisfiable and the formula τ of Example 3.7.2 is 2-Kripke-satisfiable. The following theorem shows that there exist modal systems, e.g. $S5$, in which such a stepwise procedure is interesting from a computational point of view.

Theorem 3.7.3 (uniform complexity for $S5$) *If we restrict our attention to accessibility relations which are reflexive, transitive and euclidean, then there exists one algorithm to decide if α is S-1-Kripke satisfiable and one to decide if α is S-3-Kripke satisfiable both running in $O(m \cdot |\alpha| \cdot 2^{|S|})$ time, where m is the number of occurrences of the modal operator in α.*

The above theorem shows that all the observations we made in Section 3.3 on the approximation of the 2-satisfiability of a propositional formula also hold for the approximation of the 2-Kripke-satisfiability of any formula of the modal system $S5$ (cf. Theorem 3.3.3.)

The same idea can be applied, with only minor variations, to other systems whose satisfiability test is known to be an NP-complete problem, such as $K45$ and $KD45$. The reason why this holds is that in these systems any satisfiable formula is satisfied by a 2-Kripke interpretation whose set of worlds W has size bounded by a polynomial function of the size of the formula itself.

On the other hand, as proved by the following result, there exist interesting modal systems, such as K, in which the stepwise procedure suggested by Theorems 3.7.1, 3.7.2 is not useful from a computational point of view.

Theorem 3.7.4 (non-uniform complexity for K) *If the accessibility relation is unrestricted, then deciding if α is S-1-Kripke satisfiable and deciding if α is S-3-Kripke satisfiable are PSPACE-complete problems even if the cardinality $|S|$ of S equals 1.*

This result prevents us from the development of a result analogous to Theorem 3.7.3 for unrestricted accessibility relation (unless P=PSPACE.) This is not surprising, since Ladner has shown [Ladner, 1977] that there exist formulae in the systems K, T and $S4$, which are satisfied only by 2-Kripke interpretations having a set of worlds whose size is exponential in the nesting of the modal operators.

A possible way to overcome this problem is to focus only on limited parts of the interpretations. We now present a semantics for approximation which further extends the possible-worlds semantics. The idea is that a Kripke interpretation M should satisfy a formula α in a world w iff α is satisfied in the subset $W' \subseteq W$ of the possible worlds containing only those worlds whose *distance* from w is less than or equal to i, where i is a particular integer. In this way we can limit our attention to Kripke interpretations having $O(2^i)$ worlds. The worlds which are outside the "range" i are treated differently in the S-1- and in the S-3- case. In particular S-1-Kripke interpretations are "pessimistic", since they do not validate anything in those worlds, while S-3-Kripke interpretations are "optimistic", since they validate everything.

This idea is captured by the following definition.

Definition 3.7.4 (interpretation of formulae within a range) *Let α be a formula in which each occurrence of a modal operator lies in the scope of at most n modal operators, S a subset of L, $i \leq n+1$, and $M = \langle W, R, V \rangle$ an S-3-Kripke interpretation. We define a new relation $\models^3_{S,i}$ as follows (γ is a propositional formula):*

- *$M, w \models^3_{S,i} \gamma$ if and only if $(V(w)(\gamma) = 1$ or $i < 0)$;*

- *$M, w \models^3_{S,i} \alpha \wedge \beta$ if and only if $M, w \models^3_{S,i} \alpha$ and $M, w \models^3_{S,i} \beta$;*

- $\mathcal{M}, w \models^3_{S,i} \alpha \vee \beta$ if and only if $\mathcal{M}, w \models^3_{S,i} \alpha$ or $\mathcal{M}, w \models^3_{S,i} \beta$;

- $\mathcal{M}, w \models^3_{S,i} \mathbf{K}\alpha$ if and only if $\forall t \in W \ wRt$ implies $\mathcal{M}, t \models^3_{S,i-1} \alpha$;

- $\mathcal{M}, w \models^3_{S,i} \neg\mathbf{K}\alpha$ if and only if $\exists t \in W \ wRt$ and $\mathcal{M}, t \models^3_{S,i-1} \neg\alpha$.

Note that according to the above definition, if $i < 0$ then any formula is true in any world. A modal formula α is $\langle S, i \rangle$-3-Kripke satisfiable iff there exists an S-3-interpretation $\mathcal{M} = \langle W, R, V \rangle$ and a $w \in W$ s.t. $\mathcal{M}, w \models^3_{S,i} \alpha$.

A similar definition can be given for the relation $\models^1_{S,i}$. The only difference is that now $\mathcal{M}$ is an S-1-Kripke interpretation and the definition of the base case is:

- $\mathcal{M}, w \models^1_{S,i} \gamma$ if and only if $(V(w)(\gamma) = 1$ and $i \geq 0)$.

Note that if $i < 0$ then a formula cannot be true in a world.

It is easy to show that the analogous of Theorem 3.7.1 holds for the new definitions, when we compare pairs $\langle S, i \rangle$ and $\langle S', j \rangle$ such that $S \subseteq S' \subseteq L$ and $i \leq j \leq n+1$. In other words if a modal formula α is $\langle S, i \rangle$-3-Kripke unsatisfiable, then it is $\langle S', j \rangle$-3-Kripke unsatisfiable, and if it is $\langle S, i \rangle$-1-Kripke satisfiable, then it is $\langle S', j \rangle$-1-Kripke satisfiable. Moreover, there exists a subset S of L and an integer $i \leq n + 1$ such that α is either $\langle S, i \rangle$-1-satisfiable or $\langle S, i \rangle$-3-unsatisfiable (cf. Observation 3.7.2).

We can also prove that there exists an algorithm for deciding if a modal formula α is $\langle S, i \rangle$-3-Kripke satisfiable which runs in $O(|\alpha| \cdot 2^{|S| \cdot i})$ time, provided that the constraints of either $\mathcal{K}$ or $\mathcal{T}$ or $\mathcal{S}4$ hold on the accessibility relation. The algorithm for determining $\langle S, i \rangle$-3-Kripke satisfiability of a modal formula α is based on a mapping of α into another modal formula $\psi^3_{S,i}(\alpha)$, in which the nesting of the modal operators is limited and any occurrence of a letter not in S is substituted by the literal t. More precisely, the rewriting is given by the following definition.

Definition 3.7.5 (syntactic approximation $\psi^3_{S,i}$) If $i < 0$ then $\psi^3_{S,i}(\alpha)$ is t, otherwise $\psi^3_{S,i}(\alpha)$ is obtained by:

1. substituting each occurrence of a letter in $L \setminus S$ with the literal t, thus obtaining the formula α';

2. substituting every sub-formula $\neg\mathbf{K}\beta$ of α' which is in the scope of at least i modal operators $\mathbf{K}$ with the literal t.

The relation between α and $\psi^3_{S,i}(\alpha)$ is the following.

Theorem 3.7.5 (semantics of $\psi^3_{S,i}$ approximation) *Let α be a modal formula and X be a modal system admitting the K schema and the rule of necessitation. The formula α is $\langle S,i \rangle$-3-Kripke satisfiable in the system X iff $\psi^3_{S,i}(\alpha)$ is 2-Kripke satisfiable in the system X.*

Since the 2-Kripke satisfiability of $\psi^3_{S,i}(\alpha)$ can be determined with standard algorithms, we have an effective procedure to decide $\langle S,i \rangle$-3-Kripke satisfiability. The algorithm for checking $\langle S,i \rangle$-1-Kripke satisfiability is based on a similar mapping $\psi^1_{S,i}$ in which the literal f is used instead of using t.

   Theorem 3.7.5 allows us to extend all the considerations on the approximation of the 2-satisfiability of a propositional formula to the approximation of the 2-Kripke-satisfiability of any formula of the modal systems $\mathcal{K}$, $\mathcal{T}$ and $\mathcal{S}4$.

All the results presented in this section will be proved in Appendix B.5.

The results of this section have been published in a preliminary form in [Cadoli and Schaerf, 1992b].

Chapter 4

Using complexity results for evaluating approximation techniques

In Chapters 2 and 3 we described two strategies for achieving tractable reasoning, namely language restriction and theory approximation. In this chapter we present a first attempt at linking the two techniques. Our goal is to show that the analyses of the tractability threshold for minimal reasoning and approximation techniques —that seem to be far apart— are actually related.

In particular we address Kautz and Selman's knowledge compilation method, that we already described in Section 3.1.2. We show that the Horn compilations defined by the authors are semantically close to minimal models. As a consequence, we can take advantage of the complexity analysis performed in Chapter 2 and obtain interesting computational results.

Structure of the chapter

After an introductory section in which we state precisely the goals of this chapter (Section 4.1), we study Horn GLBs and LUBs in Sections 4.2 and 4.3, respectively. We discuss our results in Section 4.4.

The results presented in this chapter have been published in [Cadoli, 1993].

4.1 Horn compilation: semantical and computational aspects

As we saw in Section 3.1.2, Selman and Kautz's method relies on the approximation of a propositional knowledge base by means of two Horn formulae, namely a Horn GLB and a Horn LUB. In this chapter we address two important questions that have not been addressed so far in the papers appeared on the subject of Horn compilation ([Selman and Kautz, 1991, Kautz and Selman, 1991a, Kautz and Selman, 1992, Greiner and Schuurmans, 1992]):

1. is it possible to describe Horn approximations with a **semantics** that does not rely on the syntactic notion of Horn clause?

2. what is the **exact complexity** of finding Horn approximations?

An answer to the first question provides a method for determining the exact meaning of the approximate answers. An answer to the second question tells in which cases it is reasonable —from the computational point of view— to use Horn approximations.

We obtain two different kinds of results, that we briefly summarize here:

semantical

- Horn GLBs of a propositional formula Σ are closely related to minimal models of Σ, i.e., to models of the circumscription of Σ;

- reasoning w.r.t. Horn GLBs is the same as reasoning by counterexamples using only minimal models;

- while *skeptical* reasoning w.r.t. the Horn GLBs of a formula Σ is the same as ordinary reasoning w.r.t. Σ, *brave* reasoning w.r.t. the Horn GLBs of Σ is the same as reasoning w.r.t. $CIRC(\Sigma)$;

- compiling more knowledge does not always give better Horn GLBs;

- reasoning w.r.t. the Horn LUB can be mapped into classical propositional reasoning;

- the Horn LUB of a formula Σ is related to the closed world assumption $CWA(\Sigma)$ of Σ.

computational

- finding a Horn GLB is "mildly" harder than inference in propositional logic, i.e., the original inference problem that one wants to approximate;

- reasoning w.r.t. the Horn LUB is exactly as hard as inference in propositional logic;

- finding the single components of a Horn UB is a search problem that cannot be done in parallel.

We believe that our results provide useful criteria that may help finding a knowledge compilation policy. In particular, we show that an interesting tradeoff seems to emerge between the computation done during the compilation time (off-line) and the computation done during the query answering time (on-line.)

4.2 Horn GLBs

In this section Σ denotes a propositional formula and Σ_{glb} denotes one of its Horn GLBs. We refer to Section 3.1.2 for the definition and examples of Horn GLB. We assume that both Σ and Σ_{glb} are in CNF.

In the following two subsections we prove that Horn GLBs of a formula Σ are closely related to the *minimal* models of Σ. In the third subsection we address some of the semantical consequences of the relations found. We refer to Section 2.2.1 for the definition of minimal models. We recall that Horn formulae have a unique minimal model (the *minimum* model), that can be found in polynomial time using the well-known algorithm by Dowling and Gallier [Dowling and Gallier, 1984].

4.2.1 From GLBs to minimal models

We prove that the minimum model M of Σ_{glb} is minimal for Σ, thus proving that if a Horn GLB of Σ is known, then it is possible to obtain a minimal model of Σ in polynomial time.

Theorem 4.2.1 (from GLBs to minimal models) *Let Σ be a propositional formula and Σ_{glb} a Horn GLB of Σ. The minimum model of Σ_{glb} is minimal for Σ.*

The above theorem shows a polynomial reduction from the search problem of finding a minimal model of Σ to the search problem of finding a Horn GLB of Σ. The computational complexity of the search problem of finding a minimal model of a propositional formula has been analyzed in Section 2.5. One of the results we have shown in that section is that finding a minimal model of a formula Σ is hard (using many-one reductions) with respect to the class $FP^{NP[O(\log n)]}$. This implies that a polynomial-time deterministic Turing machine which can use an oracle (or subroutine) that answers NP-complete queries needs at least a logarithmic number of calls to such an oracle in order to find a Horn GLB. It is interesting to remark that the original inference problem of deciding whether $\Sigma \models \alpha$ holds is co-NP-complete, i.e., it can be solved by the same machine with *a single* call to the oracle.

As shown in Theorem A.3.1, announced in Section 2.5 and proven in Appendix A.3, the task of finding a minimal model of Σ is $FP^{NP[O(\log n)]}$-hard even if a model of Σ is known. This fact can be compared with an observation by Selman and Kautz: in [Selman and Kautz, 1991, Theorem 1] they prove that Σ_{glb} is satisfiable iff Σ is satisfiable, hence finding a Horn GLB is NP-hard. We can now say that even if we know that Σ is satisfiable and have one of its models in hand, finding a Horn GLB is still $FP^{NP[O(\log n)]}$-hard. We recall that finding a model (not necessarily minimal) of a propositional formula is *per se* an NP-hard task.

We note that the result just shown gives us only a lower bound. It is reasonable to ask *how easy* is to find a Horn GLB, i.e., to give an upper bound to the problem. In [Selman and Kautz, 1991] Selman and Kautz show an algorithm for computing a Horn GLB of a formula Σ. The algorithm performs an exponential number of polynomial steps. In fact we can show that a Horn GLB can be found in polynomial time by a deterministic Turing machine with access to an NP oracle, i.e., that the problem is in the class FP^{NP} of the polynomial hierarchy.

These computational results are summarized by the following theorem.

Theorem 4.2.2 (complexity of finding a GLB) *Finding a Horn GLB of a propositional formula Σ is hard w.r.t. the class $FP^{NP[O(\log n)]}$. This holds even if a model of Σ is already known.*

Finding a Horn GLB of a propositional formula Σ is in FP^{NP}.

In other words finding a Horn GLB is "mildly" harder than inference in propositional logic, i.e., the original inference problem that one wants to approximate by means of the Horn GLB. We only need a polynomial number of queries to the GLB in order to "pay off" the overhead of the knowledge compilation.

4.2.2   From minimal models to GLBs

We now show that if we have a minimal model M of a formula Σ, then we can easily build a very good approximation of a Horn GLB of Σ. In particular we show that we can build in linear time a Horn LB of Σ whose minimum model is M. This result allows us to perform, in the following subsection, some interesting observations on the semantics of Horn GLBs.

Theorem 4.2.3 (from minimal models to GLBs) *Let M be a minimal model of Σ. We can find in linear time a Horn LB of Σ whose minimum model is M. Moreover there is a Horn GLB of Σ whose minimum model is M.*

In Section 2.5 we have shown cases in which a minimal model of a formula can be found in polynomial time. The above theorem implies that in such cases we can obtain a good approximation of a Horn GLB in polynomial time.

4.2.3   Semantical consequences

Theorems 4.2.1 and 4.2.3 implies the following result.

Corollary 4.2.4 (Horn GLBs and circumscription) *The set of minimal models of a formula Σ and the set of minimum models of the Horn GLBs of Σ are the same.*

We now address some interesting semantical consequences of the above results.

As noted in [Selman and Kautz, 1991] a traditional AI approach is *reasoning by counterexamples*, which consists in refuting a possible consequence of a theory by means of a suitable model that contradicts it (an example of this technique is in the early work by Gelernter [Gelernter, 1959].) This approach is based on the well-known property $M \not\models \alpha \implies \Sigma \not\models \alpha$, that holds for any pair of formulae α, Σ and any model M of Σ. Selman and Kautz indicate that reasoning under a specific Horn GLB is an improved version of such a reasoning schema, since a single Horn GLB captures a *set* of models of the original theory. Using Corollary 4.2.4 and the well-known fact that the minimum model of a Horn formula completely characterizes the set of its positive consequences, we can say that, as far as positive theorems are concerned, reasoning under Horn GLBs is the same as reasoning by counterexamples using only minimal models. This does not hold for negative theorems.

Selman and Kautz address briefly the issue of how reasoning with respect to a set of Horn GLBs looks like, proving [Selman and Kautz, 1991, Theorem 3] that a formula is always equivalent to the disjunction of all its Horn GLBs. The notions of *skeptical* and *brave* (also known as credulous) reasoning are frequently used in the literature (see also Section 3.6.1.) We say that a formula α skeptically follows from the Horn GLBs of a formula Σ (written $skep{-}glb(\Sigma) \vdash \alpha$) if for each of its Horn GLBs Σ_{glb} it holds $\Sigma_{glb} \models \alpha$. We also say that α bravely follows (written $brave{-}glb(\Sigma) \vdash \alpha$) if there exists a Horn GLB Σ_{glb} such that $\Sigma_{glb} \models \alpha$.

The result by Selman and Kautz can be rephrased in the following way: $skep{-}glb(\Sigma) \vdash \alpha$ holds iff $\Sigma \models \alpha$. Using Theorems 4.2.1 and 4.2.3 we can say that —as far as positive theorems are concerned— brave reasoning w.r.t. Horn GLBs is the same as brave reasoning w.r.t. minimal models. More precisely let α be a positive clause, $brave{-}glb(\Sigma) \vdash \alpha$ holds iff there exists a minimal model M of Σ s. t. $M \models \alpha$, i.e., iff $CIRC(\Sigma) \not\models \neg\alpha$, where $CIRC(\Sigma)$ denotes the circumscription of Σ in which all the letters of Σ are minimized (see [Lifschitz, 1985b] and Section 2.2.1.) Using a result shown by Eiter and Gottlob in in [Eiter and Gottlob, 1993b] (see also Appendix A.1) we can say that brave reasoning w.r.t. Horn GLBs is a decision problem which is hard w.r.t. the class Σ_2^p of the polynomial hierarchy.

Let us see how the relation with non-monotonicity just shown affects approximate inference under Horn GLBs. We consider two knowledge bases Σ, Σ^+ such that $\mathcal{M}(\Sigma^+) \subset \mathcal{M}(\Sigma)$, i.e., $\Sigma^+ \models \Sigma$ and $\Sigma \not\models \Sigma^+$. It is well known that for a generic formula α, $CIRC(\Sigma) \models \neg\alpha$ does not imply $CIRC(\Sigma^+) \models \neg\alpha$, even if $\Sigma^+ \not\models \alpha$ holds. Using the relation $(CIRC(\Sigma) \models \neg\alpha)$ iff $(brave{-}glb(\Sigma) \not\vdash \alpha)$ we prove the following result.

Proposition 4.2.5 (compiling more knowledge) *Let Σ, Σ^+ be two formulae such that $\Sigma^+ \models \Sigma$ and $\Sigma \not\models \Sigma^+$; let α be a positive clause. If $\Sigma^+ \not\models \alpha$ and $brave{-}glb(\Sigma) \not\vdash \alpha$ then it might be the case that $brave{-}glb(\Sigma^+) \vdash \alpha$.*

Let us see an example clarifying the above proposition. Let $\Sigma = \neg a \vee \neg b$ and $\Sigma^+ = \Sigma \wedge (a \vee b)$. Σ has a unique GLB, which is Σ itself. Therefore $brave{-}glb(\Sigma) \not\vdash a$. Moreover $\Sigma^+ \not\models a$. It is easy to see that $brave{-}glb(\Sigma^+) \vdash a$, as Σ^+ has two different Horn GLBs: $(a \wedge \neg b)$ and $(\neg a \wedge b)$.

We recall that reasoning using a generic Horn GLB is complete and unsound w.r.t. reasoning using the original formula. In other words if $brave-glb(\Sigma) \not\vdash \alpha$ then we know that $\Sigma \not\models \alpha$, i.e., α is disproved. Proposition 4.2.5 says that if we are able to disprove a formula α using a generic complete compilation of a "small" formula Σ, then we are not guaranteed that we are able to disprove α using a generic complete compilation of a "bigger" formula Σ^+, even if $\Sigma^+ \not\models \alpha$. In other words it is not true that compiling more knowledge we always have better complete approximations.

For the sake of completeness, we note that $brave-glb(\Sigma) \vdash \alpha$ does not imply $brave-glb(\Sigma^+) \vdash \alpha$. This is shown by the following example: $\Sigma = a \vee b$, $\Sigma^+ = \Sigma \wedge b$ and $\alpha = a$.

All the results presented in this section will be proved in Appendix C.1.

4.3   Horn LUB

In this section Σ denotes a propositional formula and Σ_{lub} denotes its unique Horn LUB. We refer to Section 3.1.2 for the definition and examples of Horn LUB.

As shown in [Kautz and Selman, 1992] in general it is not possible to store efficiently the Horn LUB of Σ. In particular the size of Σ_{lub} can be exponential in the size of Σ, and this seems to be independent on the representation used for Σ_{lub} (see [Kautz and Selman, 1992] for further details.) As a consequence any method for efficiently representing the Horn LUB is incomplete. Selman and Kautz propose in [Selman and Kautz, 1991, page 908] to *approximate* the Horn LUB with Horn upper bounds of limited length. This idea is used by Greiner and Schuurmans in [Greiner and Schuurmans, 1992], where Horn UBs with a limited number of Horn clauses are studied.

In Subsection 4.3.1 we investigate about this idea and analyze its computational properties. Other computational properties of Horn LUBs are addressed in Subsection 4.3.2. Computational results are discussed in Subsection 4.3.3. In Subsection 4.3.4 we make a brief semantical remark.

4.3.1   Horn UBs with a limited number of clauses

We remind that a prime implicate of Σ is a clause γ such that $\Sigma \models \gamma$ and for no sub-clause γ' of γ it holds that $\Sigma \models \gamma'$. Σ_{lub} is logically equivalent to the conjunction of all the Horn prime implicates of Σ (cf. [Selman and Kautz, 1991, Theorem 4].) Σ_{lub} therefore guarantees sound and complete reasoning w.r.t. Σ as far as inference of Horn formulae is concerned: for all Horn formulae α, $(\Sigma_{lub} \models \alpha)$ iff $(\Sigma \models \alpha)$. One natural choice is to approximate Σ_{lub} with a formula that guarantees sound and complete reasoning w.r.t. Σ as far as inference of *short* Horn formulae is concerned. As an example of this kind of approximation, we define the formula Σ_{ub}^1 to be the conjunction of the formulae in the set

$$\{x \mid x \text{ is a positive literal and } \Sigma \models x\}.$$

Note that Σ_{ub}^1 is a Horn UB of Σ. This formula is a reasonable approximation of Σ, since 1) at least all the positive atomic queries are answered correctly and 2) it has a nice short representation.

The goal of this subsection is to investigate about computational properties of approximations of Σ_{lub}. In particular we deal with Σ_{ub}^1, but the results we obtain can be generalized to other approximations.

An interesting question is the following: how difficult is to obtain Σ_{ub}^1? We note that finding Σ_{ub}^1 is the search problem that amounts to decide for each propositional variable x occurring in Σ whether $\Sigma \models x$ holds or not. It is well known that just deciding $\Sigma \models x$ for a single propositional variable is co-NP-complete, but it is important to understand if the task of deciding $\Sigma \models x$ for *many* propositional variables can be done in parallel (on a single processor.) In other words we are interested in the following practical problem: is it possible to obtain Σ_{ub}^1 with one —or few— queries to a propositional theorem prover, or is it the case that the best strategy is just to ask separately for each propositional variable x of Σ whether $\Sigma \models x$ holds? Clearly if it is possible to parallelize the process of building Σ_{ub}^1 —or any other approximation of Σ_{lub}— then we have better chances to obtain good approximations of Σ_{lub}. On the other hand if in order to find an approximation of Σ_{lub} with k clauses we need k calls to a theorem prover, then the complexity of query answering is completely moved to the compilation phase.

Several authors (see for example [Beigel, 1988, Gasarch, 1986, Krentel, 1988]) studied the computational complexity of search problems of the kind we are addressing here. The goal of the research in this field is to understand "how much NP-hardness" does an NP-hard problem contain. Gasarch defines in [Gasarch, 1986] (see also [Krentel, 1988] and Appendix A.3) the problem QUERY, which is a generalization of the standard satisfiability problem SAT. The input of QUERY are k propositional formulae $T_1, \ldots, T_k$ and its output are k bits $b_1, \ldots, b_k$, where for any i ($1 \leq i \leq k$), $b_i = 1$ if T_i is satisfiable, and $b_i = 0$ if T_i is not satisfiable. Beigel shows in [Beigel, 1988] that it is very unlikely that QUERY can be solved with less than k queries to a SAT oracle. More formally he shows that if this happens, then randomized polynomial algorithms for the class NP exist and the polynomial hierarchy collapses (which is conjectured to be false, cf. [Johnson, 1990].) In other words it seems that any strategy for solving QUERY cannot be better than solving independently the k corresponding SAT problems. A general property of this kind of NP-hard problems (see [Beigel, 1988] for further details) is that it is not possible to gain efficiency via parallelization.

The following theorem clarifies the relation existing between QUERY and the problem of finding Σ_{ub}^1.

Theorem 4.3.1 QUERY *can be polynomially reduced to the problem of finding the approximation Σ_{ub}^1 of a formula Σ.*

The proof of the above theorem can be easily adapted to the problem of finding other sets of Horn prime implicates of Σ.

This result can be interpreted in the following way: the task of finding short approximations of Σ_{lub} —like for example Σ_{ub}^1— contains "a lot of NP-hardness". There seems to be a direct correspondence between the size of the approximation and the computational effort that we need to obtain it. As a consequence there is little hope to obtain good approximations of Σ_{lub} by performing few calls to a theorem prover.

4.3.2   Dealing with the LUB implicitly

In the previous subsection we addressed the issue of how hard is to compile Σ, and in particular how hard is to obtain an approximation of Σ_{lub} like for example Σ_{ub}^1. In this subsection we are interested in another computational property of Σ_{lub}: we want to know how hard is to reason w.r.t. Σ_{lub}, regardless of the representation of this formula that we are currently storing in our memory. In other words we want to understand what is the exact complexity of deciding $\Sigma_{lub} \models \alpha$, assuming that the inputs are Σ and α.

As far as the lower bound is concerned, the problem is obviously co-NP-hard, since when α is Horn, then $\Sigma_{lub} \models \alpha$ iff $\Sigma \models \alpha$. The following theorem clarifies that co-NP is also the upper bound.

Theorem 4.3.2 (reduction to classical reasoning) *Given Σ and a clause α we can build in polynomial time two formulae Σ' and α' such that $\Sigma_{lub} \models \alpha$ iff $\Sigma' \models \alpha'$.*

As a consequence, deciding if $\Sigma_{lub} \models \alpha$ is a problem in co-NP.

This proves that the problem of deciding $\Sigma_{lub} \models \alpha$ can be solved by means of a single call to a propositional theorem prover. Therefore testing if $\Sigma_{lub} \models \alpha$ is a co-NP-complete problem, i.e., it has exactly the same complexity as the original problem of deciding $\Sigma \models \alpha$.

We note also that the above theorem identifies a sound and complete description of inference w.r.t. Σ_{lub} in terms of classic propositional inference. Such characterization will be formally given in Appendix C.2, equation (C.2).

4.3.3   Comments on the computational results

Summarizing all the computational results presented so far we can say that:

1. it is not possible to represent Σ_{lub} explicitly in the memory (cf.[Kautz and Selman, 1992]);

2. we can make Σ_{lub} partially explicit; this is doable off-line but it is more difficult than the original task of reasoning w.r.t. Σ (cf. Theorem 4.3.1);

3. if we keep Σ_{lub} completely implicit then reasoning w.r.t. it is exactly as hard as reasoning (on-line) w.r.t. Σ (cf. Theorem 4.3.2.)

We remark that a generic propositional formula Σ has computational properties which are very similar to the above ones. In particular 1) it is not feasible —in order to perform quick on-line reasoning— to store all of its consequences explicitly 2) it can be made partially explicit but this is going to be computationally expensive.

An interesting tradeoff therefore exists between the amount of compilation that we want to perform off-line and the amount of reasoning that we want to do on-line. This holds for the Horn LUB as well as for the original formula.

4.3.4   A semantical remark

In Subsection 4.3.2 we noted that it is possible to characterize inference w.r.t. Σ_{lub} in terms of classical propositional inference. In this subsection we make a brief remark about the relation existing between Horn LUBs and closed world reasoning (see Section 2.2.2)

The "most important" model of a Horn formula is its minimum model, as it contains necessary and sufficient information to answer all the positive queries. The following proposition clarifies the relations existing between the minimal model of Σ_{lub} and the closed world assumption $CWA(\Sigma)$ of Σ.

Proposition 4.3.3 (LUB and CWA) *Let M be the minimum model of Σ_{lub}. M is the intersection of all the minimal models of Σ. Therefore M is a model of Σ iff the closed world assumption $CWA(\Sigma)$ of Σ is consistent.*

We remind that reasoning w.r.t. Σ_{lub} is always sound. The above observation says that —as far as positive queries are concerned— it is also complete iff $CWA(\Sigma)$ is consistent. We note that $CWA(\Sigma)$ may be consistent even if Σ is non-Horn: The CWA of $\neg a \lor b \lor c$ is consistent.

Relations between Horn LUBs and closed world reasoning are implicit in the works [Borgida and Etherington, 1989, Selman and Kautz, 1991]. The complexity of testing if the CWA of a propositional formula is consistent has been studied in [Eiter and Gottlob, 1993b].

All the results presented in this section will be proved in Appendix C.2.

4.4   Discussion

The results that we have seen in Sections 4.2 and 4.3 show that Horn knowledge compilation has unexpected relations with minimal reasoning.

As for the computational results, in Section 4.2 we have seen that the computational effort of finding a Horn GLB is justified only if a significant number of queries to it will be done. In particular we have seen that the compilation is more expensive than a set of query answering tasks. The size of such a set has a lower bound which is a function logarithmic in the size of the input and an upper bound which is a function polynomial in the size of the input.

In Section 4.3 we have obtained similar results, showing that high-quality Horn UBs need a significant computational effort. Moreover we have shown that an interesting tradeoff exists between the amount of compilation that we want to perform during compile time (off-line) and the amount of reasoning that we want to do during query-answering time (on-line.)

Since compilation causes anyway loss of information (either soundness or completeness), the computational effort spent in the compilation must be compared to the quality of the inference obtained. It is an interesting open issue to find an adequate formal framework for comparing the two aspects.

Chapter 5

Conclusions

In this book we studied two popular techniques for limiting complexity of reasoning in Artificial Intelligence problems.

The first technique, known as language restriction, has been studied in Chapter 2, referring in particular to a form of non-monotonic reasoning known as minimal reasoning. The second technique we considered is logic-based approximation and has been studied in Chapter 3. In Chapter 4 we made a first attempt at integrating the two studies on tractable reasoning, showing how complexity analysis about minimal reasoning can be used as a tool for evaluating techniques for approximate reasoning.

In the present chapter we intend to comment the results we obtained and to discuss problems that are still open.

Structure of the chapter

In Section 5.1 we briefly comment the results we obtained in the book. In Section 5.2 we discuss open problems and current research.

5.1 Comments on the results obtained

In Chapter 2, we dealt with minimal reasoning. Minimal reasoning consists of a set of well-known techniques that are used for formalizing common-sense reasoning and for handling indefinite, disjunctive, implicit and negative information in knowledge bases. Such techniques are studied also in the areas of Logic Programming and Database Theory. Complexity analysis of non-monotonic formalisms like minimal reasoning is currently a very active research area (cf. [Cadoli and Schaerf, 1993b].)

In this book we focused on the analysis of the threshold between polynomiality and intractability for various forms of minimal reasoning defined in the literature. We found polynomially tractable cases —for which we gave polynomial-time algorithms— and intractable cases. We considered decision as well as constructive problems, modeling several reasoning patterns. Complexity results have been applied to practical reasoning problems such as model-based diagnosis and inheritance. Most of the results refer to propositional languages. Anyway we found semantical as well as computational results about minimal reasoning in first-order languages.

In Chapter 2 the major effort has been analytic, since we mainly studied computational and semantical properties of formal systems and techniques defined in the literature by other authors. An original language for the representation of non-monotonic inheritance networks has been introduced and analyzed in Section 2.7.1.

The second technique we considered is logic-based approximation and has been studied in Chapter 3. We started analyzing two techniques for approximation of logical problems defined by other authors. Comparing the basic aspects of those techniques we were able to make a desiderata list for a new technique for approximate reasoning. The guidelines for the new technique are semantical foundation, computational effectiveness, possibility of having more and more accurate approximations, unique approach for a wide range of deductive problems. The new technique has been introduced by showing the approximation of entailment in propositional logic. It has been extended to deal with non-monotonic and modal logics, as well as decidable fragments of first-order logic. Moreover we defined an epistemic language for representing approximate knowledge, typical of an agent with limited computational resources.

In Chapter 3 the major effort has been synthetic, since we defined original techniques for approximate reasoning and we applied them to specific deductive problems.

In Chapter 4 we made a first attempt at integrating the two studies on tractable reasoning, showing how complexity analysis about minimal reasoning can be used as a tool for evaluating techniques for approximate reasoning. In particular we showed various computational properties about the approximation technique called Horn knowledge compilation, introduced by Selman and Kautz. In such an analysis we used some of the results obtained in Chapter 2.

The analysis on worst-case complexity of various problems in minimal reasoning we studied in the first part of this book showed that the expressiveness of polynomial languages is often limited. Studies performed by other researchers about other areas in Knowledge Representation lead to similar results. At this point we had several possibilities for continuing our study in tractable reasoning. Following a well-established area, we investigated on partial —or approximate— reasoning based on logical formalizations. Starting from the simplest language in Knowledge Representation, namely propositional logic, we defined technique for approximate reasoning for various deductive problems, including minimal reasoning.

Both language restriction and theory approximation technique lead to interesting results, which are complementary in nature.

As far as problems of minimal reasoning are concerned, we found that in the propositional case polynomial languages are often strictly less expressive than polynomial languages w.r.t. classical inference. In first-order languages high degrees of undecidability are reached.

We found that the situation is better for model checking and model finding problems than in inference problems, i.e., checking validity w.r.t. all minimal models, as the former problems admit more polynomial cases than the latter. This seems to confirm the ideas expressed by Halpern and Vardi in [Halpern and Vardi, 1991], where they suggested that reasoning in AI should be modeled as a model checking activity, as opposed to the traditional idea of reasoning as a theorem proving activity.

As for theory approximation techniques, in our research we stressed the point of equipping the approximate answer with a clear semantics. We also made an attempt at defining a degree of belief specifying "how much" the user can trust an approximate answer. This has been made by means of an epistemic logic for non-omniscient agents.

We think that the idea of knowledge compilation is particularly interesting, as this is a task that can be done off-line. We plan to investigate about the possibility to integrate knowledge compilation and on-line reasoning. To this end we consider the results shown in Chapter 4 to be encouraging, as they show that a very general idea of minimality —explicit in circumscription— can capture a reasonable notion of compilation. Since minimality is a basic idea in non-monotonic logics, we think that the area of knowledge compilation will be intertwined with that of non-monotonic reasoning.

5.2   Open problems

Both in the study of language restriction and of theory approximation some interesting problems remained unsolved. Moreover there are a number of possible directions in which our research can be continued. We close our work by giving a list of topics that we consider particularly interesting for future research. For some of them preliminary results already exist but have not been included in the book.

5.2.1   Complexity of minimal reasoning

Closed world reasoning

- It is still unknown (see also [Eiter and Gottlob, 1993b]) whether CWA inference in unrestricted propositional formulae is complete for the class $P^{NP[O(\log n)]}$ (with respect to polynomial transformability.) Analogously, it is unknown whether GCWA and CCWA in unrestricted propositional formulae are complete for $P^{\Sigma_2^p[O(\log n)]}$. Finally, there is the question if CCWA inference in Dual-Horn formulae and ECWA in both Horn and Dual-Horn formulae, are complete for $P^{NP[O(\log n)]}$.

Model checking

- It would be interesting to provide an abstract characterization of all the cases where model checking for propositional circumscription can be solved in polynomial time, in the style of the "dichotomy results" shown by Schaefer in [Schaefer, 1978]. The same question is interesting also for ECWA inference and model finding.

Circumscription

- It is noted in [Kolaitis and Papadimitriou, 1990] that computing the first order sentence equivalent to the circumscription of a first-order formula F may increase the size of F exponentially. It would be interesting to determine if this happens for propositional formulae too, i.e., if the formula corresponding to the circumscription of a propositional formula T needs to have exponential size with respect to the size of T. It is worth noticing that this condition would imply that circumscription may be used to produce a compact representation of an inherently exponential boolean function.

  In a recent work [Cadoli et al., 1995] we proved that —unless the polynomial hierarchy collapses at the second level— the size of a purely propositional representation of the circumscription $CIRC(T)$ of a propositional formula T grows faster than any polynomial as the size of T increases. The significance of this result from the point of view of Knowledge Representation and Reasoning has been presented in [Cadoli et al., 1994a].

- Relational database query languages grounded on non-monotonic logics have been proposed in several papers (cf. for example [Kolaitis and Papadimitriou, 1991, Cadoli et al., 1994b].) Such works investigate on the *expressive power* of the proposed languages, i.e., the set of relations that it is possible to compute by querying. In general, the expressive power of a language is not necessarily the same as its computational complexity.

  The expressive power of circumscription on finite structures such as relational databases has been only marginally investigated. It would be interesting to know whether the tractability threshold for the complexity of inference in the propositional case (cf. Section 2.3) corresponds in some way to a threshold for the expressiveness of a properly defined query language.

Model finding

- A complexity class that characterizes the search problem of finding a minimal model of a propositional formula in terms of calls to oracles is still unknown. Moreover it is still unknown whether the search problem of finding a $(P; Z)$-minimal model is any harder than the problem of finding a minimal model.

- Analogously, it is still unknown whether the search problem of finding a Horn GLB (cf. Section 4.2) is any harder than the problem of finding a minimal model.

5.2.2 Approximation of a logical theory

Logical aspects

- We would like to provide S-1- and S-3-entailment with a proof theory, for example with a Gentzen-style system.

- We would like to give a sort of "interpolation theorem" for S-3- and S-1-entailment (cf. [Kleene, 1966, §56].) In such a way we expect to have a formalization of the gain of information that we have in the stepwise solution of the problem.

Computational aspects

- Are there propositional formulae T, γ such that $T \models \gamma$ and $\forall S \neq L$ it holds that $T \not\models^3_S \gamma$?

  Dually, are there formulae T, γ such that $T \not\models \gamma$ and $\forall S \neq L$ it holds that $T \models^1_S \gamma$?

- It would be interesting to study the computational complexity of optimization problems like:

  - given a pair of propositional formulae T, γ, find the size $|S|$ of a minimal set S such that either $T \models^3_S \gamma$ or $T \not\models^1_S \gamma$ holds. Find one such set S of minimal size;

  - given a pair of propositional formulae T, γ and the fact that both $T \not\models^3_S \gamma$ and $T \models^1_S \gamma$ for a fixed set of letters $S \neq \emptyset$, find the size $|S'|$ of a minimal set $S' \supset S$ such that either $T \models^3_{S'} \gamma$ or $T \not\models^1_{S'} \gamma$ holds. Find one such set S' of minimal size.

Integration with other approximation techniques

- We have briefly mentioned in Section 3.3 that our method has some similarities with the techniques developed in the field of abstract interpretation. Our approach is more semantics-oriented, while abstract interpretation mainly uses algebraic and syntactic methods. We believe that a more careful comparison of the relative advantages of the two methods can lead to further results.

- We think that the idea of knowledge compilation (see [Kautz and Selman, 1991a, Kautz and Selman, 1992, Selman and Kautz, 1991] and Section 3.1) is particularly interesting, as this is a task that can be done off-line. We plan to investigate about the possibility to integrate knowledge compilation and on-line approximate reasoning.

- Is there any relation between our definition of approximation and a definition of approximation based on numerical estimates?
  As an example, we know that $T \models \gamma$ iff $\mathcal{M}(T) \subseteq \mathcal{M}(\gamma)$, where $\mathcal{M}()$ denotes the models of a propositional formula. Let us define a new form of approximate entailment as follows: consider the number δ defined as the ratio $(|\mathcal{M}(T)| - |\mathcal{M}(\gamma)|)/|\mathcal{M}(T)|$. Clearly $0 \leq \delta \leq 1$ and $T \models \gamma$ iff $\delta = 0$. Intuitively we can say that an estimate of δ gives an estimate of the validity of the relation $T \models \gamma$; in particular if we suspect that δ is low, then we might be willing to accept that $T \models \gamma$ holds.
  Is there any relation between δ and S-3, S-1-entailment? Note that if we can relate a numerical parameter of this kind with the approximate inference, then we might have a heuristic "measure" of the reliability of intermediate answers.

- Studies about complexity of NMR —including those of the present book— show that inferring in non-monotonic knowledge bases is significantly harder than reasoning in monotonic ones. This contrasts with the general idea that NMR can be used to make knowledge representation and reasoning simpler, not harder. In [Cadoli *et al.*, 1994a] we showed that sometimes NMR really makes reasoning simpler. In particular we gave prototypical scenarios where closed world reasoning accounts for a faster and unsound approximation of classical reasoning.

Use of meta-knowledge

- In Section 3.4 we have presented some ideas on how an expressive language can be used to declaratively state properties of a knowledge base and help in the query answering process. In our opinion, this is a very important issue and we believe that it deserves further theoretical investigation as well as experiments in applicative domains.

- Extend the epistemic language for non-omniscient agents to a multi-agent framework. Such an extended language would be capable to formalize the interaction between several non-omniscient agents.

Approximation of other computational tasks

- Extend the work on approximation to planning problems (which are in general search problems.) In this field, there is a need for efficient inference mechanisms to be used in real-time systems. In the literature some interesting work on approximation of planning has already been done (see for example literature on any-time algorithms [Dean and Boddy, 1988, Russell and Zilberstein, 1991, Ginsberg, 1991b].) We believe that our framework can be successfully applied to planning problems by adopting a stepwise construction of plans.

Appendix to Chapter 2

A.1   Appendix to Section 2.3

The structure of this section is as follows: In Subsection A.1.1 we survey some preliminary results about CWR that are useful for our complexity analysis. In Subsection A.1.2 we discuss the upper bound of the complexity of the various forms of CWR in unrestricted propositional formulae. Moreover we describe the basic characteristics of two algorithms proposed in the literature for computing circumscription. We turn then our attention (Subsections A.1.3 through A.1.7) to the complexity analysis of all the CWR-rules in the eight propositional languages described in Section 2.3.1. First of all we analyze the complexity of the inference problem under CWA, GCWA, and EGCWA, i.e., the closed world rules that do not require the partition of the alphabet into the three subsets P, Q, Z. Then we consider the remaining closed world rules, namely CCWA and ECWA. Within each subsection we first present the intractability results, then the tractability results. Finally, in Subsection A.1.8 we analyze the various forms of CWR with respect to the possibility of inferring new positive clauses.

A.1.1   Preliminaries

The different forms of CWR are not independent on each other. In the rest of this paper we shall make use of the following facts relating the various CWR-rules.

- **Fact 1:**   (see [Gelfond *et al.*, 1989, page 84], [Lifschitz, 1985a, Theorem 3.1], [Minker, 1982, page 300]) for every formula F, if T is Horn, i.e., is constituted by clauses with at most one positive literal, then $CWA(T) \models F$ iff $GCWA(T) \models F$ iff $EGCWA(T) \models F$ iff $CCWA(T; P; \emptyset; \emptyset) \models F$ iff $ECWA(T; P; \emptyset; \emptyset) \models F$.

- **Fact 2:** (see [Gelfond *et al.*, 1989, page 84]) for every formula F, $EGCWA$ $(T) \models F$ iff $ECWA(T; P; \emptyset; \emptyset) \models F$.

- **Fact 3:** (see [Gelfond and Przymusinska, 1986, page 277]) for every formula F, $GCWA(T) \models F$ iff $CCWA(T; P; \emptyset; \emptyset) \models F$.

- **Fact 4:** (see [Gelfond and Przymusinska, 1986, Theorem 3.9], [Gelfond *et al.*, 1989, Theorem 5.1]) for every literal L belonging to $P^+ \cup P^-$, $CCWA(T; P; Q; Z)) \models L$ iff $ECWA(T; P; Q; Z) \models L$.

Fact 1 follows from the uniqueness of the minimal model in Horn formulae, while Facts 2, 3 and 4 are straightforward consequences of the definitions. Moreover, the following properties hold for CCWA and ECWA.

- **Fact 5:** (see [Gelfond *et al.*, 1989, Theorem 5.8]) for every clause γ whose literals belong to $P^+ \cup Q^+ \cup Q^-$, $ECWA(T; P; Q; Z)) \models \gamma$ iff $T \models \gamma$.

- **Fact 6:** (see [Gelfond *et al.*, 1989, Theorem 5.5]) for every clause γ, $ECWA(T; P; Q; Z)) \models \gamma$ iff both the following two conditions hold:

  1. there exist n $(n \geq 0)$ conjunctions $k_1, \ldots, k_n$ of literals belonging to $P^+ \cup Q^+ \cup Q^-$ such that $k_1, \ldots, k_n$ are ECWA-ffn in $\langle T; P; Q; Z \rangle$;

  2. $T \models \gamma \vee k_1 \vee \cdots \vee k_n$.

- **Fact 7:** (see [Gelfond and Przymusinska, 1986, Theorem 3.6]) for every literal $\neg L$ belonging to P^-, $CCWA(T; P; Q; Z) \models \neg L$ iff L is CCWA-ffn.

- **Fact 8:** (see [Gelfond *et al.*, 1989, Theorem 4.5]) for every formula of the form $\neg K$ not involving literals from Z, $ECWA(T; P; Q; Z) \models \neg K$ iff the formula K is ECWA-ffn.

Fact 6 has been used by Przymusinski in [Przymusinski, 1989] as the basis of an algorithm that we discuss in Section A.1.2.2.

A.1.2   Upper bounds and algorithms for CWR

In this subsection we discuss the upper bound of the complexity of the various forms of CWR in unrestricted propositional formulae. Moreover we describe the basic characteristics of two algorithms proposed in the literature for computing circumscription, since they can be used to compute inference under the ECWA and to some extent under the other forms of CWR.

A.1.2.1   Upper bounds of CWR

In this subsection we deal with the upper bound of the complexity of the inference problem under the various forms of CWR.

We first provide an upper bound of the complexity of the inference problem under ECWA, showing that this problem is in Π_2^p. In particular we provide a

Algorithm NonMinimal
Input a formula $\langle T; P; Q; Z \rangle$ and a model M of T
Output true, if M is not $(P; Z)$-minimal, false otherwise
begin
    guess an interpretation N of T;
    if N is a model of T and $N <_{(P;Z)} M$
    then return true;
    return false
end.

Algorithm A.1: NonMinimal

non-deterministic polynomial time algorithm for the complement of such problem, i.e., the one of deciding if $ECWA(T; P; Q; Z) \not\models \gamma$, where γ is a clause. The algorithm uses an oracle $\mathcal{L}$ for the decision problem $(P; Z)$-MINIMALITY, i.e., an oracle whose input is a formula T and a model M of T and whose answer is "yes" iff M is $(P; Z)$-minimal for T. The tractability threshold of the problem $(P; Z)$-MINIMALITY is analyzed in Section 2.4, where we consider various syntactic classes for the formula T in input.

Before describing the algorithm, we show that $(P; Z)$-MINIMALITY is in co-NP, thus showing that $\mathcal{L}$ is an NP oracle.

Note that an interpretation of T can be guessed in polynomial time. Moreover, a model M of T is not $(P; Z)$-minimal iff there exists a model N of T such that $N <_{(P;Z)} M$. Algorithm A.1 is non-deterministic and checks whether a model M of T is not $(P; Z)$-minimal.

Note that both checking whether N is a model of T and checking whether $N <_{(P;Z)} M$ are polynomial tasks. Therefore the algorithm NonMinimal is non-deterministic polynomial. This shows that the problem of determining whether a model M of T *is not* $(P; Z)$-minimal is in NP, and therefore $(P; Z)$-MINIMALITY is in co-NP. It follows that $\mathcal{L}$ is an NP oracle.

Now we return to the complexity of determining if $ECWA(T; P; Q; Z) \models \gamma$. Algorithm A.2 can be used for deciding whether $ECWA(T; P; Q; Z) \not\models \gamma$.

Note that Algorithm A.2 uses the oracle $\mathcal{L}$. Moreover, since both checking whether M is a model of T and checking whether $M \not\models \gamma$ are polynomial tasks, it has non-deterministic polynomial time complexity. It follows that deciding if $ECWA(T; P; Q; Z) \not\models \gamma$ is in Σ_2^p, and therefore the problem of deciding if $ECWA(T; P; Q; Z) \models \gamma$ is in Π_2^p.

From this result and from Fact 2, we can conclude that the problem of deciding if $EGCWA(T) \models \gamma$ is in Π_2^p too.

We now consider the CCWA, and provide an upper bound to the inference

Algorithm NotECWA
Input a formula $\langle T; P; Q; Z \rangle$ and a clause γ
Output true, if $ECWA(T; P; Q; Z) \not\models \gamma$, false otherwise
begin
    guess an interpretation M of T;
    if M is a model of T and $M \not\models \gamma$
    then if $\mathcal{L}$ answers "yes" with input T, P, Q, Z, and M
        then return true;
    return false;
end.

Algorithm A.2: NotECWA

problem under such rule. By Facts 4 and 7 a letter $p \in P$ is CCWA-ffn iff $ECWA(T; P; Q; Z) \models \neg p$. A straightforward algorithm for the problem of deciding if $CCWA(T; P; Q; Z) \models \gamma$ is reported as Algorithm A.3.

The first step of the algorithm (the for-loop) can be done by means of $|P|$ calls to Algorithm A.2, and yields the formula $CCWA(T; P; Q; Z)$, denoted T' in the algorithm. T' has a linear size with respect to T, and is used in the final step of the algorithm in order to compute the answer.

Since checking if $ECWA(T; P; Q; Z) \models \neg p$ can be done by an oracle in Σ_2^p, and checking if $CCWA(T; P; Q; Z) \models \gamma$ can be done by an oracle in NP, the problem of deciding if $CCWA(T; P; Q; Z) \models \gamma$ is in $P^{\Sigma_2^p[O(n)]}$, that is, it can be solved in deterministic polynomial time with at most $O(n)$ calls to an oracle in Σ_2^p, where n is the number of distinct letters occurring in P. It follows from Fact 3 that the above observations apply to GCWA too.

As we said in Section 2.3, in this work we are mainly interested in tractable fragments of propositional logic. However, a few words are in order about the lower bound of the complexity of CWR for unrestricted propositional formulae. Schlipf [Schlipf, 1988] noted that for unrestricted propositional formulae, the inference problem under CCWA is both NP-hard and co-NP-hard. Recently Eiter and Gottlob [Eiter and Gottlob, 1993b] established a new lower bound, proving that inference under GCWA is a Π_2^p-hard problem. By Facts 2,3,4, this applies also to CCWA, EGCWA and ECWA. Taking into account the above observations, we can conclude that the inference problem under both ECWA and EGCWA is Π_2^p-complete.

Eiter and Gottlob [Eiter and Gottlob, 1993b] have also obtained new results on the upper bound of CWR. In particular they proved (Theorem 3.13) that the inference problem under both GCWA and CCWA can be solved in polynomial time with a logarithmic number of calls to an oracle in Σ_2^p. The upper bound of

Algorithm CCWA
Input a formula $\langle T; P; Q; Z \rangle$, and a clause γ
Output true, if $CCWA(T; P; Q; Z) \models \gamma$, false otherwise
begin
    $T' := T$;
    for each $p \in P$
    do (*check if p is CCWA-ffn, and if so, add $\neg p$ to T'*)
        if $ECWA(T; P; Q; Z) \models \neg p$
        then $T' := T' \cup \{\neg p\}$;
    return $T' \models \gamma$;
end.

Algorithm A.3: CCWA

the inference problem under GCWA and CCWA is therefore $P^{\Sigma_2^p[O(\log n)]}$ where n is the number of distinct letters occurring in P.

To summarize, if no restriction is imposed on the propositional formula, then inference under both EGCWA and ECWA is a Π_2^p-complete problem, while inference under both GCWA and CCWA is Π_2^p-hard (lower bound) and in $P^{\Sigma_2^p[O(\log n)]}$ (upper bound.)

It is interesting to analyze the role played by the computational complexity of $(P; Z)$-MINIMALITY and MINIMALITY (i.e., the same problem when $Q = Z = \emptyset$) in determining the upper and the lower bounds of CWR. Let Θ be the class of formulae for which $(P; Z)$-MINIMALITY can be solved in deterministic polynomial time and Ω the class of formulae for which MINIMALITY can be solved in deterministic polynomial time. Looking at Algorithm A.2 we can realize that, for the class Θ, the inference problem under ECWA is in co-NP, and, for the class Ω, the inference problem under EGCWA is in co-NP.

Moreover, we can modify the proof of Theorem 3.13 in [Eiter and Gottlob, 1993b] and show that for the formulae in the class Θ, the inference problem under CCWA can be solved in polynomial time with a logarithmic number of calls to an oracle in NP, and therefore is in $P^{NP[O(\log n)]}$. Analogously, for the class Ω, the inference problem under GCWA is in $P^{NP[O(\log n)]}$.

The above observations show that the complexity of $(P; Z)$-MINIMALITY and MINIMALITY plays an important role in establishing the complexity of CWR. The complexity of the problem $(P; Z)$-MINIMALITY is analyzed in Section 2.4. In that section we show that both $(P; Z)$-MINIMALITY and MINIMALITY can be solved in polynomial time for all the classes of formulae we will take into account in the following subsections (cf. row γ of Table 2.6, Section 2.4.)

Using the results of that section we can build straightforward polynomial algorithms for $(P; Z)$-MINIMALITY in the case of Krom, Horn and Dual-Horn formulae. This shows that for such classes of formulae, an upper bound of the complexity of the inference problem under ECWA and EGCWA is co-NP, while the upper bound for CCWA and GCWA is $P^{NP[O(\log n)]}$.

A.1.2.2   Algorithms for computing circumscription

We briefly describe two methods for computing circumscription, namely, Przymusinski's MILO-resolution and Ginsberg's circumscriptive theorem prover. In the following the symbol $CIRC(T; P; Q; Z)$ denotes the circumscription of P in T, varying the letters in Z and keeping the letters in Q fixed.

The method proposed by Przymusinski in [Przymusinski, 1989] is essentially based on the definition of ECWA-ffn formula and on Fact 6.

The method, called *MInimal model Linear Ordered resolution* (MILO-resolution), is a variant of the ordered linear resolution and is briefly described in the following for the propositional case.

We first recall some definition from [Przymusinski, 1989]. Let T be a formula on the alphabet L, $\langle P; Q; Z \rangle$ a partition of L, and C any clause on L. A *MILO-resolution tree* on T, C is a linear ordered deduction tree such that:

1. the root is the clause C;

2. given a node N and a clause α of T, if N and α can be resolved using a literal from $P^- \cup Z^+ \cup Z^-$, then their resolvent is a successor of N;

3. nothing else is in the tree.

A node without literals from $P^- \cup Z^+ \cup Z^-$ has no children. Note that, if C is the root of the tree and D is any node, then $T \models C \rightarrow D$. Therefore D is called *MILO-deducible* from $\langle T, C \rangle$. A leaf of the tree with no literals from $P^- \cup Z^+ \cup Z^-$ is called a *MILO-leaf* of $\langle T, C \rangle$. The conjunction of all the MILO-leaves is denoted by $Deriv(T, C)$. If no such leaf exists, then $Deriv(T, C) = true$.

Given a formula T on the alphabet L, a partition $\langle P; Q; Z \rangle$ of L, and any clause γ on L, the algorithm answers *yes* iff $CIRC(T; P; Q; Z) \models \gamma$.

The algorithm splits in two sub-cases, depending on whether γ contains literals from $Z^+ \cup Z^-$, or not. We first deal with the latter case.

Case 1: γ does not contain literals from $Z^+ \cup Z^-$. We know that in this case $CIRC(T; P; Q; Z) \models \gamma$ iff $\neg\gamma$ is ECWA-ffn in $\langle T; P; Q; Z \rangle$ (see [Gelfond *et al.*, 1989, Theorem 5.2].) Consider the MILO-resolution tree having γ as root and let B be a MILO-leaf of the tree. Note that B is a clause whose literals belong to $P^+ \cup Q^+ \cup Q^-$ and that $T \models \gamma \rightarrow B$, i.e., $T \models \neg\gamma \vee B$. By definition of ECWA-ffn formula, if $T \not\models B$, then $\neg\gamma$ is not ECWA-ffn in $\langle T; P; Q; Z \rangle$. Conversely, Przymusinski (see [Przymusinski, 1989, Theorem 3.3]) shows that, if for each MILO-leaf B of the tree, $T \models B$, then $\neg\gamma$ is ECWA-ffn in $\langle T; P; Q; Z \rangle$. Therefore, the method for case 1 can be summarized as follows:

build depth-first the MILO-tree having γ as root;
for each MILO-leaf B of the tree
    if $T \not\models B$
    then return *no*;
return *yes*

The following example shows that the size of a MILO-tree on T, C can be exponential with respect to the size of T and C.

Example A.1.1 (exponential growth of the MILO-tree) Let $L = \{p_1, \ldots, p_n, q_1, \ldots, q_n\}$ be an alphabet and let $\langle P; Q \rangle$ be a partition of L, with $P = \{p_1, \ldots, p_n\}$ and $Q = \{q_1, \ldots, q_n\}$. Let T be the propositional formula

$$\{ \bigwedge_{1 \leq i \leq n} (p_i \vee \neg q_i) \bigwedge_{1 \leq i \leq n} \neg q_i \}.$$

We want to determine whether $CIRC(T; P; Q; Z) \models \gamma$, where γ is the clause $\neg p_1 \vee \cdots \vee \neg p_n$. It is easy to note that the MILO-tree having γ as root has $n + 1$ levels. The i-th $(i > 1)$ level has $\prod_{0 \leq j \leq i-2}(n - j)$ nodes. Each node in the i-th level $(i \geq 1)$ is a clause with $n - i + 1$ literals from P^- and $i - 1$ literals from Q^-. The $(n + 1)$-th level has $n!$ nodes, each node being a permutation of the literals of the clause $\neg q_1 \vee \cdots \vee \neg q_n$. Since $T \models \neg q_1 \vee \cdots \vee \neg q_n$, the algorithm must visit each leaf of the tree and then returns *yes*. Therefore the method needs exponential time in this case.

Note that T is an HornKrom$^-$ formula. Later in this paper we describe a polynomial time algorithm for computing circumscription in HornKrom$^-$ formulae (see Theorem A.1.27.) $\Diamond$

Case 2: γ contains some literal from $Z^+ \cup Z^-$. We first consider the case where γ is a single literal, and then move to the general case.

If γ is a literal, we know by Fact 6 that $CIRC(T; P; Q; Z) \models \gamma$ iff both the following conditions hold:

1. there exist n $(n \geq 0)$ conjunctions $k_1, \ldots, k_n$ whose literals belong to $P^+ \cup Q^+ \cup Q^-$ such that $k_1, \ldots, k_n$ are ECWA-ffn in $\langle T; P; Q; Z \rangle$;

2. $T \models \gamma \vee k_1 \vee \cdots \vee k_n$.

Consider the MILO-tree having $\neg \gamma$ as root. Let $Deriv(T, \neg \gamma)$ the conjunction of all the MILO-leaves of the tree. Note that $Deriv(T, \neg \gamma)$ is a conjunction of clauses whose literals belong to $P^+ \cup Q^+ \cup Q^-$. It holds that $T \models \neg \gamma \rightarrow Deriv(T, \neg \gamma)$, that is $T \models \gamma \vee Deriv(T, \neg \gamma)$. Let $k_1, \ldots, k_n$ be the DNF of $Deriv(T, \neg \gamma)$. Note that each $\neg k_i$ is a clause without literals from $Z^+ \cup Z^-$. By Fact 6, if $CIRC(T; P; Q; Z) \models \neg k_1 \wedge \cdots \wedge \neg k_n$, then $CIRC(T; P; Q; Z) \models \gamma$. Conversely, Przymusinski (see [Przymusinski, 1989] Theorem 3.7) shows that, if a k_i $(1 \leq i \leq n)$ exists such that $CIRC(T; P; Q; Z) \not\models \neg k_i$, then $CIRC(T; P; Q; Z) \not\models \gamma$.

The method proposed for this case is the following:

build the MILO-tree having $\neg\gamma$ as root;
let $k_1, \ldots, k_n$ be the DNF of $Deriv(T, \neg\gamma)$;
for each i $(1 \le i \le n)$
      use the method described in Case 1 for determining whether
      $CIRC(T; P; Q; Z) \not\models \neg k_i$;
      if the answer is *no*
      then return *no*;
return *yes*;

It remains to analyze the case where γ is a clause of the form $c_1 \vee \cdots \vee c_m$ $(m > 1)$. In this case, in order to determine whether $CIRC(T; P; Q; Z) \models \gamma$, it is necessary to build m MILO-trees. The i-th MILO-tree has the literal $\neg c_i$ as root and corresponds to the formula $T_i = T \cup \{\neg c_1 \wedge \cdots \wedge \neg c_{i-1}\}$. The algorithm answers *yes* iff $CIRC(T; P; Q; Z) \models \neg(Deriv(T_1, \neg c_1) \wedge \cdots \wedge Deriv(T_n, \neg c_n))$, and its correctness can be determined using the method sketched in Case 1. One can show that in Case 2 too, the algorithm requires to build MILO-trees that may have exponential size with respect to the size of the formula and the query.

We now turn to the method proposed by Ginsberg ([Ginsberg, 1989].) Such method is based on the notion of a sentence p *confirming* another sentence q. We recall such a notion for the propositional case.

    Let T be a formula on the alphabet L, $\langle P; Z \rangle$ a partition of L, and p, q two sentences on L. Let D be the set $\{\neg d \mid d \in P\}$. The sentence q is said to be *confirmed by p* w.r.t T and D if the following conditions hold:

1. $T \cup \{p\}$ is satisfiable;

2. $T \cup \{p\} \models q$;

3. p is in DNF with respect to the set D, i.e., $p = \bigvee_i \bigwedge_j d_{ij}$, where $d_{ij} \in D$.

If there is no p that confirms q, we say that q is *unconfirmed* in T.

    It is easy to see that the notion of confirmation is closely related to that of ECWA-freeness for negation: a sentence q is unconfirmed w.r.t T and D iff q is ECWA-ffn in $\langle T; P; \emptyset; Z \rangle$.

    Ginsberg's main theorem relates confirmation and entailment under circumscription in the case where $Q = \emptyset$. The case where $Q \ne \emptyset$ is only briefly mentioned in [Ginsberg, 1989]. The main result is the following: if γ a sentence on L, then $CIRC(T; P; \emptyset; Z) \models \gamma$ holds iff there is some p that confirms γ and such that $\neg p$ is unconfirmed.

    Note that the above property is essentially equivalent to Fact 6 in the case where $Q = \emptyset$.

    The following example shows that the number of sentences confirming a given clause γ can grow exponentially with respect to the size of the formula.

Example A.1.2 (exponential growth of the set of sentences confirming a clause) Let $L = \{p_1, \ldots, p_{2n}, z_1, \ldots, z_n\}$ be an alphabet and let $\langle P; Z \rangle$ be a partition of L, with $P = \{p_1, \ldots, p_{2n}\}$ and $Z = \{z_1, \ldots, z_n\}$. Let T be the propositional formula

$$\{ \bigwedge_{1 \leq i \leq n} (p_i \vee \neg z_i), \bigwedge_{1 \leq i \leq n} (p_{n+i} \vee \neg z_i) \}.$$

Note that, as in the previous example, T is an HornKrom$^-$ formula.

We want to determine whether $CIRC(T; P; \emptyset; Z) \models \gamma$, where γ is the clause $\neg z_1 \vee \cdots \vee \neg z_n$. It is easy to see that each clause of the set

$$C = \{ \bigvee_{1 \leq i \leq n} \neg h_i \mid h_i \in \{p_i, p_{n+i}\} \}$$

confirms γ. Note also that $|C| = 2^n$ and that no clause in C subsumes another clause in C. Since Ginsberg's method builds the *weakest* G that confirms γ, it generates each element of the set C. Therefore the method needs exponential time in this case. $\Diamond$

In [Inoue and Helft, 1990], the methods of Przymusinski and Ginsberg are shown to be similar in the sense that both try to prove that $CIRC(T; P; \emptyset; Z) \models \gamma$ by showing that a sentence G exists such that the following conditions hold:

1. all the literals of G belong to P^+;

2. $T \models G \vee \gamma$;

3. $CIRC(T; P; Q; Z) \models \neg G$.

The main difference between the two methods can be summarized as follows: Przymusinski builds a very general sentence G using MILO-trees having literals of γ as roots. Then he uses MILO-resolution again to check if $CIRC(T; P; Q; Z) \models \neg G$. On the other hand, Ginsberg builds the *weakest* sentence G that confirms γ using a backward-chaining Assumption-based Truth Maintenance System (ATMS) based on multi-valued logic (see [Ginsberg, 1989].) Then he uses the ATMS again to check if $CIRC(T; P; Q; Z) \models \neg G$.

In [Inoue and Helft, 1990] it is shown that each of the two algorithms has some feature that can be –in some case– lead to a computational behavior preferable with respect to the other one. Note that the computational complexity of Ginsberg's method relies on the performance of the backward-chaining ATMS, and in particular on the building of the *weakest* G that confirms γ (this aspect is not discussed in detail in [Ginsberg, 1989].)

A.1.3   CWA

The results reported in [Reiter, 1978] show that the application of the CWA to propositional formulae may lead to inconsistency. In [Eiter and Gottlob,

---

Algorithm CWA
Input a formula T and a clause γ
Output true, if $CWA(T) \models \gamma$, false otherwise
begin
  $T' := T$;
  for each $p \in \Gamma$
  do (*check if p is CWA-ffn, and if so, add $\neg p$ to T'*)
    if $T \not\models p$
    then $T' := T' \cup \{\neg p\}$;
  return $T' \models \gamma$;
end.

Algorithm A.4: CWA

1993b], Eiter and Gottlob present a careful analysis of the complexity of the problem of deciding whether the CWA of a formula is consistent. They show that for unrestricted propositional formulae, such problem is co-NP-hard, while the inference problem under CWA is in $P^{NP[O(\log n)]}$.

However, for the kind of formulae we are interested in, both problems are polynomial, since the CWA of a Horn (resp. Krom, Dual-Horn) formula is itself a Horn (resp. Krom, Dual-Horn) formula, and can be computed in polynomial time. Therefore, there are straightforward algorithms both for checking the satisfiability of CWA and for the inference problem under CWA. This was noted by Apt [Apt, 1990] for Definite formulae. A simple algorithm for deciding if $CWA(T) \models \gamma$ is reported as Algorithm A.4.

Since all the steps of the algorithm CWA can be performed in polynomial time if T is Horn, Krom or Dual-Horn, we have the following.

Theorem A.1.1 *The problems:* INF-CWA[HORN,CLAUSE], INF-CWA[KROM, CLAUSE], *and* INF-CWA[DHORN,CLAUSE] *can be solved in polynomial time.*

In [Rajasekar *et al.*, 1989], Rajasekar, Lobo and Minker propose a weak form of CWA, called Weak Generalized Closed World Assumption (WGCWA), which applies to disjunctive logic programs (i.e., logic programs constituted by rules whose heads are disjunctions of positive literals.) The WGCWA is only defined for formulae that do not include negative clauses. By definition, inference under WGCWA polynomially reduces to an inference problem under the CWA on a suitable definite logic program. By Apt's result [Apt, 1990], the WGCWA yields polynomial time inference algorithms in the propositional case.

A.1.4 GCWA

In this subsection we deal with the GCWA. We present the intractability results in the first part and the tractability results in the second part.

A.1.4.1 Intractable cases

The following theorem shows that in the case of Dual-Horn formulae inference under GCWA is intractable even for single literals.

Theorem A.1.2 INF-GCWA[DHORN,LIT] *is co-NP-hard.*

PROOF: We reduce the unsatisfiability problem (the complement of SAT) to our problem by exhibiting a polynomial mapping from any CNF formula π to a Dual-Horn formula π' and a literal $\neg \overline{\overline{a}}_p$ such that π is unsatisfiable iff $GCWA(\pi') \models \neg\overline{\overline{a}}_p$.

Let π be a CNF formula on the alphabet $L = \{a_1, \ldots, a_p\}$ and let L' be $L \cup \{\overline{a} \mid a \in L\} \cup \{\overline{\overline{a}} \mid a \in L\}$. We define π' on the alphabet L' according to the following rules:

1. for each letter a of L, there is a clause $a \vee \overline{a}$ in π';

2. there are the clauses $a_1 \vee \overline{\overline{a}}_1$, $\overline{a}_1 \vee \overline{\overline{a}}_1$ in π';

3. for each i $(1 \le i \le p - 1)$ there are the clauses $\neg\overline{\overline{a}}_i \vee a_{i+1} \vee \overline{\overline{a}}_{i+1}$ and $\neg\overline{\overline{a}}_i \vee \overline{a}_{i+1} \vee \overline{\overline{a}}_{i+1}$ in π';

4. for each clause $\neg w_1 \vee \cdots \vee \neg w_n \vee w_{n+1} \vee \cdots \vee w_{n+m}$ in π, there is a clause $\overline{w_1} \vee \cdots \vee \overline{w_n} \vee w_{n+1} \vee \cdots \vee w_{n+m}$ in π'.

Note that the above mapping from π to π' is clearly polynomial, and π' is a Dual-Horn formula. We will prove that:

1. given a model of π, we can build a disjunction B of positive literals of L' such that $\pi' \models B \vee \overline{\overline{a}}_p$ and $\pi' \not\models B$;

2. given a disjunction B of positive literals of L' such that $\pi' \models B \vee \overline{\overline{a}}_p$ and $\pi' \not\models B$, we can build a model of π.

Therefore, the literal $\overline{\overline{a}}_p$ is not GCWA-ffn in π' iff π is satisfiable. Taking into account Facts 3 and 7, $GCWA(\pi') \models \neg\overline{\overline{a}}_p$ iff $\overline{\overline{a}}_p$ is GCWA-ffn in π', hence $GCWA(\pi') \models \neg\overline{\overline{a}}_p$ iff π is unsatisfiable.

Proof of 1: let M be a model of π and let B be the clause on the alphabet L' defined as follows:

for each letter a of L
    if $M \models a$, then $\overline{a}$ is a literal of B;
    if $M \models \neg a$, then a is a literal of B.

We first prove that $\pi' \not\models B$. Let M' be the truth assignment defined as follows:

- $M' \models a_i$ iff $M \models a_i$

- $M' \models \overline{a}_i$ iff $M \models \neg a_i$

- $M' \models \overline{\overline{a}}_i$.

It is easy to see that M' is a model of $\pi' \wedge \neg B$, and therefore, $\pi' \not\models B$.

In order to prove that $\pi' \models B \vee \overline{\overline{a}}_p$, note that for each model N of π', either $N \models B$ or $N \not\models B$. In the latter case, for each a_i, either $N \not\models a_i$ or $N \not\models \overline{a}_i$. It follows from rule 2 above, that $N \models \overline{\overline{a}}_1$. By rule 3, this implies that for each $i\,(1 \leq i \leq p)$, $N \models \overline{\overline{a}}_i$. Since every model N of π' that does not satisfy B satisfies $\overline{\overline{a}}_p$, we can conclude that $\pi' \models B \vee \overline{\overline{a}}_p$.

Proof of 2: let B be a disjunction of positive literals of L' such that both $\pi' \models B \vee \overline{\overline{a}}_p$ and $\pi' \not\models B$. Note first of all that $\pi' \not\models B$ implies that for each letter a_i of L, either a_i or $\overline{a}_i$ does not occur in B. Moreover, since $\pi' \models B \vee \overline{\overline{a}}_p$, it follows that $\pi' \wedge \neg B \wedge \neg \overline{\overline{a}}_p$ is unsatisfiable. We now show that this implies that for each a_i, either a_i or $\overline{a}_i$ occur in B. Suppose that there is an a_i such that both a_i and $\overline{a}_i$ are not in B. Remember that $\pi' \wedge \neg B$ is satisfiable. Let N be any model of $\pi' \wedge \neg B$, and let N' be the same as N except for the fact that $N \models a_i$, $N \models \overline{a}_i$ and $N \models \neg \overline{\overline{a}}_j$ for each $i \leq j \leq p$. It is easy to see that N' is a model of $\pi' \wedge \neg B \wedge \neg \overline{\overline{a}}_p$. Since this contradicts the above hypothesis, we can conclude that for each a_i, either a_i or $\overline{a}_i$ occur in B.

Now let M be a truth assignment of π defined as follows:

for each letter a of L

if a occurs in B, then $M \models \neg a$;

if $\overline{a}$ occurs in B, then $M \models a$.

Clearly, M assigns exactly one truth value to each letter of L. We now prove that M is a model of π. Suppose that a clause $\gamma = \neg w_1 \vee \cdots \vee \neg w_n \vee w_{n+1} \vee \cdots \vee w_{n+m}$ of π exists such that $M \not\models \gamma$. This implies that the following conditions hold: $\overline{w_1}$ occurs in $B, \cdots, \overline{w_n}$ occurs in B, w_{n+1} occurs in $B, \cdots, w_{n+m}$ occurs in B, i.e., all the literals of a clause of π' introduced according to rule 4 above occur in B. Therefore $\pi' \models B$, contradicting the hypothesis. $\diamond$

Using Facts 2, 3 and 4, the above theorem delivers intractability results for EGCWA, CCWA and ECWA as well. Such derived results will be shown in detail in Sections A.1.5, A.1.6 and A.1.7, in which those formalisms are analyzed.

A.1.4.2 Tractable cases

Minker [Minker, 1982] shows that, when the CWA is consistent, it is equivalent to the GCWA (see also Fact 1.) Since the CWA of a Horn formula is always consistent, it follows from Theorem A.1.1 that INF-GCWA[HORN,CLAUSE] is a polynomial problem.

The only case left for GCWA is inference for Krom formulae. We shall see in Section A.1.6.2 that this is indeed a polynomial problem even when clauses are inferred (see Corollary A.1.9, Section A.1.6.2.)

A.1.5   EGCWA

In this subsection we deal with the EGCWA. We present the intractability results in the first part and the tractability results in the second part.

A.1.5.1   Intractable cases

The first intractability result follows from the analysis performed in Section A.1.4.1.

Corollary A.1.3 INF-EGCWA[DHORN,LIT] *is co-NP-hard.*

PROOF: Use Theorem A.1.2 and Facts 2, 3 and 4. ◇

The second intractability result deals with inference of clauses from Krom formulae.

Theorem A.1.4 INF-EGCWA[2POSK,CLAUSE] *is co-NP-hard.*

PROOF: We reduce the unsatisfiability problem to our problem by exhibiting a polynomial mapping from any CNF formula π to a 2-positive-Krom formula π' and a clause $\neg K$ such that π is unsatisfiable iff $EGCWA(\pi') \models \neg K$.

Let π be a CNF formula on the alphabet L. Let L' be the alphabet $L \cup \{\bar{a} \mid a \in L\} \cup \{g_i \mid \gamma_i$ is a clause of $\pi\}$. We define π' on the alphabet L' according to the following rules:

1. for each letter a of L, there is a clause $a \vee \bar{a}$ in π';

2. for each clause $\gamma_i = \neg w_1 \vee \cdots \vee \neg w_n \vee w_{n+1} \vee \cdots \vee w_{n+m}$ in π, there are $n + m$ clauses $g_i \vee \overline{w_1}, \ldots, g_i \vee \overline{w_n}, g_i \vee w_{n+1}, \ldots, g_i \vee w_{n+m}$ in π'.

Note that the above mapping from π to π' is clearly polynomial, and π' is a 2-positive-Krom formula. Let K be the conjunction $g_1 \wedge \cdots \wedge g_h$, where $g_1, \ldots, g_h$ are all the letters of L' corresponding to the clauses in π. We now prove that:

1. given a model of π, we can build a disjunction B of positive literals of L' such that both $\pi' \models B \vee K$ and $\pi' \not\models B$;

2. given a disjunction B of positive literals of L' such that both $\pi' \models B \vee K$ and $\pi' \not\models B$, we can build a model M of π.

Therefore, the conjunction K is not EGCWA-ffn in π' iff π is satisfiable. Taking into account Facts 2 and 8 and that $\neg K$ is a clause, $EGCWA(\pi') \models \neg K$ iff K is EGCWA-ffn in π', hence $EGCWA(\pi') \models \neg K$ iff π is unsatisfiable.

Proof of 1: let M be a model of π, and let B be a clause on the alphabet L' defined as follows:

for each letter a of L
    if $M \models a$, then a is in B;
    if $M \models \neg a$, then $\bar{a}$ is in B.

Note that for each letter a in L, either a or $\bar{a}$ does not occur in B.

We first prove that $\pi' \not\models B$. Let M' be the truth assignment to the letters of L' defined as follows:

- for each $a \in L$, $M' \models a$ iff $M \models \neg a$

- for each $a \in L$, $M' \models \bar{a}$ iff $M \models a$

- for each g_i, $M' \models g_i$.

It is easy to see that M' is a model of $\pi' \wedge \neg B$, and therefore, $\pi' \not\models B$. In order to prove that $\pi' \models B \vee K$, consider any model N of $\pi' \wedge \neg B$. Since for each clause $\gamma_i = \neg w_1 \vee \cdots \vee \neg w_n \vee w_{n+1} \vee \cdots \vee w_{n+m}$ of π at least one literal l in $\{\overline{w_1} \ldots \overline{w_n}, w_{n+1}, \ldots, w_{n+m}\}$, occurs in B and the clause $l \vee g_i$ occurs in π', every g_i must be true in N and therefore $\pi' \wedge \neg B \wedge \neg K$ is unsatisfiable.

Proof of 2: let B be a disjunction of positive literals of L' such that both $\pi' \models B \vee K$ and $\pi' \not\models B$. Define an interpretation M of π as follows:

for each letter a of L
    if a occurs in B, then $M \models a$
            else $M \models \neg a$.

Note first of all that M assigns exactly one truth value to each letter of L. Suppose that M is not a model of π, i.e., a clause $\gamma_i = \neg w_1 \vee \cdots \vee \neg w_n \vee w_{n+1} \vee \cdots \vee w_{n+m}$ of π exists such that $M \not\models \gamma_i$. This implies that $w_1, \ldots, w_n$ occur in B, and that $w_{n+1}, \ldots, w_{n+m}$ do not occur in B. Since $\pi' \not\models B$, the first condition implies that $\overline{w_1}, \ldots, \overline{w_n}$ do not occur in B. Therefore $\pi' \wedge \neg B \wedge \neg g_i$ is satisfiable, where g_i corresponds to γ_i, but this contradicts the hypothesis that $\pi' \models B \vee K$ holds. $\diamond$

Using Fact 2 the above theorem gives an intractability result for ECWA as well. Such derived result will be shown in detail in Section A.1.7.

A.1.5.2   Tractable cases

The equivalence of EGCWA and CWA for Horn formulae (see Fact 1) and Theorem A.1.1 imply that INF-EGCWA[HORN,CLAUSE] is polynomial.

The only case left for EGCWA is inference of literals for Krom formulae. We shall see in Section A.1.7.2 that this is indeed a polynomial problem (see Corollary A.1.20, Section A.1.7.2.) Note that Corollary A.1.20 shows the first case in which inference of literals is easier than inference of clauses.

A.1.6   CCWA

In this subsection, we analyze the complexity of the CCWA. In particular we present one new intractability result in the first part and the tractability results in the second part. We recall that the CCWA requires the partition of the alphabet into the three subsets P, Q, Z.

A.1.6.1 Intractable cases

The first intractability result follows from the analysis performed in Section A.1.4.1.

Corollary A.1.5 INF-CCWA[DHORN,LIT,$Q = Z = \emptyset$] *is co-NP-hard.*

PROOF: Use Theorem A.1.2 and Fact 3. $\diamond$

The next theorem shows the intractability of the CCWA for Horn formulae, even if $Z = \emptyset$ and the inferred formula is a literal.

Theorem A.1.6 INF-CCWA[HORN,LIT,$Z = \emptyset$] *is co-NP-hard.*

PROOF: We reduce the unsatisfiability problem to our problem by exhibiting a polynomial mapping from any CNF formula π to a Horn formula π' on the alphabet L', a partition $\langle P; Q; \emptyset \rangle$ of L' and a literal $\neg p$ such that π is unsatisfiable iff $CCWA(\pi'; P; Q; \emptyset) \models \neg p$.

Let π be a CNF formula on the alphabet L. Let L' be $L \cup \{\bar{a} \mid a \in L\} \cup \{g_i \mid \gamma_i$ is a clause of $\pi\} \cup \{p\}$. We define π' on the alphabet L' according to the following rules:

1. for each letter a of L, there is a clause $\neg a \vee \neg \bar{a}$ in π';

2. for each clause $\gamma_i = \neg w_1 \vee \ldots \vee \neg w_n \vee w_{n+1} \vee \cdots \vee w_{n+m}$ in π, there are $n + m$ clauses $\neg \overline{w_1} \vee g_i, \ldots, \neg \overline{w_n} \vee g_i, \neg w_{n+1} \vee g_i, \ldots, \neg w_{n+m} \vee g_i$ in π';

3. there is the clause $\neg g_1 \vee \cdots \vee \neg g_h \vee p$ in π', where $g_1, \ldots, g_h$ are the letters of L' corresponding to the clauses $\gamma_1, \ldots, \gamma_h$ of π.

Moreover, we let P be the set of letters $\{g_i \mid \gamma_i$ is a clause of $\pi\} \cup \{p\}$, and Q the set of letters $L' \setminus P$. Note that the above mapping from π to π' is clearly polynomial, and π' is a Horn formula. We now prove that:

1. given a model M of π, we can build a disjunction B whose literals belong to $P^+ \cup Q^+ \cup Q^-$ such that both $\pi' \models B \vee p$ and $\pi' \not\models B$;

2. given a disjunction B whose literals belong to $P^+ \cup Q^+ \cup Q^-$ such that both $\pi' \models B \vee p$ and $\pi' \not\models B$, we can build a model M of π.

Therefore, the literal p is not CCWA-ffn in $\langle \pi'; P; Q; \emptyset \rangle$ iff π is satisfiable. Taking into account Fact 7, $CCWA(\pi'; P; Q; \emptyset) \models \neg p$ iff p is CCWA-ffn in $\langle \pi'; P; Q; \emptyset \rangle$, hence $CCWA(\pi'; P; Q; \emptyset) \models \neg p$ iff π is unsatisfiable.

Proof of 1: let M be a model of π and let B be a clause on the alphabet L' defined as follows:

for each letter a of L
    if $M \models a$, then $\neg a$ is in B;
    if $M \models \neg a$, then $\neg \bar{a}$ is in B.

Note first of all that all the literals of B belong to Q^-. Since for each letter a of L, either $\neg a$ or $\neg \overline{a}$ does not occur in B, $\pi' \not\models B$. Moreover, since for each clause $\gamma_i = \neg w_1 \vee \cdots \vee \neg w_n \vee w_{n+1} \vee \cdots \vee w_{n+m}$ in π it holds that $M \models \gamma_i$, at least one literal among $\neg \overline{w}_1, \ldots, \neg \overline{w}_n, \neg w_{n+1}, \ldots, \neg w_{n+m}$ occurs in B. Therefore for each i $(1 \leq i \leq h)$, it holds that $\pi' \models B \vee g_i$, where g_i is the letter of L' corresponding to γ_i. This implies that $\pi' \models B \vee p$.

Proof of 2: let B be a disjunction whose literals belong to $P^+ \cup Q^+ \cup Q^-$ such that both $\pi' \models B \vee p$ and $\pi' \not\models B$, and let M be an interpretation of π defined as follows:

for each letter a of L
    if $\neg a$ occurs in B, then $M \models a$
                else $M \models \neg a$.

Note first of all that M assigns exactly one truth value to each letter of L. We show that M is a model of π. Suppose that M is not a model of π, i.e., a clause $\gamma_i = \neg w_1 \vee \cdots \vee \neg w_n \vee w_{n+1} \vee \cdots \vee w_{n+m}$ of π exists such that $M \not\models \gamma_i$. This implies that $\neg w_1, \ldots, \neg w_n$ occur in B and that $w_{n+1}, \ldots, w_{n+m}$ do not occur in B. Since $\pi' \not\models B$, the first n conditions imply that $\neg \overline{w}_1, \ldots, \neg \overline{w}_n$ do not occur in B. Therefore $\pi' \not\models B \vee g_i$, where g_i is the letter of L' corresponding to γ_i, but this contradicts the hypothesis that $\pi' \models B \vee p$. $\diamond$

Using Fact 4 the above theorem gives an intractability result for ECWA as well. Such derived result will be shown in detail in Section A.1.7.

A.1.6.2 Tractable cases

In this subsection we show that the inference problem under CCWA can be solved in polynomial time both for Definite and for Krom formulae.

Theorem A.1.7 INF-CCWA[DEF,CLAUSE] *can be solved in polynomial time.*

PROOF: Note that the application of the CCWA to $\langle T; P; Q; Z \rangle$ results in adding to T negative literals of the form $\neg p$, where $p \in P^+$ is a CCWA-ffn literal in $\langle T; P; Q; Z \rangle$. It follows that if T is Definite, then $CCWA(T; P; Q; Z)$ is a Horn formula whose size is $O(|T| + |P|)$. We now show that if T is Definite, then the problem of determining whether a given literal $p \in P^+$ is CCWA-ffn in $\langle T; P; Q; Z \rangle$ can be solved in polynomial time. As a consequence, we can compute the formula $CCWA(T; P; Q; Z)$ in polynomial time. Moreover checking if any clause follows from it is a polynomial task.

Let D be the disjunction $\models \neg q_1 \vee \cdots \vee \neg q_n$, where $q_1, \ldots, q_n$ are all the literals of Q. Since T is Definite, no negative clause can be derived from it, hence $T \not\models D$. If $T \models D \vee p$, then p is obviously not CCWA-ffn in $\langle T; P; Q; Z \rangle$. We now show that the converse is true, i.e., we show that if $T \not\models D \vee p$, then p is CCWA-ffn in $\langle T; P; Q; Z \rangle$. Suppose the contrary, i.e., suppose that $T \not\models D \vee p$ and a disjunction B whose literals belong to $P^+ \cup Q^+ \cup Q^-$ exists such that

Algorithm DefCCWA
Input a Definite formula $\langle T; P; Q; Z \rangle$ (where $Q = \{q_1, \ldots, q_n\}$),
and a clause γ
Output true, if $CCWA(T; P; Q; Z) \models \gamma$, false otherwise
begin
   $T' := T$;
   for each $p \in P^+$
   do (* check if p is CCWA-ffn, and if so, add $\neg p$ to T' *)
     if $T \not\models p \vee \neg q_1 \vee \cdots \vee \neg q_n$
     then $T' := T' \cup \{\neg p\}$;
   return $T' \models \gamma$
end.

Algorithm A.5: DefCCWA

both $T \not\models B$ and $T \models B \vee p$. Since $T \not\models D \vee p$ by hypothesis, some positive literal must occur in B, so B has the form $B' \vee p_1 \vee \cdots \vee p_h$, where the literals $p_1, \ldots, p_h$ $(h > 0)$ are positive, while the remaining in B' are negative hence belong to Q^- and B' is sub-clause of D. We observe that the fact that T is Definite implies that the clauses minimally derivable from T contain exactly one positive literal. Now, since by hypothesis $T \not\models B$ and $T \models B \vee p$, it follows that $T \models B' \vee p$, that implies $T \models D \vee p$, so contradicting the former hypothesis. $\diamond$

The above theorem allows us to develop a polynomial time algorithm for checking if $CCWA(T; P; Q; Z) \models \gamma$, where T is Definite, and γ is a clause. The algorithm, called DefCCWA, is reported as Algorithm A.5.

Theorem A.1.8 INF-CCWA[KROM,CLAUSE] *can be solved in polynomial time.*

PROOF: Note that if T is Krom, then $CCWA(T; P; Q; Z)$ is a Krom formula whose size is $O(|T| + |P|)$. We now show that if T is Krom, then the problem of determining whether a given literal $p \in P^+$ is CCWA-ffn in $\langle T; P; Q; Z \rangle$ can be solved in polynomial time. As a consequence, we can compute the formula $CCWA(T; P; Q; Z)$ in polynomial time. Moreover checking if any clause follows from it is a polynomial task.

Consider a literal q belonging to $P^+ \cup Q^+ \cup Q^-$. If both $T \models p \vee q$ and $T \not\models q$, then p is not CCWA-ffn in $\langle T; P; Q; Z \rangle$. We now show that the converse is true, i.e., we show that if for any literal q belonging to $P^+ \cup Q^+ \cup Q^-$, either $T \not\models p \vee q$ or $T \models q$, then p is CCWA-ffn in $\langle T; P; Q; Z \rangle$. Suppose the contrary, i.e., suppose that for any literal q belonging to $P^+ \cup Q^+ \cup Q^-$, either $T \not\models p \vee q$ or $T \models q$, and a disjunction B whose literals belong to $P^+ \cup Q^+ \cup Q^-$ exists such that both $T \not\models B$ and $T \models B \vee p$. We observe that since T is a Krom

---

Algorithm KromCCWA
Input a Krom formula $\langle T; P; Q; Z \rangle$ and a clause γ
Output true if $CCWA(T; P; Q; Z) \models \gamma$, false otherwise
begin
  $T' := T$;
  for each $p \in P^+$
  do begin
      (* check if p is CCWA-ffn *)
      flag := true;
      for each $q \in P^+ \cup Q^+ \cup Q^-$
      do if $(T \models p \vee q) \wedge (T \not\models q)$
        then *flag* := false;
      (* if p is CCWA-ffn then add $\neg p$ to T *)
      if *flag* **then** $T' := T' \cup \{\neg p\}$;
    end;
  return $T' \models \gamma$
end.

Algorithm A.6: KromCCWA

---

formula, the clauses minimally derivable from T contain at most two literals. Therefore, B is simply a literal q belonging to $P^+ \cup Q^+ \cup Q^-$ such that $T \not\models q$ and $T \models p \vee q$. But this contradicts the former hypothesis. $\Diamond$

As mentioned in Section A.1.4.2, the above theorem gives a polynomial result for inference under GCWA.

Corollary A.1.9 INF-GCWA[KROM,CLAUSE] *can be solved in polynomial time.*

PROOF: Use Theorem A.1.8 and Fact 3. $\Diamond$

    Theorem A.1.8 allows us to develop a polynomial time algorithm for checking if $CCWA(T; P; Q; Z) \models \gamma$, where T is Krom, and γ is a clause. The algorithm, called KromCCWA, is reported as Algorithm A.6.

    The only case left for CCWA is inference of clauses for Horn formulae when $Q = \emptyset$, which is indeed a polynomial problem (see Corollary A.1.22, Section A.1.7.2.) This follows from a stronger result (Theorem A.1.19) that we shall see in Section A.1.7.2.

A.1.7   ECWA

In this subsection we analyze the complexity of the inference problem under ECWA and —like in the previous subsections— we distinguish between intractable and tractable cases. In the first part we present five new intractable cases. After this analysis, only four cases remain. They are considered in the second part, where all of them are shown to be solvable in polynomial time.

A.1.7.1   Intractable cases

Three intractability results follow from the analysis performed in Sections A.1.4.1, A.1.5.1 and A.1.6.1.

Corollary A.1.10 INF-ECWA[DHORN,LIT,$Q = Z = \emptyset$] *is co-NP-hard.*

PROOF: Use Theorem A.1.2 and Facts 3 and 4. $\diamond$

Corollary A.1.11 INF-ECWA[2POSK,CLAUSE,$Q = Z = \emptyset$] *is co-NP-hard.*

PROOF: Use Theorem A.1.4 and Fact 2. $\diamond$

Corollary A.1.12 INF-ECWA[HORN,LIT,$Z = \emptyset$] *is co-NP-hard.*

PROOF: In the proof of Theorem A.1.6 the inferred literal $\neg p$ belongs to P^-, hence we can use Fact 2. $\diamond$

As far as the new intractable cases are concerned, we first deal with Definite formulae. In particular, we analyze the case of clause inference in Definite formulae with $Z = \emptyset$, and the case of literal inference in Definite formulae with no restriction on Q and Z.

Theorem A.1.13 INF-ECWA[DEF,CLAUSE,$Z = \emptyset$] *is co-NP-hard.*

PROOF: We reduce the unsatisfiability problem to our problem by exhibiting a polynomial mapping from any CNF formula π to a Definite formula π' on the alphabet L', a partition $\langle P; Q \rangle$ of L' and a clause $\neg K$ such that π is unsatisfiable iff $ECWA(\pi'; P; Q; \emptyset) \models \neg K$.

Let π be a CNF formula on the alphabet L and let L' be $L \cup \{\overline{a} \mid a \in L\} \cup \{\overline{\overline{a}} \mid a \in L\} \cup \{r\}$. We define π' on the alphabet L' according to the following rules:

1. for each letter a of L, there are the clauses $\neg a \vee \overline{\overline{a}}, \neg \overline{a} \vee \overline{\overline{a}}$ in π';

2. for each clause $\neg w_1 \vee \cdots \vee \neg w_n \vee w_{n+1} \vee \cdots \vee w_{n+m}$ in π, there is the clause $\neg \overline{w_1} \vee \cdots \vee \neg \overline{w_n} \vee \neg w_{n+1} \vee \cdots \vee \neg w_{n+m} \vee r$ in π'.

Note that the above mapping from π to π' is clearly polynomial, and π' is a Definite formula. Let us partition the letters of L' into $\langle P; Q; Z \rangle$, where P is the set of letters $\{\overline{\overline{a}} \mid a \in L\} \cup \{r\}$, Q is $L' \setminus P$, and $Z = \emptyset$. Let K be the conjunction $\neg r \bigwedge_{\overline{\overline{a}} \in \{\overline{\overline{a}} \mid a \in L\}} \overline{\overline{a}}$. We prove that:

1. given a model M of π, we can build a disjunction B whose literals belong to $P^+ \cup Q^+ \cup Q^-$ such that both $\pi' \models B \vee K$ and $\pi' \not\models B$;

2. given a disjunction B whose literals belong to $P^+ \cup Q^+ \cup Q^-$ such that both $\pi' \models B \vee K$ and $\pi' \not\models B$, we can build a model M of π.

Therefore, the conjunction K is not ECWA-ffn in $\langle \pi'; P; Q; \emptyset \rangle$ iff π is satisfiable. Taking into account that $ECWA(\pi'; P; Q; \emptyset) \models \neg K$ iff K is ECWA-ffn in $\langle \pi'; P; Q; \emptyset \rangle$, it follows that $ECWA(\pi'; P; Q; \emptyset) \models \neg K$ iff π is unsatisfiable.

Proof of 1: let M be a model of π, and let B be a clause on the alphabet L' defined as follows:

r is in B;
for each letter a of L
    if $M \models a$, then $\neg \bar{a}$ is in B
           else $\neg a$ is in B.

Note first of all that all the literals of B belong to $P^+ \cup Q^-$. Moreover, for each a, either $\neg a$ or $\neg \bar{a}$ is in B. Therefore, It is easy to prove that $\pi' \models B \vee K$. We will now prove that $\pi' \not\models B$. Suppose that $\pi' \models B$. This implies that a clause $\gamma = \neg w_1 \vee \cdots \vee \neg w_n \vee w_{n+1} \vee \cdots \vee w_{n+m}$ of π exists such that all the literals $\neg \overline{w_1}, \ldots, \neg \overline{w_n}, \neg w_{n+1}, \cdots, \neg w_{n+m}$ of the clause of π' corresponding to γ occur in B. Therefore, the following conditions hold: $M \models w_1, \ldots, M \models w_n, M \not\models w_{n+1}, \ldots, M \not\models w_{n+m}$. These conditions imply that $M \not\models \gamma$, thus contradicting the hypothesis that M is a model of π.

Proof of 2: let B be a disjunction whose literals belong to $P^+ \cup Q^+ \cup Q^-$ such that both $\pi' \models B \vee K$ and $\pi' \not\models B$. We can easily show that r occurs in B, and for each letter a of L, either $\neg a$ or $\neg \bar{a}$ occurs in B. We build an interpretation M of π as follows:

for each letter a of L
    if $\neg a$ occurs in B, then $M \models \neg a$

Note first of all that M assigns exactly one truth value to each letter of L. Suppose that M is not a model of π, i.e., a clause $\gamma = \neg w_1 \vee \cdots \vee \neg w_n \vee w_{n+1} \vee \cdots \vee w_{n+m}$ of π exists such that $M \not\models \gamma$. This implies that all the literals $\neg \overline{w_1}, \ldots, \neg \overline{w_n}, \neg w_{n+1}, \ldots, \neg w_{n+m}$ occur in B. Since r occurs in B, it follows that $\pi' \models B$, contradicting the above hypothesis. $\diamond$

Theorem A.1.14 INF-ECWA[DEF,LIT] *is co-NP-hard.*

PROOF: We refer to the proof of Theorem A.1.13, and reduce the problem of determining if $ECWA(T; P; Q; \emptyset) \models \gamma$, where T is a Definite formula and γ is a clause, to our problem.

Let $L, L', r, K, P, Q, \pi, \pi'$ be as in the proof of Theorem A.1.13, and let L'' be $L' \cup \{z, p\}$, with z, p not appearing in L'. We define π'' on the alphabet L'' according to the following rules:

1. each clause of π' is a clause of π'';

2. for each literal a_i of $L = \{a_1, \ldots, a_h\}$, there is the clause $\bar{\bar{a}}_i \vee \neg z$ in π'';

3. the clause $\neg z \vee \neg r \vee p$ is in π'';

Note that the above mapping from π' to π'' is clearly polynomial, and π'' is a Definite formula. Let P' be the set of letters $P \cup \{p\}$, and Z be the set $L'' \setminus (P' \cup Q)$, that is $Z = \{z\}$. Note also that p is ECWA-ffn in $\langle \pi''; P'; Q; Z \rangle$. We will prove that:

1. $ECWA(\pi''; P'; Q; Z) \models \neg z$ iff K is ECWA-ffn in $\langle \pi''; P'; Q; Z \rangle$;

2. K is ECWA-ffn in $\langle \pi''; P'; Q; Z \rangle$ iff K is ECWA-ffn in $\langle \pi'; P; Q; \emptyset \rangle$.

Therefore, $ECWA(\pi''; P'; Q; Z) \models \neg z$ iff K is ECWA-ffn in $\langle \pi'; P; Q; \emptyset \rangle$. Taking into account that K is ECWA-ffn in $\langle \pi'; P; Q; \emptyset \rangle$ iff π is unsatisfiable (see Theorem A.1.13), it follows that $ECWA(\pi''; P'; Q; Z) \models \neg z$ iff π is unsatisfiable.

Proof of 1 (if part): suppose that $K = \neg r \wedge \bar{\bar{a}}_1 \wedge \cdots \wedge \bar{\bar{a}}_h$ is ECWA-ffn in $\langle \pi''; P'; Q; Z \rangle$. It follows that, for each $(P'; Z)$-minimal model M of π'', $M \models r \vee \neg \bar{\bar{a}}_1 \vee \cdots \vee \neg \bar{\bar{a}}_h$. Since $\bar{\bar{a}}_1 \vee \neg z, \ldots, \bar{\bar{a}}_h \vee \neg z$ are clauses of π'', we have that $M \models \bar{\bar{a}}_1 \vee \neg z, \ldots, M \models \bar{\bar{a}}_h \vee \neg z$. Since p is ECWA-ffn in $\langle \pi''; P'; Q; Z \rangle$, and $\neg z \vee \neg r \vee p$ is a clause of π'', $M \models \neg z \vee \neg r$ and therefore $M \models \neg z$, implying that $ECWA(\pi''; P'; Q; Z) \models \neg z$.

Proof of 1 (only if part): suppose that $ECWA(\pi''; P'; Q; Z) \models \neg z$. We will prove that no $(P'; Z)$-minimal model M of π'' exists such that $M \models \neg r \wedge \bar{\bar{a}}_1 \wedge \cdots \wedge \bar{\bar{a}}_h$, thus proving that $K = \neg r \wedge \bar{\bar{a}}_1 \wedge \cdots \wedge \bar{\bar{a}}_h$ is ECWA-ffn in $\langle \pi''; P'; Q; Z \rangle$. Suppose that such an M exists. Note that $ECWA(\pi''; P'; Q; Z) \models \neg z$ implies $M \models \neg z$. Moreover, since p is ECWA-ffn in $\langle \pi''; P'; Q; Z \rangle$, it follows that $M \models \neg p$. We build an interpretation M' of π'' as follows:

$M' \models z$;
$M' \models \neg p$;
for each letter c of L'
$\quad$ if $M \models c$ then $M' \models c$
$\quad\quad\quad$ else $M' \models \neg c$.

Note first of all that M' assigns exactly one truth value to each letter of L''. Moreover, since M' satisfies all the clauses of π'', M' is a model of π''. Since M' differs from M only in the interpretation of literals in the set Z, it follows that, if M is a $(P'; Z)$-minimal model of π'', then M' is a $(P'; Z)$-minimal model of π'', thus contradicting the hypothesis that $ECWA(\pi''; P'; Q; Z) \models \neg z$.

Proof of 2 (if part): suppose that K is not ECWA-ffn in $\langle \pi''; P'; Q; Z \rangle$. Then a disjunction B whose literals belong to $P'^+ \cup Q^+ \cup Q^-$ exists such that both $\pi'' \models B \vee K$ and $\pi'' \not\models B$. We assume without loss of generality that p does not occur in B, and therefore all the literals of B belong to $P^+ \cup Q^+ \cup Q^-$. For the monotonicity of the relation $\models$, $\pi' \not\models B$. We will now prove that $\pi' \models B \vee K$, thus proving that K is not ECWA-ffn in $\langle \pi'; P; Q; \emptyset \rangle$. The condition $\pi'' \models B \vee K$ is equivalent to $\pi' \wedge (\bar{\bar{a}}_1 \vee \neg z) \wedge \cdots \wedge (\bar{\bar{a}}_h \vee \neg z) \wedge (\neg z \vee \neg r \vee p) \models B \vee K$, that, for the deduction theorem, is equivalent to $\pi' \models (\neg\bar{\bar{a}}_1 \wedge z) \vee \cdots \vee (\neg\bar{\bar{a}}_h \wedge z) \vee (z \wedge r \wedge \neg p) \vee B \vee K$. This condition implies that $\pi' \models z \vee B \vee K$ and therefore, since z does not occur in π', $\pi' \models B \vee K$.

Proof of 2 (only if part): suppose that K is not ECWA-ffn in $\langle \pi'; P; Q; \emptyset \rangle$. Then a disjunction B whose literals belong to $P^+ \cup Q^+ \cup Q^-$ exists such that both $\pi' \models B \vee K$ and $\pi' \not\models B$. For the monotonicity of the relation $\models$, $\pi'' \models B \vee K$. We will now prove that $\pi'' \not\models B$, thus proving that K is not ECWA-ffn in $\langle \pi''; P'; Q; Z \rangle$. Suppose that $\pi'' \models B$. This implies that $\pi' \wedge (\bar{a}_1 \vee \neg z) \wedge \cdots \wedge (\bar{a}_h \vee \neg z) \wedge (\neg z \vee \neg r \vee p) \models B$, that, for the deduction theorem, implies $\pi' \models (\neg\bar{\bar{a}}_1 \wedge z) \vee \cdots \vee (\neg\bar{\bar{a}}_h \wedge z) \vee (z \wedge r \wedge \neg p) \vee B$. This condition implies that $\pi' \models z \vee B$, and therefore, since z does not occur in π', $\pi' \models B$, contradicting the above hypothesis. $\diamond$

The next case we consider is the literal inference in 2-positive-Krom formulae with $Q = \emptyset$.

Theorem A.1.15 INF-ECWA[2POSK,LIT,$Q = \emptyset$] *is co-NP-hard.*

PROOF: We refer to the proof of Theorem A.1.4, and reduce the problem of determining if $EGCWA(T) \models \gamma$, where T is a 2-positive-Krom formula and γ is a clause, to our problem. Note first of all that, taking into account Fact 2, Theorem A.1.4 implies that INF-ECWA[2POSK,CLAUSE,$Q = Z = \emptyset$] is a co-NP-hard problem.

Let $L, L', g_1, \ldots, g_h, K, \pi, \pi'$ be as in the proof of Theorem A.1.4 and let L'' be $L' \cup \{z\}$, with z not appearing in L'. We define π'' on the alphabet L'' according to the following rules:

1. each clause of π' is a clause of π'';

2. for each literal g_i $(1 \leq i \leq h)$, there is the clause $g_i \vee z$ in π''.

Note that the above mapping from π' to π'' is clearly polynomial, and π'' is a 2-positive-Krom formula. Let P be the set of letters L', and Z be the set $L'' \setminus L'$, i.e., $Z = \{z\}$. We will prove that:

1. $ECWA(\pi''; P; \emptyset; Z) \models z$ iff K is ECWA-ffn in $\langle \pi''; P; \emptyset; Z \rangle$;

2. K is ECWA-ffn in $\langle \pi''; P; \emptyset; Z \rangle$ iff K is EGCWA-ffn in π'.

Therefore, $ECWA(\pi''; P; \emptyset; Z) \models z$ iff K is EGCWA-ffn in π'. Taking into account that K is EGCWA-ffn in π' iff π is unsatisfiable (see Theorem A.1.4), it follows that $ECWA(\pi''; P; \emptyset; Z) \models z$ iff π is unsatisfiable.

Proof of 1 (if part): suppose that $K = g_1 \wedge \ldots \wedge g_h$ is ECWA-ffn in $\langle \pi''; P; \emptyset; Z \rangle$. It follows that, for each $(P; Z)$-minimal model M of π'', $M \models \neg g_1 \vee \ldots \vee \neg g_h$. Since $g_1 \vee z, \ldots, g_h \vee z$ are clauses of π'', we have that $M \models g_1 \vee z, \ldots, M \models g_h \vee z$. Therefore $M \models z$, implying that $ECWA(\pi''; P; \emptyset; Z) \models z$.

Proof of 1 (only if part): suppose that $ECWA(\pi''; P; \emptyset; Z) \models z$. We will prove that no $(P; Z)$-minimal model M of π'' exists such that $M \models g_1 \wedge \ldots \wedge g_h$, thus proving that $K = g_1 \wedge \ldots \wedge g_h$ is ECWA-ffn in $\langle \pi''; P; \emptyset; Z \rangle$. Suppose that such an M exists. Since $ECWA(\pi''; P; \emptyset; Z) \models z$, $M \models z$. We build an interpretation M' of π'' using the following rules:

$M' \models \neg z$;
for each letter c of L'
    if $M \models c$ then $M' \models c$

Note first of all that M' assigns exactly one truth value to each letter of L''. Moreover, since M' satisfies all the clauses of π'', M' is a model of π''. Since M' differs from M only in the interpretation of literals in the set Z, it follows that, if M is a $(P; Z)$-minimal model of π'', then M' is a $(P; Z)$-minimal model of π'', thus contradicting the hypothesis that $ECWA(\pi''; P; \emptyset; Z) \not\models z$.

    Proof of 2 (if part): suppose that K is not ECWA-ffn in $\langle \pi''; P; \emptyset; Z \rangle$. Then a disjunction B whose literals belong to P^+ exists such that both $\pi'' \models B \vee K$ and $\pi'' \not\models B$. Note that all the literals of B are positive literals of L'. Moreover, for the monotonicity of the relation $\models$, $\pi' \not\models B$. We will now prove that $\pi' \models B \vee K$, thus proving that K is not EGCWA-ffn in π'. The condition $\pi'' \models B \vee K$ is equivalent to $\pi' \wedge (g_1 \vee z) \wedge \cdots \wedge (g_h \vee z) \models B \vee K$, that, for the deduction theorem, is equivalent to $\pi' \models (\neg g_1 \wedge \neg z) \vee \cdots \vee (\neg g_h \wedge \neg z) \vee B \vee K$. This condition implies that $\pi' \models \neg z \vee B \vee K$ and therefore, since z does not occur in π', $\pi' \models B \vee K$.

    Proof of 2 (only if part): suppose that K is not EGCWA-ffn in π'. Then a disjunction B of positive literals of L' exists such that both $\pi' \models B \vee K$ and $\pi' \not\models B$. Note that all the literals of B belong to P^+. Moreover, for the monotonicity of the relation $\models$, $\pi'' \models B \vee K$. We now prove that $\pi'' \not\models B$, thus showing K is not ECWA-ffn in $\langle \pi''; P; \emptyset; Z \rangle$. Suppose that $\pi'' \models B$; this implies that $\pi' \wedge (g_1 \vee z) \wedge \cdots \wedge (g_h \vee z) \models B$, that, for the deduction theorem, implies that $\pi' \models (\neg g_1 \wedge \neg z) \vee \cdots \vee (\neg g_h \wedge \neg z) \vee B$. The last condition implies that $\pi' \models \neg z \vee B$, and therefore, since z does not occur in π', $\pi' \models B$, contradicting the above hypothesis. $\diamond$

Finally, we consider the case of HornKrom formulae. We first deal with clause inference in HornKrom formulae with $Z = \emptyset$, and then with literal inference in HornKrom formulae with no restrictions on Q and Z.

Theorem A.1.16 INF-ECWA[HK,CLAUSE,$Z = \emptyset$] *is co-NP-hard.*

PROOF: We reduce the unsatisfiability problem to our problem by exhibiting a polynomial mapping from any CNF formula π to a HornKrom formula π' on the alphabet L', a partition $\langle P; Q \rangle$ of L' and a clause $\neg K$, such that π is unsatisfiable iff $ECWA(\pi'; P; Q; \emptyset) \models \neg K$.

    Let π be a CNF formula on the alphabet L and let L' be $L \cup \{\overline{a} \mid a \in L\} \cup \{g_i \mid \gamma_i \text{ is a clause of } \pi\}$. We define π' on the alphabet L' according to the following rules:

    1. for each letter a of L, there is a clause $\neg a \vee \neg \overline{a}$ in π';

2. for each clause $\gamma_i = \neg w_1 \vee \ldots \vee \neg w_n \vee w_{n+1} \vee \cdots \vee w_{n+m}$ in π, there are $n + m$ clauses $\neg \overline{w_1} \vee g_i, \ldots, \neg \overline{w_n} \vee g_i, \neg w_{n+1} \vee g_i, \ldots, \neg w_{n+m} \vee g_i$ in π'.

Note that the above mapping from π to π' is clearly polynomial, and π' is a HornKrom formula. Let K be the conjunction $g_1 \wedge \cdots \wedge g_h$, where $g_1, \ldots, g_h$ are all the letters of L' corresponding to the clauses in π. Let P be the set of letters $\{g_i \mid \gamma_i$ is a clause of $\pi\}$, and Q the set of letters $L' \setminus P$. We will prove that:

1. given a model M of π, we can build a disjunction B whose literals belong to $P^+ \cup Q^+ \cup Q^-$ such that both $\pi' \models B \vee K$ and $\pi' \not\models B$;

2. given a disjunction B whose literals belong to $P^+ \cup Q^+ \cup Q^-$ such that both $\pi' \models B \vee K$ and $\pi' \not\models B$, we can build a model M of π.

Therefore, the conjunction K is not ECWA-ffn in $\langle \pi'; P; Q; \emptyset \rangle$ iff π is satisfiable. Taking into account that $\neg K$ is a disjunction, and $ECWA(\pi'; P; Q; \emptyset) \models \neg K$ iff K is ECWA-ffn in $\langle \pi'; P; Q; \emptyset \rangle$, it follows that $ECWA(\pi'; P; Q; \emptyset) \models \neg K$ iff π is unsatisfiable.

Proof of 1: let M be a model of π, and let B be a clause on the alphabet L' defined as follows:

for each letter a of L
    if $M \models a$, then $\neg a$ is in B;
    if $M \models \neg a$, then $\neg \overline{a}$ is in B.

Note first of all that all the literals of B belong to Q^-. Since for each letter a of L, $\neg a, \neg \overline{a}$ cannot occur together in B, $\pi' \not\models B$. Moreover, since for each clause $\gamma_i = \neg w_1 \vee \cdots \vee \neg w_n \vee w_{n+1} \vee \cdots \vee w_{n+m}$ in π it holds that $M \models \gamma_i$, at least one literal among $\neg \overline{w}_1, \ldots, \neg \overline{w}_n, \neg w_{n+1}, \ldots, \neg w_{n+m}$ occurs in B. Therefore for each i $(1 \leq i \leq h)$, it holds that $\pi' \models B \vee g_i$, where g_i corresponds to γ_i. This implies that $\pi' \models B \vee K$.

Proof of 2: let B be a disjunction whose literals belong to $P^+ \cup Q^+ \cup Q^-$ such that both $\pi' \models B \vee K$ and $\pi' \not\models B$. We build an interpretation M of π using the following rule:

for each letter a of L
    if $\neg a$ occurs in B, then $M \models a$
            else $M \models \neg a$.

Note first of all that M assigns exactly one truth value to each letter of L. Suppose that M is not a model of π and a clause $\gamma_i = \neg w_1 \vee \cdots \vee \neg w_n \vee w_{n+1} \vee \cdots \vee w_{n+m}$ of π exists such that $M \not\models \gamma_i$. This implies that $\neg w_1, \ldots, \neg w_n$ occur in B and that $w_{n+1}, \ldots, w_{n+m}$ do not occur in B. Since $\pi' \not\models B$, the first conditions imply that $\neg \overline{w}_1, \ldots, \neg \overline{w}_n$ do not occur in B. Therefore $\pi' \not\models B \vee g_i$, where g_i corresponds to γ_i, but this contradicts the hypothesis that $\pi' \models B \vee K$.

$\diamond$

Theorem A.1.17 INF-ECWA[HK,LIT] *is co-NP-hard.*

PROOF: We refer to the proof of Theorem A.1.16, reducing the problem of determining if $ECWA(T; P; Q; \emptyset) \models \gamma$, where T is a HornKrom formula and γ is a clause, to our problem.

Let $L, L', g_1, \ldots, g_h, K, P, Q, \pi, \pi'$ be as in the proof of Theorem A.1.16 and let L'' be $L' \cup \{z\}$, with z not appearing in L'. We define π'' on the alphabet L'' according to the following rules:

1. each clause of π' is a clause of π'';

2. for each literal g_i $(1 \leq i \leq h)$, there is the clause $g_i \vee \neg z$ in π''.

Note that the above mapping from π' to π'' is clearly polynomial, and π'' is a HornKrom formula. Let Z be the set of letters $L'' \setminus (P \cup Q)$, i.e., $Z = \{z\}$. We will prove that:

1. $ECWA(\pi''; P; Q; Z) \models \neg z$ iff K is ECWA-ffn in $\langle \pi''; P; Q; Z \rangle$;

2. K is ECWA-ffn in $\langle \pi''; P; Q; Z \rangle$ iff K is ECWA-ffn in $\langle \pi'; P; Q; \emptyset \rangle$.

Therefore, $ECWA(\pi''; P; Q; Z) \models \neg z$ iff K is ECWA-ffn in $\langle \pi'; P; Q; \emptyset \rangle$. Taking into account that K is ECWA-ffn in $\langle \pi'; P; Q; \emptyset \rangle$ iff π is unsatisfiable (see Theorem A.1.16), it follows that $ECWA(\pi''; P; Q; Z) \models \neg z$ iff π is unsatisfiable.

Proof of 1 (if part): suppose that $K = g_1 \wedge \ldots \wedge g_h$ is ECWA-ffn in $\langle \pi''; P; Q; Z \rangle$. It follows that, for each $(P; Z)$-minimal model M of π'', $M \models \neg g_1 \vee \ldots \vee \neg g_h$. Since $g_1 \vee \neg z, \ldots, g_h \vee \neg z$ are clauses of π'', we have that $M \models g_1 \vee \neg z, \ldots, M \models g_h \vee \neg z$. Therefore $M \models \neg z$, implying that $ECWA(\pi''; P; Q; Z) \models \neg z$.

Proof of 1 (only if part): suppose that $ECWA(\pi''; P; Q; Z) \models \neg z$. We will prove that no $(P; Z)$-minimal model M of π'' exists such that $M \models g_1 \wedge \ldots \wedge g_h$, thus proving that $K = g_1 \wedge \ldots \wedge g_h$ is ECWA-ffn in $\langle \pi''; P; Q; Z \rangle$. Suppose that such an M exists. Since $ECWA(\pi''; P; Q; Z) \models \neg z$, it follows that $M \models \neg z$. We build an interpretation M' of π'' using the following rules:

$M' \models z$;
for each letter c of L'
   if $M \models c$ then $M' \models c$

Note first of all that M' assigns exactly one truth value to each letter of L''. Moreover, since M' satisfies all the clauses of π'', M' is a model of π''. Since M' differs from M only in the interpretation of literals in the set Z, it follows that, if M is a $(P; Z)$-minimal model of π'', then M' is a $(P; Z)$-minimal model of π'', thus contradicting the hypothesis that $ECWA(\pi''; P; Q; Z) \models \neg z$.

Proof of 2 (if part): suppose that K is not ECWA-ffn in $\langle \pi''; P; Q; Z \rangle$. Then a disjunction B whose literals belong to $P^+ \cup Q^+ \cup Q^-$ exists such that both $\pi'' \models B \vee K$ and $\pi'' \not\models B$. For the monotonicity of the relation $\models$, $\pi' \not\models B$. We will now prove that $\pi' \models B \vee K$, thus proving that K is not ECWA-ffn in $\langle \pi'; P; Q; \emptyset \rangle$. The condition $\pi'' \models B \vee K$ is equivalent to $\pi' \wedge (g_1 \vee \neg z) \wedge \cdots \wedge (g_h \vee \neg z) \models B \vee K$, that, for the deduction theorem, is equivalent to $\pi' \models (\neg g_1 \wedge z) \vee \cdots \vee (\neg g_h \wedge z) \vee B \vee K$. The last condition implies that $\pi' \models z \vee B \vee K$ and therefore, since z does not occur in π', $\pi' \models B \vee K$.

Proof of 2 (only if part): suppose that K is not ECWA-ffn in $\langle \pi'; P; Q; \emptyset \rangle$. Then a disjunction B whose literals belong to $P^+ \cup Q^+ \cup Q^-$ exists such that both $\pi' \models B \vee K$ and $\pi' \not\models B$. For the monotonicity of the relation $\models$, $\pi'' \models B \vee K$. We will now prove that $\pi'' \not\models B$, thus proving that K is not ECWA-ffn in $\langle \pi''; P; Q; Z \rangle$. Suppose that $\pi'' \models B$. This implies that $\pi' \wedge (g_1 \vee \neg z) \wedge \cdots \wedge (g_h \vee \neg z) \models B$, that, for the deduction theorem, implies that $\pi' \models (\neg g_1 \wedge z) \vee \cdots \vee (\neg g_h \wedge z) \vee B$. The last condition implies that $\pi' \models z \vee B$ and therefore, since z does not occur in π', $\pi' \models B$, contradicting the former hypothesis. $\diamond$

A.1.7.2 Tractable cases

In this subsection we deal with the classes of formulae where ECWA and circumscription can be computed in polynomial time. To the best of our knowledge, the results presented here are the first tractability results on ECWA and circumscription, with the exception of the polynomial time algorithm for CWA in Horn formulae.

We first analyze two tractable cases of literal inference, concerning Definite formulae with $Z = \emptyset$, and Krom formulae with $Z = \emptyset$, respectively.

Theorem A.1.18 INF-ECWA[DEF,LIT,$Z = \emptyset$] *can be solved in polynomial time.*

PROOF: Note first of all that, by Fact 5, if l belongs to $P^+ \cup Q^+ \cup Q^-$, then $ECWA(T; P; Q; \emptyset) \models l$ iff $T \models l$. If l belongs to P^-, then, by Fact 4, $ECWA(T; P; Q; \emptyset) \models l$ iff $\neg l$ is CCWA-ffn in $\langle T; P; Q; \emptyset \rangle$. Checking if $\neg l$ is CCWA-ffn in $\langle T; P; Q; \emptyset \rangle$ can be done in polynomial time (see Theorem A.1.7.) $\diamond$

Theorem A.1.19 INF-ECWA[KROM,LIT,$Z = \emptyset$] *can be solved in polynomial time.*

PROOF: Note first of all that, by Fact 5, if l belongs to $P^+ \cup Q^+ \cup Q^-$, then $ECWA(T; P; Q; \emptyset) \models l$ iff $T \models l$. If l belongs to P^-, then, by Fact 4, $ECWA(T; P; Q; \emptyset) \models l$ iff $\neg l$ is CCWA-ffn in $\langle T; P; Q; \emptyset \rangle$. Checking if $\neg l$ is CCWA-ffn in $\langle T; P; Q; \emptyset \rangle$ can be done in polynomial time (see Theorem A.1.8.) $\diamond$

As mentioned in Section A.1.5.2, the above theorem gives a polynomial result for inference under EGCWA.

Corollary A.1.20 INF-EGCWA[KROM,LIT] *can be solved in polynomial time.*

PROOF: Use Theorem A.1.19 and Fact 2. $\diamond$

We now show that clause inference in Horn formulae with $Q = \emptyset$ is solvable in polynomial time.

Theorem A.1.21 INF-ECWA[HORN,CLAUSE,$Q = \emptyset$] *can be solved in polynomial time.*

PROOF: Since $Q = \emptyset$, the ECWA-ffn formulae are constituted by literals from P. By Fact 6, we can consider, without loss of generality, only those ECWA-ffn formulae which are conjunction of literals from P^+. Let $p_1, \ldots, p_n$ be n literals from P^+. We prove that:

1. for each i $(1 \leq i \leq n)$ p_i is ECWA-ffn in $\langle T; P; \emptyset; Z \rangle$ iff $T \not\models p_i$;

2. $p_1 \wedge \cdots \wedge p_n$ is ECWA-ffn in $\langle T; P; \emptyset; Z \rangle$ iff at least one p_i $(1 \leq i \leq n)$ is ECWA-ffn in $\langle T; P; \emptyset; Z \rangle$.

Therefore, the application of the ECWA to $\langle T; P; \emptyset; Z \rangle$ results always in adding to T unit clauses of the form $\neg p$, where $p \in P^+$ is an ECWA-ffn literal in $\langle T; P; \emptyset; Z \rangle$ (point 2.) Note that this fact implies that applying the ECWA to $\langle T; P; \emptyset; Z \rangle$ is equivalent to applying the CCWA to the same formula. It follows that $ECWA(T; P; \emptyset; Z)$ is a Horn formula whose size is $O(|T| + |P|)$. Moreover, determining whether a given literal $p \in P^+$ is ECWA-ffn in $\langle T; P; \emptyset; Z \rangle$ can be done in polynomial time by checking whether $T \models p$ holds (point 1.)

Proof of 1: the only if part is trivial. We now show that the if part is true, that is, if for each $p \in P^+, T \not\models p$, then p is ECWA-ffn in $\langle T; P; \emptyset; Z \rangle$. Suppose the contrary, that is $T \not\models p$, and a disjunction B whose literals belong to P^+ exists such that both $T \not\models B$ and $T \models B \vee p$. Since T is a Horn formula, the clauses minimally derivable from T contain at most one positive literal. Therefore, if both $T \not\models B$ and $T \models B \vee p$, then $T \models p$, thus contradicting the above hypothesis.

Proof of 2: the if part is trivial. We now show that the only if part is true, that is, if for each i $(1 \leq i \leq n)$ p_i is not ECWA-ffn in $\langle T; P; \emptyset; Z \rangle$, then $p_1 \wedge \cdots \wedge p_n$ is not ECWA-ffn in $\langle T; P; \emptyset; Z \rangle$. If each p_i $(1 \leq i \leq n)$ is not ECWA-ffn in $\langle T; P; \emptyset; Z \rangle$, then $T \models p_i$ (see proof of point 1.) Therefore $T \models p_1 \wedge \cdots \wedge p_n$, and $p_1 \wedge \cdots \wedge p_n$ is clearly not ECWA-ffn in $\langle T; P; \emptyset; Z \rangle$. ◇

As mentioned in Section A.1.6.2, the above theorem gives a polynomial result for inference under CCWA.

Corollary A.1.22 INF-CCWA[HORN,CLAUSE,$Q = \emptyset$] *can be solved in polynomial time.*

PROOF: As shown in the proof of Theorem A.1.21 above, applying the ECWA to $\langle T; P; \emptyset; Z \rangle$ where T is Horn, is equivalent to applying the CCWA to the same formula. ◇

The whole method for checking if $ECWA(T; P; \emptyset; Z) \models \gamma$ is represented by Algorithm A.7 (HornECWA), which runs in polynomial time. According to Corollary A.1.22, the same algorithm can be used for checking if $CCWA(T; P; \emptyset; Z) \models \gamma$.

Algorithm HornECWA
Input a Horn formula $\langle T; P; \emptyset; Z \rangle$ and a clause γ
Output true, if $ECWA(T; P; \emptyset; Z) \models \gamma$, false otherwise
begin
  $T' := T;$
  for each $p \in P^+$
  do (* if p is ECWA-ffn then $\neg p$ is added to T *)
    if $T \not\models p$
    then $T' := T' \cup \{\neg p\};$
  return $T' \models \gamma$
end.

Algorithm A.7: HornECWA

In the rest of this subsection we concentrate our attention to the last problem left for ECWA, namely inference in HornKrom$^-$ formulae. In the following we make use of the fact that the the clauses minimally derivable from a HornKrom$^-$ formula contain at most two literals. At most one of such literals is positive, and at most one is negative.

We show that ECWA inference is polynomial for HornKrom$^-$ formulae. In order to prove this result, we need four lemmas.

Lemma A.1.23 *Let $\langle T; P; Q; Z \rangle$ be a HornKrom$^-$ formula, and let $k = p_1 \wedge \cdots \wedge p_l \wedge \neg q_1 \wedge \cdots \wedge \neg q_m \wedge q_{m+1} \wedge \cdots \wedge q_{m+n}$ be a conjunction of literals, with $\{p_1, \ldots, p_l\} \subseteq P$, and $\{q_1, \ldots, q_m, q_{m+1}, \ldots, q_{m+n}\} \subseteq Q$. Then k is ECWA-ffn in $\langle T; P; Q; Z \rangle$ iff either $k' = p_1 \wedge \cdots \wedge p_l \wedge \neg q_1 \wedge \cdots \wedge \neg q_m$ or $k'' = \neg q_1 \wedge \cdots \wedge \neg q_m \wedge q_{m+1} \wedge \cdots \wedge q_{m+n}$ is ECWA-ffn in $\langle T; P; Q; Z \rangle$.*

PROOF: The *if* part is trivial. For the *only if* part, we suppose that k is ECWA-ffn in $\langle T; P; Q; Z \rangle$ and that both k' and k'' are not ECWA-ffn in $\langle T; P; Q; Z \rangle$, and show that this leads to a contradiction.

If k' is not ECWA-ffn in $\langle T; P; Q; Z \rangle$, then a clause B whose literals belong to $P^+ \cup Q^+ \cup Q^-$ exists such that both $T \models B \vee k'$ and $T \not\models B$. The first condition implies that the following conditions hold: $T \models B \vee p_1, \ldots, T \models B \vee p_l, T \models B \vee \neg q_1, \ldots, T \models B \vee \neg q_m$. Note that we can assume, without loss of generality, that $T \not\models p_1, \ldots, T \not\models p_l, T \not\models \neg q_1, \ldots, T \not\models \neg q_m$ (otherwise we can delete from k' every literal which is derivable from T, and the resulting conjunction is ECWA-ffn in $\langle T; P; Q; Z \rangle$ iff the original is.) Therefore, the above conditions imply that:

1. at least l negative literals $\neg r_1, \ldots, \neg r_l$ –possibly not distinct– occur in B such that $T \models \neg r_1 \vee p_1, \ldots, T \models \neg r_l \vee p_l$; note that $\{\neg r_1, \ldots, \neg r_l\} \subseteq Q^-$;

2. at least m positive literals $s_1, \ldots, s_m$ —possibly not distinct— occur in B such that $T \models s_1 \vee \neg q_1, \ldots, T \models s_m \vee \neg q_m$.

We now prove that $T \models \neg r_1 \vee \cdots \vee \neg r_l \vee q_1 \vee \cdots \vee q_m$. This implies that there exist i, j $(1 \leq i \leq l, 1 \leq j \leq m)$ such that $T \models \neg r_i \vee q_j$. Since $T \models s_j \vee \neg q_j$, then $T \models s_j \vee \neg r_i$, and the hypothesis that $T \not\models B$ is contradicted.

Note first of all that $T \not\models \neg k''$, otherwise k'' is ECWA-ffn in $\langle T; P; Q; Z \rangle$ and the former hypothesis is contradicted. Note also that $\neg k'' = q_1 \vee \cdots \vee q_m \vee \neg q_{m+1} \vee \cdots \vee \neg q_{m+n}$. Let C be the disjunction $\neg r_1 \vee \cdots \vee \neg r_l \vee \neg k''$. Note that all the literals of C belong to $Q^+ \cup Q^-$ and $T \models C \vee k$. Since k is ECWA-ffn in $\langle T; P; Q; Z \rangle$, it follows that $T \models C$, and therefore $T \models \neg r_1 \vee \cdots \vee \neg r_l \vee q_1 \vee \cdots q_m$. $\diamond$

Lemma A.1.24 *Let $\langle T; P; Q; Z \rangle$ be a HornKrom⁻ formula, and let $k = p_1 \wedge \cdots \wedge p_l \wedge \neg q_1 \wedge \cdots \wedge \neg q_m$ be a conjunction with $\{p_1, \ldots, p_l\} \subseteq P$ and $\{q_1, \ldots, q_m\} \subseteq Q$. Then k is ECWA-ffn in $\langle T; P; Q; Z \rangle$ iff at least one of the conjunctions $k_i = p_i \wedge \neg q_1 \wedge \cdots \wedge \neg q_m$ $(1 \leq i \leq l)$ is ECWA-ffn in $\langle T; P; Q; Z \rangle$.*

PROOF: The *if* part is trivial. For the *only if* part, we suppose that k is ECWA-ffn in $\langle T; P; Q; Z \rangle$ and that each k_i $(1 \leq i \leq l)$ is not ECWA-ffn in $\langle T; P; Q; Z \rangle$ and show that this leads to a contradiction.

If k_i $(1 \leq i \leq l)$ is not ECWA-ffn in $\langle T; P; Q; Z \rangle$, then a clause B_i whose literals belong to $P^+ \cup Q^+ \cup Q^-$ exists such that both $T \models B_i \vee k_i$ and $T \not\models B_i$. The first condition implies that $T \models B_i \vee p_i, T \models B_i \vee \neg q_1, \ldots, T \models B_i \vee \neg q_m$. Note that we can assume, without loss of generality, that $T \not\models p_i, T \not\models \neg q_1, \ldots, T \not\models \neg q_m$. Therefore, the above conditions imply that:

1. at least one negative literal $\neg r_i$ occurs in B_i such that $T \models \neg r_i \vee p_i$; note that $\neg r_i \in Q^-$;

2. at least m positive literals $s_1^i, \ldots, s_m^i$ —possibly not distinct— occur in B_i such that $T \models s_1^i \vee \neg q_1, \ldots, T \models s_m^i \vee \neg q_m$.

Let B be the disjunction $\neg r_1 \vee \cdots \vee \neg r_l \vee q_1 \vee \cdots q_m$, where each r_i $(1 \leq i \leq l)$ corresponds to k_i. Since $T \models B \vee k$, and k is ECWA-ffn in $\langle T; P; Q; Z \rangle$, $T \models B$. This implies that there exist i, j $(1 \leq i \leq l, 1 \leq j \leq m)$ such that $T \models \neg r_i \vee q_j$. We noted before that the hypothesis that k_i $(1 \leq i \leq l)$ is not ECWA-ffn in $\langle T; P; Q; Z \rangle$ implies that a literal s_j^i $(1 \leq j \leq m)$ exists such that $T \models s_j^i \vee \neg q_j$. This implies that $T \models s_j^i \vee \neg r_i$, thus contradicting the hypothesis that $T \not\models B_i$ holds. $\diamond$

Lemma A.1.25 *Let $\langle T; P; Q; Z \rangle$ be a HornKrom⁻ formula and let γ be a clause. Then $ECWA(T; P; Q; Z) \models \gamma$ iff at least one of the following properties hold:*

1. $T \models \gamma$;

2. a conjunction $k = p \wedge \neg q_1 \wedge \cdots \wedge \neg q_m$ exists such that $p \in P, \{q_1, \ldots, q_m\} \subseteq Q$, k is ECWA-ffn in $\langle T; P; Q; Z \rangle$ and $T \models \gamma \vee k$.

PROOF: The *if* part is trivial. For the *only if* part, observe that Fact 6 states that if $ECWA(T; P; Q; Z) \models \gamma$, then n $(n \geq 0)$ conjunctions $k_1, \ldots, k_n$ whose literals belong to $P^+ \cup Q^+ \cup Q^-$ exist such that $k_1, \ldots, k_n$ are ECWA-ffn in $\langle T; P; Q; Z \rangle$ and $T \models \gamma \vee k_1 \vee \cdots \vee k_n$.

Note first of all that we can assume without loss of generality that at least one literal from P^+ occurs in each k_i $(1 \leq i \leq n)$, otherwise, by Fact 5, $T \models \neg k_i$ holds, and $T \models \gamma \vee k_1 \vee \cdots \vee k_{i-1} \vee k_{i+1} \vee \cdots \vee k_n$. Therefore, by Lemmas A.1.23 and A.1.24, we can assume without loss of generality that exactly one literal from P^+ occurs in each k_i $(1 \leq i \leq n)$, while the remaining literals belong to Q^-.

If $n \leq 1$, then the theorem is proven. We now show that if $n > 1$, it is impossible that for each i $(1 \leq i \leq n)$ $T \not\models \gamma \vee k_i$.

If $T \not\models \gamma \vee k_i$, then a literal a_i occurs in k_i such that $T \not\models \gamma \vee a_i$. Rewriting the condition $T \models \gamma \vee k_1 \vee \cdots \vee k_n$ –which belongs to our set of hypotheses– in conjunctive normal form, it follows that $T \models \gamma \vee a_1 \vee \cdots \vee a_n$. Taking into account that the clauses minimally derivable in T contain at most two literals, it follows that $T \models a_1 \vee \cdots \vee a_n$. Therefore, two literals a_i, a_j $(1 \leq i, j \leq n)$ exist such that $T \models a_i \vee a_j, T \not\models a_i$, and $T \not\models a_j$. One of these literals is positive, the other is negative. Taking into account the structure of each k_i, and in order to simplify the notation, we assume that $i = 1$ and $a_1 = \neg q_1$ $(q_1 \in Q^+)$, $j = 2$ and $a_2 = p_2$ $(p_2 \in P^+)$.

Since $T \models \neg q_1 \vee p_2$ and $T \not\models \neg q_1$, it follows that p_2 is not ECWA-ffn in $\langle T; P; Q; Z \rangle$. Therefore k_2 must be of the form $p_2 \wedge k_2'$, where k_2' is a non-empty conjunction whose literals belong to Q^-.

We now prove that $T \models \neg q_1 \vee \neg k_2'$. Note that $\neg k_2'$ is a disjunction whose literals belong to Q^+. Since both $T \models \neg q_1 \vee p_2$ and $T \models k_2' \vee \neg k_2'$, $T \models (p_2 \wedge k_2') \vee (\neg q_1 \vee \neg k_2')$, that is, $T \models k_2 \vee (\neg q_1 \vee \neg k_2')$. Therefore, if $T \models \neg q_1 \vee \neg k_2'$ does not hold, then the hypothesis that k_2 is ECWA-ffn in $\langle T; P; Q; Z \rangle$ is contradicted.

$T \models \neg q_1 \vee \neg k_2'$ implies that a literal $q_2 \in Q^+$ occurs in $\neg k_2'$ such that $T \models \neg q_1 \vee q_2$. Note that $T \not\models \neg q_2 \vee \gamma$, otherwise the hypothesis that $T \not\models \neg q_1 \vee \gamma$ is contradicted.

Let us summarize all the facts we have proven so far: a literal $\neg q_1 \in Q^-$ occurs in k_1 such that $T \not\models \neg q_1 \vee \gamma$; a literal $\neg q_2 \in Q^-$ occurs in k_2 such that $T \not\models \neg q_2 \vee \gamma$; a literal $a_i \in P^+ \cup Q^-$ occurs in each k_i $(3 \leq i \leq n)$ such that $T \not\models \neg a_i \vee \gamma$.

Rewriting the condition $T \models \gamma \vee k_1 \vee \cdots \vee k_n$ –which belongs to our set of hypotheses– in conjunctive normal form, it follows that $T \models \gamma \vee \neg q_1 \vee \neg q_2 \vee a_3 \vee \cdots \vee a_n$. Taking into account that the clauses minimally derivable from T contain at most two literals, we have that $T \models \neg q_1 \vee \neg q_2 \vee a_3 \vee \cdots \vee a_n$. This implies that at least one of the following conditions hold:

1. $T \models \neg q_1 \vee a_i$ for some i $(3 \leq i \leq n)$;

2. $T \models \neg q_2 \vee a_i$ for some i $(3 \leq i \leq n)$;

3. $T \models a_i \vee a_j$ for some i, j $(3 \leq i, j \leq n)$.

In the first two cases we can prove with a similar argument that a literal $\neg q_3 \in Q^-$ occurs in k_3 such that both $T \not\models \gamma \vee \neg q_3$ and $T \models \gamma \vee \neg q_1 \vee \neg q_2 \vee \neg q_3 \vee a_4 \vee \cdots \vee a_n$. In the third case we can prove with a similar argument that a literal $\neg q_3 \in Q^-$ and a literal $\neg q_4 \in Q^-$ occur in k_3 and k_4 respectively, such that $T \not\models \gamma \vee \neg q_3$, $T \not\models \gamma \vee \neg q_4$ and $T \models \gamma \vee \neg q_1 \vee \neg q_2 \vee \neg q_3 \vee \neg q_4 \vee a_5 \vee \cdots \vee a_n$. Therefore, after at most $n - 2$ iterations, we can prove that n literals $\neg q_1, \ldots, \neg q_n \in Q^-$ exist such that $\neg q_i$ occurs in k_i $(1 \leq i \leq n)$, $T \models \gamma \vee \neg q_1 \vee \cdots \vee \neg q_n$, and for each i, $T \not\models \gamma \vee \neg q_i$. This implies that $T \models \neg q_1 \vee \cdots \vee \neg q_n$. Since a clause minimally derivable in T cannot contain two negative literals this is a contradiction. $\diamond$

Lemma A.1.26 Let $\langle T; P; Q; Z \rangle$ be a HornKrom$^-$ formula, and let $k = p \wedge \neg q_1 \wedge \cdots \wedge \neg q_m$ be a conjunction with $p \in P$, $\{q_1, \ldots, q_m\} \subseteq Q$ and $T \not\models p$, $T \not\models q_1, \ldots, T \not\models q_m$. Let $\mathcal{L} = \{\neg d \in Q^- \mid T \models p \vee \neg d\}$ and $\mathcal{M} = \{\neg d \in Q^- \mid \exists j \ (1 \leq j \leq m) : T \models q_j \vee \neg d\}$. Then k is ECWA-ffn in $\langle T; P; Q; Z \rangle$ iff $\mathcal{L} \subseteq \mathcal{M}$.

PROOF: (only if part) Suppose that $\mathcal{L} \not\subseteq \mathcal{M}$ and let $\neg d$ be a literal in $\mathcal{L} \setminus \mathcal{M}$. Let B be the disjunction $q_1 \vee \cdots \vee q_m \vee \neg d$. Note that each literal of B belongs to $Q^+ \cup Q^-$. Since $\neg d \notin \mathcal{M}$, it follows that $T \not\models B$. Moreover $T \models (q_1 \vee \cdots \vee q_m \vee \neg d) \vee (p \wedge \neg q_1 \wedge \cdots \wedge \neg q_m)$, that is, $T \models B \vee k$. Therefore k is not ECWA-ffn in $\langle T; P; Q; Z \rangle$.

(if part) Suppose that k is not ECWA-ffn in $\langle T; P; Q; Z \rangle$. It follows that a disjunction B whose literals belong to $P^+ \cup Q^+ \cup Q^-$ exists such that both $T \not\models B$ and $T \models B \vee k$. The last condition implies that:

1. a literal $\neg d \in Q^-$ occurs in B such that $T \models p \vee \neg d$;

2. m literals r_j $(1 \leq j \leq m) \in P^+ \cup Q^+$ –possibly not distinct– occur in B such that $T \models \neg q_j \vee r_j$.

Note that $\neg d$ belongs to $\mathcal{L}$. We now prove that $\neg d$ does not belong to $\mathcal{M}$, thus showing that $\mathcal{L} \not\subseteq \mathcal{M}$.

Suppose that $\neg d$ belongs to $\mathcal{M}$ and $T \models q_j \vee \neg d$ for some j $(1 \leq j \leq m)$. Since a literal r_j occurs in B such that $T \models \neg q_j \vee r_j$, it follows that $T \models \neg d \vee r_j$, thus contradicting the hypothesis that $T \not\models B$. $\diamond$

Theorem A.1.27 INF-ECWA[HK$^-$,CLAUSE] can be solved in polynomial time.

PROOF: Let H be the conjunction $p_1 \wedge \cdots \wedge p_l \wedge \neg q_1 \wedge \cdots \wedge \neg q_m$, where $\{p_1, \ldots, p_l\} \subseteq P$, $\{q_1, \ldots, q_m\} \subseteq Q$, such that a literal l occurs in H iff both $T \not\models l$ and $T \models l \vee \gamma$.

We prove that $ECWA(T; P; Q; Z) \models \gamma$ iff either $T \models \gamma$, or H is ECWA-ffn in $\langle T; P; Q; Z \rangle$. The if part is trivial. For the only if part we recall Lemma A.1.25: if both $ECWA(T; P; Q; Z) \models \gamma$ and $T \not\models \gamma$, then a conjunction $k = p \wedge \neg q_1 \wedge \cdots \wedge \neg q_r$ exists such that $p \in P$, $\{q_1, \ldots, q_r\} \subseteq Q$, k is ECWA-ffn in $\langle T; P; Q; Z \rangle$ and $T \models \gamma \vee k$. If such a formula k exists, then it must be a sub-conjunction of H; therefore H is ECWA-ffn in $\langle T; P; Q; Z \rangle$.

Hence, in order to determine whether $ECWA(T; P; Q; Z) \models \gamma$, we first of all check whether $T \models \gamma$, and, if not, we build the above formula H. Note that, since the clauses which are minimally derivable from a HornKrom$^-$ formula contain at most one positive literal and at most one negative literal, H can be constructed in polynomial time by checking, for each positive literal x of γ, if there exists a $y \in Q^-$ such that $x \vee y$ is minimally derivable from T, and for each negative literal z of γ, if there exists a $w \in P^+$ such that $z \vee w$ is minimally derivable from T.

Now the problem reduces to one of checking H for freeness for negation. By Lemma A.1.24, in order for H to be free for negation, there must exist one i $(1 \leq i \leq l)$ such that $k_i = p_i \wedge \neg q_1 \wedge \cdots \wedge \neg q_n$ is so. By Lemma A.1.26, an efficient method for performing such a test is based on the idea of building the $l + 1$ sets $\mathcal{M} = \{\neg d \in Q^- \mid \exists j \ (1 \leq j \leq m) : \ T \models q_j \vee \neg d\}$, and $\mathcal{L}_i = \{\neg d \in Q^- \mid T \models p_i \vee \neg d\}$ $(1 \leq i \leq l)$ and checking whether $\mathcal{L}_i \subseteq \mathcal{M}$. Note that such sets can be computed in polynomial time. $\diamondsuit$

Taking into account the above result, we can solve the inference problem under ECWA in HornKrom$^-$ formulae by means of the polynomial time Algorithm A.8 (HK$^-$ECWA.)

A.1.8   Inference of·new positive clauses

In this subsection we analyze the various forms of CWR with respect to the possibility of inferring new positive clauses. We remind the reader that the main motivation leading to the study of CCWA and ECWA was the impossibility for previous forms of closed world reasoning, namely, CWA, GCWA, and EGCWA, of inferring from a formula T any positive clause that is not monotonically derivable by T. The following propositions state a number of results which allow us to establish whether new positive clauses are derivable or not using a given CWR-rule.

The first proposition states that, as we said before, no new positive clause can be inferred from a propositional formula using the simple forms of CWR.

Proposition A.1.28 ([Minker, 1982, Yahya and Henschen, 1985] [Reiter, 1978, Rajasekar *et al.***, 1989])** *Let T be a formula and let γ be a positive clause. Then the following properties hold:*

1. *if $CWA(T)$ is satisfiable, then $CWA(T) \models \gamma$ iff $T \models \gamma$;*

2. *if the WGCWA is applicable to T, then $WGCWA(T) \models \gamma$ iff $T \models \gamma$;*

3. *$GCWA(T) \models \gamma$ iff $EGCWA(T) \models \gamma$ iff $T \models \gamma$.*

The next proposition states that new positive clauses cannot be inferred from a propositional formula $\langle T; P; Q; Z \rangle$ where $Z = \emptyset$, even using the strongest forms of CWR.

Proposition A.1.29 ([Gelfond   and   Przymusinska,   1986] [Gelfond *et al.***, 1989])** *Let $\langle T; P; Q; \emptyset \rangle$ be a formula, and let γ be a positive*

Algorithm HK⁻ECWA
Input a HornKrom⁻ formula $\langle T; P; Q; Z \rangle$,
     and a clause $\gamma = \neg r_1 \vee \cdots \vee \neg r_u \vee s_1 \vee \cdots \vee s_v$
Output true, if $ECWA(T; P; Q; Z) \models \gamma$, false otherwise
begin
   if $T \models \gamma$
   then return true
   else begin
        (* build H *)
        $H := \emptyset$;
        for $i := 1$ **to** u
        do $H := H \cup \{p_j \in P^+ \mid T \models \neg r_i \vee p_j, T \not\models p_j\}$;
        for $i := 1$ **to** v
        do $H := H \cup \{\neg q_j \in Q^- \mid T \models s_i \vee \neg q_j, T \not\models \neg q_j\}$;
        (* build $\mathcal{M}$ *)
        $\mathcal{M} := \emptyset$;
        for each $\neg q_j \in H$
        do $\mathcal{M} := \mathcal{M} \cup \{\neg d \in Q^- \mid T \models q_j \vee \neg d\}$;
        (* check if $H = p_1 \wedge \cdots \wedge p_l \wedge \neg q_1 \wedge \cdots \wedge \neg q_m$ is free for negation *)
        for each $p_i \in H$
        do begin
            (* check if $p_i \wedge \neg q_1 \wedge \cdots \wedge \neg q_m$ is free for negation *)
            $\mathcal{L}_i := \{\neg d \in Q^- \mid T \models p_i \vee \neg d\}$;
            if $\mathcal{L}_i \subseteq \mathcal{M}$
            then return true
        end;
        return false
   end
end.

Algorithm A.8: HK⁻ECWA

clause. Then the three conditions are equivalent: (1) $(CCWA(T; P; Q; \emptyset) \models \gamma)$, (2) $(ECWA(T; P; Q; \emptyset) \models \gamma)$, (3) $(T \models \gamma)$.

We now show that no CWR-rule allows us to derive new positive clauses from a Horn formula.

Proposition A.1.30 *Let $\langle T; P; Q; Z \rangle$ be a Horn formula, and let γ be a positive clause. Then $(CCWA(T; P; Q; Z) \models \gamma)$ iff $(ECWA(T; P; Q; Z) \models \gamma)$ iff $(T \models \gamma)$.*

PROOF: Let us consider the case of ECWA. The argument for CCWA is similar. The *if* part is trivial. For the *only if* part, we know by Fact 6 that $ECWA(T; P; Q; Z) \models \gamma$ implies that there exist n $(n \geq 0)$ conjunctions $k_1, \ldots, k_n$ of literals belonging to $P^+ \cup Q^+ \cup Q^-$ such that $k_1, \ldots, k_n$ are ECWA-ffn in $\langle T; P; Q; Z \rangle$, and $T \models \gamma \vee k_1 \vee \cdots \vee k_n$. By Fact 5 we can assume that at least one literal p_i from P^+ occurs in each k_i $(1 \leq i \leq n)$. Moreover we can assume without loss of generality that $T \not\models p_i$. Now, since $T \models \gamma \vee k_1 \vee \cdots \vee k_n$, it follows that $T \models \gamma \vee p_1 \vee \cdots \vee p_n$. Since T is Horn and γ is positive, this implies that $T \models \gamma$. $\diamond$

Finally, we show that when the formula $\langle T; P; Q; Z \rangle$ contains clauses with at least two positive literals, then it is possible to infer new positive clauses by using both CCWA and ECWA, even if $Q = \emptyset$.

Proposition A.1.31 *Let $\langle T; P; \emptyset; Z \rangle$ be a formula such that T contains clauses with at least two positive literals, and let γ be a positive clause. Then it is possible that both $(T \not\models \gamma)$ and $(CCWA(T; P; Q; Z) \models \gamma)$, even if $Q = \emptyset$.*

PROOF: Let T be the formula constituted by the single clause $(p \vee z)$, and let $P = \{p\}$, $Z = \{z\}$. It is easy to see that p is CCWA-ffn in $\langle T, P, \emptyset, Z \rangle$. Therefore $CCWA(T; P; \emptyset; Z) \models z$, but $T \not\models z$. A similar argument applies both when $Q \neq \emptyset$ holds, and when we deal with the ECWA. $\diamond$

A.2   Appendix to Section 2.4

The structure of this section is as follows: In the first subsection we show proofs for the intractable cases. In the second subsection we deal with polynomial subcases. As for the upper bound of the $(P; Q; Z)$-MIN(S) problem, we refer the reader to the analysis performed in Section A.1.2 (cf. algorithm in Figure 3.)

A.2.1   Intractable cases

Theorem A.2.1 *If condition β holds for S, then $(P; Q; Z)$-MIN(S) is co-NP-complete even if $Q = Z = \emptyset$.*

PROOF: Let S be the singleton $\{R_1\}$, where R_1 is the 3-ary relation "one-in-three", denoted by the set $\{\langle 1,0,0\rangle, \langle 0,1,0\rangle, \langle 0,0,1\rangle\}$. We reduce the NP-complete problem $SAT(S)$ (see [Schaefer, 1978, Lemma 3.5]) to the complement of our problem by exhibiting a polynomial mapping from any S-formula π on the alphabet L, into an S'-formula π' on the same alphabet L and a model M of π' such that every relation in S' is 1-valid and M is not minimal for π' iff π is satisfiable.

S' is constituted by three logical relations R_2, R_3, R_4. R_2 is the 3-ary relation "at-least-one-in-three", denoted by the set $\{0,1\}^3 \backslash \{\langle 0,0,0\rangle\}$, which corresponds to $x \vee y \vee z$. R_3 is the 3-ary relation "not-two-in-three", denoted by the set $\{0,1\}^3 \backslash \{\langle 1,1,0\rangle \langle 1,0,1\rangle \langle 0,1,1\rangle\}$. R_4 is the 6-ary relation defined in such a way that $R_4(x_1,y_1,z_1,x_2,y_2,z_2) \equiv (R_1(x_1,y_1,z_1) \rightarrow R_1(x_2,y_2,z_2))$, where $\rightarrow$ is the sign for logical implication. Intuitively, $R_4(x_1,y_1,z_1,x_2,y_2,z_2)$ is falsified by exactly those truth assignments that map exactly one variable in $\{x_1,y_1,z_1\}$ into 1 and map zero, two or three variables in $\{x_2,y_2,z_2\}$ into 1. Note that every relation in S' is 1-valid.

Let π be an S-formula whose clauses are $R_1(x_1,y_1,z_1) \wedge \cdots \wedge R_1(x_n,y_n,z_n)$. The alphabet L of π is $\{x_1,y_1,z_1,\ldots,x_n,y_n,z_n\}$. We define π' on the same alphabet L to be the S'-formula which is the conjunction of the formulae π'_1, π'_2, π'_3 defined in the following way:

$$
\begin{aligned}
\pi'_1 &= R_2(x_1,y_1,z_1) \wedge \cdots \wedge R_2(x_n,y_n,z_n) \\
\pi'_2 &= R_3(x_1,y_1,z_1) \wedge \cdots \wedge R_3(x_n,y_n,z_n) \\
\pi'_3 &= R_4(x_1,y_1,z_1,x_2,y_2,z_2) \wedge \\
&\quad R_4(x_2,y_2,z_2,x_3,y_3,z_3) \wedge \cdots \wedge \\
&\quad R_4(x_{n-1},y_{n-1},z_{n-1},x_n,y_n,z_n) \wedge \\
&\quad R_4(x_n,y_n,z_n,x_1,y_1,z_1).
\end{aligned}
$$

Note that the mapping from π to π' is polynomial, and that the truth assignment M mapping every variable of L into 1 is a model of π'. Intuitively, the conjunction $\pi'_1 \wedge \pi'_2$ states that for each triple x_i, y_i, z_i $(1 \leq i \leq n)$, a model of π' either assigns exactly one variable in x_i, y_i, z_i to 1, or it assigns x_i, y_i and z_i to 1. Moreover, π'_3 states that if a model of π' assigns to 1 exactly one variable in a triple x_i, y_i, z_i, then it assigns to 1 exactly one variable in every triple x_i, y_i, z_i $(1 \leq i \leq n)$. Therefore –making an exception for M– the only truth assignments which can be models of π' are those which assign to 1 exactly one variable in every triple x_i, y_i, z_i $(1 \leq i \leq n)$. Note that such truth assignments –if existing– are exactly the set of models of π, and that for each such truth assignment N, it holds that $N <_{P;Z} M$, where $P = L, Q = Z = \emptyset$. Therefore M is a minimal model of π' iff such a truth assignment does not exist iff π is unsatisfiable. This completes the proof. $\diamond$

Theorem A.2.2 *If none of the conditions α, β, γ holds for S, then $(P;Q;Z)$-MIN(S) is co-NP-complete even if $Q = Z = \emptyset$.*

PROOF: Throughout this proof we refer to the notation in the proof of Theorem A.2.1. The main idea is to modify that proof by specifying a new set S'' of logical relations and a S''-formula π''. S'' is obtained from S' by adding "unmeaningful" logical relations in such a way that none of the conditions α, β, γ holds for S''. π'' is obtained from π' in such a way that the minimal models of π'' correspond to those of π' and vice-versa.

We remind the reader that R_1 is the "one-in-three" relation. Obviously R_1 is neither 0-valid nor 1-valid. By [Schaefer, 1978, Theorem 3.0, Lemma 3.5], R_1 is neither weakly positive, nor weakly negative, nor bijunctive, nor affine. Let S'' be $S' \cup \{R_1\}$. We provide a polynomial mapping from the S'-formula π', the alphabet L of π' and the model M of π' into a S''-formula π'' on a different alphabet O and a model N of π'' such that N is minimal for π'' iff M is minimal for π'.

We want to point out that we are not obliged to choose the set $\{R_1\}$. Any set of relations will work, provided that it contains at least one relation which is not 0-valid, at least one not 1-valid, ... and at least one not affine.

Let O be the set $L \cup \{v_1, v_2, v_3\}$, where v_1, v_2, v_3 are distinct and do not occur in L. The S''-formula π'' is obtained by conjoining π' with the formula $R_1(v_1, v_2, v_3)$. The truth assignment N to the variables of O is defined in the following way:

- for each $x \in L$, $N(x) = M(x)$;

- $N(v_1) = 1$, $N(v_2) = 0$, $N(v_3) = 0$.

Note that N is a model of π''. The assignment of N to the variables v_1, v_2, v_3 is minimal and "does not interfere" with the assignment to the letters of L. Therefore N is minimal for π'' iff M is minimal for π'. Note also that the mapping from L, π' and M into O, π'' and N is polynomial. This completes the proof.

As a final remark we note that the set S'' is not arbitrary, since it contains the relations in the set S'. The present theorem is therefore not a dichotomy result in the sense of [Schaefer, 1978]. $\diamond$

Theorem A.2.3 *If condition α on S holds, then $(P; Q; Z)$-MIN(S) is co-NP-complete even if $Z = \emptyset$.*

PROOF: Throughout this proof we refer to the notation in the proof of Theorem A.2.1. The only difference is that we use the symbol U to denote the set of relations $\{R_2, R_3, R_4\}$. We reduce the co-NP-complete problem $(P; Q; Z)$-MIN(U) in the case $Q = Z = \emptyset$ to our problem by exhibiting a polynomial mapping from any U-formula ψ on the alphabet O and a model N of ψ, into a U'-formula ψ' on a different alphabet O', a partition $\langle P; Q \rangle$ of O' and a model N' of ψ' such that every relation in U' is 0-valid and N' is $(P; Z)$-minimal for ψ' iff N is minimal for ψ.

First of all we define the logical relations of U'. For each relation R_i ($2 \leq i \leq 4$) of U, having arity k, the corresponding relation R'_i of U' has arity $k + 1$ and is defined in the following way:

- $\langle 0, v_1, \ldots, v_k \rangle \in R'_i$ iff $v_1 = \cdots = v_k = 0$;

- for each $v_1, \ldots, v_k \in \{0, 1\}$, $\langle 1, v_1, \ldots, v_k \rangle \in R'_i$ iff $\langle v_1, \ldots, v_k \rangle \in R_i$.

Note that every relation in U' is 0-valid. Secondly, we define the clauses of ψ'. Let O' be the set $O \cup \{q\}$, where q does not occur in O. O' is partitioned into the sets $P = O, Q = \{q\}$. For each clause $\gamma = R_i(x_1, \ldots, x_k)$ of ψ, there exists the clause $\gamma' = R'_i(q, x_1, \ldots, x_k)$ in ψ'. Finally, the truth assignment N' to the variables of O' is defined in the following way:

- $N'(q) = 1$;

- for each $x \in O$, $N'(x) = N(x)$.

Note that the mapping from O, ψ and N into O', ψ' and N' is polynomial. Moreover N' is a model of ψ'. As a straightforward application of Theorem A.2.4, N' is $(P; Z)$-minimal for ψ' iff N is minimal for ψ. This completes the proof. $\Diamond$

A.2.2 Tractable cases

The following theorem provides a characterization of the $(P; Z)$-minimal models of a propositional formula.

Theorem A.2.4 *Let S be any set of relations and T any S-formula. Let $\langle P; Q; Z \rangle$ be a partition of the alphabet of T, M a model of T, P^+ the set $\{p \in P \mid M(p) = 1\}$, Q^+ the set $\{q \in Q \mid M(q) = 1\}$, and T' the formula*

$$T \wedge \left(\bigwedge_{p \in P \setminus P^+} R_0(p) \right) \wedge \left(\bigwedge_{q \in Q \setminus Q^+} R_0(q) \right) \wedge \left(\bigwedge_{q \in Q^+} R_1(q) \right)$$

where R_0 is the 1-ary logical relation denoted by $\{0\}$, while R_1 is the 1-ary logical relation denoted by $\{1\}$. Then M is $(P; Z)$-minimal for T iff for each $s \in P^+$, the formula $T'_s \equiv T' \wedge R_0(s)$ is unsatisfiable.

PROOF: *(if part)* Suppose that M is a $(P; Z)$-minimal model of T and that an $s \in P^+$ exists such that $T' \wedge R_0(s)$ is satisfiable. We show that this leads to a contradiction. Let N be a model of $T' \wedge R_0(s)$. Clearly N is also a model of T, and moreover $N <_{(P;Z)} M$. This contradicts the hypothesis that M is $(P; Z)$-minimal for T.

(only if part) Suppose that for each $s \in P^+$, $T' \wedge R_0(s)$ is unsatisfiable, and suppose that a model N of T exists such that $N <_{(P;Z)} M$. We show that this leads to a contradiction. Since $N <_{(P;Z)} M$, there exists at least one $t \in P$, such that $N(t) = 0$ and $M(t) = 1$. Now N is obviously a model of $T' \wedge R_0(t)$. Since $t \in P^+$, it follows that there exists one $s \in P^+$ such $T' \wedge R_0(s)$ is satisfiable, which contradicts the above hypothesis. $\Diamond$

We observe that a similar result was cited without proof by Eiter and Gottlob [Eiter and Gottlob, 1993b, Lemma 3.2] for the restricted case in which $Q = Z = \emptyset$ and T is a CNF formula with at most two literals per disjunction.

Schaefer [Schaefer, 1978] analyzed the complexity of *satisfiability with constants* problems, in which the constants 0 and 1 are allowed to occur in the formulae (e.g. the formula $R(x, 0, y)$ is allowed.) The corresponding decision problem is denoted by $SAT_C(S)$. The only polynomial case for $SAT_C(S)$ is case γ; the other cases are NP-complete (see [Schaefer, 1978, Lemma 4.1].)

Theorem A.2.4 shows that $(P; Q; Z)$-MIN(S) is similar to satisfiability with constants problems. In particular for any set S for which $SAT_C(S)$ is polynomial, $(P; Q; Z)$-MIN(S) is polynomial too, since it can be decided by deciding $|P^+|$ instances of $SAT_C(S)$. We note also that if every relation in S is 0-valid, then any relation in $S' = S \cup \{R_0\}$ is 0-valid too, and that if $Q = \emptyset$, then $(P; Q; Z)$-MIN(S) can be decided by deciding $|P^+|$ instances of $SAT(S')$. This implies that if every relation in S is 0-valid and $Q = \emptyset$, then $(P; Q; Z)$-MIN(S) is polynomial.

Corollary A.2.5 *If condition γ holds for S, then $(P; Q; Z)$-MIN(S) is polynomial. If condition α holds for S and $Q = \emptyset$, then $(P; Q; Z)$-MIN(S) is polynomial.*

A.3   Appendix to Section 2.5

The structure of this section is as follows: In the first subsection we recall definitions about polynomial reducibility among search problems. In the second subsection we show the $\text{FP}^{\text{NP}[O(\log n)]}$-hardness proof. Finally, in the third subsection we deal with polynomial sub-cases.

A.3.1   Preliminaries

We deal with the problem $(P; Q; Z)$-**FIND**(S), as defined in Section 2.5.

Papadimitriou [Papadimitriou, 1991, Section 3] deals with the case $Q = \emptyset$ and uses the term *X-minimal* for referring to the $(P; Z)$-minimal models, where X denotes the subset of the letters that are minimized. He shows that finding a minimal model of a propositional formula is in Δ_2^p. This terminology is a little bit unusual for a search problem, since Δ_2^p has been defined in [Stockmeyer, 1976] as a class of decision problems (see Krentel in [Krentel, 1988] and Megiddo and Papadimitriou in [Megiddo and Papadimitriou, 1991] for the definition of some classes of search problems.) Membership in $\text{F}\Delta_2^p$ (or equivalently in FP^{NP}) for a search problem means that it can be computed by a deterministic, polynomial time Turing machine with access to an NP oracle (using the terminology of [Krentel, 1988] it is a problem in FP^{SAT}.)

For defining hardness w.r.t. a class of search problems, for example w.r.t. $\text{F}\Delta_2^p$, we need to consider the usual polynomial reduction between search problems, as found for example in [Megiddo and Papadimitriou, 1991, Section 2]. For the sake of clarity we recall here such reduction.

Definition A.3.1 ([Megiddo and Papadimitriou, 1991]) *Let Π_R and Π_S be two search problems, represented respectively by the sets $R, S \subseteq \Sigma^* \times \Sigma^*$, where Σ is an alphabet with two or more symbols. Π_R reduces to Π_S if there is a pair of polynomially computable functions f and g such that, for any $x \in \Sigma^*$, $(x, g(y)) \in R$ iff $(f(x), y) \in S$.*

Given a class of decision problems X (e.g., Δ_2^p, $\mathrm{P}^{\mathrm{NP}[O(\log n)]}$), a search problem is hard w.r.t. the class of search problems FX if any *decision* problem (considered as a search problem, i.e., a single-valued function) in X can be reduced according to Definition A.3.1 to it. Intuitively, a search problem Π_S is $\mathrm{F}\Delta_2^p$-hard if any decision problem in Δ_2^p can be solved by means of a polynomial-time Turing machine that makes a single call to an oracle that solves Π_S. The same intuition holds for $\mathrm{FP}^{\mathrm{NP}[O(\log n)]}$-hardness.

A.3.2 Intractable cases

In this subsection we prove that the search problem of finding a minimal model of a propositional, 1-valid CNF formula is hard —in the sense specified by Definition A.3.1— w.r.t. the class of decision problems TT[NP]. The class TT[NP], defined by Kadin in [Kadin, 1988], contains the languages polynomial time truth-table reducible to a language in NP(the definition of truth-table reducibility is given in the following.) In the same paper (see also Wagner in [Wagner, 1990]) it is shown that TT[NP] is the same as the class $\mathrm{P}^{\mathrm{NP}[O(\log n)]}$ of languages recognizable in deterministic polynomial time with $O(\log n)$ queries to an NP oracle and the same as the class $\mathrm{P}^{\mathrm{NP}\|}$ of languages recognizable by deterministic polynomial time machines that make polynomially many parallel queries to an NP oracle.

It is interesting to note that the number of calls to an NP oracle that a deterministic polynomial time machine needs for finding any (not necessarily minimal) model of a propositional formula is not known. A trivial algorithm takes $O(n)$ calls. Moreover in [Gottlob and Fermüller, 1993] it is shown that if it is possible to perform the computation with $O(\log n)$ calls, then P = NP.

First of all we note that, since every propositional formula T has a minimal model iff it is satisfiable, then the above consideration holds for finding minimal models also. By the way, the $\mathrm{P}^{\mathrm{NP}[O(\log n)]}$-hardness result we give holds even if a model of T is already known. This confirms the empirical consideration that a non-monotonic reasoning task is more difficult than the corresponding monotonic task.

In order to prove the TT[NP]-hardness result, first of all we show that the search problem **QUERY**, defined by Gasarch in [Gasarch, 1986] can be polynomially reduced to the problem of finding a minimal model. The problem **QUERY** (see also [Krentel, 1988]) takes as input k propositional formulae $T_1, \ldots, T_k$ and outputs $b_1, \ldots, b_k$, where $b_i = 1$ if T_i is satisfiable, and $b_i = 0$ if T_i is not satisfiable. Given $T_1, \ldots, T_k$, we build in polynomial time a formula Φ such that, if we have a minimal model of Φ, then we can compute in polynomial time the above specified array $b_1, \ldots, b_k$.

Hyp: We assume that none of $T_1, \ldots, T_k$ is satisfied by mapping into 1 all of its letters. We don't lose any generality with this assumption, since we can consider the k formulae $T_i^+ \doteq T_i \wedge \neg l_i$ ($1 \leq i \leq k$) in which l_i is a letter occurring in no T_i. Clearly the T_i^+ satisfy the assumption and are satisfiable iff the corresponding T_i are satisfiable.

Let $\mathcal{L}_1, \ldots, \mathcal{L}_k$ be the sets of letters occurring in $T_1, \ldots T_k$, respectively. We assume —again no loss of generality because we can rename letters— that $\mathcal{L}_i \cap \mathcal{L}_j = \emptyset$ for each $i, j \in [1..k]$. By L_i we denote the conjunction $\bigwedge_{l \in \mathcal{L}_i} l$.

We define the formula Φ in the following way:

$$(T_1 \vee L_1) \ \wedge \cdots \wedge \ (T_k \vee L_k)$$

and denote the k conjuncts of Φ with $\phi_1, \ldots, \phi_k$, respectively.

Note that, if $T_1, \ldots, T_k$ are in CNF, then Φ can be rewritten in an equivalent CNF form of size $(|T_1| \cdot |L_1|) + \cdots + (|T_k| \cdot |L_k|)$, since all the T_i's and the L_i's are conjunctions and $(c_1 \wedge \cdots \wedge c_n) \vee (d_1 \wedge \cdots \wedge d_m) \equiv \bigwedge_{1 \leq i \leq n, \ 1 \leq j \leq m} (c_i \vee d_j)$.

A truth assignment $\mathcal{I}$ to the letters of a formula is denoted with the set of letters that $\mathcal{I}$ maps into 1. Note that $\mathcal{M} \doteq \mathcal{L}_1 \cup \cdots \cup \mathcal{L}_k$ is a model of Φ. In other words Φ is 1-valid.

We now prove that if we have a minimal model of Φ, then we can compute in polynomial time the k bits $b_1, \ldots, b_k$ required by **QUERY**.

In fact, if T_1 is unsatisfiable, then ϕ_1 is satisfied only by the truth assignment $\mathcal{L}_1$. As a consequence every minimal model of Φ is of the type $\mathcal{L}_1 \cup \mathcal{N}_2 \cup \cdots \cup \mathcal{N}_k$, where $\mathcal{N}_2, \ldots, \mathcal{N}_k$ are models of $\phi_2, \ldots, \phi_k$, respectively. On the other hand if T_1 is satisfiable, then —by **Hyp**— $\mathcal{L}_1$ is not the only model of ϕ_1. As a consequence every minimal model of Φ is of the type $\mathcal{N}_1 \cup \mathcal{N}_2 \cup \cdots \cup \mathcal{N}_k$, where $\mathcal{N}_1$ is a model of T_1 and $\mathcal{N}_1 \subset \mathcal{L}_1$.

The same kind of argument applies —in a completely independent way— to the satisfiability of each formula T_i ($i \in [2..k]$). Therefore —regardless of the minimal model $\mathcal{P}$ of Φ that we have— for each $i \in [1..k]$, T_i is satisfiable iff $\mathcal{P}$ does not contain all the letters of $\mathcal{L}_i$, i.e., $\mathcal{L}_i \not\subseteq \mathcal{P}$. As a consequence we can solve the **QUERY** problem on $T_1, \ldots, T_k$ with a single call to an oracle that returns any minimal model of Φ, followed by a polynomial-time computation.

We recall that **QUERY** is $\text{FP}^{\text{NP}[O(\log n)]}$-hard under the metric reduction defined in [Krentel, 1988] (see also [Gasarch, 1986]) and it is not known whether it is $\text{FP}^{\text{NP}[O(\log n)]}$-complete. Therefore, using the results on metric reductions of [Krentel, 1988], the problem of finding a minimal model is $\text{FP}^{\text{NP}[O(\log n)]}$-hard as well.

It is interesting to note that a single call to an oracle that returns a minimal model of Φ lets us know for each i:

(i) whether T_i is satisfiable or not;

(ii) a minimal model of T_i, if it is satisfiable.

Point (ii) shows intuitively that finding a minimal model of Φ gives more information than solving the original **QUERY** problem.

We now give a direct proof of TT[NP]-hardness for the problem of finding a minimal model. More precisely, we show that any decision problem $\mathcal{T}$ such that $\mathcal{T} \leq^p_{tt} \text{SAT}$, where $\leq^p_{tt}$ is the "truth-table" polynomial reduction defined by Ladner, Lynch and Selman in [Ladner *et al.*, 1975], can be reduced in the sense specified in the previous subsection, to the search problem of finding a minimal model. We now briefly recall the definition of $\leq^p_{tt}$: Let $A, B \subset \Sigma^*$. $A \leq^p_{tt} B$ if the following hold:

1. There exists a polynomial-time mapping g (the *generator*) from Σ^* into $\Delta^* \# (\# \Sigma^*)^*$, where Δ is a fixed alphabet and $\# \notin \Sigma \cup \Delta$.

2. There exists a polynomial-time mapping e (the *evaluator*) from $\Delta^* \# \{0, 1\}^*$ into $\{0, 1\}$.

3. $(\forall x \in \Sigma^*)[x \in A \iff$
   $(g(x) = w \# \# \alpha_1 \# \alpha_2 \# \cdots \# \alpha_k \implies e(w \# \chi_B(\alpha_1) \chi_B(\alpha_2) \cdots \chi_B(\alpha_k)) = 1)]$,
   where $\chi_B(\alpha) = 1 \iff \alpha \in B$.

Less formally, any instance $\mathcal{T}$ of a generic problem in TT[NP] can be transformed in polynomial time (by the generator) in a string w and a sequence of propositional formulae $\langle \alpha_1, \alpha_2, \ldots, \alpha_k \rangle$ such that, if we know for each of the α_i's if it is satisfiable or not, then we can decide for any input x if $x \in \mathcal{T}$ in polynomial time (using the evaluator.) [1]

Now, let $\mathcal{T} \subset \Sigma^*$ be a generic problem in TT[NP], i.e., a set s.t. $\mathcal{T} \leq^p_{tt} \text{SAT}$. We show that there exists a propositional formula Ψ and two polynomial functions f_1, f_2 s.t. (1) $f_1(\mathcal{T}) = \Psi$, (2) $\mathcal{M}$ is a minimal model of Ψ and (3) $(\forall x \in \Sigma^*)(x \in \mathcal{T} \iff x \in f_2(\mathcal{M}))$. In other words we can decide whether $x \in \mathcal{T}$ with a polynomial computation, followed by a single call to an oracle that returns the minimal model of a propositional formula, followed by another polynomial computation. This shows that the problem of finding a minimal model of a propositional CNF[2] formula is TT[NP]-hard. The function f_1 can be obtained by using the function g and the polynomial construction developed in the previous proof for building Φ out of $T_1, \ldots, T_k$. The function f_2 is e combined with the polynomial algorithm for deciding the satisfiability of each of the T_i's out of the minimal model of Φ.

Theorem A.3.1 *Let Φ be a propositional formula which is in CNF. Finding a minimal model of Φ is TT[NP]-hard, or equivalently $P^{\text{NP}[O(\log n)]}$-hard, $P^{\text{NP}\|}$-hard, even if we have a model of Φ. The same result holds if Φ is 1-valid.*

---

[1] Note that this is a polynomial-time computation with an oracle for SAT, but the oracle can be used in a restricted form: All the queries have to be done at the same time i.e., are *non-adaptive* in the terminology of [Wagner, 1990]. As shown in [Ladner *et al.*, 1975], the polynomial-time Turing reduction $\leq^p_T$ is stronger than $\leq^p_{tt}$ when recursive sets are taken into account. We recall that the sets in Δ^p_2 are exactly those sets $\mathcal{T}$ such that $\mathcal{T} \leq^p_T \text{SAT}$, that TT[NP] $\subseteq \Delta^p_2$ and it is not known whether the containment is strict.

[2] By Cook's theorem we can assume that the α_i's generated by g are in CNF.

A.3.3   Tractable cases

In this subsection we briefly describe some polynomial sub-cases of the search problem we are taking into account.

Polynomiality of the problem $(P;Q;Z)$-**FIND**(S) in in the case α trivially follows from the fact that the assignment that maps all the letters into 0 is a model.

Proposition A.3.2 *Let Φ be a 0-valid formula. Finding a $(P;Z)$-minimal model of Φ is polynomial.*

In [Papadimitriou, 1991] it is noted that the lexicographically smallest model of a formula is also $(P;\emptyset;Z)$-minimal. Since finding the lexicographically smallest model is well-known to be in $F\Delta_2^p$, this gives the upper bound for finding a $(P;\emptyset;Z)$-minimal model. It is easy to see that, provided that the letters in Z are the least significant and those in Q the most significant, the lexicographically smallest model is also a $(P;Q;Z)$-minimal model, hence $F\Delta_2^p$ is an upper bound also when $Q \neq \emptyset$. Algorithm A.9 can be used for finding the lexicographically smallest model. The algorithm is also useful for showing that the case γ is also polynomial.

If T is satisfiable, then in every moment of the computation all the bits of the lexicographically smallest model from the j-th to the n-th (with $j = smallest\text{-}fixed\text{-}bit$) are stored into the variables $l_j, \ldots, l_n$, respectively and are not changed any more.

The algorithm uses the subroutine (or oracle) SAT_C, whose inputs are a propositional formula T on the alphabet $\{l_1, \ldots, l_n\}$, a truth assignment M that maps $\{l_1, \ldots, l_n\}$ into $\{0, 1\}$ and an index $1 \leq i \leq n$. SAT_C returns YES iff the following formula is true (N is a truth assignment to $\{l_1, \ldots, l_n\}$):

$$\exists N \left[(N \models T) \wedge (N(l_i) = M(l_i)) \wedge \cdots \wedge (N(l_n) = M(l_n)) \right]$$

where $\models$ denotes boolean satisfaction. The above formula is existentially quantified, therefore SAT_C performs an NP computation. More precisely SAT_C solves a *satisfiability with constants* problem (see [Schaefer, 1978]), i.e., satisfiability in which a partial truth assignment is given as part of the input.

The algorithm builds the lexicographically smallest model fixing one bit at a time, starting from the most significant one. The algorithm runs in $O(n^2)$ steps, making also $O(n^2)$ calls to the oracle SAT_C. As shown in [Schaefer, 1978], the computation performed by SAT_C can be done in polynomial time in the case γ. As a consequence also $(P;Q;Z)$-**FIND**(S) is polynomial in such case.

Proposition A.3.3 *Let Φ be a propositional formula which is weakly positive, weakly negative, bijunctive or affine. Finding a $(P;Z)$-minimal model of Φ is polynomial.*

In [Ben-Eliyahu and Dechter, 1993] Ben-Eliyahu and Dechter show an algorithm that finds a generic minimal model (not necessarily the lexicographically smallest one) with $O(n)$ calls to an oracle in NP.

Algorithm Lexicographically smallest model
Input a propositional formula T on the alphabet $\{l_1, \ldots, l_n\}$.
Output The lexicographcally smallest model of T, if T is satisfiable,
        NO otherwise. The least significant bit is l_1.
begin
    (* M is always an abbreviation for $\langle l_1, \ldots, l_n \rangle$ *);
    for $i := 1$ **to** n **do** $l_i := 0$;
    $smallest\text{-}fixed\text{-}bit := n + 1$; (* no fixed bits *)
    $i := 1$;
    while $i < smallest\text{-}fixed\text{-}bit$
    do begin
        if $M \models T$ (* this check is meaningful only when $i = 1$ *)
        then return M;
        (* else every model of T –if any– is strictly greater than M *)
        $l_i := 1$;
        if $SAT_C(T, M, i)$=YES
        then begin
            (* The smallest model of T is M or greater.
              The bit l_i of such a model is 1 *)
            $smallest\text{-}fixed\text{-}bit := i$;
            $i := 1$;
        end
        else begin
            $l_i := 0$; (* the bit l_i is not fixed *)
            $i := i + 1$;
        end
    end;
    if $smallest\text{-}fixed\text{-}bit = n + 1$
    then return NO (* T is unsatisfiable *)
    else return M
end.

Algorithm A.9: Lexicographically smallest model

A.4   Appendix to Section 2.6

The structure of this section is as follows: In the first subsection we present the
method for the elimination of the varying predicates. In the second subsection
we show how the method works by means of the "Tweety" example.

A.4.1   The reduction

In this subsection we exhibit a transformation of a pair of first-order formulae
T and F into a first-order formula $\Gamma(T; F; P; Z)$ such that F follows from the
circumscription of T where the P predicates are minimized and the Z predicates
vary if and only if $\neg u$ follows from the circumscription of $\Gamma(T; F; P; Z)$ under
minimization of all predicates, where u is a new 0-ary predicate symbol not
occurring in T or F.

General formulations of circumscription allow arbitrary expressions $E(P, \mathbf{x})$
to be minimized [McCarthy, 1986] or functions to be varied [Lifschitz, 1985b,
Lifschitz, 1986b]. These extensions are inessential, cf. Etherington [Etherington,
1987, p.132,Theorem 6.3] and de Kleer and Konolige [de Kleer and Konolige,
1989], however, and will be disregarded in the following.

We introduce some notation first, specifying more precisely the notions of
minimal model and circumscription we already gave in Section 2.2.1. In the
following, predicate constants and predicate variables are both referred to as
predicate symbols. If A denotes a list $a_1, \ldots, a_n$ of predicate symbols occurring
in a formula $\mathcal{G}$, then A' and A'' denote the lists $a'_1, \ldots, a'_n$ and $a''_1, \ldots, a''_n$, respectively, where it is assumed that for $1 \leq i \leq n$, a'_i and a''_i are new distinct
predicate symbols not occurring in $\mathcal{G}$ such that a_i, a'_i, a''_i are of the same arity.
AB denotes the concatenation of lists A and B of predicate symbols. If A, B are
the respective lists $a_1, \ldots, a_n$ and $b_1, \ldots, b_n$ of predicate symbols where a_i and
b_i are of the same arity, $1 \leq i \leq n$, we use the following notation:

$$(A \equiv \neg B) \quad \text{stands for} \quad \bigwedge_{1 \leq i \leq n} (\forall \mathbf{x}_i . a_i(\mathbf{x}_i) \equiv \neg b_i(\mathbf{x}_i)),$$

$$(A < B) \quad \text{stands for} \quad [\bigwedge_{1 \leq i \leq n} (\forall \mathbf{x}_i . a_i(\mathbf{x}_i) \rightarrow b_i(\mathbf{x}_i))] \wedge$$

$$[\bigvee_{1 \leq i \leq n} (\exists \mathbf{x}_i . \neg a_i(\mathbf{x}_i) \wedge b_i(\mathbf{x}_i))],$$

$$(A \equiv true) \quad \text{stands for} \quad [\bigwedge_{1 \leq i \leq n} (\forall \mathbf{x}_i . a_i(\mathbf{x}_i))].$$

We follow Lifschitz's notion of parallel circumscription in [Lifschitz, 1985b]. For
the reader's convenience we state more accurately the notions already given
in Section 2.2.1. For the definition of second order structures and models see
[Lifschitz, 1985b]; as Lifschitz, we denote the universe of a structure M by $|M|$.
For each list A of predicate constants, we denote by $[\![A]\!]_M$ the extension of
the A-predicates in structure M. We write $[\![A]\!]_M \leq [\![A]\!]_{M'}$ if and only if for

each a in A the extension of a in M is a subset of the extension of a in M'; $[A]_M < [A]_{M'}$ means $[A]_M \leq [A]_{M'}$ and $[A]_M \neq [A]_{M'}$. We write $M <_{P;Z} M'$ for models M, M' iff $|M| = |M'|$, the interpretation of functions and predicates not in PZ is identical and $[P]_M < [P]_{M'}$, where P, Z are disjoint lists of predicate constants. Model M is $P; Z$-minimal iff there is no model M' such that $M' <_{P;Z} M$. If P covers all predicates, minimal means $P; \emptyset$-minimal and $M < M'$ stands for $M <_{P;\emptyset} M'$.

$CIRC(T; P; Z)$ is defined by the second-order formula

$$T[P; Z] \wedge (\forall P'Z'. T[P'; Z'] \to \neg(P' < P)),$$

where P and Z are disjoint lists of predicate constants and $T[P'; Z']$ is T with each predicate symbol p in PZ replaced by p'. All remaining predicates not in PZ (the Q predicates) are fixed. Note that unlike in [Lifschitz, 1985b, Lifschitz, 1986a], functions are not allowed to vary. For convenience, we denote the circumscription of T under minimization of all predicates ($Q = Z = \emptyset$) by $CIRC(T)$.

de Kleer and Konolige have shown how to eliminate fixed predicates from a circumscription efficiently (even in linear time) [de Kleer and Konolige, 1989]; thus we may assume that no fixed predicates occur in T. Further, we may assume without loss of generality that in any instance of $CIRC(T; P; Z) \models F$ all predicates in the formula F occur in T: if a predicate p does not occur in T, simply join a tautology involving only p (e.g., $\forall x(p(x) \to p(x))$) to T.

The transformation is as follows:

Definition A.4.1 (reduction) *Let T, F be first-order formulae, and let the lists P, Z partition the predicate symbols in T. The first-order formula $\Gamma(T; F; P; Z)$ is defined as follows:*

$$\Gamma(T; F; P; Z) = (PZ \equiv \neg P''Z'') \wedge$$
$$[(u \wedge (P'Z' \equiv true)) \vee (\neg u \wedge \Theta(P, Z, P', Z'))]$$

where $\Theta(P, Z, P', Z')$ is the formula $(T \to F) \vee (T[P'; Z'] \wedge (P' < P))$.

Let us first give a rough intuitive explanation of this transformation. The predicates P'' and Z'' and the formula $PZ \equiv \neg P''Z''$ are added in order to make structures with different extensions of PZ incomparable. Hence, minimization has no effect on the predicates from $PZP''Z''$. This allows us to "simulate" standard semantics within a circumscription where all predicates are minimized. The only predicates in $CIRC(\Gamma(T; F; P; Z))$ that are effectively minimized are those in $P'Z'$ and u. Therefore, $CIRC(\Gamma(T; F; P; Z)) \models \neg u$ holds iff in each $P; Z$-minimal model of $\Gamma(T; F; P; Z)$, the formula $\Theta(P, Z, P', Z')$ is satisfied. This means that for each extension of P and Z, either $T \to F$, or the extension is not $P; Z$-minimal; in other words, $CIRC(T; P; Z) \models F$ holds.

For examples of this transformation, refer to the the following subsection, where its application is demonstrated for two well-known examples for inferencing under circumscription.

In the sequel, we formally prove that $CIRC(T; P; Z) \models F$ iff $CIRC(\Gamma(T; F; P; Z)) \models \neg u$. To this end, we first show a lemma stating that testing the validity of formulae belonging to a certain fragment of second order logic can be reduced to an inference problem under circumscription where all predicates are minimized. In order to show our main result, we then make use of this transformation.

Definition A.4.2 Let Ψ be a second-order formula of the form $\forall A \exists B \, \Phi(A, B)$ where A, B are disjoint lists of predicate variables and $\Phi(A, B)$ is a first-order formula. Denote by $\tau(\Psi)$ the following first-order formula:

$$(A \equiv \neg A'') \wedge [(u \wedge (B \equiv true)) \vee (\neg u \wedge \Phi(A, B))].$$

Lemma A.4.1 (from second-order validity to basic circumscription)
Let Ψ be a second-order formula of the form $\forall A \exists B \, \Phi(A, B)$ where A, B are disjoint lists of predicate variables and $\Phi(A, B)$ is a first-order formula containing no other predicate symbols except those in A and B. Then, Ψ is valid if and only if $CIRC(\tau(\Psi)) \models \neg u$.

PROOF: We first observe that for any possible universe U, $\tau(\Psi)$ has for any interpretation of the function symbols and any extension $\mathcal{E}$ of the A-predicates over U, a unique model M such that $|M| = U$, $[\![A]\!]_M = \mathcal{E}$, $M \models u$, and $M \models (\forall \mathbf{x}.b(\mathbf{x}))$ for every b from B. Furthermore, if any two models M, M' of $\tau(\Psi)$ satisfy $[\![A]\!]_M \neq [\![A]\!]_{M'}$, then neither $M < M'$ nor $M' < M$.

Now assume that Ψ is valid but $CIRC(\tau(\Psi)) \models \neg u$ is false. This means that there is a minimal model M of $\tau(\Psi)$ such that u is true in M. Observe that $[\![B]\!]_M$ is the maximum possible extension of B over $|M|$ because M satisfies $(B \equiv true)$. Since Ψ is valid, for the same extension of all function symbols, there must exist an extension $\mathcal{E}$ of B over $|M|$ such that $\Phi([\![A]\!]_M, \mathcal{E})$ is true over $|M|$. Now consider the structure M' with the same interpretation of functions as M and $[\![AA'']\!]_{M'} = [\![AA'']\!]_M$, $[\![B]\!]_{M'} = \mathcal{E}$, and u is false. Since $M' \models \neg u$, and $M' \models \Phi([\![A]\!]_M, \mathcal{E})$, it is a model of $\tau(\Psi)$. As $[\![AA'']\!]_{M'} = [\![AA'']\!]_M$, $[\![B]\!]_{M'} \leq [\![B]\!]_M$ and $[\![u]\!]_{M'} < [\![u]\!]_M$, we have $M' < M$. This is a contradiction to the minimality of M, however.

Conversely, assume that $CIRC(\tau(\Psi)) \models \neg u$ holds. Let $\mathcal{E}$ be an arbitrary extension of the A-predicates over some universe U. By our observation from above, there exists for any U and any function interpretation over U a model M of $\tau(\Psi)$ such that $|M| = U$, $[\![A]\!]_M = \mathcal{E}$, and $M \models u$. From $CIRC(\tau(\Psi)) \models \neg u$ it follows that M cannot be minimal; hence there exists a model $M' < M$ with $[\![A]\!]_{M'} = [\![A]\!]_M$ where u is not satisfied. (Clearly u cannot be satisfied in any model $M' < M$: Any such M' must satisfy $|M'| = |M| = U$ and $[\![A]\!]_{M'} = [\![A]\!]_M$, and since M is for this function interpretation the unique model of $\tau(\Psi)$

over U satisfying $[\![A]\!]_M = \mathcal{E}$ and $M \models u$, $M' \models \neg u$ must hold; hence, M' must satisfy $\neg u \wedge \Phi(A, B)$, the second term of the disjunction in $\tau(\Psi)$.) Consequently, $\Phi([\![A]\!]_{M'}, [\![B]\!]_{M'})$ is true over U under that function interpretation. Since U, the function interpretation and the extension $\mathcal{E} = [\![A]\!]_{M'}$ of the A-predicates over U were arbitrary, it follows that $\forall A \exists B\, \Phi(A, B)$ is true over any universe U under any function interpretation, and hence Ψ is valid. $\diamond$

Theorem 2.6.1 *Let T, F be first-order formulae such that all predicates in F appear in T, and let the lists P, Z partition the predicates in T. Then, $CIRC(T; P; Z) \models F$ if and only if $CIRC(\Gamma(T; F; P; Z)) \models \neg u$.*

PROOF: $CIRC(T; P; Z) \models F$ holds iff F is valid in every $P; Z$-minimal model of T [Lifschitz, 1985b, Proposition 1], that is $CIRC(T; P; Z) \models F$ is true iff every model of T is also a model of F or not a $P; Z$-minimal model of T. Thus $CIRC(T; P; Z) \models F$ is true iff the second-order formula $(\forall PZ.(T[P; Z] \rightarrow F) \vee (\exists P'Z'.(T[P'; Z'] \wedge (P' < P))))$ is valid, which is equivalent to the following formula $\Psi[T; F; P; Z]$:

$$(\forall PZ\, \exists P'Z'.(T[P; Z] \rightarrow F) \vee (T[P'; Z'] \wedge (P' < P))).$$

Note that $\Psi[T; F; P; Z]$ is of the form $\forall A \exists B\, \Phi(A, B)$, where $\Phi(A, B)$ is a first-order formula and $A = PZ, B = P'Z'$. Note that $\forall A \exists B \Phi(A, B)$ satisfies the conditions on the formula Ψ in Lemma A.4.1. Since $\tau(\forall A \exists B\, \Phi(A, B))$ is the first-order formula $(A \equiv \neg A'') \wedge [(u \wedge (B \equiv true)) \vee (\neg u \wedge \Phi(A, B))]$, we thus get by Lemma A.4.1 that $CIRC(T; F; Z) \models F$ iff $\neg u$ follows from the circumscription of the first-order formula

$$(PZ \equiv \neg P''Z'')\wedge$$

$$[(u \wedge (P'Z' \equiv true)) \vee (\neg u \wedge ((T \rightarrow F) \vee (T[P'; Z'] \wedge (P' < P)))))].$$

The latter formula is just the formula $\Gamma(T; F; P; Z)$; thus $CIRC(T; P; Z) \models F$ iff $CIRC(\Gamma(T; F; P; Z)) \models \neg u$. $\diamond$

Lemma A.4.1 and Theorem 2.6.1 put together are a simple proof for the fact that the problem of inferencing under circumscription, whether or not varying predicates are used, is precisely equivalent to the problem of checking the validity of a second-order formula belonging to the Π_2^1-level of the prenex hierarchy of second-order logic. By a well-known result of Hintikka [Hintikka, 1955], this problem (as well as validity checking for *any* higher-order formula) can be effectively reduced to validity checking of a monadic Σ_1^1 second-order formula as long as standard models are considered (see also [van Benthem and Doets, 1983].) Thus, under standard model semantics in the sense of [van Benthem and Doets, 1983], the inference problem under circumscription, with varying predicates as well as without, is complete for the class Σ_1^1. This complements a result shown by Schlipf [Schlipf, 1987], who proved that the same problem restricted to countably infinite models is $\Pi_2^1(\mathcal{N})$-complete, that is Π_2^1-complete over the natural numbers. (Note that the class $\Pi_2^1(\mathcal{N})$ of the analytical hierarchy is strictly more expressive than the class $\Sigma_1^1(\mathcal{N})$.)

The transformation as a syntactic reduction is feasible in linear time and hence very efficient. The question of how it affects the complexity of the *derivation* is rather intricate, however. On the one hand, our transformation adds new predicate symbols to the initial formula that lead to additional computational overhead. Also, some methods require the input to be in a special form. As an example, Przymusinski's method requires the circumscribed formula to be in clausal form. Hence, in order to use our transformation, the first step is to compute the clausal form of $\Gamma(T; F; P; Z)$. This computation may be very expensive, sometimes more expensive than transforming T itself into clause form. On the other hand, our transformation eliminates the handling of varying predicates, which constitutes a substantial part of most derivation algorithms. In Przymusinski's algorithm for instance, this step may cause exponential overhead. In summary, our transformation shifts the burden of handling varying predicates to predicate minimization.

A.4.2   Example

To illustrate the transformation, we consider the classic example of Tweety the bird (cf. Examples 2.2.1 and 2.2.2 in Section 2.2.)

Example A.4.1 (Tweety and circumscription (II)) Let our knowledge base be the following:

$$T = b(Tweety) \land \forall x (b(x) \land \neg ab(x) \to f(x))$$

(cf. formulae (2.2) and (2.3) in Section 2.1.) The intended meaning of b is "is a bird", of ab is "is abnormal", and of f is "flies".) The list P of the predicates to be minimized contains only ab, while the remaining predicates b and f are the varying predicates Z. It is well-known that $CIRC(T; P; Z) \models f(Tweety)$ (see, for example [Gelfond and Przymusinska, 1986, Lifschitz, 1985b].) The transformation we defined previously yields the following formula:

$$\begin{aligned}
\Gamma(T; f(Tweety); P; Z) \;=\; & [(ab, b, f) \equiv \neg(ab'', b'', f'')] \land \\
& [(u \land (ab', b', f' \equiv true)) \lor \\
& (\neg u \land \Theta(ab, b, f, ab', b', f'))],
\end{aligned}$$

where $\Theta(ab, b, f, ab', b', f') = [(T \to f(Tweety)) \lor (T[ab'; b', f'] \land (ab' < ab))]$. Substituting for our notation, we get

$$\Gamma(T; f(Tweety); P; Z) = C_1 \land C_2 \land C_3 \land [(u \land D_1) \lor (\neg u \land (D_2 \lor D_3))],$$

where

$$C_1 \;=\; \forall x\,(b(x) \equiv \neg b''(x)),$$

$$C_2 = \forall x \ (f(x) \equiv \neg f''(x)),$$
$$C_3 = \forall x \ (ab(x) \equiv \neg ab''(x)),$$
$$D_1 = \forall x \ (b'(x)) \wedge \forall x \ (f'(x)) \wedge \forall x \ (ab'(x)),$$
$$D_2 = [b(Tweety) \wedge \forall x \ (b(x) \wedge \neg ab(x) \rightarrow f(x))] \rightarrow f(Tweety),$$
$$D_3 = [b'(Tweety) \wedge \forall x \ (b'(x) \wedge \neg ab'(x) \rightarrow f'(x)) \wedge$$
$$\forall x \ (ab'(x) \rightarrow ab(x)) \wedge \exists x \ (\neg ab'(x) \wedge ab(x))].$$

We show that $CIRC(\Gamma(T; f(Tweety); P; Z)) \models \neg u$: Suppose that there exists a minimal model M of $\Gamma(T; f(Tweety); P; Z)$ such that $M \models u$; clearly $M \not\models D_2 \vee D_3$, otherwise the interpretation N of T which is equivalent to M everywhere but not in u ($N \not\models u$) would be a model of $\Gamma(T; f(Tweety); P; Z)$ such that $N < M$, but this contradicts the hypothesis that M is a minimal model of $\Gamma(T; f(Tweety); P; Z)$. Note that $M \not\models D_2$ implies $M \models ab(Tweety)$. Moreover $M \models D_1$, since M is a model of $\Gamma(T; f(Tweety); P; Z)$. We can define a new interpretation L of $\Gamma(T; f(Tweety); P; Z)$ such that L is equivalent to M everywhere but not in u or in ab' such that $L \models \neg u \wedge \forall x \ \neg ab'(x)$. Since $M \models D_1$, it follows that $L \models \forall x \ (b'(x)) \wedge \forall x \ (f'(x))$. Since $M \models ab(Tweety)$, it follows that $L \models ab(Tweety)$. It follows from this $L \models D_3$; this means that L is a model of $\Gamma(T; f(Tweety); P; Z)$. But $L < M$, which contradicts the hypothesis that M is minimal. $\diamond$

A.5 Appendix to Section 2.7

A.5.1 Appendix to Section 2.7.1

The structure of this subsection is as follows: In the first part we prove a semantic result (Theorem 2.7.1.) In the second part we provide the proofs for the intractable cases. Finally we provide the proofs for the tractable cases.

A.5.1.1 Semantics of NINs

Theorem 2.7.1 *Let $T = \langle \Gamma, \Omega, \Sigma \rangle$ be a NIN, $A(z)$ a ground literal of T^E, $E_1, \ldots, E_n$ all the exception predicates of T^E and T_z^E the projection of T^E w.r.t. z. Then*

$$CIRC(T^E; \{E_1, ..., E_n\}; \Gamma) \models A(z) \quad \text{if and only if}$$

$$ECWA(T_z^E; \{E_1, ..., E_n\}; \emptyset; \Gamma) \models A(z)$$

PROOF: We denote the set of predicates minimized in $CIRC(T^E; \{E_1, ..., E_n\}; \Gamma)$ with the symbol $\mathcal{P}$ and the set of letters minimized in $ECWA(T_z^E; \{E_1, ..., E_n\}; \Gamma)$ with the symbol P.

(*only if part:*) We assume that $A(z)$ is true in all $(\mathcal{P}; \Gamma)$-minimal models of T^E, that there exists a $(P; \Gamma)$-minimal model M of T_z^E such that $M \not\models A(z)$ and prove that a contradiction follows.

We build a Herbrand interpretation M' of T^E as follows:

- for each unary predicate symbol A and each constant symbol c of T^E:
  $M' \models A(c) \Longleftrightarrow M \models A(c)$;

- for each pair of constant symbols c_i, c_j of T^E such that $i \neq j$: $M' \models c_i \neq c_j$;

- for each constant symbol c_i of T^E: $M' \models c_i = c_i$.

M' is clearly a model of T^E and $M' \not\models A(z)$. As a consequence a Herbrand model M'' of T^E such that $M'' \leq_{(\mathcal{P};\Gamma)} M'$ must exist. Let us consider the interpretation of T_z^E defined as follows:

- for each unary predicate A and each constant symbol c of T^E: $M''' \models A(c) \Longleftrightarrow M'' \models A(c)$

M''' is clearly a model of T_z^E and $M''' \leq_{(P;\Gamma)} M$, but this contradicts the assumption that M is a $(P;\Gamma)$-minimal model of T_z^E.

(*if part:*) We assume that $A(z)$ is true in all $(P;\Gamma)$-minimal models of T_z^E, that there exists a $(\mathcal{P};\Gamma)$-minimal model M of T^E such that $M \not\models A(z)$ and prove that a contradiction follows.

Let U be the universe of interpretation of M. For each constant symbol c we denote with c_M the element of U which c is mapped to by M. For each unary (binary) predicate symbol S of T^E we denote with S_M the subset of U (of $U \times U$) which S is mapped to by M. We build an interpretation M' of T_z^E as follows:

- for each unary predicate A and each constant symbol c of T^E: $M' \models A(c) \Longleftrightarrow c_M \in A_M$

M' is clearly a model of T_z^E and $M' \not\models A(z)$. As a consequence a model M'' of T_z^E such that $M'' \leq_{(P;\Gamma)} M'$ must exist. We define an interpretation M''' of T_E, with universe U defined as follows:

- for each constant symbol c of T^E: $c_{M'''} \equiv c_M$.

- for each constant symbol c of T^E such that M' and M'' do not agree in c (i.e., there exists a literal $L(c)$ such that $M' \models L(c)$, $M'' \not\models L(c)$), for each element e of U such that $M \models c_M = e$, for each unary predicate symbol A of T^E: $M''' \models A(e) \Longleftrightarrow M'' \models A(c)$;

- M''' is the same as M on everything else.

We note that $M''' \leq_{(P;\Gamma)} M$ We show now that M''' is a model of T^E, thus proving a contradiction. First of all we note that the interpretation of the predicate symbol "$=$" is the same in M and in M'''. Moreover for each unary predicate B of T^E and each pair of elements $a, b \in U$

$$M'' \models a = b \Longrightarrow [M''' \models B(a) \Longleftrightarrow M''' \models B(b)]$$

This proves that M''' satisfies the equality axioms and the unique name axioms for T^E.

We prove now that M''' satisfies all proper axioms of T^E. M''' must satisfy ground axioms of T^E: let us assume that a ground axiom $\gamma(c)$ of T^E exists such that $M''' \not\models \gamma(c)$; two cases may occur

1. there exists a literal $L(c)$ such that $M' \models L(c)$, $M'' \not\models L(c)$; in this case $M'' \models \gamma(c) \Longleftrightarrow M''' \models \gamma(c)$. Since $M'' \models \gamma(c)$ there is a contradiction;

2. there is no literal $L(c)$ such that $M' \models L(c)$, $M'' \not\models L(c)$; in this case $M \models \gamma(c) \Longleftrightarrow M''' \models \gamma(c)$. Since $M \models \gamma(c)$ there is a contradiction.

Let us consider now the case of universally quantified axioms $\delta = \forall x\, (\neg B_1(x) \vee \neg B_2(x) \vee A(x))$ of T^E. If $M''' \not\models \delta$ an element $e \in U$ exists such that $M''' \models B_1(e) \wedge B_2(e) \wedge \neg A(e)$. Two cases may occur:

1. a constant symbol c of T^E exists such that $M''' \models c_{M'''} = e$ (this happens iff $M \models c_M = e$) and such that M' and M'' do not agree on c. In this case $M''' \models \neg A(c_{M'''}) \wedge B_1(c_{M'''}) \wedge B_2(c_{M'''})$, that —by construction of M''— implies $M'' \models \neg A(c) \wedge B_1(c) \wedge B_2(c)$, which is a contradiction;

2. such a constant symbol does not exists. In this case —by construction of M'''— $M \models \neg A(e) \wedge B_1(e) \wedge B_2(e)$, that is $M \not\models \delta$. Since M is a model of T^E this is a contradiction.

The proof is complete. $\Diamond$

A.5.1.2   Intractable cases

First of all we make a brief observation on the upper bound of the inference problem. According to Theorem 2.7.1 the inference problem can be polynomially reduced to ECWA in a propositional formula. As a consequence (see Appendix A.1.2) the upper bound of the inference problem is Π_2^p.

Theorem 2.7.2   *Let T be a NIN including only one assertion $A(z)$ of type 1, and any number of assertions of type 4 (negative strict assertions) and 5 (positive defeasible assertions.) Then, both checking whether $T \vdash B(z)$ (where B is a class symbol) and checking whether $T \vdash \neg B(z)$ are co-NP-hard problems.*

PROOF: We reduce the unsatisfiability problem to our problem by exhibiting a polynomial mapping from any CNF formula π to two literals $B(z), \neg C(z)$ and a NIN T with only one assertion of type 1, and any number of assertions of type 4 and 5 such that π is unsatisfiable iff $T \vdash B(z)$ iff $T \vdash \neg C(z)$.

Let π be a CNF formula on the alphabet L. Let L' be the set of classes $L \cup \{\overline{a} \mid a \in L\} \cup \{g_i \mid \gamma_i$ is a clause of $\pi\} \cup \{y\}$. Let $\Omega = \{z\}$ be a set of symbol objects. We define the NIN $T = \langle L', \Omega, \Sigma \rangle$, were the set of assertions Σ is obtained according to the following rules:

1. for each letter a of L, there are in Σ:

(a) two defeasible assertions y _gen_ a and y _gen_ $\overline{a}$;

(b) the strict assertion a _is − not_ $\overline{a}$;

2. for each clause $\gamma_i = \neg w_1 \vee \cdots \vee \neg w_n \vee w_{n+1} \vee \cdots \vee w_{n+m}$ in π, there are in Σ:

(a) $n + m$ strict assertions

g_i _is − not_ $\overline{w_1}, \ldots, g_i$ _is − not_ $\overline{w_n}, g_i$ _is − not_ $w_{n+1}, \ldots,$
g_i _is − not_ w_{n+m};

(b) the defeasible assertion y _gen_ g_i;

(c) the defeasible assertion g_i _gen_ B;

(d) the strict assertion g_i _is − not_ C;

Note that the above mapping from π to T is clearly polynomial, and T contains only one assertion of type 1, and assertions of type 4 and 5.

Let us consider now the propositional formula T_z^E. Let K be the conjunction $E_{g_1}(z) \wedge \cdots \wedge E_{g_h}(z)$, where $g_1, \ldots, g_h$ are all the classes of T corresponding to the clauses in π. Using Theorem 2.7.1 and the proof of Theorem A.1.4 in Appendix A.1.5.1 it is immediate to prove that K is ECWA-ffn in T_z^E iff π is unsatisfiable.

Moreover $T \vdash B(z)$ iff K is ECWA-ffn in T_z^E and $T \vdash \neg C(z)$ iff K is ECWA-ffn in T_z^E. This completes the proof. $\diamond$

Theorem 2.7.3   *Let T be a NIN including only one assertion $A(z)$ of type 1, and any number of assertions of type 5 and 6 (positive and negative defeasible assertions.) Then, both checking whether $T \vdash B(z)$ (where B is a class symbol) and checking whether $T \vdash \neg B(z)$ are co-NP-hard problems.*

PROOF: The proof is similar to that of Theorem 2.7.2. In particular we reduce the unsatisfiability problem to our problem by exhibiting a polynomial mapping from any CNF formula π to two literals $B(z), \neg C(z)$ and a NIN W with only one assertion of type 1, and any number of assertions of type 5 and 6 such that π is unsatisfiable iff $W \vdash B(z)$ iff $W \vdash \neg C(z)$.

Let π be a CNF formula on the alphabet L. Let L' and Ω like in the proof of Theorem 2.7.2. We define the NIN $W = \langle L', \Omega, \Sigma' \rangle$, were the set of assertions Σ' is obtained according to the following rules:

1. for each letter a of L, there are in Σ:

(a) two defeasible assertions y _gen_ a and y _gen − not_ $\overline{a}$;

2. for each clause $\gamma_i = \neg w_1 \vee \cdots \vee \neg w_n \vee w_{n+1} \vee \cdots \vee w_{n+m}$ in π, there are in Σ:

(a) $n + m$ defeasible assertions

g_i _gen_ $\overline{w_1}, \ldots, g_i$ _gen_ $\overline{w_n}, g_i$ _gen − not_ $w_{n+1}, \ldots, g_i$ _gen − not_ w_{n+m};

(b) the defeasible assertion g_i *gen* B;

(c) the defeasible assertion g_i *gen − not* C;

Note that the above mapping from π to W is clearly polynomial, and W contains only one assertion of type 1, and assertions of type 5 and 6.

Let us consider now the propositional formula W_z^E. Let K be the conjunction $E_{g_1}(z) \wedge \cdots \wedge E_{g_h}(z)$, where $g_1, \ldots, g_h$ are all the classes of W corresponding to the clauses in π. Using Theorem 2.7.1 and the proof of Theorem A.1.4 in Appendix A.1.5.1 it is immediate to prove that K is ECWA-ffn in W_z^E iff π is unsatisfiable.

Moreover $W \vdash B(z)$ iff K is ECWA-ffn in W_z^E and $W \vdash \neg C(z)$ iff K is ECWA-ffn in W_z^E. This completes the proof. $\diamond$

A.5.1.3 Tractable cases

Theorem 2.7.4 *Let T be a NIN including no assertion of type 5 (positive defeasible.) Then, both checking whether $T \vdash B(z)$ (where B is a class symbol) and checking whether $T \vdash \neg B(z)$ are polynomial-time problems.*

PROOF: First of all we note that in the NINs considered in this theorem there cannot be conflicting exceptions. In other words

$$ECWA(T_z^E; \{E_1, ..., E_n\}; \Gamma) \models B(z) \Longleftrightarrow CCWA(T_z^E; \{E_1, ..., E_n\}; \Gamma) \models B(z)$$

and the same holds for the inference of $\neg B(z)$. The basic computational problem in this kind of NINs is therefore to decide whether a literal $E_i(z)$ is CCWA-ffn in T_z^E, where E_i is the exception predicate corresponding to a negative defeasible assertion $\sigma_i : A$ *gen − not* B. Clearly if $T_z^E \models A(z) \wedge B(z)$ $E_i(z)$ is not CCWA-ffn in T_z^E. On the other hand if $T_z^E \not\models A(z) \wedge B(z)$ we cannot build a $(P; Z)$-minimal model of T_z^E in which $E_i(z)$ is true. As a consequence $E_i(z)$ is CCWA-ffn in T_z^E iff $T_z^E \not\models A(z) \wedge B(z)$. Since this test can be performed in polynomial time, we have a polynomial method for deciding whether both $CCWA(T_z^E; \{E_1, ..., E_n\}; \Gamma) \models B(z)$ and $CCWA(T_z^E; \{E_1, ..., E_n\}; \Gamma) \models \neg B(z)$ holds, i.e., for deciding $T \vdash B(z)$ and $T \vdash \neg B(z)$. $\diamond$

Theorem 2.7.5 *Let T be a NIN including no assertion of type 4 (negative strict assertions), and no assertion of type 6 (negative defeasible.) Suppose that T is acyclic (i.e., no cycle exists in the graph corresponding to T, considering only edges coming from is-a and gen assertions.) Then, both checking whether $T \vdash B(z)$ (where B is a class symbol) and checking whether $T \vdash \neg B(z)$ are polynomial-time problems.*

PROOF: First of all we can prove that for the NINs considered in this theorem it holds

$$ECWA(T_z^E; \{E_1, ..., E_n\}; \Gamma) \models B(z) \Longleftrightarrow CCWA(T_z^E; \{E_1, ..., E_n\}; \Gamma) \models B(z)$$

even if conflicting exceptions may occur. The same holds for the inference of $\neg B(z)$. The basic computational problem in this kind of NINs is therefore to decide whether a literal $E_i(z)$ is CCWA-ffn in T_z^E, where E_i is the exception predicate corresponding to a negative defeasible assertion $\sigma_i : A$ gen B.

We introduce now a representation of T_z^E as a directed graph G. There is a node A for each class symbol A in T. There are two special nodes Y, N in G. There is an edge from A to B for each assertion A gen B or A is $-$ a B in T. There is an edge from Y to A for an assertion $A(z)$ and an edge from A to N for an assertion $\neg A(z)$. We can prove that $E_i(z)$ —corresponding to A gen B— is CCWA-ffn in T_z^E iff for each cycle-free path from Y to N passing through A gen B there exists a node D in the path from B to N and a node C in the path from Y to A such that there is a path from C to D that uses only is-a edges.

Let us consider the set of cycle-free paths from Y to A not containing the edge A gen B. If $\alpha = \emptyset$ then $E_i(z)$ is CCWA-ffn in T_z^E. Let α be the set of nodes touched by such paths. Let σ be a cycle-free path from B to N. If such a path does not exist then $E_i(z)$ is CCWA-ffn in T_z^E. Let K be a node in σ and let β be the set of nodes from which β is reachable using only is-a edges. If $\alpha \cap \beta \neq \emptyset$ then we can safely eliminate K from the graph G and $E_i(z)$ is CCWA-ffn iff it is CCWA-ffn in the resulting formula. If $\alpha \cap \beta = \emptyset$ then we consider another node H in σ. If for each node of σ we find $\alpha \cap \beta = \emptyset$ then $E_i(z)$ is not CCWA-ffn in T_z^E. As a consequence for each step of this computation we can either eliminate a node or conclude that $E_i(z)$ is not CCWA-ffn in T_z^E.

We note that each step in the above computation is polynomial but the computation of α. If the graph G is cycle-free then α can be computed in linear time. Therefore we have a polynomial method for deciding whether both $CCWA(T_z^E; \{E_1, ..., E_n\}; \Gamma) \models B(z)$ and $CCWA(T_z^E; \{E_1, ..., E_n\}; \Gamma) \models \neg B(z)$ holds, i.e., for deciding $T \vdash B(z)$ and $T \vdash \neg B(z)$. $\diamond$

A.5.2   Appendix to Section 2.7.2

Theorem 2.7.6   *The following facts hold:*

1. *for every diagnosis Δ for $\langle SD, OBS, COMP \rangle$ there is a $(P; Z)$-minimal model M of $SD \cup OBS$ such that $\Delta = \{c \in COMP \mid M \models ab(c)\}$;*

2. *for every $(P; Z)$-minimal model M of $SD \cup OBS$ there is a diagnosis Δ for $\langle SD, OBS, COMP \rangle$ such that $\Delta = \{c \in COMP \mid M \models ab(c)\}$.*

PROOF:
   (Proof of 1) According to [Reiter, 1987, Definition 2.4] the formula

$$T = SD \cup OBS \cup \{ab(c) | c \in \Delta\} \cup \{\neg ab(c) | c \in COMP \setminus \Delta\}$$

is satisfiable. Let M be a model of T. M is clearly a model of $SD \cup OBS$.

We prove that M is a $(P; Z)$-minimal model for $SD \cup OBS$. Let us assume that M is not a $(P; Z)$-minimal model for $SD \cup OBS$ and let N be a model of

$SD \cup OBS$ such that $N <_{(P;Z)}$. Let Σ be the set $\{c \in COMP \mid N \models ab(c)\}$. Clearly $\Sigma \subset \Delta$. Moreover $OBS \cup \{ab(c)|c \in \Sigma\} \cup \{\neg ab(c)|c \in COMP \setminus \Sigma\}$ is satisfiable, N being one of its models. This contradicts the hypothesis that Δ is a diagnosis.

(Proof of 2) Let M be a $(P;Z)$-minimal model of $SD \cup OBS$ and Δ be the set $\{c \in COMP \mid M \models ab(c)\}$. First of all we note that the formula $SD \cup OBS \cup \{\neg ab(c)|c \in COMP \setminus \Delta\}$ is consistent, as M satisfies it.

Let us assume that Δ is not a diagnosis. According to [Reiter, 1987, Proposition 3.3] a set Σ must exist such that the formula $T \doteq SD \cup OBS \cup \{\neg ab(c)|c \in COMP \setminus \Sigma\}$ is satisfiable. Let N be a model of T. Clearly $N \models \neg ab(c)$ for each $c \in COMP \setminus \Sigma$. In other words the set of letters of P satisfied by N is a subset of the analogous set for M, i.e., N is a model of $SD \cup OBS$ and $N <_{(P;Z)} M$, but this is a contradiction. $\Diamond$

Appendix to Chapter 3

B.1   Appendix to Section 3.3

In the first subsection we prove the theorems announced in Section 3.3. In the second subsection we show how to reduce S-entailment to S-unsatisfiability. In the last subsection we analyze algorithms for testing S-1- and S-3-satisfiability of formulae.

B.1.1   Proofs of theorems

First of all we prove two lemmata that originally appeared in [Levesque, 1989] without proof. The lemmata have already been referenced in Section 3.1.1.

Lemma B.1.1 (soundness of $\models^3$) *If $T \models^3 \gamma$ holds, then $T \models \gamma$ holds.*

PROOF: Each 3-interpretation of T is also an interpretation of T. Therefore the set of interpretations satisfying T is a subset of the set of 3-interpretations satisfying T. The same holds for γ. Hence if γ is true in all the 3-interpretations satisfying T, then it is also true in all the interpretations satisfying T. ◇

Lemma B.1.2 (polynomiality of $\models^3$) *$T \models^3 \gamma$ holds iff either a clause subsumed by γ (i.e., such that all its literals also occur in γ) occurs in T or a pair $p, \neg p$ of literals occurs in γ. Therefore, determining if $T \models^3 \gamma$ holds can be checked in $O(|T| \cdot |\gamma|)$ time.*

PROOF: Let L' be the alphabet $L \cup \{\bar{p} \mid p \in L\}$. Let T' be the formula obtained from T by substituting each occurrence of a negative literal $\neg p$ with the corresponding letter $\bar{p}$ of L'. Let γ' be the clause obtained from γ in the same way. Let T'' be the formula obtained by conjoining T' with all the clauses of the set $\{(p \vee \bar{p}) \mid p \in L\}$. Let γ'' be the clause obtained from γ' in the same way. It is easy to note that there is a 1-1 correspondence between the set of 3-interpretations of T and the set of interpretations of T'': in each 3-interpretation of T the unique constraint on the truth values of a pair of corresponding literals $p, \neg p$ is that they cannot be both 0; moreover, in each interpretation of T'' the unique constraint on the truth values of a pair of corresponding literals $p, \overline{p}$ is that they cannot be both 0. The same property holds for the set of 3- interpretations of γ and the set of interpretations of γ''. Therefore $T \models^3 \gamma$ holds iff $T'' \models \gamma''$ holds. Since negative literals do not occur either in T'' or in γ'', the last relation holds iff either a clause subsumed by γ' (i.e., such that all its literals also occur in γ') occurs in T' or a pair $p, \overline{p}$ of literals occurs in γ'. Therefore $T \models^3 \gamma$ holds iff either a clause subsumed by γ occurs in T or a pair $p, \neg p$ of literals occurs in γ. This can be checked in $O(|T| \cdot |\gamma|)$ time. $\Diamond$

Theorem 3.3.1   *For any S, S' such that $S \subseteq S' \subseteq L$, if $T \models^3_S \gamma$ holds, then $T \models^3_{S'} \gamma$ (hence $T \models \gamma$.) Moreover if $T \not\models^1_S \gamma$ holds and both a letter l of $S' \setminus S$ and its negation $\neg l$ do not occur in γ, then $T \not\models^1_{S'} \gamma$ holds (hence $T \not\models \gamma$.)*

PROOF: As far as $\models^3_S$ is concerned, the proof is the same as that of Lemma B.1.1.

As for $\models^1_S$, we prove that $T \models^1_{S'} \gamma$ implies $T \models^1_S \gamma$.

Suppose that $T \models^1_{S'} \gamma$ holds and that there exists an S-1-interpretation M satisfying T but not satisfying γ. We show that this leads to a contradiction.

We build an S'-1-interpretation N of the alphabet L of T in the following way:

- for each $l \in S$, N maps l into 1 iff M maps l into 1; moreover it maps $\neg l$ into the opposite value;

- for each $l \in S' \setminus S$ such that l occurs in γ, N maps l into 0 and $\neg l$ into 1;

- for each $l \in S' \setminus S$ such that $\neg l$ occurs in γ, N maps l into 1 and $\neg l$ into 0;

- for each remaining letter l, N maps l and $\neg l$ into 0.

Note that N is an S'-1-interpretation of L, since it maps every letter l of S' and its negation $\neg l$ into opposite values and it maps each remaining literal into 0. Moreover, it satisfies T, since M maps at least one literal per clause of T into 1, and the set of literals that N maps into 1 is a superset of the set of literals M maps into 1. It is easy to note that N does not satisfy γ, but this contradicts the hypothesis that $T \models^1_{S'} \gamma$ holds. $\Diamond$

Theorem 3.3.3   *There exists an algorithm for deciding if $T \models^3_S \gamma$ and deciding if $T \models^1_S \gamma$ which runs in $O(|T| \cdot |\gamma| \cdot 2^{|S|})$ time.*

PROOF: As far as $\models^3_S$ is concerned, forthcoming Theorem B.1.3 states that $T \models^3_S \gamma$ can be tested by performing $2^{|S|}$ tests of the kind $T \models^3 \delta$, where δ has size proportional to the size of γ. Using Lemma B.1.2, we obtain the desired upper bound for the complexity of $\models_S^3$.

As for $\models_S^1$, forthcoming Theorem B.1.5 reduces $T \models_S^1 \gamma$ to the problem of testing S-1-unsatisfiability of $T \wedge \delta$, where δ is a CNF formula with size proportional to the size of γ. As we already showed in Section 3.3, S-1-satisfiability of a formula Γ in NNF can be tested in time $O(|\Gamma| \cdot 2^{|S|})$ by: 1) substituting each positive or negative literal whose corresponding letter occurs in S with the propositional constant false; 2) running any satisfiability algorithm on the resulting formula. Algorithms for testing S-1-satisfiability will be further analyzed in the following. $\diamond$

Theorem B.1.3 (from S-3-entailment to 3-entailment) *Let S be the set* $\{a_1, \ldots, a_m\}$. $T \models_S^3 \gamma$ *iff* $T \models^3 \gamma \vee [(a_1 \wedge \neg a_1) \vee \cdots \vee (a_m \wedge \neg a_m)]$ *holds, or equivalently* $T \models^3 \gamma \vee (c_1 \vee \cdots \vee c_m)$ *holds for any combination* $\{c_1, \ldots, c_m\}$, *where each* c_i $(1 \leq i \leq m)$ *is either* a_i *or* $\neg a_i$.

PROOF: (*only if part*) Suppose that $T \models_S^3 \gamma$ holds and a set $\{c_1, \ldots, c_m\}$ exists where each c_i $(1 \leq i \leq m)$ is either a_i or $\neg a_i$, such that $T \not\models^3 c_1 \vee \cdots \vee c_m$ holds. We show that this leads to a contradiction.

If $T \not\models^3 c_1 \vee \cdots \vee c_m$ holds, then a 3-interpretation M satisfying T exists such that T does not satisfy $c_1 \vee \cdots \vee c_m$. Note that M maps each literal c_i $(1 \leq i \leq m)$ into 0. This implies that it maps each literal $\neg c_i$ $(1 \leq i \leq m)$ into 1. Therefore, M is also a S-3-interpretation, but this contradicts the hypothesis that $T \models_S^3 \gamma$.

(*if part*) Suppose that both $T \models^3 (a_1 \wedge \neg a_1) \vee \cdots \vee (a_m \wedge \neg a_m)$ and $T \not\models_S^3 \gamma$. We show that this leads to a contradiction.

If $T \not\models_S^3 \gamma$, then an S-3-interpretation M satisfying T and not satisfying γ exists. We build a set H of literals in the following way: for each i $(1 \leq i \leq m)$, if M maps a_i into 0, then put a_i in H; if M maps $\neg a_i$ into 0, then put $\neg a_i$ in H. Note that exactly one literal in $\{a_i, \neg a_i\}$ $(1 \leq i \leq m)$ occurs in H. Let H be $\{c_1, \ldots, c_m\}$, where each c_i $(1 \leq i \leq m)$ is either a_i or $\neg a_i$. Since M is a 3-interpretation satisfying T, $T \not\models^3 c_1 \vee \cdots \vee c_m$ holds, but this contradicts the hypothesis that $T \models^3 (a_1 \wedge \neg a_1) \vee \cdots \vee (a_m \wedge \neg a_m)$ holds. $\diamond$

Theorem 3.3.4 *For any S, S' such that $S \subseteq S' \subseteq L$, if T is S-1-satisfiable, then T is S'-1-satisfiable (hence satisfiable.) Moreover if T is S-3-unsatisfiable, then T is S'-3-unsatisfiable (hence unsatisfiable.)*

PROOF: A formula T is S-1-satisfiable if and only if $T \not\models_S^1 \square$, where $\square$ denotes the empty clause. Analogously, T is S-3-satisfiable if and only if $T \not\models_S^3 \square$. The thesis follows by using Theorem 3.3.1. $\diamond$

B.1.2   Reducing S-entailment to S-unsatisfiability

In this subsection we deal with a different computational aspect of S-entailment. By taking into account that $T \models \gamma$ holds iff $T \cup \{\neg \gamma\}$ is unsatisfiable —i.e., for 2-valued semantics entailment can be reduced to unsatisfiability—

we develop methods for testing S-1- and S-3-entailment based on S-1- and S-3-unsatisfiability, respectively. First of all, we introduce a set describing the clause γ.

Definition B.1.1 *We denote with letters(γ) the set $\{l \in L \mid l$ occurs in $\gamma\} \cup \{l \in L \mid \neg l$ occurs in $\gamma\}$.*

The next lemma shows that, when dealing with S-3-entailment, we can safely choose an S such that $letters(\gamma) \subseteq S$.

Lemma B.1.4 *Suppose letters(γ) $\not\subseteq S$ holds. Let S' be the set $S \cup letters(\gamma)$. $T \models^3_S \gamma$ holds iff $T \models^3_{S'} \gamma$ holds.*

PROOF: (*only if part*) See Theorem 3.3.1.
   (*if part*) Suppose both $T \not\models^3_S \gamma$ and $T \models^3_{S'} \gamma$. We will show that this leads to a contradiction. An S-3-interpretation M exists such that M satisfies T and it does not satisfy γ. It follows that M maps each literal of γ into 0. This implies that M maps each literal of $\neg\gamma$ into 1, therefore M is also an S'-3-interpretation, but this contradicts the hypothesis that $T \models^3_{S'} \gamma$ holds. $\Diamond$.

The next two theorems show that S-1- and S-3-entailment can be reduced to S-1- and S-3-unsatisfiability, respectively.

Theorem B.1.5 (reducing S-1-entailment to S-1-unsatisfiability) *Let γ be $\gamma_S \vee \gamma_{\overline{S}}$, where both letters($\gamma_S$) $\subseteq S$ and letters($\gamma_{\overline{S}}$) $\cap S = \emptyset$ hold. $T \models^1_S \gamma$ holds iff $T \cup \{\neg\gamma_S\}$ is not S-1-satisfiable.*

PROOF: (*only if part*) Suppose that $T \cup \{\neg\gamma_S\}$ is S-1-satisfiable; let M be the S-1-interpretation satisfying it. M satisfies T, but it does not satisfy γ_S. Moreover, M does not satisfy $\gamma_{\overline{S}}$ because it maps all its literals into 0. Therefore $T \not\models^1_S \gamma_S \vee \gamma_{\overline{S}}$ holds.
   (*if part*) Suppose that $T \cup \{\neg\gamma_S\}$ is not S-1-satisfiable and that $T \not\models^1_S \gamma$ holds. We show that this leads to a contradiction. An S-1-interpretation M exists such that M satisfies T and does not satisfy γ. M maps each literal of γ into 0. Since no literal of γ_S is in $L \setminus S$, M satisfies $\neg\gamma_S$. Therefore M satisfies $T \cup \{\neg\gamma_S\}$, but this contradicts the former hypothesis. $\Diamond$

Theorem B.1.6 (reducing S-3-entailment to S-3-unsatisfiability) *Let letters(γ) $\subseteq S$ hold. $T \models^3_S \gamma$ holds iff $T \cup \{\neg\gamma\}$ is not S-3-satisfiable.*

PROOF: Analogous to that of Theorem B.1.5 with $\gamma = \gamma_S$. $\Diamond$

We now present some simple observations leading to significant simplifications of the formulae whose S-1- and S-3-unsatisfiability we must check in order to prove S-1- and S-3-entailment.

We define an operation on formulae; we say that $\Theta = simplify(\Gamma, \delta)$, where Θ and Γ are CNF formulae and δ is a set or a conjunction of literals, if Θ is obtained from Γ through the following steps:

1. delete all clauses of Γ that contain a literal occurring in δ;

2. in any clause β of Γ delete all literals l whose negation $\neg l$ occurs in δ.

This operation can be done in $O(|\Gamma| \cdot |\delta|)$ time. Note that no literal p of δ or its negation $\neg p$ occurs in Θ. Moreover, the simplified CNF formula Θ is always smaller than the original formula Γ, since some of the clauses of the latter disappeared, and some of the remaining clauses contain less literals. We can now prove a simple result about simplified formulae, stating that the simplifying process does not lead to loss of information.

Theorem B.1.7 (simplifying) *Let δ be a set of literals such that letters$(\delta) \subseteq S$ holds and both a letter l and its negation $\neg l$ do not occur in δ; $simplify(T, \delta)$ is S-1-satisfiable iff $T \cup \delta$ is S-1-satisfiable. In addition, $simplify(T, \delta)$ is S-3-satisfiable iff $T \cup \delta$ is S-3-satisfiable.*

PROOF: (*if part for both properties*) Suppose that $T \cup \delta$ is S-x-satisfiable (x = 1 or 3.) Let M be a S-x-interpretation satisfying it. M maps each literal of δ into 1. Since $\delta \subseteq S$ holds, M maps the negation of each literal of δ into 0. Therefore, given any clause β of T in which the negation of a literal of δ occurs, M satisfies one of the remaining literals of β. Taking into account that the only clauses of $simplify(T, \delta)$ are sub-clauses of those in which the negation of a literal of δ occurs, we can easily note that M satisfies $simplify(T, \delta)$.

(*only if part for both properties*): Suppose that $simplify(T, \delta)$ is S-x-satisfiable. Let M be a S-x-interpretation satisfying it. Note that M satisfies every clause of T in which no literal of δ occurs. Recall that no literal of δ occurs in $simplify(T, \delta)$. We build a S-x-interpretation N according to the following rule: N maps any literal l of δ into 1 and its negation $\neg l$ into 0; moreover, N is equivalent to M for any remaining literal. M satisfies every clause of T in which no literal of δ occurs; therefore N satisfies the same clauses. Moreover, N satisfies all the literals in δ and every clause of T in which at least one literal of δ occurs. Therefore N satisfies $T \cup \delta$. $\diamond$

The above theorem is intuitive when $S = L$ holds, that is, for the 2-valued logic. By taking into account Theorems B.1.5 and B.1.6, the above result shows that, in order to prove whether $T \not\models_S^1 \gamma$ and $T \models_S^3 \gamma$ holds, we can focus our attention on S-1-satisfiability of $simplify(T, \neg\gamma_S)$ and on S-3-unsatisfiability of $simplify(T, \neg\gamma)$, respectively. The role of simplification of T is that of reducing its dimensions, thus gaining efficiency in the whole process of determining the validity of the entailment relation $\models$. Anyway, the simplification can be done if the following hypotheses hold:

1. γ is not a tautology;

2. $letters(\gamma) \subseteq S$ [only for $\models^3_S$].

Since checking entailment of tautologies is a trivial problem, the first hypothesis can be assumed without loss of generality. Lemma B.1.4 shows that also the second hypothesis can be assumed without loss of generality.

The following theorems provide two methods for testing S-1-satisfiability and S-3-unsatisfiability of a formula.

Theorem B.1.8 (testing S-3-satisfiability) *Let S be the set $\{a_1, \ldots, a_m\}$. T is S-3-unsatisfiable iff $T \models^3 (a_1 \wedge \neg a_1) \vee \cdots \vee (a_m \wedge \neg a_m)$ holds, or equivalently $T \models^3 (c_1 \vee \cdots \vee c_m)$ holds for any combination $\{c_1, \ldots, c_m\}$, where each c_i $(1 \leq i \leq m)$ is either a_i or $\neg a_i$.*

PROOF: See proof of Theorem B.1.3. $\Diamond$

Theorem B.1.9 (testing S-1-satisfiability) *Let S be the set $\{a_1, \ldots, a_m\}$. T is S-1-satisfiable iff there exists a set $\alpha = \{c_1, \ldots, c_m\}$, where each c_i $(1 \leq i \leq m)$ is either a_i or $\neg a_i$, such that $simplify(T, \alpha)$ contains no clauses.*

PROOF: (*if part*) Suppose that for a set $\alpha = \{c_1, \ldots, c_m\}$, where each c_i $(1 \leq i \leq m)$ is either a_i or $\neg a_i$, such that $simplify(T, \alpha)$ does not contain any clause. We define an S-1-interpretation M according to the following rule: M maps every letter l of $L \setminus S$ and its negation $\neg l$ into 0; M maps every letter a_i of $L \setminus S$ into 1 iff a_i occurs in α, otherwise it maps a_i into 0; M maps $\neg a_i$ into the opposite value. Taking into account that the process of simplification deletes all the clauses of T which contain a literal appearing in α, we can easily note that M maps at least one literal per clause of T into 1. Therefore M is a S-1-interpretation satisfying T.

    (*only if part*) Suppose that T is S-1-satisfiable and let M be a S-1-interpretation satisfying it. We define a set of literals α according to the following rule: if M maps a letter a_i of S into 1 then a_i occurs in α; if M maps a letter a_i of S into 0 then $\neg a_i$ occurs in α. Note that α is the set $\{c_1, \ldots, c_m\}$, where each c_i $(1 \leq i \leq m)$ is either a_i or $\neg a_i$. Taking into account that M maps at least one literal per clause of T into 1, we can easily note that $simplify(T, \alpha)$ does not contain any clause, since the process of simplification deletes all the clauses of T which contain a literal occurring in α. $\Diamond$

B.1.3   Algorithms for testing S-satisfiability

As we showed in the last subsection, testing S-entailment can always be reduced to testing S-satisfiability. In this subsection we focus on the development of an algorithm for checking S-1- and S-3-satisfiability. In the first part we show the relations existing between S-satisfiability and famous algorithms for satisfiability. In the second part we design an original algorithm.

B.1.3.1 Resolution and Enumeration

Satisfiability of CNF formulae is a very well-known problem in 2-valued propositional logic, extensively studied and discussed in the specialized literature. Here we focus on two of the major types of algorithms for satisfiability:

1. Resolution-based algorithms (e.g. [Robinson, 1965]): they try to prove unsatisfiability of a formula T by deriving the empty clause from it. If the empty clause cannot be derived, then T is satisfiable;

2. Enumeration-based algorithms (e.g. [Davis and Putnam, 1960]): they try to prove satisfiability of a formula T by generating an interpretation which satisfies T. If such an interpretation is not found, then T is unsatisfiable.

The first type of algorithms is more directed to proving unsatisfiability, hence we expect that they are well suited to check S-3-unsatisfiability, while we expect that the latter ones are well suited to check S-1-satisfiability. We now state formally the correspondence between these algorithms and the checks we are interested in. In the following we denote with $\square$ the empty clause, and with Ω the CNF formula with no clauses.

In order to show the link existing between S-satisfiability and resolution-based algorithms, we introduce a collection of CNF formulae T^i ($1 \leq i \leq m$), defined as follows (we denote with $\{a_1, \ldots, a_m\}$ the set S):

- $T^0 = T$;

- $T^{i+1} = \{x | \exists y_1, y_2 \in T^i \text{ and } x \text{ is the resolvent of } y_1 \text{ and } y_2 \text{ upon } a_{i+1}\} \cup \{x | x \in T^i, a_{i+1} \notin x \text{ and } \neg a_{i+1} \notin x\}$.

The CNF formula T^i ($1 \leq i \leq m$) is the conjunction of all the resolvents at i-th level of the resolution tree having T as the root and which have been produced by resolving upon all the literals in $\{a_1, \ldots, a_i\}$ in any order. Note that T^i has $O(2^i)$ times the number of clauses T has. Note also that no literal of $\{a_1, \ldots, a_i\}$ occurs in T^i. The next theorem shows how S-satisfiability of a CNF formula T can be computed using the resolution method.

Theorem B.1.10 (S-satisfiability and resolution) *A formula T is S-3-satisfiable iff T^m is S-3-satisfiable iff $\square \notin T^m$. A formula T is S-1-satisfiable iff T^m is S-1-satisfiable iff $T^m = \Omega$.*

PROOF: We divide the proof into two parts, first of all we prove, at the same time, the two equivalences : T is S-3-satisfiable iff T^m is S-3-satisfiable and T is S-1-satisfiable iff T^m is S-1-satisfiable. In the last part we prove the other two equivalences: T^m is S-3-satisfiable iff $\square \notin T^m$ and T^m is S-1-satisfiable iff $T^m = \Omega$. We prove the first part by induction on m. The base case is trivial since $T^0 = T$, in the inductive case we have:

(*if part for both properties*) Suppose that there is an S-x-interpretation I satisfying T^i ($0 < i < m$) then I maps into 1 at least one literal of any clause of T^i. Let us assume that there is one clause β of T^{i+1} which is not satisfied by I we show that this leads to a contradiction. This clause β cannot belong to T^i because it would be satisfied by I, so it must be the resolvent of two clauses $\beta_1 = \{d_1, \ldots, d_k, a_{i+1}\}$ and $\beta_2 = \{f_1, \ldots, f_j, \neg a_{i+1}\}$ of T^i which resolved upon a_{i+1}. Since I satisfies β but not β_1 and β_2 then it must be the case that I maps a_{i+1} and $\neg a_{i+1}$ into 1, but this contradicts the hypothesis that I is an S-x-interpretation.

(*only if part for both properties*) Suppose that there is an S-x-interpretation I satisfying T^{i+1} $(0 < i < m)$ then I maps into 1 at least one literal of any clause of T^{i+1}. Let us assume that there is one clause β of T^i which is not satisfied by I we show that this leads to a contradiction. This clause β_1 cannot belong to T^{i+1} because it would be satisfied by I, so in it must occur a_{i+1} and I maps a_{i+1} into 0, or in it occurs $\neg a_{i+1}$ and I maps $\neg a_{i+1}$ into 0. In the first case define a new S-x-interpretation I' which is equivalent to I except that it maps a_{i+1} into 1, note that this new interpretation I' satisfies T^{i+1} because a_{i+1} does not occur in it. If there is another clause $\beta_2 \in T^i$ which is not satisfied by I' then in β_2 must occur $\neg a_{i+1}$ and now we have that the resolvent of β_1 and β_2 belongs to T^{i+1}, but this resolvent is not satisfied by I' hence contradiction.

We now show that T^m is S-3-satisfiable iff $\Box \notin T^m$ and T^m is S-1-satisfiable iff $T^m = \Omega$. Note that T^m does not contain any of the letters of S, hence T^m is S-3-satisfiable iff it is 3-satisfiable, but any formula not containing $\Box$ is 3-satisfiable because the 3-interpretation mapping all the literals into 1 will satisfy it. For the same reason, T^m is S-1-satisfiable iff it is 1-satisfiable, but any formula containing at least one clause is 1-unsatisfiable because the 1-interpretation maps all the literals into 0 and, therefore, does not satisfy it. $\Diamond$

Similar considerations enable us to relate S-satisfiability of a CNF formula T to the Davis-Putnam algorithm for checking satisfiability [Davis and Putnam, 1960]. For this aim we introduce a collection Φ^i $(1 \leq i \leq m)$ of sets of CNF formulae defined as follows:

- $\Phi^0 = \{T\}$;

- $\Phi^{i+1} = \{W | \exists H \in \Phi^i$ and $W = simplify(H, \{a_{i+1}\})\} \cup \{W | \exists H \in \Phi^i$ and $W = simplify(H, \{\neg a_{i+1}\})\}$.

The collection Φ^i $(1 \leq i \leq m)$ is the set of all the CNF formulae H obtained by simplifying T with any set of literals representing a 2-interpretation of the letters in $\{a_1, \ldots, a_i\}$. In the generation of Φ^{i+1} any formula H belonging to Φ^i is replaced by the two formulae $simplify(H, \{a_{i+1}\})$ and $simplify(H, \{\neg a_{i+1}\})$. Note that Φ^i has 2^i CNF formulae, each being smaller than T.

Theorem B.1.11 (S-satisfiability and Davis-Putnam algorithm) *A formula T is S-3-satisfiable iff there exists a $H \in \Phi^m$ that is S-3-satisfiable; H is S-3-satisfiable iff $\Box \notin H$. A formula T is S-1-satisfiable iff there exists a $H \in \Phi^m$ that is S-1-satisfiable; H is S-1-satisfiable iff $H = \Omega$.*

PROOF: We divide the proof into two parts, first of all we prove, at the same time, the two equivalences : T is S-3-satisfiable iff there exists a $H \in \Phi^m$ that is S-3-satisfiable and T is S-1-satisfiable iff there exists a $H \in \Phi^m$ that is S-1-satisfiable. In the last part we prove that any $H \in \Phi^m$ is S-3-satisfiable iff $\square \notin H$ and it is H is S-1-satisfiable iff $H = \Omega$. We prove the first part by induction on m. The base case is trivial since $T^0 = T$, in the inductive case we have:

(*if part for both properties*) Suppose that there is an S-x-interpretation I satisfying an $H \in \Phi^i$ $(0 < i < m)$ then I maps into 1 at least one literal of any clause of H. There are two formulae $H_1 = simplify(H, \{a_{i+1}\})$ and $H_2 = simplify(H, \{\neg a_{i+1}\})$ which occur in Φ^{i+1}. Since I is an S-x-interpretation it maps a_{i+1} into 1 and $\neg a_{i+1}$ into 0 or the reverse; we show that in the first case I satisfies H_1, while in the second case I satisfies H_2. We examine the first case, the other case is similar. We assume that there is a clause β in H_1 which is not satisfied by I and show that this leads to a contradiction. It is clear that β does not belong to H, hence β has been obtained by $\beta_1 = \beta \cup \{\neg a_{i+1}\}$ where $\beta_1 \in H$, but now we have that I does not validate β_1 because I maps into 0 all literals of β and also maps $\neg a_{i+1}$ into 0, hence we obtain a contradiction.

(*only if part for both properties*) Suppose that there is an S-x-interpretation I satisfying an $H_1 \in \Phi^{i+1}$ $(0 < i < m)$ then I maps into 1 at least one literal of any clause of H_1. Since in H_1 the literals a_{i+1} and $\neg a_{i+1}$ do not occur then also the interpretation I' which is equal to I, except that it maps these two literals into the opposite of the value of I, satisfies H_1. We know that there exist an $H \in \Phi^i$ s.t. either $H_1 = simplify(H, \{a_{i+1}\})$ or $H_1 = simplify(H, \{\neg a_{i+1}\})$, we show that in the first case I satisfies H while in the second case I' satisfies H. We examine the first case, the other case is similar. We assume that there is a clause β in H which is not satisfied by I and show that this leads to a contradiction. It is clear that β has been eliminated in the simplifying process, because otherwise it would be satisfied by I. But the only reason why it may have been eliminated is because in it occurs a_{i+1} and in this case β is satisfied by I, hence contradiction.

The last part is immediately proven noticing that any $H \in \Phi^m$ will not contain any literal of the set S, hence the result trivially follows from the proof of the last part of the Theorem B.1.10. $\diamond$

B.1.3.2 The algorithm

We briefly sketch our desiderata about an algorithm for testing S-satisfiability:

- the algorithm must compute at the same time both S-1-satisfiability and S-3-unsatisfiability of a generic formula;

- it should benefit from previous computations. In other words, if for a given S, T is still S-1-unsatisfiable and S-3-satisfiable, we probably want to try with a set $S' \supset S$. In principle this may happen after hours or days, depending on our computing resources; therefore we want our algorithm to compute satisfiability *incrementally*, using information gained in previous steps;

- although we expect that the algorithm runs in time exponential in $|S|$, we want the algorithm to use polynomial space.

By taking into account that we want to accommodate a stepwise extension of the set S, an important issue for an efficient algorithm is that this extension does not require to perform all the computations from scratch. In other words, some form of *history* must be kept from the past computations.

Theorems B.1.10 and B.1.11 provide a semantics, based on S-3-unsatisfiability and on S-1-satisfiability respectively, for each step of the algorithms for satisfiability based on resolution principle and on enumeration of truth assignments. These two theorems also provide the basis for straightforward algorithms for checking S-3-unsatisfiability and S-1-satisfiability. Simply by generating the CNF formula T^m we can determine at the same time S-3-unsatisfiability and S-1-satisfiability of the formula T simply by checking whether T^m contains $\Box$ or T^m is equal to Ω, in the same way this can be done through the generation of the set of formulae Φ^m. Moreover, both algorithms are incremental: if for a given S, T is still S-1-unsatisfiable and S-3-satisfiable and we take into account the set $S' = S \cup \{a_{m+1}\}$, then, in order to compute T^{m+1}, we only need T^m; in the same way, in order to compute Φ^{m+1} we only need Φ^m. These two algorithms fulfill our first two desiderata, but unfortunately they fail to accomplish the third one, because both algorithms use an amount of space which grows exponentially with the size of S. Note that this is not to say that the resolution algorithm and the Davis-Putnam algorithm necessarily need to use an exponential amount of space, since this is avoided if the associated search tree is visited depth-first rather than breadth-first.

This is particularly evident in the Davis-Putnam algorithm. In fact, we can perform both checks using a polynomially-bounded amount of space if we generate every combination $\delta = \{c_1, \ldots, c_m\}$, where each c_i $1 \leq i \leq m$ is either a_i or $\neg a_i$, one at the time. S-1-satisfiability is proven when we find a δ such that $simplify(T, \delta) = \Omega$. On the other hand, S-3-unsatisfiability is proven if for all δ we have that $simplify(T, \delta)$ contains the clause $\Box$. This procedure fulfills the first and the third desiderata, but fails to fulfill the second one, since when we take into account a set $S' = S \cup \{a_{m+1}\}$ we are not able to exploit the previous computations and we must generate each combination $\{c_1, \ldots, c_m, c_{m+1}\}$.

A further possibility for determining S-1- and S-3-satisfiability is to reduce T to T_S^1 and T_S^3, respectively, as sketched in the last part of Section 3.3.2, and check their 2-satisfiability. These reductions may simplify the computations, but they force us to work on two different formulae, thus making difficult the integration of the checks. Furthermore, it is not clear how to make these computations incremental, since the reduced formulae T_S^3 and T_S^1 vary with the set S.

Our analysis has shown that all of the above algorithms fail to fulfill all of the desiderata, hence, we now develop an enumeration algorithm for performing the satisfiability check based on Theorems B.1.8 and B.1.9. The basic idea of this algorithm is that, given any set $S = \{a_1, \ldots, a_m\}$, at any step we generate a combination $\alpha = \{c_1, \ldots, c_m\}$ of literals such that each c_i $(1 \leq i \leq m)$ is either a_i or $\neg a_i$. To generate all the combinations $\{c_1, \ldots, c_m\}$ we use the binary coding of an integer j varying between 0 and $2^m - 1$. If $simplify(T, \alpha)$ does not contain any clause then T is S-1-satisfiable. Conversely, if $T \not\models^3 (c_1 \vee \cdots \vee c_m)$, then T is S-3-satisfiable. In the first case we have a definite answer, while in the second case we can stop our check of S-3-unsatisfiability. Note that, if $\{c_1, \ldots, c_m\}$ is the first combination such that $T \not\models^3 (c_1 \vee \cdots \vee c_m)$ holds, then for any other combination $\{g_1, \ldots, g_m\}$ previously generated, $T \models^3 (g_1 \vee \cdots \vee g_m)$ holds. If $S' = S \cup \{a_{m+1}\}$ is the next set that we consider, we already know that $T \models^3 (g_1 \vee \cdots \vee g_m \vee \neg a_{m+1})$ and $T \models^3 (g_1 \vee \cdots \vee g_m \vee a_{m+1})$. Hence, in order to prove S'-3-satisfiability, we can start to generate combinations from $\{c_1, \ldots, c_m, \neg a_{m+1}\}$. Therefore, the combination $\{c_1, \ldots, c_m\}$ represents the history of our computation and is provided as an output through an integer j_{out}, which will be used as an input of the next call of the algorithm. In the same way, we suppose to have the integer j_{in} as input, representing the history of the previous call. Note that if every clause of T does not contain at least one literal of S (i.e., T_S^1 contains the empty clause), then T is clearly S-1-unsatisfiable, therefore we do not need to generate its simplifications.

Algorithm B.1 formalizes the procedure sketched above. In this algorithm we assume that the set S is incremented of a single unit at any step, its generalization is obvious.

We note that, if we restrict the algorithm to check S-3-unsatisfiability and we extend S through successive calls to the algorithm, then the number of checks of 3-entailment is less or equal than $2^{|L|}$.

B.2   Appendix to Section 3.4

In this section we prove the results announced in Section 3.4.

Theorem 3.4.1 $(\models \Box_S^3 \alpha \rightarrow \Box_S^3 \gamma)$ iff $(\Box_S^3 \alpha \wedge \neg \Box_S^3 \gamma$ is unsatisfiable) iff $(\alpha \models_S^3 \gamma)$.

PROOF: We prove the theorem by showing the following three properties:

1. $(\Box_S^3 \alpha \wedge \neg \Box_S^3 \gamma$ is unsatisfiable) implies $(\models \Box_S^3 \alpha \rightarrow \Box_S^3 \gamma)$;

2. $(\models \Box_S^3 \alpha \rightarrow \Box_S^3 \gamma)$ implies $(\alpha \models_S^3 \gamma)$;

3. $(\alpha \models_S^3 \gamma)$ implies $(\Box_S^3 \alpha \wedge \neg \Box_S^3 \gamma$ is unsatisfiable.)

Proof of 1: Assume that $\Box_S^3 \alpha \wedge \neg \Box_S^3 \gamma$ is unsatisfiable. The property can be proven by means of the following steps:

1. $\not\models \Box_S^3 \alpha \rightarrow \Box_S^3 \gamma$.

Algorithm S-3-unsat/S-1-sat;
Input an alphabet L, a subset $S = \{a_1, \ldots, a_m\}$ of L, a CNF formula T
     and an integer j_{in} such that $0 \leq j_{in} \leq (2^{m-1} - 1)$;
Output true, iff T is S-1-satisfiable, false iff T is S-3-unsatisfiable,
     an integer j_{out} such that $0 \leq j_{out} \leq (2^m - 1)$ otherwise;
begin
  if T_S^1 contains $\square$ (* if there is a clause of T that does not
                                contain at least one literal of S *)
  then S-1-unsat := $true$ (* then it cannot be S-1-satisfiable *)
  else S-1-unsat := $false$; (* else T could be S-1-satisfiable *)
  S-1-sat := $false$;   (* S-1-sat is $false$ until we prove S-1-satisfiability *)
  S-3-unsat := $true$;   (* S-3-unsat is $true$ until we prove S-3-satisfiability *)
  $exit$:= $false$;   (* this flag is used to control the loop *)
  $j := 0$;
  while $(j < 2^m)$ **and** (**not** $exit$)
  do begin
       let $d_1 \cdots d_m$ be the binary coding of j; (* d_m is the least significant bit *)
       for $i := 1$ **to** m **do**   (* computation of a combination of literals *)
          if $d_i = 1$
          then $c_i := a_i$
          else $c_i := \neg a_i$;
       if $(j \geq 2 * j_{in})$ **and** (S-3-unsat)
       then if $T \not\models^3 (c_1 \vee \cdots \vee c_m)$
          then begin
               S-3-unsat := $false$;
               $j_{out} := j$
               if S-1-unsat (* T is both S-3-satisfiable
                             and S-1-unsatisfiable *)
               then $exit$:= $true$; (* hence we exit the loop *)
             end;
       if not S-1-unsat
       then if $simplify(T; \{c_1, \ldots, c_m\})$ contains no clauses
          then begin
               S-1-sat := $true$; (* T is S-1-satisfiable *)
               $exit$:= $true$ (* hence we exit the loop *)
          end
      $j := j + 1$
    end;   (* while *)
  if S-1-sat **then return** $true$;
  if S-3-unsat **then return** $false$
          else return j_{out}
end;

Algorithm B.1: S-3-unsat/S-1-sat

2. $\exists \mathcal{M}.\exists s.\mathcal{M}, s \not\models \Box_S^3\alpha \to \Box_S^3\gamma$.

3. $\exists \mathcal{M}.\exists s.(\mathcal{M}, s \not\models \neg\Box_S^3\alpha)$ and $(\mathcal{M}, s \not\models \Box_S^3\gamma)$.

4. $\exists \mathcal{M}.\exists s.\neg(\exists t \in S\text{-}3(Sit) \; sRt$ and $\mathcal{M}, t \not\models \alpha)$ and $\neg(\forall t \in S\text{-}3(Sit) \; sRt$ implies $\mathcal{M}, t \models \gamma)$

5. $\exists \mathcal{M}.\exists s.(\forall t \in S\text{-}3(Sit) \; sRt$ implies $\mathcal{M}, t \models \alpha)$ and $(\exists t \in S\text{-}3(Sit) \; sRt$ and $\mathcal{M}, t \not\models \gamma)$

6. $\exists \mathcal{M}.\exists s.\mathcal{M}, s \models \Box_S^3\alpha$ and $\mathcal{M}, s \models \neg\Box_S^3\gamma$

7. $\exists \mathcal{M}.\exists s.\mathcal{M}, s \models \Box_S^3\alpha \wedge \neg\Box_S^3\gamma$

8. $\Box_S^3\alpha \wedge \neg\Box_S^3\gamma$ is satisfiable, hence contradiction.

Proof of 2: Assume that $(\models \Box_S^3\alpha \to \Box_S^3\gamma)$ and $(\alpha \not\models_S^3 \gamma)$. Hence, there exists an S-3-interpretation I s. t. $I \models \alpha$ and $I \not\models \gamma$. Let $\mathcal{M} = (Sit, R, V)$ where $Sit = \{s\}$, $R = \{(s, s)\}$ and $V(s) = I$. We have that $\mathcal{M}, s \models \alpha$ and $\mathcal{M}, s \not\models \gamma$. Since s is the only situation in Sit, we also have that $\mathcal{M}, s \models \Box_S^3\alpha$ and $\mathcal{M}, s \models \neg\Box_S^3\gamma$. Therefore, $\mathcal{M}, s \not\models \Box_S^3\alpha \to \Box_S^3\gamma$, but this contradicts the assumptions.

Proof of 3: Assume that $\alpha \models_S^3 \gamma$. The property can be proven by means of the following steps:

1. $\Box_S^3\alpha \wedge \neg\Box_S^3\gamma$ is satisfiable.

2. $\exists \mathcal{M}.\exists s.\mathcal{M}, s \models \Box_S^3\alpha \wedge \neg\Box_S^3\gamma$.

3. $\exists \mathcal{M}.\exists s.(\mathcal{M}, s \models \Box_S^3\alpha)$ and $(\mathcal{M}, s \models \neg\Box_S^3\gamma)$.

4. $\exists \mathcal{M}.\exists s.(\forall t \in S\text{-}3(Sit) \; sRt$ implies $\mathcal{M}, t \models \alpha)$ and $(\exists t \in S\text{-}3(Sit) \; sRt$ and $\mathcal{M}, t \not\models \gamma)$

5. $\exists \mathcal{M}.\exists s.\exists t \in S\text{-}3(Sit) \; sRt$ and $\mathcal{M}, t \not\models \gamma \wedge \mathcal{M}, t \models \alpha)$

6. There exists an x s. t. x is an S-3-interpretation and $x \not\models \alpha$ and $x \models \gamma$

7. $\alpha \not\models_S^3 \gamma$, hence contradiction. $\Diamond$

Theorem 3.4.2 $(\models \Box_S^1\alpha \to \Box_S^1\gamma)$ iff $(\Box_S^1\alpha \wedge \neg\Box_S^1\gamma$ is unsatisfiable) iff $(\alpha \models_S^1 \gamma)$.

PROOF: Simply replace S-1 for S-3 in the previous proof. $\Diamond$

Proposition 3.4.3   *The following relations hold*

Nec : $\models \alpha$ *does not imply* $\models \Box_S^1\alpha$

$K \ : \ \models \Box_S^1(\alpha \to \beta) \to (\Box_S^1\alpha \to \Box_S^1\beta)$

$T \ : \ \not\models \Box_S^1\alpha \to \alpha$

$4 \ : \ \models \Box_S^1\alpha \to \Box_S^1\Box_S^1\alpha$

$5 \ : \ \models \neg\Box_S^1\alpha \to \Box_S^1\neg\Box_S^1\alpha$

PROOF: The validity of the schemata 4 and 5 is a straightforward consequence of the properties of the accessibility relation, while the schema K follows from the semantic definition of $\Box_S^1$. We now show counterexamples for the properties which do not hold.

$Nec \ : \ $ Let $\alpha = q \vee \neg q$, $S = \emptyset$, $\mathcal{M} = (Sit, R, V)$, $Sit = \{s_1, s_2\}$, $R = \{(s_1, s_1),$ $(s_1, s_2), (s_2, s_1), (s_2, s_2)\}$, $V(s_1)(q) = 1$ and $V(s_1)(\neg q) = V(s_2)(q) = V(s_2)(\neg q) = 0$. We have that $\models \alpha$ holds but $\models \Box_S^1\alpha$ does not hold, in fact $\mathcal{M}, s_1 \not\models \Box_S^1\alpha$.

$T \ : \ $ Let $S = \emptyset$, $\mathcal{M} = (Sit, R, V)$, $Sit = \{s_1\}$, $R = \{(s_1, s_1)\}$, $V(s_1)(\neg p) = 1$ and $V(s_1)(p) = 0$. $\Box_S^1 p \to p$ is valid iff $\forall N \ \forall w \in W(Sit) \ N, w \models \neg\Box_S^1 p \vee$ $N, w \models p$. Since by instantiating N to $\mathcal{M}$ and w to s_1 we obtain that $\mathcal{M}, s_1 \not\models \neg\Box_S^1 p$ and $\mathcal{M}, s_1 \not\models p$ then it is not the case that $\Box_S^1\alpha \to \alpha$ is valid. $\Diamond$

Proposition 3.4.4 *The following relations hold:*

$Nec \ : \ \models \alpha \ implies \models \Box_S^3\alpha$

$K \ : \ \not\models \Box_S^3(\alpha \to \beta) \to (\Box_S^3\alpha \to \Box_S^3\beta)$

$T \ : \ \models \Box_S^3\alpha \to \alpha$

$4 \ : \ \models \Box_S^3\alpha \to \Box_S^3\Box_S^3\alpha$

$5 \ : \ \models \neg\Box_S^3\alpha \to \Box_S^3\neg\Box_S^3\alpha$

PROOF: Again, the schemata 4 and 5 are a straightforward consequence of the properties of the accessibility relation, while the schema T and the rule Nec follow from the semantic definition of $\Box_S^3$. We now show a counterexample for the property K. Let $S = \emptyset$, $\mathcal{M} = (Sit, R, V)$, $Sit = \{s_1, s_2\}$, $R = \{(s_1, s_1), (s_1, s_2), (s_2, s_1), (s_2, s_2)\}$, $V(s_1)(p) = V(s_1)(q) = V(s_2)(p) = V(s_2)(\neg p) = V(s_2)(\neg q) = 1$ and $V(s_1)(\neg p) = V(s_1)(\neg q) = V(s_2)(q) = 0$. We have that $\mathcal{M}, s_1 \models \Box_S^3(p \to q)$ and $\mathcal{M}, s_1 \models \Box_S^3 p$ but $\mathcal{M}, s_1 \models \Box_S^3 q$ does not hold. $\Diamond$

Proposition 3.4.5 *Let* $S \subseteq S' \subseteq L.$ $\models (\Box_S^3\alpha \to \Box_{S'}^3\alpha).$

PROOF: Assume that

1. $\not\models \Box_S^3\alpha \rightarrow \Box_{S'}^3\alpha$.

2. $\exists\mathcal{M}.\exists s.\mathcal{M}, s \not\models \Box_S^3\alpha \rightarrow \Box_{S'}^3\alpha$.

3. $\exists\mathcal{M}.\exists s.\mathcal{M}, s \models \Box_S^3\alpha$ and $\mathcal{M}, s \not\models \Box_{S'}^3\alpha$.

4. $\exists\mathcal{M}.\exists s.(\forall t \in S\text{-}3(Sit)\ sRt$ implies $\mathcal{M}, t \models \alpha)$ and $(\exists x \in S'\text{-}3(Sit)\ sRx$ and $\mathcal{M}, x \not\models \alpha)$.

5. Since $S'\text{-}3(Sit) \subseteq S\text{-}3(Sit)$, we have that $\exists x \in S\text{-}3(Sit)\ sRx$ and $\mathcal{M}, x \not\models \alpha$. But for such an x we also have that $\mathcal{M}, x \models \alpha$, hence contradiction. $\diamond$

B.3   Appendix to Section 3.5

The structure of this section is the following: in the first subsection we give a preliminary result and some definitions; in the second and the third subsections we prove the results announced in Section 3.5.

B.3.1   Preliminaries

Some of the proofs given in the following use the standard semantics of concept languages based on extension functions. Now we briefly recall this semantics (for more details see [Schmidt-Schauß and Smolka, 1991].)

An interpretation $\mathcal{I} = (\Delta^{\mathcal{I}}, \cdot^{\mathcal{I}})$ consists of a set $\Delta^{\mathcal{I}}$ (the domain) and a function $\cdot^{\mathcal{I}}$ that maps every concept to a subset of $\Delta^{\mathcal{I}}$ and every role to a subset of $\Delta^{\mathcal{I}} \times \Delta^{\mathcal{I}}$ such that $\top^{\mathcal{I}} = \Delta^{\mathcal{I}}$, $\bot^{\mathcal{I}} = \emptyset$, $(C\sqcap D)^{\mathcal{I}} = C^{\mathcal{I}} \cap D^{\mathcal{I}}$, $(\neg A)^{\mathcal{I}} = \Delta^{\mathcal{I}} \setminus A^{\mathcal{I}}$, $(\forall R.C)^{\mathcal{I}} = \{a \in \Delta^{\mathcal{I}} \mid \forall b.(a, b) \in R^{\mathcal{I}} \rightarrow b \in C^{\mathcal{I}}\}$, and $(\exists R.C)^{\mathcal{I}} = \{a \in \Delta^{\mathcal{I}} \mid \exists b.(a, b) \in R^{\mathcal{I}} \wedge b \in C^{\mathcal{I}}\}$.

A concept C is satisfiable if and only if there exists an interpretation $\mathcal{I}$ such that $C^{\mathcal{I}}$ is non empty. We say C is subsumed by D ($C \sqsubseteq D$) if for every interpretation $\mathcal{I}$ we have $C^{\mathcal{I}} \subseteq D^{\mathcal{I}}$.

In order to prove some of the results of the paper we need the following lemma. Let C be an $\mathcal{ALC}$ concept and D one of its sub-concepts, we denote with $C(D/G)$ the concept obtained by replacing every occurrence of D in C with the concept G.

Lemma B.3.1 (replacing sub-concepts) *Let C be an $\mathcal{ALC}$ concept and D one of its sub-concepts which is in the scope of no $\neg$ operators. Let G be another $\mathcal{ALC}$ concept. If $D \sqsubseteq G$ then $C(D/G)$ is satisfiable if C is satisfiable. On the other hand, if $G \sqsubseteq D$ then C is satisfiable if $C(D/G)$ is satisfiable.*

PROOF: The proof is done by induction on the structure of C. In the base case we have that $C = D$, thus $C(D/G) = G$ and $D \sqsubseteq G$ then satisfiability of C implies satisfiability of $C(D/G)$. In the general case we have to show that all the language constructors except negation preserve this property. In particular $D \sqsubseteq G$ implies $C' \sqcap D \sqsubseteq C' \sqcap G$, $C' \sqcup D \sqsubseteq C' \sqcup G$, $\exists R.D \sqsubseteq \exists R.G$

and $\forall R.D \sqsubseteq \forall R.G$. The proof is straightforward for all cases. A dual argument holds for the case of $G \sqsubseteq D$. $\diamond$

Dealing with an S-1-interpretation M, when an atom $\alpha \in B_h \setminus S$ belongs neither to M^+ nor to M^-, we say that α is mapped into *undefined*.

Dealing with an S-3-interpretation M, when an atom $\alpha \in B_h \setminus S$ belongs both to M^+ and to M^-, we say that α is mapped into *inconsistent*.

B.3.2   Appendix to Section 3.5.3

Theorem 3.5.1   *For each i $(0 \le i \le n+1)$, if $C_i^\top$ is unsatisfiable then $C_j^\top$ is unsatisfiable for all $j \ge i$, hence C is unsatisfiable.*
   For each i $(0 \le i \le n+1)$, if $C_i^\perp$ is satisfiable then $C_j^\perp$ is satisfiable for all $j \ge i$, hence C is satisfiable.

PROOF: It follows from Lemma B.3.1. In on case we are replacing sub-concepts of C with $\top$ and it is always the case that a concept is subsumed by $\top$. Furthermore, even if $\mathcal{ALE}$ allows negation, we never replace sub-concepts which are under the scope of $\neg$ operator so the proof of Lemma B.3.1 still holds. In the other case, in which we replace sub-concepts of C with $\perp$, the other part of Lemma B.3.1 is used. $\diamond$

Theorem 3.5.3   *For all i $(0 \le i \le n+1)$ C is S_i-3-satisfiable iff $C_i^\top$ is satisfiable.*

PROOF: *(only if part)* Suppose that $C_i^\top$ is satisfiable, i.e., that $SNF(\Gamma(C_i^\top))$ is satisfiable. Let $M = \langle M^+, M^- \rangle$ be an Herbrand model of $SNF(\Gamma(C_i^\top))$. We define an S_i-3-interpretation $N = \langle N^+, N^- \rangle$ of $SNF(\Gamma(C))$ according to the following rules:

- for each atom $\alpha \in S_i$:

    - $\alpha \in M^+ \Longrightarrow \alpha \in N^+$;
    - $\alpha \in M^- \Longrightarrow \alpha \in N^-$;

- for each atom $\alpha \in H_b \setminus S_i$: $\alpha \in N^+$ and $\alpha \in N^-$.

Note that N is necessarily an S_i-3-interpretation of $SNF(\Gamma(C))$, since the Herbrand base of $SNF(\Gamma(C_i^\top))$ is equal to S_i. We now show that N is also an S_i-3-model, thus proving that C is S_i-3-satisfiable. Since $SNF(\Gamma(C))$ is an universally quantified formula, it is sufficient to show that N satisfies all its ground instances. We split the proof in two sub-cases:

1. all the variables of $SNF(\Gamma(C))$ are bound to terms belonging to U_i. In this case for every instance g of $SNF(\Gamma(C))$ there exists a corresponding instance h of $SNF(\Gamma(C_i^\top))$, where the same variables are bound to the same

terms. More precisely, all the atoms of h belong to S_i, and h is obtained from g by substituting some of its sub-formulae with $\top$. All the atoms occurring in these sub-formulae are instantiated on terms of $U_k \setminus U_i$, where $k > i$ and U_k is a stratum of the Herbrand base of $SNF(\Gamma(C))$. Therefore all these atoms belong to $S_k \setminus S_i$, hence are mapped into *inconsistent* by N. Since $M \models SNF(\Gamma(C_i^\top))$, we know that $M \models h$, hence $N \models h$. Since g differs from h in some literals which are anyway mapped into *inconsistent* by N, it follows that $N \models g$.

2. at least one variable of $SNF(\Gamma(C))$ is bound to a term not belonging to U_i. By definition of N, we know that all the atoms instantiated to those terms are mapped by N to *inconsistent*. Since the Herbrand universe of $SNF(\Gamma(C_i^\top))$ is equal to U_i, some instances g of $SNF(\Gamma(C))$ do not have a corresponding instance of $SNF(\Gamma(C_i^\top))$. Let us consider an instance g' of $SNF(\Gamma(C_i^\top))$ obtained from g by binding any variable not bound to terms belonging to U_i to terms of U_i in an arbitrary way. From the previous item we know that $N \models g'$. Remember all the atoms instantiated to terms not belonging to U_i are mapped into *inconsistent* by N. Therefore g differs from g' in some literals which are mapped into *inconsistent* by N, hence it follows that $N \models g$.

(if part) Suppose that C is S_i-3-satisfiable, i.e., that $SNF(\Gamma(C))$ is S_i-3-satisfiable. Let $N = \langle N^+, N^- \rangle$ be an S_i-3 Herbrand model of $SNF(\Gamma(C))$. We define an Herbrand interpretation $M = \langle M^+, M^- \rangle$ of $SNF(\Gamma(C_i^\top))$ according to the following rule. For each atom $\alpha \in S_i$:

- $\alpha \in N^+ \implies \alpha \in M^+$;

- $\alpha \in N^- \implies \alpha \in M^-$;

Note that M is necessarily an Herbrand interpretation of $SNF(\Gamma(C_i^\top))$, since the Herbrand base of $SNF(\Gamma(C_i^\top))$ is equal to S_i. We now show that M is also an Herbrand model, thus proving that $C_i^\top$ is satisfiable. Since $SNF(\Gamma(C_i^\top))$ is an universally quantified formula, it is sufficient to show that M satisfies all its ground instances g. Let h be any instance of $SNF(\Gamma(C))$ which corresponds to g, where the same variables are bound to the same terms. Since $N \models SNF(\Gamma(C))$, we know that $N \models h$. Moreover h is obtained from g by substituting each occurrence of $\top$ with a formula. Since $\top$ occurs always positively in g and is satisfied by M, it follows that $M \models g$. $\diamond$

Theorem 3.5.4   *For all i $(0 \leq i \leq n+1)$ C is S_i-1-satisfiable iff $C_i^\perp$ is satisfiable.*

PROOF: *(only if part)* Suppose that $C_i^\perp$ is satisfiable, i.e., that $SNF(\Gamma(C_i^\perp))$ is satisfiable. Let $M = \langle M^+, M^- \rangle$ be an Herbrand model of $SNF(\Gamma(C_i^\perp))$. We define an S_i-1-interpretation $N = \langle N^+, N^- \rangle$ of $SNF(\Gamma(C))$ according to the following rules:

- for each atom $\alpha \in S_i$:

  - $\alpha \in M^+ \Longrightarrow \alpha \in N^+$;
  - $\alpha \in M^- \Longrightarrow \alpha \in N^-$;

- for each atom $\alpha \in H_b \setminus S_i$: $\alpha \notin N^+$ and $\alpha \notin N^-$.

Note that N is necessarily an S_i-1-interpretation of $SNF(\Gamma(C))$, since the Herbrand base of $SNF(\Gamma(C_i^{\perp}))$ is equal to S_i. We now show that N is also an S_i-1-model, thus proving that C is S_i-1-satisfiable. Since $SNF(\Gamma(C))$ is an universally quantified formula, it is sufficient to show that N satisfies all its ground instances. We recall that, by definition of S-1-satisfiability, we have only to consider ground instances of $SNF(\Gamma(C))$ in which variables are substituted by terms of the set $Terms(S_i)$, which are the terms occurring in the set S_i, i.e., are the terms of U_i. Therefore we know that all the variables of $SNF(\Gamma(C))$ are bound to terms belonging to U_i. This implies that for every instance g of $SNF(\Gamma(C))$ there exists a corresponding instance h of $SNF(\Gamma(C_i^{\perp}))$, where the same variables are bound to the same terms. More precisely, all the atoms of h belong to S_i, and h is obtained from g by substituting some of its sub-formulae with $\perp$. Since $M \models SNF(\Gamma(C_i^{\top}))$, we know that $M \models h$, hence $N \models h$. Note that $\perp$ is not satisfied by N, therefore $N \models g$ even if the sub-formulae in which g differs from h are not satisfied. Since this is the "worst" case, it follows that $N \models g$.

(if part) Suppose that C is S_i-1-satisfiable, i.e., that $SNF(\Gamma(C))$ is S_i-1-satisfiable. Let $N = \langle N^+, N^- \rangle$ be an S_i-1 Herbrand model of $SNF(\Gamma(C))$. We define an Herbrand interpretation $M = \langle M^+, M^- \rangle$ of $SNF(\Gamma(C_i^{\perp}))$ according to the following rule. For each atom $\alpha \in S_i$:

- $\alpha \in N^+ \Longrightarrow \alpha \in M^+$;

- $\alpha \in N^- \Longrightarrow \alpha \in M^-$;

Note that M is necessarily an Herbrand interpretation of $SNF(\Gamma(C_i^{\perp}))$, since the Herbrand base of $SNF(\Gamma(C_i^{\perp}))$ is equal to S_i. We now show that M is also an Herbrand model, thus showing that $C_i^{\perp}$ is satisfiable. Since $SNF(\Gamma(C_i^{\perp}))$ is an universally quantified formula, it is sufficient to show that M satisfies all its ground instances g. Let h be any instance of $SNF(\Gamma(C))$ which corresponds to g, where the same variables are bound to the same terms. Since $N \models SNF(\Gamma(C))$, we know that $N \models h$. Moreover h is obtained from g by substituting each occurrence of $\perp$ with a formula. All the atoms occurring in this formula are instantiated on terms of $U_k \setminus U_i$, where $k > i$ and U_k is a stratum of the Herbrand base of $SNF(\Gamma(C))$. Therefore all these atoms belong to $S_k \setminus S_i$, hence are mapped into *undefined* by N. Since M maps $\perp$ into 0, it follows that $M \models g$.
$\diamond$

B.3.3   Appendix to Section 3.5.4

Theorem 3.5.5 *Let P be a subset of $\mathcal{A}$ and i be an index such that $0 \leq i \leq n+1$. If $C_{P,i}^{\top}$ is unsatisfiable then any subconcept D of C such that $C_{P,i}^{\top} \preceq D$ is* *unsatisfiable. If $C_{P,i}^{\perp}$ is satisfiable then any subconcept D of C such that $C_{P,i}^{\perp} \preceq D$ is satisfiable.*

PROOF: The same proof of Theorem 3.5.1 applies also in this case. In fact, we only allow negation in front of primitive concepts. Hence, we never replace sub-concepts that are in the scope of the $\neg$ operator. $\diamond$

Theorem 3.5.7   *For all i ($0 \leq i \leq n+1$) and $P \subseteq \mathcal{A}$ the concept C is $S_{P,i}$-3-satisfiable iff $C_{P,i}^{\top}$ is satisfiable.*

PROOF: The proof is very similar to that of Theorem 3.5.3 with the additional complication of replacing some of the primitive concepts and their negation with $\top$. This is however already taken into account when we define the Herbrand base H_b of a simplified concept $C_{P,i}^{\top}$. In fact, H_b will only contain atoms of concepts appearing in $C_{P,i}^{\top}$ and, even in this case, is equal to $S_{P,i}$. Hence, the same proof of Theorem 3.5.3 applies. $\diamond$

Theorem 3.5.8   *For all i ($0 \leq i \leq n+1$) and $P \subseteq \mathcal{A}$ the concept C is $S_{P,i}$-1-satisfiable iff $C_{P,i}^{\perp}$ is satisfiable.*

PROOF: The proof is very similar to that of Theorem 3.5.4 since similar considerations to the ones done in the proof of Theorem 3.5.7 hold. $\diamond$

B.4   Appendix to Section 3.6

B.4.1   Appendix to Section 3.6.1

Lemma 3.6.1   *Let $S \subseteq S' \subseteq L$, $\langle D, W \rangle$ be a normal default theory and E be one of its S-3-extensions. There exists an E' s.t. $E' \supseteq E$ and E' is an S'-3-extension of $\langle D, W \rangle$.*

PROOF : Let $GD_S^3(E, D, W) \subseteq D$ be the set of generating defaults associated to E. As a consequence of the monotonicity of S-3-entailment and S-1-satisfiability all the defaults in this set are applicable also for S' together, possibly, with other defaults. Furthermore, since the property of semi-monotonicity of normal default theories ([Reiter, 1980b, Theorem 3.2]) holds for S-3-extensions as well, there exists an S'-3-extension E' s. t. $GD_{S'}^3(E', D, W) \supseteq GD_S^3(E, D, W)$, hence, $E' \supseteq E$. $\diamond$

Lemma 3.6.2   *Let $S \subseteq S' \subseteq L$ and $\langle D, W \rangle$ be a normal default theory. For all E' being an S'-1-extension there exists an E being an S-1-extension s.t. $E' \subseteq E$.*

PROOF: Let $GD_S^1(E, D, W) \subseteq D$ be the set of generating defaults associated to E. Since S-1-entailment implies S'-1-entailment and S-3-satisfiability implies

S'-3-satisfiability, then it follows that all the defaults in $D \setminus GD_S^1(E, D, W)$ are not applicable also for S' together, possibly, with other defaults. In other words, $GD_{S'}^1(E', D, W) \subseteq GD_S^1(E, D, W)$, from which $E' \subseteq E$. $\Diamond$

Theorem 3.6.3 *Let* $\langle D, W \rangle$ *be a normal default theory and* $S \subseteq L$ *be a non empty set of letters. If* W *is* S-3-satisfiable then all the S-3-extensions of $\langle D, W \rangle$ *are also* S-3-satisfiable. *If* W *is* S-1-satisfiable then all the S-1-extensions of $\langle D, W \rangle$ *are also* S-1-satisfiable.

PROOF : Assume that W is S-3-satisfiable and let E be an S-3-unsatisfiable set s. t. $E = \{\epsilon | \epsilon$ is a non-tautological clause and $E \models_S^3 \epsilon\}$. Let $p \in S$. Since E is S-3-unsatisfiable, both p and $\neg p$ belong to E and E is also S-1-unsatisfiable. We now show that such a set E cannot be an extension, to this end we compute $\Gamma_S^3(E)$. Using Definition 3.6.3 to build the least set that respects points 1 to 3, we end up with $\Gamma_S^3(E) = \{\epsilon | \epsilon$ is a non-tautological clause and $W \models_S^3 \epsilon\}$ since for all the defaults $E \cup \{\gamma\}$ is S-1-unsatisfiable. In other words, no default rule is applied, but it cannot be the case that $E = \Gamma_S^3(E)$, because E is S-3-unsatisfiable and $\Gamma_S^3(E)$ is S-3-satisfiable.

The second part of the theorem can be proved in a similar way. $\Diamond$

Lemma 3.6.6 *Any normal default theory* $\langle D, W \rangle$ *has at most* $2^{|S|}$ S-3-extensions. *The same bound holds for the number of* S-1-extensions.

PROOF: Given two S-3-extensions E_1 and E_2, it is always the case that their union $E_1 \cup E_2$ is S-1-unsatisfiable. This easily follows from the definition of S-3-extension and from [Reiter, 1980b, Theorem 3.3 (Orthogonality of extensions)]. By analogy with the propositional case, where it can be easily shown that there exist at most $2^{|L|}$ distinct sets of formulae that are pairwise inconsistent, we show that there exist at most $2^{|S|}$ distinct sets which are S-1-satisfiable but the union of any two of them is S-1-unsatisfiable. Let's denote with A and B two S-1-satisfiable sets of formulae and with $M(A)$ and $M(B)$ the set of S-1-interpretations satisfying A and B, respectively. The two sets of formulae A and B are mutually S-1-inconsistent if and only if $M(A) \cap M(B) = \emptyset$. Since there are only $2^{|S|}$ S-1-interpretations the maximum number of distinct sets being pairwise S-1-inconsistent is $2^{|S|}$. The same argument applies to S-1-extensions as well. $\Diamond$

Lemma 3.6.7 *Let* $\langle D, W \rangle$ *be a normal default theory and* $D' \subseteq D$ *a set of defaults. Deciding whether* $E = W \cup CONSEQ(D')$ *is an* S-3 *or* S-1-extension of $\langle D, W \rangle$ *can be done in* $O(|D|^3 \cdot |E| \cdot 2^{|S|})$ *time.*

PROOF: To decide whether E is an S-3-extension we compute the minimal set D'' of defaults which is applicable w.r.t. E and check whether $D'' = D'$. This can be done via a double loop through the set of defaults by setting $D'' = \emptyset$ at the beginning and adding to any default that becomes applicable. This check needs to be repeated because a default that at a certain moment is not applicable may become so later on when other defaults have been applied. However, the loop can only be repeated $|D|$ times hence the number of applicability tests is at most $|D|^2$. Any applicability test requires both an S-3-entailment and an S-1-satisfiability check whose cost, according to Theorem 3.3.3, is $O(|E| \cdot |D| \cdot 2^{|S|})$ time. ◇

B.4.2 Appendix to Section 3.6.2

Theorem 3.6.9 *For any S, S' such that $S \subseteq S' \subseteq L$, $CIRC_S^3(T) \vdash \neg u$ implies $CIRC_{S'}^3(T) \vdash \neg u$ (hence $CIRC(T) \models \neg u$). Moreover $CIRC_S^1(T) \not\vdash \neg u$ implies $CIRC_{S'}^1(T) \not\vdash \neg u$ (hence $CIRC(T) \not\models \neg u$).*

PROOF: $CIRC_S^3(T) \vdash \neg u$ implies that for each positive clause B, $(T \models_S^3 B) \vee (T \not\models_S^1 B \vee u)$. By Theorem 3.3.1, this implies that for each positive clause B, $(T \models_{S'}^3 B) \vee (T \not\models_{S'}^1 B \vee u)$, that is $CIRC_{S'}^3(T) \vdash \neg u$.

$CIRC_S^1(T) \not\vdash \neg u$ implies that there exists a positive clause B such that $(T \not\models_S^1 B) \wedge (T \models_S^3 B \vee u)$. By Theorem 3.3.1 this implies that $(T \not\models_{S'}^1 B) \wedge (T \models_{S'}^3 B \vee u)$, that is $CIRC_{S'}^1(T) \not\vdash \neg u$. ◇

Lemma B.4.1 *Let $S \subseteq L$. Let B, C be clauses. Let $letters(C) \subseteq L \setminus S$. $T \models_S^1 B \Longleftrightarrow T \models_S^1 B \vee C$.*

PROOF: ($\longrightarrow$) trivial.
($\longleftarrow$) $B \vee C$ is assigned 1 in all the S-1-models of T. All those S-1-models assign 0 to C, hence they assign 1 to B. ◇

Lemma 3.6.11 *$CIRC_S^3(T) \vdash \neg u$ iff for all the positive clauses B whose letters belong to S it holds $(T \not\models_S^3 B) \Longrightarrow (T \not\models_S^1 B \vee u)$.*

PROOF: ($\longrightarrow$) is a straightforward consequence of Definition 3.6.6.
($\longleftarrow$) Assume that for all the positive clauses B whose letters belong to S it holds $(T \not\models_S^3 B) \Longrightarrow (T \not\models_S^1 B \vee u)$ and $CIRC_S^3(T) \not\vdash \neg u$. The latter assumption implies that there exists a positive clause D such that $(T \not\models_S^3 D) \wedge (T \models_S^1 D \vee u)$. Let D be $B \vee C$, where $letters(B) \subseteq S$ and $letters(C) \cap S = \emptyset$. By Lemma B.4.1, $T \models_S^1 B \vee C \vee u$ implies $T \models_S^1 B \vee u$. Obviously $T \not\models_S^3 B \vee C$ implies $T \not\models_S^3 B$, hence we have a contradiction. ◇

Lemma 3.6.13 *$CIRC_S^1(T) \not\vdash \neg u$ iff there exists a positive clause B whose letters belong to S such that $(T \not\models_S^1 B) \wedge (T \models_S^3 B \vee u \vee \delta)$, where $\delta = \bigvee_{p \in L \setminus S} p$.*

PROOF: ($\longleftarrow$) is a straightforward consequence of Definition 3.6.7 and Lemma B.4.1.
($\longrightarrow$) $CIRC_S^1(T) \not\vdash \neg u$ implies that there exists a positive clause D such that $(T \not\models_S^1 D) \wedge (T \models_S^3 D \vee u)$. Let D be $B \vee C$, where $letters(B) \subseteq S$ and $letters(C) \cap S = \emptyset$. By Lemma B.4.1, $T \not\models_S^1 B \vee C$ implies $T \not\models_S^1 B$. Obviously $T \models_S^3 B \vee C \vee u$ implies $T \models_S^3 B \vee \delta \vee u$, hence the thesis. ◇

B.5   Appendix to Section 3.7

In this section we prove the results announced in Section 3.7.

Theorem 3.7.3   *If we restrict our attention to accessibility relations which are reflexive, transitive and euclidean, then there exists one algorithm to decide if α is S-1-Kripke satisfiable and one to decide if α is S-3-Kripke satisfiable both running in $O(m \cdot |\alpha| \cdot 2^{|S|})$ time, where m is the number of occurrences of the modal operator in α.*

PROOF: The algorithms for checking S-1- and S-3-Kripke satisfiability are based on a mapping π from any modal formula α on the alphabet L into a propositional formula $\pi(\alpha)$ on the alphabet $\pi(L)$ such that $|\pi(L)| = (m+1) \cdot |L|$ and $|\pi(\alpha)| \leq (m+1) \cdot |\alpha|$.

The alphabet $\pi(L)$ is defined as $\bigcup_{i=1}^{m+1} \bigcup_{p \in L} p^i$, that is it contains $m+1$ copies of each letter of L. If S is a subset of L, then $\pi(S)$ is defined as $\bigcup_{i=1}^{m+1} \bigcup_{p \in S} p^i$. The mapping $\pi(\alpha)$ is defined by the following rewriting rules, where $\alpha, \alpha_1, \alpha_2$ are modal formulae, and p is in L:

$$
\begin{aligned}
\alpha &\mapsto (\alpha, 1) \\
(\alpha_1 \wedge \alpha_2, i) &\mapsto (\alpha_1, i) \wedge (\alpha_2, i) \\
(\alpha_1 \vee \alpha_2, i) &\mapsto (\alpha_1, i) \vee (\alpha_2, i) \\
(\neg(\alpha_1 \wedge \alpha_2), i) &\mapsto (\neg\alpha_1, i) \vee (\neg\alpha_2, i) \\
(\neg(\alpha_1 \vee \alpha_2), i) &\mapsto (\neg\alpha_1, i) \wedge (\neg\alpha_2, i) \\
(\mathbf{K}\alpha, i) &\mapsto (\alpha, 1) \wedge \cdots \wedge (\alpha, m+1) \\
(\neg\mathbf{K}\alpha, i) &\mapsto (\neg\alpha, 1) \vee \cdots \vee (\neg\alpha, m+1) \\
(p, i) &\mapsto p^i \\
(\neg p, i) &\mapsto \neg p^i
\end{aligned}
$$

It is easy to prove that the S-1-Kripke satisfiability of the modal formula α is equivalent to the S'-1-satisfiability of the propositional formula $\pi(\alpha)$, where $S' = \pi(S)$. In fact the mapping π is based on a generalization of a property of the system $S5$, stating that if β is a 2-Kripke satisfiable formula with m occurrences of the modal operator, then there exists a 2-Kripke interpretation $\mathcal{M} = \langle W, R, V \rangle$ and a $w \in W$ such that $\mathcal{M}, w \models \beta$ and where the size of W is less than $m+1$ (see [Ladner, 1977, Lemma 6.1].)

The S'-1-satisfiability of $\pi(\alpha)$ can be determined in $O(m \cdot |\alpha| \cdot 2^{|S|})$ time with the algorithms presented in Appendix B.1. Analogous properties hold for the S-3-Kripke satisfiability of α. $\diamond$

Theorem 3.7.4   *If the accessibility relation is unrestricted, then deciding if α is S-1-Kripke satisfiable and deciding if α is S-3-Kripke satisfiable are PSPACE-complete problems even if $|S| = 1$.*

PROOF: It is proven in [Schild, 1991] that any formula of the $\mathcal{K}$ system can be polynomially mapped into a concept of the language $\mathcal{ALC}$ such that satisfiability is preserved. It is proven in [Schmidt-Schauß and Smolka, 1991] that satisfiability of an $\mathcal{ALC}$ concept is a PSPACE-complete problem, even if only one primitive concept is used. As a consequence, satisfiability of a formula of the $\mathcal{K}$ system in which only one propositional letter occur is PSPACE-complete. $\diamondsuit$

Theorem 3.7.5 *Let α be a modal formula and X be a modal system admitting the K schema and the rule of necessitation. The formula α is $\langle S, i \rangle$-3-Kripke satisfiable in the system X iff $\psi^3_{S,i}(\alpha)$ is 2-Kripke satisfiable in the system X.*

PROOF:

($\Rightarrow$) Assume that α is $\langle S, i \rangle$-3-Kripke satisfiable. Hence, there exists a model (over the alphabet L) $\mathcal{M} = \langle W, R, V \rangle$ and a world $w \in W$ s. t. $\mathcal{M}, w \models^3_{S,i} \alpha$. Let $\mathcal{M}_1 = \langle W_1, R_1, V_1 \rangle$ be a new model (over the alphabet S) where $W_1 = W$, $R_1 = R$, $V_1(x) = V(x)$ and $V_1(\neg x) = V(\neg x)$ if $x \in S$. Note that $\mathcal{M}_1$ is a 2-Kripke interpretation.

We prove that $\mathcal{M}_1, w \models \psi^3_{S,i}(\alpha)$ by a double induction on i and the size of α. When i is smaller than 0 $\psi^3_{S,i}(\alpha) = t$ and, therefore, $\mathcal{M}_1, w \models \psi^3_{S,i}(\alpha)$. If $\alpha = p$ or $\alpha = \neg p$ it is clearly the case that $\mathcal{M}_1, w \models \psi^3_{S,i}(\alpha)$. If $\alpha = \alpha_1 \wedge (\vee)\alpha_2$ then $\mathcal{M}_1, w \models \psi^3_{S,i}(\alpha)$ iff $\mathcal{M}_1, w \models \psi^3_{S,i}(\alpha_1)$ and (or) $\mathcal{M}_1, w \models \psi^3_{S,i}(\alpha_2)$.

If $\alpha = \mathbf{K}\beta$ then it is the case that $\forall t.wRt$ implies $\mathcal{M}, t \models^3_{S,i-1} \beta$. By the inductive hypothesis, $\mathcal{M}, t \models^3_{S,i-1} \beta$ implies $\mathcal{M}_1, t \models \psi^3_{S,i-1}\beta$, hence $\forall t.wRt$ implies $\mathcal{M}_1, t \models \psi^3_{S,i-1}\beta$. Therefore, we also have that $\mathcal{M}_1, w \models \mathbf{K}\psi^3_{S,i-1}(\beta)$. Since it is easy to show that $\psi^3_{S,i}(\alpha) = \mathbf{K}\psi^3_{S,i-1}(\beta)$, we also have $\mathcal{M}_1, w \models \psi^3_{S,i}(\alpha)$.

A similar proof also applies to $\alpha = \neg \mathbf{K}\beta$.

($\Leftarrow$) Assume that $\psi^3_{S,i}(\alpha)$ is satisfiable. Hence, there exists a model, over the alphabet S, $\mathcal{M}_1 = \langle W_1, R_1, V_1 \rangle$ and a world $w \in W_1$ s. t. $\mathcal{M}, w \models \psi^3_{S,i}(\alpha)$. Let $\mathcal{M} = \langle W, R, V \rangle$ be a new model over the alphabet L, where $W = W_1$, $R = R_1$, $V(x) = V_1(x)$ and $V(\neg x) = V_1(\neg x)$ if $x \in S$ and $V(x) = V(\neg x) = 1$ if $x \in L \setminus S$. Note that $\mathcal{M}$ is an S-3-Kripke interpretation.

We prove that $\mathcal{M}, w \models^3_{S,i} \alpha$ by a double induction on i and the size of α. When i is smaller than 0 $\mathcal{M}, w \models^3_{S,i} \alpha$ holds by definition. If $\alpha = p$ or $\alpha = \neg p$ it is clearly the case that $\mathcal{M}, w \models^3_{S,i} \alpha$. If $\alpha = \alpha_1 \wedge (\vee)\alpha_2$ then $\mathcal{M}, w \models^3_{S,i} \alpha$ iff $\mathcal{M}, w \models^3_{S,i} \alpha_1$ and (or) $\mathcal{M}, w \models^3_{S,i} \alpha_2$.

If $\alpha = \mathbf{K}\beta$ then it is the case that $\forall t.wRt$ implies $\mathcal{M}_1, t \models \psi^3_{S,i-1}(\beta)$. By the inductive hypothesis, $\mathcal{M}_1, t \models \psi^3_{S,i-1}\beta$ implies $\mathcal{M}, t \models^3_{S,i-1} \beta$, hence $\forall t.wRt$ implies $\mathcal{M}, t \models^3_{S,i-1} (\beta)$. Therefore, we also have that $\mathcal{M}, w \models^3_{S,i-1} \mathbf{K}\beta$ which in turn implies that $\mathcal{M}, w \models^3_{S,i} \alpha$.

A similar proof also applies to $\alpha = \neg \mathbf{K}\beta$. $\diamondsuit$

Appendix to Chapter 4

C.1 Appendix to Section 4.2

In [Selman and Kautz, 1991] Selman and Kautz define a clause γ_H to be a *Horn-strengthening* of a clause γ if 1) γ_H is Horn, 2) $\gamma_H \subseteq \gamma$ and 3) there exists no clause γ'_H such that $\gamma_H \subset \gamma'_H \subseteq \gamma$. As noted in [Selman and Kautz, 1991, Lemma 2], every clause in Σ_{glb} is a Horn-strengthening of a clause in Σ. In other words each clause of Σ_{glb} is the "witness" of a clause in Σ.

As shown in the following example, the syntactic form of the GLB may vary.

Example C.1.1 Let us consider the formula $\Phi = a \wedge (\neg a \vee b) \wedge (\neg c \vee b)$ The following are three equivalent Horn GLBs of Φ: $\Phi_{glb1} = a \wedge b$, $\Phi_{glb2} = a \wedge (\neg a \vee b)$ and $\Phi_{glb3} = \Phi$. $\diamond$

We show now that we can assume without loss of generality that each clause in Σ has a Horn-strengthening in Σ_{glb}, i.e., that every clause in Σ has at least one "witness" clause in Σ_{glb}. By definition $\Sigma_{glb} \models \Sigma$, therefore $\Sigma_{glb} \models \gamma$ for each clause γ in Σ. By a well-known property of Horn formulae, there exists a Horn-strengthening γ' of γ such that $\Sigma_{glb} \models \gamma'$. Σ_{glb} and $\Sigma_{glb} \wedge \gamma'$ are equivalent. From now on we assume that for each clause γ of Σ there is at least one Horn-strengthening of γ in Σ_{glb}. In the previous example both Φ_{glb1} and Φ_{glb3} satisfy this requirement, while Φ_{glb2} doesn't.

Theorem 4.2.1 *Let Σ be a propositional formula and Σ_{glb} a Horn GLB of Σ. The minimum model of Σ_{glb} is minimal for Σ.*

PROOF: First of all we note that M is also a model of Σ. Now, let's assume that M is not minimal, and let N be a model of Σ such that $N < M$. We prove that we can build a Horn formula U such that $\mathcal{M}(\Sigma_{glb}) \subset \mathcal{M}(U) \subseteq \mathcal{M}(\Sigma)$, thus contradicting the assumption that Σ_{glb} a Horn GLB of Σ.

The Horn formula U is built as follows:

begin
    unmark all the clauses of Σ;
    $U :=$ **true**;
    for each clause $\gamma = a_1 \vee \cdots \vee a_m \vee \neg b_1 \vee \cdots \vee \neg b_n$ of Σ **do**
        for $i := 1$ to m **do**
            if $N(a_i) = 1$
            then begin
                (* add a Horn-strengthening of γ *)
                $U := U \wedge (a_i \vee \neg b_1 \vee \cdots \vee \neg b_n)$;
                mark γ
            end;
    for each unmarked clause γ of Σ
    do begin
        let γ' be (one of) the witness(es) of γ in Σ_{glb};
        $U := U \wedge \gamma'$;
    end;
end.

Since U is a collection of Horn-strengthenings of Σ, $\mathcal{M}(U) \subseteq \mathcal{M}(\Sigma)$ holds. It is easy to prove that N is a model of U: 1) N clearly satisfies all the clauses in U that come from marked clauses of Σ; 2) N must satisfy at least one negative literal of each clause γ' in U that comes from an unmarked clause γ of Σ, otherwise γ would have been marked.

Now we prove that $\mathcal{M}(\Sigma_{glb}) \subset \mathcal{M}(U)$ holds. Since $N \in \mathcal{M}(U)$ and $N \notin \mathcal{M}(\Sigma_{glb})$, it is sufficient to prove that $\mathcal{M}(\Sigma_{glb}) \subseteq \mathcal{M}(U)$. Let's take a generic model P of Σ_{glb}; we prove that it is also a model of U. Since P is a model of Σ_{glb}, $M < P$ must hold, hence $N < P$ holds too. As a consequence P satisfies all the clauses in U that come form marked clauses of Σ. As far as the other clauses of U are concerned, they are clauses of Σ_{glb} as well, therefore P satisfies all of them. The proof is complete. $\diamond$

Theorem 4.2.2 *Finding a Horn GLB of a propositional formula Σ is hard w.r.t. the class $FP^{NP[O(\log n)]}$. This holds even if a model of Σ is already known. Finding a Horn GLB of a propositional formula Σ is in FP^{NP}.*

PROOF: The lower bound is a corollary of Theorems A.3.1 and 4.2.1.

As far as the upper bound is concerned, we show that a Horn GLB can be found in polynomial time by a deterministic Turing machine with access to an NP oracle. As noted in [Selman and Kautz, 1991], a Horn LBs of Σ is a collection of Horn-strengthenings of it. Each Horn-strengthening can be characterized as a tuple of digits, by using a digit per clause which denotes the selected positive literal. The Horn-strengthenings of a formula can therefore be ordered lexicographically. Let Σ_1 and Σ_2 be two Horn-strengthenings of Σ; we write $\Sigma_1 \succ \Sigma_2$ if Σ_1 follows Σ_2 in the lexicographical order. Let Σ_0 be the lexicographically first LB and let Σ_{lb} be a symbol that denotes a generic Horn LB. Σ_0 is a Horn GLB if and only if the following holds:

$$\forall \Sigma_{lb} | \Sigma_{lb} \succ \Sigma_0 \to \Sigma_{lb} \not\models \Sigma_0$$

Note that testing the validity of the above formula is clearly a problem in co-NP, as the formula inside the quantifier can be tested in polynomial time. As a consequence the test can be done with a single query to an oracle in NP. This fact can be used as the basis for designing an algorithm that finds the lexicographically smallest Horn GLB. In particular we can use the schema of the algorithm for finding the lexicographically smallest model of a propositional formula, shown in Appendix A.3.3. The algorithm for finding the lexicographically smallest Horn GLB runs in $O(n^2)$ steps, making also $O(n^2)$ calls to an oracle that checks the validity of a formula of this kind

$$\forall \Sigma_{lb} | \Sigma_{lb} \succ \Sigma_i \to \Sigma_{lb} \not\models \Sigma_i$$

Basically Σ_i represents an estimate for the Horn GLB and it is updated in each cycle. Validity of the above formula can be clearly checked by an oracle in NP. $\Diamond$

Theorem 4.2.3 *Let M be a minimal model of Σ. We can build in linear time a Horn LB of Σ whose minimum model is M. Moreover there is a Horn GLB of Σ whose minimum model is M.*

PROOF: We build a Horn LB W of Σ, whose minimum model is M. Moreover we prove that there is a Horn GLB of Σ whose minimum model is M. Algorithm C.1 shows how to build W.

M is clearly a model of W, since 1) M satisfies all of the clauses in W that come from marked clauses of Σ, 2) M must satisfy at least one negative literal of each clause γ' in W that comes from an unmarked clause γ of Σ, otherwise γ would have been marked. Since W is a collection of Horn-strengthenings of Σ, $\mathcal{M}(W) \subseteq \mathcal{M}(\Sigma)$ holds. As a consequence M is the minimum model of W.

W is a LB of Σ, but it might be not a Horn GLB. Let V be a Horn GLB of Σ such that $\mathcal{M}(W) \subset \mathcal{M}(V)$ holds. It is easy to prove that M is the minimum model of V: all of the models of V must be greater or equal than its minimum model; since M is a model of V and no model of Σ is smaller than M, M is the minimum model of V.

The proof is complete. $\Diamond$

C.2   Appendix to Section 4.3

Theorem 4.3.1 QUERY *can be polynomially mapped into the problem of finding the approximation Σ_{ub}^1 of a formula Σ.*

Algorithm MinimalModel2LB
Input a formula Σ and one of its minimal models M
Output a Horn LB W of Σ whose minimum model is M
begin
    unmark all the clauses of Σ;
    $W :=$ **true**;
    for each clause $\gamma = a_1 \vee \cdots \vee a_m \vee \neg b_1 \vee \cdots \vee \neg b_n$ of Σ **do**
        for $i := 1$ to m **do**
            if $M(a_i) = 1$
            then begin
                $W := W \wedge (a_i \vee \neg b_1 \vee \cdots \vee \neg b_n)$;
                mark γ
            end;
    for each unmarked clause $\gamma = a_1 \vee \cdots \vee a_m \vee \neg b_1 \vee \cdots \vee \neg b_n$ of Σ **do**
        $W := W \wedge (\neg b_1 \vee \cdots \vee \neg b_n)$;
    return W;
end.

Algorithm C.1: MinimalModel2LB

PROOF: Let Σ be the formula $(T_1 \vee v_1) \wedge \cdots \wedge (T_k \vee v_k)$, where $v_1, \ldots, v_k$ are propositional variables that do not occur in any of the $T_1, \ldots, T_k$. We assume without loss of generality that the alphabets of $T_1, \ldots, T_k$ are disjoint. Clearly for each i $(1 \leq i \leq k)$ $\Sigma \models v_i$ iff T_i is unsatisfiable. Therefore computing whether $\Sigma \models v_i$ for each v_i amounts to find the array of bits $b_1, \ldots, b_k$, where for any i $(1 \leq i \leq k)$, $b_i = 1$ if T_i is satisfiable, and $b_i = 0$ if T_i is not satisfiable. Since for no propositional letter $x \notin \{v_1, \ldots, v_k\}$ it may happen that $\Sigma \models x$, solving the QUERY problem for $T_1, \ldots, T_k$ is the same as finding the Horn UB Σ_{ub}^1 of Σ. $\diamond$

Theorem 4.3.2 *Given Σ and a clause α we can build in polynomial time two formulae Σ' and α' such that $\Sigma_{lub} \models \alpha$ iff $\Sigma' \models \alpha'$.*
    As a consequence deciding whether $\Sigma_{lub} \models \alpha$ holds is in co-NP.

PROOF: Let α be a clause $\neg b_1 \vee \cdots \vee \neg b_m \vee a_1 \vee \cdots \vee a_n$, that we denote as $\beta \to a_1 \vee \cdots \vee a_n$, where β is a shorthand for the conjunction $b_1 \wedge \cdots \wedge b_m$. By well-known properties of Horn formulae, $\Sigma_{lub} \models \alpha$ holds iff

$$(\Sigma_{lub} \quad \models \quad \beta \to a_1), \quad \text{or}$$

$$\vdots$$

$$(\Sigma_{lub} \quad \models \quad \beta \to a_n)$$

By [Selman and Kautz, 1991, Theorem 4], the above condition is equivalent to

$$(\Sigma \models \beta \rightarrow a_1), \quad \text{or}$$

$$\vdots$$

$$(\Sigma \models \beta \rightarrow a_n)$$

It is easy to see that this complicated condition can be compacted into a single entailment checking. First of all, it is equivalent to

$(\Sigma \wedge \beta \wedge \neg a_1)$ is unsatisfiable, or ..., or $(\Sigma \wedge \beta \wedge \neg a_n)$ is unsatisfiable

which means that its negation $\Sigma_{lub} \not\models \alpha$ holds iff

$(\Sigma \wedge \beta \wedge \neg a_1)$ is satisfiable, and ..., and $(\Sigma \wedge \beta \wedge \neg a_n)$ is satisfiable   (C.1)

Such a conjunction of satisfiability checkings can be easily compacted into a single satisfiability checking, provided we use disjoint sets of letters for each conjunct. More precisely, let $\mathcal{L}$ be the set of letters that occur in Σ, $\mathcal{L}_1, \ldots, \mathcal{L}_n$ be n disjoint sets of letters of the same arity of $\mathcal{L}$ and $\Sigma^1, \ldots, \Sigma^n$ be n duplicates of Σ built on $\mathcal{L}_1, \ldots, \mathcal{L}_n$, respectively. In an analogous way we define $\beta^1, \ldots, \beta^n$. Condition (C.1) holds iff the formula

$$(\Sigma^1 \wedge \beta^1 \wedge \neg a_1^1) \wedge \cdots \wedge (\Sigma^n \wedge \beta^n \wedge \neg a_n^n)$$

is satisfiable. Going back to the original formulation, we can say that $\Sigma_{lub} \models \alpha$ holds iff

$$\Sigma^1 \wedge \cdots \wedge \Sigma^n \models (\beta^1 \wedge \cdots \wedge \beta^n) \rightarrow (a_1^1 \vee \cdots \vee a_n^n) \qquad \text{(C.2)}$$

The proof is complete. $\diamond$

Proposition 4.3.3 *Let M be the minimum model of Σ_{lub}. M is the intersection of all the minimal models of Σ. Therefore M is a model of Σ iff the closed world assumption $CWA(\Sigma)$ of Σ is consistent.*

PROOF: For each atom a occurring in Σ, $(M \models a) \Longrightarrow (\Sigma_{lub} \models a) \Longrightarrow (\Sigma \models a) \Longrightarrow a$ is true in the intersection of all minimal models of Σ. On the other hand, $(M \not\models a) \Longrightarrow (\Sigma_{lub} \not\models a) \Longrightarrow (\Sigma \not\models a) \Longrightarrow a$ is not in the intersection of all minimal models of Σ.

It is well-known (see [Reiter, 1978]) that $CWA(\Sigma)$ is consistent iff the intersection of all minimal models of Σ is a model of Σ. $\diamond$

Bibliography

[Aho and Ullman, 1979] A. Aho and J. D. Ullman. Universality of data retrieval languages. In *Proceedings of the 6th ACM Symposium on Principles of Programming Languages*, pages 110–117, 1979.

[Aït-Kaci and Nasr, 1986] H. Aït-Kaci and R. Nasr. Login: a logic programming language with built-in inheritance. *Journal of Logic Programming*, 3:185–215, 1986.

[Anderson and Belnap, 1975] A. Anderson and N. Belnap. *Entailment: The Logic of Relevance and Necessity*. Princeton University Press, Princeton NJ, 1975.

[Apt and Blair, 1990] K. R. Apt and H. A. Blair. Arithmetic classification of perfect models of stratified programs. *Fundamenta Informaticae*, XIII:1–18, 1990. (with addendum in vol. XIV:339–343, 1991).

[Apt, 1990] K. R. Apt. Introduction to logic programming. In J. van Leeuwen, editor, *Handbook of Theoretical Computer Science*, volume B, chapter 10. Elsevier Science Publishers B. V. (North Holland), 1990.

[Atzeni and Parker, 1988] P. Atzeni and D. S. Parker. Set containment inference and syllogisms. *Theoretical Computer Science*, 62:39–65, 1988.

[Bäckström and Nebel, 1993] C. Bäckström and B. Nebel. Complexity results for SAS⁺ planning. In *Proceedings of the Thirteenth International Joint Conference on Artificial Intelligence (IJCAI-93)*, pages 1430–1453, 1993.

[Bäckström, 1992] C. Bäckström. Equivalence and tractability results for SAS⁺ planning. In *Proceedings of the Third International Conference on the Principles of Knowledge Representation and Reasoning (KR-92)*, pages 126–137, 1992.

[Beeri, 1988] C. Beeri. Data models and languages for databases. In *Proceedings of the International Conference on Database Theory (ICDT-88)*, pages 19–40, 1988.

[Beigel, 1988] R. Beigel. NP-hard sets are p-terse unless R=NP. Technical Report 88-04, The Johns Hopkins University, Department of Computer Science, August 1988.

[Ben-Eliyahu and Dechter, 1991] R. Ben-Eliyahu and R. Dechter. Default logic, propositional logic and constraints. In *Proceedings of the Ninth National Conference on Artificial Intelligence (AAAI-91)*, pages 379–385, 1991.

[Ben-Eliyahu and Dechter, 1992] R. Ben-Eliyahu and R. Dechter. Propositional semantics for default logic. Technical Report R-163, Cognitive Systems Laboratory, Computer Science Department, University of California at Los Angeles, July 1992. Also presented at the 4th International Workshop on Nonmonotonic Reasoning, Vermont, May 1992. Notes edited by H. Kautz and D. W. Etherington.

[Ben-Eliyahu and Dechter, 1993] R. Ben-Eliyahu and R. Dechter. On computing minimal models. In *Proceedings of the Eleventh National Conference on Artificial Intelligence (AAAI-93)*, pages 2–8, 1993.

[Bertossi, 1994] L. E. Bertossi. Circumscription in data logic for data type specification. *Journal of Logic and Computation*, 4:89–96, 1994.

[Besnard and Cordier, 1992] P. Besnard and M. Cordier. Explanatory diagnoses and their computation by circumscription. In *Proceedings of the Tenth European Conference on Artificial Intelligence (ECAI-92)*, pages 725–728, 1992.

[Bidoit and Froidevaux, 1991] N. Bidoit and C. Froidevaux. General logic databases and programs: default logic semantics and stratification. *Information and Computation*, 91:15–54, 1991.

[Borgida and Etherington, 1989] A. Borgida and D. W. Etherington. Hierarchical knowledge bases and efficient disjunctive reasoning. In *Proceedings of the First International Conference on the Principles of Knowledge Representation and Reasoning (KR-89)*, pages 33–43, 1989.

[Borgida et al., 1989] A. Borgida, R. J. Brachman, D. L. McGuinness, and L. A. Resnick. CLASSIC: A structural data model for objects. In *Proceedings of the ACM SIGMOD International Conference on the Management of Data*, pages 58–67, 1989.

[Bossu and Siegel, 1985] P. Bossu and P. Siegel. Saturation, nonmonotonic reasoning and the closed world assumption. *Artificial Intelligence Journal*, 25:16–63, 1985.

[Brachman and Levesque, 1984] R. J. Brachman and H. J. Levesque. The tractability of subsumption in frame-based description languages. In *Proceedings of the Fourth National Conference on Artificial Intelligence (AAAI-84)*, pages 34–37, 1984.

[Brachman and Levesque, 1985] R. J. Brachman and H. J. Levesque. A fundamental tradeoff in knowledge representation and reasoning. In R. J. Brachman and H. J. Levesque, editors, *Readings in knowledge representation*, pages 41–70. Morgan Kaufmann, 1985.

[Brachman and Schmolze, 1985] R. J. Brachman and J. Schmolze. An overview of the KL-ONE knowledge representation system. *Cognitive Science*, 9:171–216, 1985.

[Brachman, 1992] R. J. Brachman. "Reducing" CLASSIC to practice: Knowledge representation theory meets reality. In *Proceedings of the Third International Conference on the Principles of Knowledge Representation and Reasoning (KR-92)*, pages 247–258, 1992.

[Brewka, 1987] G. Brewka. The logic of inheritance in frame systems. In *Proceedings of the Eleventh International Joint Conference on Artificial Intelligence (IJCAI-89)*, pages 483–488, 1987.

[Brewka, 1991] G. Brewka. *Nonmonotonic Reasoning: Logical Foundations of Commonsense*. Cambridge University Press, Cambridge, 1991.

[Brooks, 1991] R. A. Brooks. Inference without representation. *Artificial Intelligence Journal*, 47:139–159, 1991.

[Bylander *et al.*, 1991] T. Bylander, D. Allemang, M. C. Tanner, and J. R. Josephson. The computational complexity of abduction. *Artificial Intelligence Journal*, 49:25–60, 1991.

[Bylander, 1991] T. Bylander. The monotonic abduction problem: A functional characterization on the edge of tractability. In *Proceedings of the Second International Conference on the Principles of Knowledge Representation and Reasoning (KR-91)*, pages 70–77, 1991.

[Cadoli and Lenzerini, 1990] M. Cadoli and M. Lenzerini. The complexity of closed world reasoning and circumscription. In *Proceedings of the Eighth National Conference on Artificial Intelligence (AAAI-90)*, pages 550–555, July 1990. Preliminary version of [Cadoli and Lenzerini, 1994].

[Cadoli and Lenzerini, 1994] M. Cadoli and M. Lenzerini. The complexity of propositional closed world reasoning and circumscription. *Journal of Computer and System Sciences*, 48:255–310, 1994.

[Cadoli and Schaerf, 1991] M. Cadoli and M. Schaerf. Approximate entailment. In *Trends in Artificial Intelligence: Proceedings of the 2nd Conference of the Italian Association for Artificial Intelligence*, number 549 in Lecture Notes In Artificial Intelligence, pages 68–77. Springer-Verlag, 1991.

[Cadoli and Schaerf, 1992a] M. Cadoli and M. Schaerf. Approximate inference in default reasoning and circumscription. In *Proceedings of the Tenth European Conference on Artificial Intelligence (ECAI-92)*, pages 319–323, August 1992. Extended version to appear on *Fundamenta Informaticae*.

[Cadoli and Schaerf, 1992b] M. Cadoli and M. Schaerf. Approximate reasoning and non-omniscient agents. In *Proceedings of the Fourth Conference on Theoretical Aspects of Reasoning about Knowledge (TARK-92)*, pages 169–183, 1992.

[Cadoli and Schaerf, 1992c] M. Cadoli and M. Schaerf. Approximation in concept description languages. In *Proceedings of the Third International Conference on the Principles of Knowledge Representation and Reasoning (KR-92)*, pages 330–341, October 1992.

[Cadoli and Schaerf, 1993a] M. Cadoli and M. Schaerf. The complexity of entailment in propositional multivalued logics. In *Proceedings of the 1993 AAAI Spring Symposium Series Workshop on: AI and NP-hard problems*, pages 15–21, 1993. Extended version to appear on *Annals of Mathematics and Artificial Intelligence*.

[Cadoli and Schaerf, 1993b] M. Cadoli and M. Schaerf. A survey on complexity results for of non-monotonic logics. *Journal of Logic Programming*, 17:127–160, 1993.

[Cadoli *et al.*, 1990a] M. Cadoli, F.M. Donini, and M. Schaerf. Closed world reasoning in hybrid systems. In *Proceedings of the 5th International Symposium on Methodologies for Intelligent Systems (ISMIS-90)*, pages 474–481. North Holland, 1990.

[Cadoli *et al.*, 1990b] M. Cadoli, M. Lenzerini, D. Nardi, and F. Pirri. Circumscription and nonmonotonic inheritance. In *Proceedings of the 1st Pacific Rim Conference on Artificial Intelligence (PRICAI-90)*, pages 760–765, November 1990.

[Cadoli *et al.*, 1992] M. Cadoli, T. Eiter, and G. Gottlob. An efficient method for eliminating varying predicates from a circumscription. *Artificial Intelligence Journal*, 54:397–410, 1992.

[Cadoli *et al.*, 1994a] M. Cadoli, F. M. Donini, and M. Schaerf. Is intractability of non-monotonic reasoning a real drawback? In *Proceedings of the Twelfth National Conference on Artificial Intelligence (AAAI-94)*, pages 946–951, 1994.

[Cadoli et al., 1994b] M. Cadoli, T. Eiter, and G. Gottlob. Default logic as a query language. In *Proceedings of the Fourth International Conference on the Principles of Knowledge Representation and Reasoning (KR-94)*, pages 99–108, 1994.

[Cadoli et al., 1995] M. Cadoli, F. Donini, and M. Schaerf. On compact representations of propositional circumscription. In *Twelfth Symposium on Theoretical Aspects of Computer Science (STACS-95)*, 1995. To appear.

[Cadoli, 1990] M. Cadoli. Adding failure priority knowledge to Reiter's diagnosis. In *Proceedings of the 3rd International Symposium on Artificial Intelligence (SIIA-90)*, pages 90–95, October 1990.

[Cadoli, 1992a] M. Cadoli. The complexity of model checking for circumscriptive formulae. *Information Processing Letters*, 44:113–118, 1992.

[Cadoli, 1992b] M. Cadoli. On the complexity of model finding for nonmonotonic propositional logics. In *Proceedings of the Fourth Italian Conference on Theoretical Computer Science*, pages 125–139. World Scientific Publishing Co., October 1992.

[Cadoli, 1993] M. Cadoli. Semantical and computational aspects of Horn approximations. In *Proceedings of the Thirteenth International Joint Conference on Artificial Intelligence (IJCAI-93)*, pages 39–44, 1993.

[Chan, 1993] E. P. F. Chan. A possible world semantics for disjuncitve databases. *IEEE Transactions on Knowledge and Data Engineering*, 5:282–292, 1993.

[Chellas, 1980] B. Chellas. *Modal Logic: an introduction*. Cambridge University Press, 1980.

[Chen and Toda, 1991] Z. Chen and S. Toda. On the complexity of computing optimal solutions. *International Journal of Foundations of Computer Science*, 2:207–220, 1991.

[Chen and Toda, 1993] Z. Chen and S. Toda. The complexity of selecting maximal solutions. In *Proceedings of the Eighth IEEE Conference on Structure in Complexity Theory*, pages 313–325, 1993.

[Chenoweth, 1991] S. V. Chenoweth. On the NP-hardness of blocks world. In *Proceedings of the Ninth National Conference on Artificial Intelligence (AAAI-91)*, pages 623–628, 1991.

[Chomicki and Subrahmanian, 1990] J. Chomicki and V. S. Subrahmanian. Generalized closed world assumption is Π_2^0-complete. *Information Processing Letters*, 34:289–291, 1990.

[Clark, 1978] K. L. Clark. Negation as failure. In H. Gallaire and J. Minker, editors, *Logic and Data Bases*, pages 293–322. Plenum, 1978.

[Cook, 1971] S. A. Cook. The complexity of theorem-proving procedures. In *Proceedings of the 3rd ACM Symposium on Theory Of Computing (STOC-71)*, pages 151–158, 1971.

[Cousot and Cousot, 1977] P. Cousot and R. Cousot. Abstract interpretation: A unified lattice model for static analysis of programs by construction or approximation of fixpoints. In *Proceedings of the 4th ACM Symposium on Principles of Programming Languages (POPL 77)*, pages 238–252, 1977.

[Crawford and Kuipers, 1989] J. M. Crawford and B. Kuipers. Towards a theory of access limited reasoning. In *Proceedings of the First International Conference on the Principles of Knowledge Representation and Reasoning (KR-89)*, pages 67–78, 1989.

[Dalal and Etherington, 1992] M. Dalal and D. W. Etherington. A hierarchy of tractable satisfiability problems. *Information Processing Letters*, 44:173–180, 1992.

[Dalal, 1992] M. Dalal. Tractable instances of some hard deduction problems. In *Proceedings of the Tenth European Conference on Artificial Intelligence (ECAI-92)*, pages 354–358, 1992.

[Davis and Putnam, 1960] M. Davis and H. Putnam. A computing procedure for quantification theory. *Journal of the ACM*, 7:201–215, 1960.

[de Kleer and Konolige, 1989] J. de Kleer and K. Konolige. Eliminating the fixed predicates from a circumscription. *Artificial Intelligence Journal*, 39:391–398, 1989.

[de Kleer, 1986] J. de Kleer. An assumption-based TMS. *Artificial Intelligence Journal*, 28:127–162, 1986.

[Dean and Boddy, 1988] T. Dean and M. Boddy. An analysis of time-dependent planning. In *Proceedings of the Seventh National Conference on Artificial Intelligence (AAAI-88)*, pages 49–54, 1988.

[Dechter and Pearl, 1988] R. Dechter and J. Pearl. Network-based heuristics for constraint-satisfaction problems. *Artificial Intelligence Journal*, 34:1–38, 1988.

[Doherty and Lukaszewicz, 1992] P. Doherty and W. Lukaszewicz. NML3. A nonmonotonic logic with explicit default. *Journal of Applied Non-Classical Logics*, 2:9–48, 1992.

[Donini et al., 1991a] F. M. Donini, M. Lenzerini, D. Nardi, and W. Nutt. The complexity of concept languages. In *Proceedings of the Second International Conference on the Principles of Knowledge Representation and Reasoning (KR-91)*, pages 151–162. Morgan Kaufmann, 1991.

[Donini et al., 1991b] F. M. Donini, M. Lenzerini, D. Nardi, and W. Nutt. Tractable concept languages. In *Proceedings of the Twelfth International Joint Conference on Artificial Intelligence (IJCAI-91)*, pages 458–463, 1991.

[Donini et al., 1992] F. M. Donini, B. Hollunder, M. Lenzerini, A. Marchetti Spaccamela, D. Nardi, and W. Nutt. The complexity of existential quantification in concept languages. *Artificial Intelligence Journal*, 53:309–327, 1992.

[Dowling and Gallier, 1984] W. P. Dowling and J. H. Gallier. Linear-time algorithms for testing the satisfiability of propositional Horn formulae. *Journal of Logic Programming*, 1:267–284, 1984.

[Doyle and Patil, 1991] J. Doyle and R. S. Patil. Two theses of knowledge representation: Language restrictions, taxonomic classification, and the utility of representation services. *Artificial Intelligence Journal*, 48:261–297, 1991.

[Doyle, 1985] J. Doyle. Circumscription and implicit definability. *Journal of Automated Reasoning*, 1:391–405, 1985.

[Dreben and Goldfarb, 1979] B. Dreben and W. D. Goldfarb. *The decision problem. Solvable classes of quantificational formulas*. Addison-Wesley, 1979.

[Dunn, 1976] M. Dunn. Intuitive semantics for first-degree entailments and 'coupled trees'. *Philosophical Studies*, 29:149–168, 1976.

[Eiter and Gottlob, 1992] T. Eiter and G. Gottlob. On the complexity of propositional knowledge base revision, updates and counterfactuals. *Artificial Intelligence Journal*, 57:227–270, 1992.

[Eiter and Gottlob, 1993a] T. Eiter and G. Gottlob. The complexity of logic-based abduction. In *Proceedings of the 10th Symposium on Theoretical Aspects of Computer Science (STACS-93)*, Lecture Notes in Computer Science. Springer-Verlag, 1993.

[Eiter and Gottlob, 1993b] T. Eiter and G. Gottlob. Propositional circumscription and extended closed world reasoning are Π_2^p-complete. *Theoretical Computer Science*, pages 231–245, 1993.

[Enderton, 1972] H. B. Enderton. *A mathematical introduction to logic*. Academic Press, New York, 1972.

[Etherington and Crawford, 1992] D. W. Etherington and J. M. Crawford. Towards efficient default reasoning. Presented at the 4th International Workshop on Nonmonotonic Reasoning, Vermont, May 1992. Notes edited by Kautz H. and Etherington D., 1992.

[Etherington et al., 1985] D. W. Etherington, R. E. Mercer, and R. Reiter. On the adequacy of predicate circumscription for closed world reasoning. *Computational Intelligence*, 1:11–15, 1985.

[Etherington et al., 1991] D. W. Etherington, S. Kraus, and D. Perlis. Nonmonotonicity and the scope of reasoning. *Artificial Intelligence Journal*, 52:221–261, 1991.

[Etherington, 1987] D. W. Etherington. *Reasoning with incomplete information*. Morgan Kaufman Publishers, Los Altos, CA, 1987.

[Even et al., 1976] S. Even, A. Itai, and A. Shamir. On the complexity of timetable and multicommodity flow problems. *SIAM Journal of Computing*, 5:691–703, 1976.

[Fagin and Halpern, 1988] R. Fagin and J. Y. Halpern. Belief, awareness and limited reasoning. *Artificial Intelligence Journal*, 34:39–76, 1988.

[Fagin et al., 1990] R. Fagin, J. Y. Halpern, and M. Y. Vardi. A nonstandard approach to the logical omniscience problem. In *Proceedings of the Third Conference on Theoretical Aspects of Reasoning about Knowledge (TARK-90)*, pages 41–55, 1990.

[Frisch, 1985] A. M. Frisch. Using model theory to specify AI programs. In *Proceedings of the Ninth International Joint Conference on Artificial Intelligence (IJCAI-85)*, pages 148–154, 1985.

[Frisch, 1987] A. M. Frisch. Inference without chaining. In *Proceedings of the Tenth International Joint Conference on Artificial Intelligence (IJCAI-87)*, pages 515–519, 1987.

[Gabbay and Ohlbach, 1992] D. Gabbay and H. J. Ohlbach. Quantifier elimination in second-order predicate logic. In *Proceedings of the Third International Conference on the Principles of Knowledge Representation and Reasoning (KR-92)*, pages 425–435, 1992.

[Gallier, 1987] J. H. Gallier. *Logic for Computer Science: Foundations of Automatic Theorem Proving*. John Wiley, New York, 1987.

[Gallo and Scutellà, 1988] G. Gallo and M. G. Scutellà. Polynomially solvable satisfiability problems. *Information Processing Letters*, 29:221–227, 1988.

[Garey and Johnson, 1979] M. R. Garey and D. S. Johnson. *Computers and Intractability, A Guide to the Theory of NP-Completeness*. W.H. Freeman and Company, San Francisco, Ca, 1979.

[Gasarch, 1986] W. Gasarch. The complexity of optimization functions. Technical Report 1652, Dept. of Computer Science, University of Maryland, 1986.

[Gelernter, 1959] H. Gelernter. Realization of a geometry theorem-proving machine. In *Proceedings of the International Conference on Information Processing*, pages 273–282, Paris, 1959. UNESCO House.

[Gelfond and Lifschitz, 1988] M. Gelfond and V. Lifschitz. The stable model semantics for logic programming. In *Proceedings of the Fifth Logic Programming Symposium*, pages 1070–1080. MIT Press, 1988.

[Gelfond and Przymusinska, 1986] M. Gelfond and H. Przymusinska. Negation as failure: Careful closure procedure. *Artificial Intelligence Journal*, 30:273–287, 1986.

[Gelfond et al., 1989] M. Gelfond, H. Przymusinska, and T. Przymusinski. On the relationship between circumscription and negation as failure. *Artificial Intelligence Journal*, 38:49–73, 1989.

[Genesereth and Nilsson, 1987] M. R. Genesereth and N. J. Nilsson. *Logical foundations of Artificial Intelligence*. Morgan Kaufmann Puublishers Inc., Los Altos, Ca, 1987.

[Ginsberg, 1987] M. L. Ginsberg, editor. *Readings in Nonmonotonic Reasoning*. Morgan Kaufmann Puublishers Inc., Los Altos, Ca, 1987.

[Ginsberg, 1989] M. L. Ginsberg. A circumscriptive theorem prover. *Artificial Intelligence Journal*, 39:209–230, 1989.

[Ginsberg, 1991a] M. L. Ginsberg. Anytime declarativism. Technical report, Stanford University, Dept. of Computer Science, 1991.

[Ginsberg, 1991b] M. L. Ginsberg. Computational considerations in reasoning about action. In *Proceedings of the Second International Conference on the Principles of Knowledge Representation and Reasoning (KR-91)*, pages 250–261, 1991.

[Ginsberg, 1993] M. L. Ginsberg. *Essentials of Artificial Intelligence*. Morgan Kaufmann Publishers Inc., San Mateo, CA, 1993.

[Giunchiglia and Walsh, 1992] F. Giunchiglia and T. Walsh. A theory of abstraction. *Artificial Intelligence Journal*, 57:323–389, 1992.

[Golumbic and Shamir, 1992] M. C. Golumbic and R. Shamir. Algorithms and complexity fo reasoning about time. In *Proceedings of the Tenth National Conference on Artificial Intelligence (AAAI-92)*, pages 741–747, 1992.

[Gottlob and Fermüller, 1993] G. Gottlob and C. G. Fermüller. Removing redundancy from a clause. *Artificial Intelligence Journal*, 61:263–289, 1993.

[Gottlob, 1992] G. Gottlob. Complexity results for nonmonotonic logics. *Journal of Logic and Computation*, 2:397–425, 1992.

[Grahne, 1991] G. Grahne. *The Problem of Incomplete Information in Relational Databases*, volume 554 of *Lecture Notes in Computer Science*. Springer-Verlag, 1991.

[Greiner and Schuurmans, 1992] R. Greiner and D. Schuurmans. Learning useful Horn approximations. In *Proceedings of the Third International Conference on the Principles of Knowledge Representation and Reasoning (KR-92)*, pages 383–392, 1992.

[Grosof, 1984] B. Grosof. Default reasoning as circumscription. Presented at the First International Workshop on Nonmonotonic Reasoning, 1984.

[Gupta and Nau, 1992] N. Gupta and D. S. Nau. On the complexity of blocks-world planning. *Artificial Intelligence Journal*, 56:223–254, 1992.

[Halpern and Moses, 1992] J. Y. Halpern and Y. Moses. A guide to completeness and complexity for modal logic of knowledge and belief. *Artificial Intelligence Journal*, 54:319–379, 1992.

[Halpern and Vardi, 1991] J.Y. Halpern and M.Y. Vardi. Model checking vs. theorem proving: A manifesto. In *Proceedings of the Second International Conference on the Principles of Knowledge Representation and Reasoning (KR-91)*, 1991. Also in Lifschitz V. *Artificial Intelligence and Mathematical Theory of Computation. Papers in Honor of John McCarthy*, Academic Press, San Diego, 1991.

[Halpern, 1991] J. Y. Halpern. Reasoning about knowledge: A survey circa 1991. In A. A. Kent and J. G. Williams, editors, *Encyclopedia of Computer Science and Technology*. Marcel Dekker, 1991.

[Haugh, 1988] B. A. Haugh. Tractable theories of multiple defeasible inheritance in ordinary nonmonotonic logics. In *Proceedings of the Seventh National Conference on Artificial Intelligence (AAAI-88)*, pages 421–426, 1988.

[Hintikka, 1955] J. Hintikka. Recursion in the theory of types. *Acta Philosophica Fennica*, 8:61–151, 1955.

[Hintikka, 1962] J. Hintikka. *Knowledge and belief.* Cornell University Press, Ithaca, New York, 1962.

[Horty and Thomason, 1988] J. F. Horty and R. H. Thomason. Mixing strict and defeasible inheritance. In *Proceedings of the Seventh National Conference on Artificial Intelligence (AAAI-88)*, pages 427–432, 1988.

[Horty et al., 1990] J. F. Horty, R. H. Thomason, and D. S. Touretzky. A skeptical theory of inheritance in nonmonotonic semantic networks. *Artificial Intelligence Journal*, 42:311–348, 1990.

[Imielinski, 1987a] T. Imielinski. Domain abstraction and limited reasoning. In *Proceedings of the Tenth International Joint Conference on Artificial Intelligence (IJCAI-87)*, pages 997–1003, 1987.

[Imielinski, 1987b] T. Imielinski. Results on translating defaults to circumscription. *Artificial Intelligence Journal*, 32:131–146, 1987.

[Inoue and Helft, 1990] K. Inoue and N. Helft. On theorem provers for circumscription. In *Proceedings of the Eight Biennal Conference of the Canadian Society for Computational Studies of Intelligence (CSCSI '90)*. Morgan Kaufmann Publishers, 1990.

[Jeroslow and Wang, 1990] R. G. Jeroslow and J. Wang. Solving propositional satisfiability problems. *Annals of Mathematics and Artificial Intelligence*, 1:167–187, 1990.

[Johnson, 1990] D. S. Johnson. A catalog of complexity classes. In J. van Leeuwen, editor, *Handbook of Theoretical Computer Science*, volume A, chapter 2. Elsevier Science Publishers B. V. (North Holland), 1990.

[Kadin, 1988] J. Kadin. The polynomial time hierarchy collapses if the boolean hierarchy collapses. *SIAM Journal of Computing*, 17:1263–1282, 1988.

[Kannelakis, 1990] P. Kannelakis. Elements of Relational Database Theory. In J. van Leeuwen, editor, *Handbook of Theoretical Computer Science*, volume B, chapter 17. Elsevier Science Publishers B. V. (North Holland), 1990.

[Kautz and Selman, 1991a] H. A. Kautz and B. Selman. A general framework for knowledge compilation. In *Proc. of International Workshop on Processing Declarative Knowledge (PDK-91)*, number 567 in Lecture Notes In Artificial Intelligence, pages 287–300. Springer Verlag, 1991.

[Kautz and Selman, 1991b] H. A. Kautz and B. Selman. Hard problems for simple default logics. *Artificial Intelligence Journal*, 49:243–279, 1991.

[Kautz and Selman, 1992] H. A. Kautz and B. Selman. Forming concepts for fast inference. In *Proceedings of the Tenth National Conference on Artificial Intelligence (AAAI-92)*, pages 786–793, 1992.

[Kirsh, 1991] D. Kirsh, editor. *Special volume of* Artificial Intelligence Journal *on foundations of Artificial Intelligence*, 1991. Volume 47.

[Kleene, 1966] S. C. Kleene. *Mathematical Logic*. John Wiley and Sons, 1966.

[Kolaitis and Papadimitriou, 1990] P. G. Kolaitis and C. H. Papadimitriou. Some computational aspects of circumscription. *Journal of the ACM*, 37:1–14, 1990.

[Kolaitis and Papadimitriou, 1991] P. G. Kolaitis and C. H. Papadimitriou. Why not negation by fixpoint? *Journal of Computer and System Sciences*, 43:125–144, 1991.

[Konolige, 1988] K. Konolige. On the relationship between default and autoepistemic logic. *Artificial Intelligence Journal*, 35:343–382, 1988.

[Krentel, 1988] M. V. Krentel. The complexity of optimization problems. *Journal of Computer and System Sciences*, 36:490–509, 1988.

[Kripke, 1963] S. A. Kripke. Semantical considerations on modal logic. *Acta Philosophica Fennica*, 16:83–94, 1963.

[Krishnaprasad et al., 1989] T. Krishnaprasad, M. Kifer, and D. S. Warren. On the circumscriptive semantics of inheritance networks. In *Proceedings of the 4th International Symposium on Methodologies for Intelligent Systems (ISMIS-89)*, pages 448–457, 1989.

[Krishnaprasad, 1988] T. Krishnaprasad. On the computability of circumscription. *Information Processing Letters*, 27:237–243, 1988.

[Ladner et al., 1975] R. E. Ladner, N. A. Lynch, and A. L. Selman. A comparison of polynomial time reducibilities. *Theoretical Computer Science*, 1:103–123, 1975.

[Ladner, 1977] R. Ladner. The computational complexity of provability in systems of modal propositional logic. *SIAM Journal of Computing*, 6:467–480, 1977.

[Lakemeyer, 1987] G. Lakemeyer. Tractable meta-reasoning in propositional logics of belief. In *Proceedings of the Tenth International Joint Conference on Artificial Intelligence (IJCAI-87)*, pages 402–408, 1987.

[Lenzerini, 1988] M. Lenzerini. Reasoning about inheritance networks. Technical Report RAP.22.88, Università di Roma La Sapienza, Dipartimento di Informatica e Sistemistica, 1988.

[Levesque, 1984] H. J. Levesque. A logic of implicit and explicit belief. In *Proceedings of the Fourth National Conference on Artificial Intelligence (AAAI-84)*, pages 198–202, 1984.

[Levesque, 1986] H. J. Levesque. Knowledge representation and reasoning. *Annual Reviews in Computer Science*, 1:255–287, 1986.

[Levesque, 1988] H. J. Levesque. Logic and the complexity of reasoning. *Journal of Philosophical Logic*, 17:355–389, 1988.

[Levesque, 1989] H. J. Levesque. A knowledge-level account of abduction. In *Proceedings of the Eleventh International Joint Conference on Artificial Intelligence (IJCAI-89)*, pages 1061–1067, 1989.

[Lewis, 1979] H. R. Lewis. *Unsolvable classes of quantificational formulas*. Addison-Wesley, 1979.

[Lifschitz, 1985a] V. Lifschitz. Closed-world databases and circumscription. *Artificial Intelligence Journal*, 27:229–235, 1985.

[Lifschitz, 1985b] V. Lifschitz. Computing circumscription. In *Proceedings of the Ninth International Joint Conference on Artificial Intelligence (IJCAI-85)*, pages 121–127, 1985.

[Lifschitz, 1986a] V. Lifschitz. On the satisfiability of circumscription. *Artificial Intelligence Journal*, 28:17–27, 1986.

[Lifschitz, 1986b] V. Lifschitz. Pointwise circumscription. In *Proceedings of the Fifth National Conference on Artificial Intelligence (AAAI-86)*, pages 406–410, 1986.

[Lisitsa, 1993] A. Lisitsa. Complexity of universal circumscription. *International Journal of Foundations of Computer Science*, 4:241–244, 1993.

[Lobo and Subrahmanian, 1992] J. Lobo and V. S. Subrahmanian. Relating minimal models and pre-requisite-free normal defaults. *Information Processing Letters*, 44:129–133, 1992.

[Loveland, 1978] D. Loveland. *Automated Theorem Proving: A Logical basis*. North Holland, Amsterdam, New York, 1978.

[Lukaszewicz, 1990] W. Lukaszewicz. *Non-Monotonic Reasoning*. Ellis-Horwood, Chichester, West Sussex, England, 1990.

[MacGregor, 1991] R. M. MacGregor. Inside the LOOM description classifier. *SIGART Bulletin*, 2:88–92, 1991.

[Marek and Truszczyński, 1993] W. Marek and M. Truszczyński. *Nonmonotonic Logics; Context-Dependent Reasoning*. Springer Verlag, 1993.

[McCarthy, 1959] J. McCarthy. Programs with common sense. In *Proceedings of the Teddington Conference on the Mechanization of Thought Processes*, pages 75–91, London, 1959. Her Majesty Stationery Office, London. Reprinted in *Formalizing common sense*. V. Lifschitz, editor. Ablex Publishing Corporation.

[McCarthy, 1980] J. McCarthy. Circumscription - a form of non-monotonic reasoning. *Artificial Intelligence Journal*, 13:27–39, 1980.

[McCarthy, 1986] J. McCarthy. Applications of circumscription to formalizing common-sense knowledge. *Artificial Intelligence Journal*, 28:89–116, 1986.

[Megiddo and Papadimitriou, 1991] N. Megiddo and C. H. Papadimitriou. On total functions, existence theorems and computational complexity. *Theoretical Computer Science*, 81:317–324, 1991.

[Minker, 1982] J. Minker. On indefinite databases and the closed world assumption. In *Proceedings of the Sixth Conference on Automated Deduction (CADE-82)*, pages 292–308, 1982.

[Nebel and Smolka, 1990] B. Nebel and G. Smolka. Representation and reasoning with attributive descriptions. In *Sorts and Types in Artificial Intelligence*, number 422 in Lecture Notes In Artificial Intelligence, pages 112-139. Springer Verlag, 1990.

[Nebel, 1988] B. Nebel. Computational complexity of terminological reasoning in BACK. *Artificial Intelligence Journal*, 34(3):371-383, 1988.

[Nebel, 1990] B. Nebel. Terminological reasoning is inherently intractable. *Artificial Intelligence Journal*, 43:235-249, 1990.

[Nebel, 1991] B. Nebel. Belief revision and default reasoning: Syntax-based approaches. In *Proceedings of the Second International Conference on the Principles of Knowledge Representation and Reasoning (KR-91)*, pages 417-428, 1991.

[Nilsson, 1991] N. J. Nilsson. Logic and artificial intelligence. *Artificial Intelligence Journal*, 47:31-56, 1991.

[Papadimitriou and Sideri, 1992] C. H. Papadimitriou and M. Sideri. On finding extensions of default theories. In *Proceedings of the International Conference on Database Theory (ICDT-92)*, pages 276-281, 1992.

[Papadimitriou, 1991] C. H. Papadimitriou. On selecting a satisfying truth assignment (extended abstract). In *Proceedings of the 32nd Annual Symposium on the Foundations of Computer Science (FOCS-91)*, pages 163-169, 1991.

[Papadimitriou, 1994] C. H. Papadimitriou. *Computational Complexity*. Addison Wesley Publishing Company, 1994.

[Papalaskari and Weinstein, 1990] M. Papalaskari and S. Weinstein. Minimal consequence in sentential logic. *Journal of Logic Programming*, 9:19-31, 1990.

[Patel-Schneider, 1989] P. F. Patel-Schneider. A four-valued semantics for terminological logic. *Artificial Intelligence Journal*, 38:319-351, 1989.

[Patel-Schneider, 1990] P. F. Patel-Schneider. A decidable first-order logic for knowledge representation. *Journal of Automated Reasoning*, 6:361-388, 1990.

[Przymusinski, 1988] T. Przymusinski. On the declarative semantics of stratified deductive databases and logic programs. In J. Minker, editor, *Foundation of Deductive Databases and Logic Programming*, pages 193-216. Morgan Kaufmann, 1988.

[Przymusinski, 1989] T. Przymusinski. An algorithm to compute circumscription. *Artificial Intelligence Journal*, 38:49-73, 1989.

[Rabinov, 1989] A. Rabinov. A generalization of collapsible cases of circumscription. *Artificial Intelligence Journal*, 38:111-117, 1989.

[Raiman, 1990] O. Raiman. A circumscribed diagnosis engine. In *Proceedings of the International Workshop on Expert Systems in Engineering*, volume 462 of *Lecture Notes In Artificial Intelligence*, pages 90-101. Springer-Verlag, 1990.

[Rajasekar et al., 1989] A. Rajasekar, J. Lobo, and J. Minker. Weak generalized closed world assumption. *Journal of Automated Reasoning*, 5:293-307, 1989.

[Reiter, 1978] R. Reiter. On closed world data bases. In H. Gallaire and J. Minker, editors, *Logic and Data Bases*, pages 119-140. Plenum, 1978.

[Reiter, 1980a] R. Reiter. Equality and domain closure in first-order databases. *Journal of the ACM*, 27(2), 1980.

[Reiter, 1980b] R. Reiter. A logic for default reasoning. *Artificial Intelligence Journal*, 13:81-132, 1980.

[Reiter, 1984] R. Reiter. Towards a logical reconstruction of relational database theory. In M. Brodie, J. Mylopoulos, and J. Schmidt, editors, *On Conceptual Modeling*. Springer, Berlin, 1984.

[Reiter, 1987] R. Reiter. A theory of diagnosis from first principles. *Artificial Intelligence Journal*, 32:57–95, 1987.

[Rich and Knight, 1991] E. Rich and K. Knight. *Artificial Intelligence*. McGraw Hill, Inc., second edition, 1991.

[Robinson, 1965] J. A. Robinson. A machine oriented logic based on the resolution principle. *Journal of the ACM*, 12:397–415, 1965.

[Rogers, 1967] H. Rogers. *Theory of Recursive Functions and Effective Computability*. McGraw-Hill, 1967.

[Roth, 1993] D. Roth. On the hardness of approximate reasoning. In *Proceedings of the Thirteenth International Joint Conference on Artificial Intelligence (IJCAI-93)*, pages 613–618, 1993.

[Russell and Zilberstein, 1991] S. J. Russell and S. Zilberstein. Composing real-time systems. In *Proceedings of the Twelfth International Joint Conference on Artificial Intelligence (IJCAI-91)*, pages 212–217, 1991.

[Rutenburg, 1991] V. Rutenburg. Computational complexity of truth maintenance systems. In *Eight Symposium on Theoretical Aspects of Computer Science (STACS-91)*, volume 480 of *Lecture Notes in Computer Science*. Springer-Verlag, 1991.

[Schaefer, 1978] T. J. Schaefer. The complexity of satisfiability problems. In *Proceedings of the 10th ACM Symposium on Theory Of Computing (STOC-78)*, pages 216–226, 1978.

[Schaerf and Cadoli, 1995] M. Schaerf and M. Cadoli. Tractable reasoning via approximation. *Artificial Intelligence Journal*, 1995. To appear.

[Schild, 1991] K. Schild. A correspondence theory for terminological logics: Preliminary report. In *Proceedings of the Twelfth International Joint Conference on Artificial Intelligence (IJCAI-91)*, pages 466–471, 1991.

[Schlipf, 1987] J. S. Schlipf. Decidability and definability with circumscription. *Annals of Pure and Applied Logic*, 35:173–191, 1987.

[Schlipf, 1988] J. S. Schlipf. When is closed world reasoning tractable? In *Proceedings of the 3rd International Symposium on Methodologies for Intelligent Systems (ISMIS-88)*, pages 485–494, New York, 1988. North Holland.

[Schmidt-Schauß and Smolka, 1991] M. Schmidt-Schauß and G. Smolka. Attributive concept descriptions with complements. *Artificial Intelligence Journal*, 48(1):1–26, 1991.

[Scott, 1970] D. Scott. Advice on modal logic. In K. Lambert, editor, *Philosophical problems in logic*, pages 143–173. Reidel, Dordrecht, Netherlands, 1970.

[Selman and Kautz, 1990] B. Selman and H. A. Kautz. Model-preference default theories. *Artificial Intelligence Journal*, 45:287–322, 1990.

[Selman and Kautz, 1991] B. Selman and H. A. Kautz. Knowledge compilation using Horn approximations. In *Proceedings of the Ninth National Conference on Artificial Intelligence (AAAI-91)*, pages 904–909, 1991.

[Selman and Levesque, 1989] B. Selman and H. J. Levesque. The tractability of path-based inheritance. In *Proceedings of the Eleventh International Joint Conference on Artificial Intelligence (IJCAI-89)*, pages 1140–1145, 1989.

[Stillman, 1990] J. Stillman. It's not my default: The complexity of membership problems in restricted propositional default logics. In *Proceedings of the Eighth National Conference on Artificial Intelligence (AAAI-90)*, pages 571–578, 1990.

[Stillman, 1992] J. Stillman. The complexity of propositional default logics. In *Proceedings of the Tenth National Conference on Artificial Intelligence (AAAI-92)*, pages 794–799, 1992.

[Stockmeyer, 1976] L. J. Stockmeyer. The polynomial-time hierarchy. *Theoretical Computer Science*, 3:1–22, 1976.

[Touretzky, 1984] D.S. Touretzky. Implicit ordering of defaults in inheritance systems. In *Proceedings of the Fourth National Conference on Artificial Intelligence (AAAI-84)*, pages 322–325, 1984.

[van Benthem and Doets, 1983] J. van Benthem and K. Doets. Higher order logic. In D. Gabbay and F. Guenthner, editors, *Handbook of Philosophical Logic*, volume 1, chapter 4. Reidel, Dordrecht, Netherlands, 1983.

[Van Gelder et al., 1991] A. Van Gelder, K. A. Ross, and J. S. Schlipf. The well-founded semantics for general logic programs. *Journal of the ACM*, 38:620–650, 1991.

[Van Gelder, 1988] A. Van Gelder. A satisfiability tester for non-clausal propositional calculus. *Information and Computation*, 79:1–21, 1988.

[Vardi, 1986a] M. Y. Vardi. On the integrity of databases with incomplete information. In *Proceedings of the Fifth Conference on Principle Of Database Systems (PODS-86)*, 1986.

[Vardi, 1986b] M. Y. Vardi. Querying logical databases. *Journal of Computer and System Sciences*, 33:142–160, 1986.

[Wagner, 1990] K. W. Wagner. Bounded query classes. *SIAM Journal of Computing*, 19:833–846, 1990.

[Weyhrauch et al., 1993] R. W. Weyhrauch, M. Cadoli, and C. L. Talcott. Using abstract resources to control reasoning. Technical report, Computer Science Department, Stanford University, March 1993.

[Winslett, 1989] M. Winslett. Sometimes updates are circumscription. In *Proceedings of the Eleventh International Joint Conference on Artificial Intelligence (IJCAI-89)*, 1989.

[Winston, 1992] P.H. Winston. *Artificial Intelligence*. Addison-Wesley, third edition, 1992.

[Yahya and Henschen, 1985] A. Yahya and L. J. Henschen. Deduction in non-horn databases. *Journal of Automated Reasoning*, 1:141–160, 1985.

[Yuan and Wang, 1988] L. Y. Yuan and C. H. Wang. On reducing parallel circumscription. In *Proceedings of the Seventh National Conference on Artificial Intelligence (AAAI-88)*, pages 460–464, 1988.

[Zadrozny, 1987] W. W. Zadrozny. Intended models, circumscription and common-sense reasoning. In *Proceedings of the Sixth National Conference on Artificial Intelligence (AAAI-87)*, pages 909–916, 1987.

Index

Springer-Verlag
and the Environment

We at Springer-Verlag firmly believe that an international science publisher has a special obligation to the environment, and our corporate policies consistently reflect this conviction.

We also expect our business partners – paper mills, printers, packaging manufacturers, etc. – to commit themselves to using environmentally friendly materials and production processes.

The paper in this book is made from low- or no-chlorine pulp and is acid free, in conformance with international standards for paper permanency.

Lecture Notes in Artificial Intelligence (LNAI)

Lecture Notes in Computer Science